BATTLES AND HONOURS

OF THE

ROYAL NAVY

DAVID A. THOMAS has also written:

Naval History
WITH ENSIGNS FLYING
SUBMARINE VICTORY
BATTLE OF THE JAVA SEA
CRETE 1941: THE BATTLE AT SEA
JAPAN'S WAR AT SEA: PEARL HARBOUR TO
THE CORAL SEA
ROYAL ADMIRALS
A COMPANION TO THE ROYAL NAVY
THE ILLUSTRATED ARMADA HANDBOOK
THE ATLANTIC STAR 1939–1945
CHRISTOPHER COLUMBUS: MASTER
OF THE ATLANTIC
QUEEN MARY AND THE CRUISER:
THE CURACOA DISASTER
(With Patrick Holmes)

Social History
THE CANNING STORY 1785–1985
CHURCHILL: THE MEMBER FOR WOODFORD

Bibliography
COMPTON MACKENZIE: A BIBLIOGRAPHY
(With Joyce Thomas)

Juvenile
HOW SHIPS ARE MADE

BATTLES AND HONOURS
OF THE
ROYAL NAVY

by

DAVID A. THOMAS

LEO COOPER

First published in Great Britain 1998 by
LEO COOPER
an imprint of
Pen & Sword Books Ltd
47 Church Street
Barnsley, S. Yorkshire S70 2AS

ISBN 085052 623 X

A CIP record for this book is available from the British Library

Typeset in 10.5/13.5pt Sabon by
Phoenix Typesetting, Ilkley, West Yorkshire.
Printed in England by Redwood Books Ltd. Trowbridge, Wilts.

Contents

Introduction and Acknowledgements

It was 1660, the year of the restoration of King Charles II to the throne, which finds most support from claimants for the Navy's founding year, if only because it was Charles who granted the Royal prefix in that year.

It may strike a discordant note to the purists, therefore, to read here about battles which pre-date this datum point of 1660, by as much as seventy-two years in the case of the Armada (1588). But the Armada, as the Admiralty Fleet Order puts it with inconsistency but good sense, and with studied understatement, "is in all respects worthy of inclusion".

The Admiralty goes further, and this book is content to follow in its wake, by including Cadiz (1596), Kentish Knock (1652) and Santa Cruz (1657). We read of Drake, of Howard and of Frobisher, but none of these, neither the battles nor their commanders, represented a Navy that was Royal or even British – simply English.

Much of the information presented here first appeared in *A Companion to the Royal Navy*, a comprehensive volume published by Harrap in 1988. The opportunity has been taken to thoroughly revise and up-date every entry relating to battles and honours of the Royal Navy.

Several other points call for comment in order to clarify what at first glance appear to be anomalies, omissions or difficulties.

The first difficulty to resolve is the definition of a battle when applied to the Royal Navy. Few would question the general guiding principle of including in such a compilation a battle fought at sea between a fleet or squadron and an enemy. This seems perfectly sensible and acceptable at first sight, but if this definition is observed strictly it eliminates landing assaults such as combined

I

operations, single or very-few-ship actions, evacuations and air-sea engagements, and patently this is not good enough. How then can this problem be resolved?

I confess to some inconsistency here and make no excuses for introducing into this collection of battles a category which the Admiralty disallows, namely battles which have not been awarded an honour. For example, no compilation such as this could excuse omitting the clash of Force Z and squadrons of Japanese aircraft in the South China Sea when the battleship HMS *Prince of Wales* and the battlecruiser HMS *Repulse* were sunk in December, 1941, simply because no enemy ships were engaged.

The engagement was a benchmark in naval history: two capital ships, apparently efficiently worked up, adequately armed, with plenty of sea room, with well-trained crews and good visibility, succumbed to the assault.

The operation a year earlier by aircraft squadrons of the Fleet Air Arm on the Italian battle fleet at Taranto was against capital ships secured safely but slumbrous in a well-defended port.*

The Force Z clash is not considered worthy of the Admiralty award of a battle honour, while, by contrast, the successful Fleet Air Arm attack at Taranto is justly recognized by an honour. Both engagements are included.

For equally compelling reasons no true list of battles can exclude a paragraph or two on the evacuations from Dunkirk (1940) and Crete (1941), although the principal enemy forces were German aircraft.

Other examples of such anomalies occur quite frequently and when the Admiralty battle honours list is challenged other difficulties loom. Some explanations are still wanting where the Admiralty record itself shows some inconsistencies, such as *Atlantic Conveyor* in the Falklands in 1982; and 899 Squadron of the Fleet Air Arm probably ought not to have Aegean 1943; and 801 Squadron surely

---

* Somewhere in this equation mention ought to be made of the almost simultaneous air attack on the US Navy at Pearl Harbor on 7 December, 1941, made worse in this case by the fact that the opposing countries were officially at peace.

deserves a North Africa honour. However, these anomalies have been allowed to stand until formally corrected.

Convoy battles across the Atlantic, through the Mediterranean and to and from Russia call for special comment. The Battle of the Atlantic (1939–1945) deserves a full and detailed classification in its own right. Winston Churchill described the battle as "a war of groping and drowning, of ambuscade and stratagem, of science and seamanship". On another occasion he wrote: "The only thing that really frightened me during the war was the U-boat peril."

It is evident that this is not the place for the full classification: hundreds of convoys were escorted and operated during the Second World War, with many scores of them resulting in significant engagements on a scale transcending by far many of the honour-worthy battles of the past. Yet these individual convoy battles go unrecognized; they are simply classified by the all-embracing honour Malta Convoys 1941–2, or Arctic 1941–5, or Atlantic 1939–45.

As a compromise, to give a fairer balance to the entries and to bring home the anguish, violence and horror of these clashes a few convoy battles from the Malta, Russian and Atlantic battle fronts have been selected for inclusion.

Other problems arise. British submarine activity is only honoured by campaign awards and this seems to me inadequate recognition when some patrols equated to battles. To redress the balance, partially at least, I have described two patrols one from each World War. For WWI I have chosen Commander Martin Nasmith's exciting and extraordinary foray into the Sea of Marmara in HM Submarine *E 11* (May – June, 1915) and for WWII (May, 1941) Lieutenant-Commander David Wanklyn's gallant exploits in *Upholder* in the Mediterranean.

Other limitations imposed by the Admiralty result in the exclusion of some single-ship actions, yet these were the dominant feature of the Naval War of 1812 against America. So one such battle has been selected for inclusion here – the celebrated *Chesapeake* v *Shannon*. Purists may cavil at the biased choice of this engagement, the first British success after a series of five incredible American single-ship successes. It earns inclusion because it has just about all the qualities needed in fighting at sea during the days of sail.

The document which helps set out the criteria and lists the awards of battle honours is Admiralty Fleet Order (AFO) 2565/54 Issue 98/54 dated 1 October, 1954, and it is entitled *Battle Honours for HM Ships and FAA Squadrons*. Subsequent Orders and memoranda have added to these lists.

In promulgating this AFO the Lords Commissioners of the Admiralty approved a definitive list of battle honours for the Navy for the first time in history and in doing so they rationalized what had been for centuries a slipshod arrangement. Prior to this date commanding officers of HM ships often displayed honours on their own authority, often inaccurately, perpetuating errors and without standards of presentation or display. The AFO put matters right once and for all.

The terms under which battle honours would be awarded were clearly defined. "A battle honour will be awarded," the Order instructed in its guidelines, "for those actions which resulted in the defeat of the enemy, or when the action was inconclusive but well fought, and in exceptional circumstances where outstanding efforts were made against overwhelming odds."

It was not the Admiralty's intention to award honours for a British defeat (thus, for example, excluding the Force Z battle), or when the action was inconclusive and badly fought. "Successful service" is a term used in the AFO to differentiate between active participation and simple presence at an action or operation. "Successful service" clearly approved operations which resulted in the more or less complete frustration of the enemy's intention at the time, although no warship may have been sunk.

There were six types of service approved by the Lords for rating as a battle honour:

1. Fleet or Squadron actions.
2. Single-ship or Boat Service actions.
3. Major Bombardments.
4. Combined Operations.
5. Campaign Awards.
6. Area Awards.

Fleet and Squadron Actions

Prior to WWI ships "participating in an action" needed little further definition: the extent of the participation was immaterial. In the days of sail it was even more clearly defined: physical or visual contact with the enemy was the criterion.

But more modern warfare demands more detailed definition. Since the introduction of air-sea battles, when opposing fleets or squadrons with carrier forces may not have been in visual contact at all, indeed may have been a hundred miles apart or away from the scene of close action, the word "present" is ruled as "at sea under the direct orders of the Senior Officer controlling the operation". Thus, ships may have won an award without having actually opened fire on the enemy. More precisely, the term "present" relates to the ship being mentioned in the Despatch of the C-in-C, a Flag Officer's War Diary, a Battle Summary of the Naval Staff History (BR 1736 series), the Report of Proceedings of the Commanding Officer, or the ship's log.

Single-Ship Actions and Bombardments

The most outstanding of single-ship actions when the enemy was of equal or superior force are considered to be worthy of a battle honour and have been shown by citing the name of the enemy ship sunk or captured or engaged plus the year. For example, in the action between the destroyer *Glowworm* and the enemy heavy cruiser *Admiral Hipper* the *Glowworm* is awarded the battle honour *Admiral Hipper* 1940.

In the case of Bombardments honours are only awarded where the enemy retaliation was appreciable or substantial, such as at Algiers in 1816.

Combined Operations

In order to win an award in this category the Admiralty rightly considers a large number of seamen, marines and troops have to be landed on an enemy coast. Simply transporting troops to the landing area and engaging the enemy as a minor element of the whole operation does not qualify for an award. This allows of anomalies: for example, a ship transporting and landing troops may not be awarded an honour while the troops she landed fought successfully and earned their regiment an honour.

The capture of Havana in 1762 and the assault at St Nazaire in 1942 are examples of this class of award. A curious omission from the official list is Corsica 1794. Hood's seamen gave notable service ashore under Captain Horatio Nelson: evidence of the fighting ashore is given by the loss of Nelson's right eye at the siege of Calvi.

Campaign Awards

These are largely self-explanatory. Such an award was approved for a ship or ships which served in a campaign often with little or no distinction. Simply having served for a specific period earned an award. In the days of sail such service could be grindingly awful, with long periods, extending to many months at sea, without shore leave, with near-inedible, rotting victuals and a cruel discipline to contend with. Seamen of the more modern campaigns of the Second World War suffered different but awesome experiences enduring the horrors of the Arctic convoys, the treachery of the North Atlantic and the fierce ordeals of warfare in the Mediterranean. Ships' companies display campaign awards, both ancient and modern, with worthy pride.

Fireships

The use of fireships calls for a passing reference. Where they were used to good effect and influenced the course of an engagement, reference is made to them under the battle entry. See, for example, their use in the Basque and Aix Roads 1809 entry, and for the Calais Roads fire attack of 1588 see the Armada entry.

Rating of Ships

A few words of explanation may be helpful in understanding the nomenclature of the days of sail. The following table was compiled specially for *A Companion to the Royal Navy* and is a typical example of a system that was subject to many changes. Anson, for example, when appointed First Lord of the Admiralty in 1751 raised the line status to exclude 50-gun ships. At that time 4th rates of 60 guns were virtually obsolete, so that for practical purposes the British line of battle comprised only ships of the first three rates, the majority of which were the splendid 'seventy-fours'.

The most numerous ships were the frigates – the 5th and 6th rates – mounting from 28 to 38 guns on a single deck. The smaller 6th rates of 20 to 24 guns were also known as frigates for a time, but they became classified as post-ships, the smallest ships commanded by post captains. The French classified their small ships of this class as corvettes, a name adopted by the Royal Navy nearly two centuries later.

RATES OF SHIPS					
Rate	No. of guns	Wt of Broadside (lb)	Complement	Tonnage	Length of lower gun deck (ft)
1st	100+	2,500	850–900	2,000–2,600	180
2nd	98	2,300	750	2,000	180
	90	2,050	750	2,000	170
3rd	80	1,974	720	2,000	
	74	1,764	640	1,700	170–160
	60	1,200	490	1,300	
4th	50	800	350	1,100	150
DIVISION BETWEEN SHIPS OF THE LINE AND 5TH AND 6TH RATE SHIPS					
5th	44				
	40				
	38	636–350	320–215	900–700	150–130
	36				
	32				
6th	28				
	24	250–180	200–160	650–550	130–120
	20				

A further word of explanation may clear away any confusion about the use of French and Spanish names for British ships. The naming of captured enemy ships, or prizes, was settled in a logical but at times confusing manner. When a prize was ready for Royal Navy service her name was often unchanged, unless it was unpronounceable in English or unless it was already in use. Once adopted, however, in the passage of time it became used for succeeding ships.

France followed the same policy and this resulted in some instances of enemy names becoming anglicized – such as *Gloire* to *Glory* and *Renommée* to *Renown*. It was all quite reasonable and, when put to the test, it worked.

Nevertheless it led to the curious situation at Trafalgar, for example, of the undoubtedly British ship *Berwick* fighting for the French, while a *Swiftsure* and *Achille* served in both fleets, and a *Temeraire* and *Belleisle* fought under the British flag.

Finally, I wish to acknowledge with thanks the help given by the staff of the Naval Historical Branch, Ministry of Defence for their customary help in the compilation of this book. David Brown, David Ashby and the late Alan Francis have always been most attentive.

I am also grateful for the professional help given by the staff of the Reading Room of the National Maritime Museum, Greenwich.

I owe much to the staff of several libraries for their perseverance and diligence in seeking out information. The Cambridge University Library provided a harvest of information and the reference sections of the Chelmsford, Harlow and Redbridge libraries gave unstinting help for which I am grateful.

I am grateful to Matthew Little, Archivist of the Royal Marine Museum, Southsea, and also indebted to Commander Hilary Foxworthy, OBE, RN, who read the book in typescript and gave most helpful advice.

I also acknowledge the help I have derived from *The Royal Navy Day by Day*, edited by Lieutenant-Commander R.E.A. Shrubb and Captain A.B. Sainsbury VRD MA RNR.

David A Thomas
Sheering
Essex

SECTION ONE

Battle and Campaign Honours

A

ABOUKIR BAY – see NILE, THE, 1798

ABYSSINIA 1868
13 April
19th Century Colonial Wars
A tyrannical Abyssinian ruler using the unlikely name of Theodore aroused widespread rebellion throughout the country. Inter-tribal rivalry was fought out with merciless ferocity. Britain intervened, but when peaceful overtures were rejected an expedition force under the command of Lieutenant-General Sir Charles Napier was despatched to restore peace. Naval brigades from those ships marked with an asterisk were landed and soon captured Magdala. Theodore committed suicide. However, soon after the British departed, the inter-tribal rivalry was resumed with savage butchery.
Ships engaged:

Argus	Daphne	Dryad*	Nymphe	Octavia*
Satellite*	Spiteful	Star	Vigilant.	

Battle Honour: *Dryad*   *Octavia*   *Satellite*

ACRE 1799
17 March – 20 May
French Revolutionary War 1793 – 1803
After Napoleon had conquered Egypt in 1799 he marched against Turkish forces manning the fortress of St Jean d'Acre in the Bay of Haifa in Syria. He then planned to return to Egypt to repel an anticipated reprisal assault from the sea.

Plans went horribly awry. His army started off well enough: its 13,000 men captured Gaza and Jaffa. But, as in the past, he underestimated the Royal Navy. Commodore Sir Sydney Smith commanded a small squadron blockading Alexandria. He correctly identified Acre as Bonaparte's destination – it had a commanding position – and promptly set off there in his 80-gun flagship *Tigre* and the *Alliance* and *Theseus*. En route he captured a flotilla carrying Bonaparte's siege guns. At Acre he positioned two of his ships to enfilade the landward approaches.

Smith took command of 3,000 Turks and added 500 English seamen and marines. When the French arrived they laid siege to Acre, but gave up in despair after sixty-three days, returning to Alexandria with 5,000 casualties. Bonaparte was dismayed: 'If it had not been for you English I should have been Emperor of the East . . . but wherever there is water to float a ship we are sure to find you in the way.'

<u>Battle Honour:</u>   *Alliance*   *Theseus*   *Tigre*

ADEN 1839
19 January
19th Century Colonial Wars

When the Sultan of Aden found himself reduced to penury he resolved to sell the town and port of Aden to Britain. Captain Haines of the Indian Navy was despatched from Bombay to take possession of the colony. However, the Sultan's son opposed the handover. A British naval and military force was sent to overwhelm the rebels and to formally take charge of Aden which then became annexed to British India.

Ships engaged in the expedition were *Cruizer* and *Volage* plus the Indian ships *Coote* and *Mahé*. Troops from the Bombay Artillery, the 1st Bombay European Regiment and the 24th Bombay Native Infantry participated.

<u>Battle Honour:</u>   *Coote*   *Cruizer*   *Mahé*   *Volage*

ADRIATIC 1944
World War II 1939–45

The qualifying area for this campaign honour of the Second World War is defined as all waters of the Adriatic Sea to the north of 40°N.

Ships and submarines which engaged the enemy in this area during 1944 were granted the honour.

Campaign Honour:

Aldenham	Aphis	Atherstone	Avon Vale ·	Belvoir
Bicester	Blackmore	Blean	Brocklesbury	Cleveland
Colombo	Delhi	Eggesford	Grenville	Janus
Jervis	Kimberley	Lamerton	Lauderdale	Ledbury
Loyal	Quantock	Scarab	Teazer	Tenacious
Termagant	Terpsichore	Tetcott	Troubridge	Tumult
Tuscan	Tyrian	Ulster	Undine	Urchin
Whaddon	Wheatland	Wilton	Zetland	

AEGEAN 1943–44
World War II 1939–45

The Campaign Honour Aegean 1943–44 was awarded to all ships and submarines which were engaged in the Aegean Archipelago between 35° N and 22° to 30° E, during the period 7 September to 28 November 1943, and during 1944. An example of such activity was during September and October 1943 when a force of seven escort carriers, seven cruisers and nineteen destroyers and frigates attacked the German evacuation routes from Greece and destroyed the last remnants of German naval units in the Aegean.

Campaign Honour:

Ajax	Aldenham	Argonaut	Attacker	Aurora
Beaufort	Belvoir	Beves	Bicester	Black Prince
Blankney	Blencathra	Brecon	Bruiser	Caledon
Calpe	Carlisle	Catterick	Cleveland	Clinton
Colombo	Croome	Dido	Dulverton	Eastern
Echo	Eclipse	Emperor	Exmoor	Farndale
Faulknor	Fury	Gribb	Hambleton	Haydon
Hedgehog	Hursley	Hunter	Hurworth	Intrepid
Jervis	Kelvin	Khedive	Kimberley	Lamerton
Langlaate	Larne	Ledbury	Liddesdale	Marne
Meteor	Musketeer	Orion	Panther	Pathfinder
Penelope	Penn	Petard	Phoebe	Prince David
Protea	Pursuer	Rinaldo	Rockwood	Rorqual
Royalist	Saksern	Saxifrage	Searcher	Seraph

Severn	Shakespeare	Sibyl	Sickle	Simoon
Sirius	Southern Maid		Sportsman	Stalker
Teazer	Termagant	Terpsichore	Tetcott	Thruster
Torbay	Treern	Trespasser	Trooper	Troubridge
Tumult	Tuscan	Tyrian	Ulster Queen	Ultimatum
Ultor	Unrivalled	Unruly	Unsparing	Unswerving
Vampire	Vigorous	Virtue	Vivid	Vox
Whaddon	Wilton	Zetland		

FAA Squadrons:

800,   807,   809,   879,   881,   899

AIX ROADS – see BASQUE AND AIX ROADS and OLÉRON ROADS

ALEXANDRIA 1882
11 July
19th Century Colonial Wars

The British Mediterranean Fleet comprising eight armoured ships and several smaller vessels bombarded the installations and the port of Alexandria to quell anti-foreign riots. Captain Lord Charles Beresford (later Admiral) distinguished himself in his ship *Condor*. The whole operation was commanded by the C-in-C himself, Admiral Sir Frederick Beauchamp Seymour, in his flagship *Alexandra*. A gunner aboard the flagship earned a VC for picking up a live shell and putting it in a bucket of water.

Battle Honour:

Alexandra	Beacon	Bittern	Condor
Cygnet	Decoy	Hecla	Helicon
Inflexible	Invincible	Monarch	Penelope
Sultan	Superb	Temeraire	

ALGECIRAS (AND THE STRAITS) – See GUT OF GIBRALTAR 1801

ALGIERS 1816
27 August
19th Century Anti-Slavery Operations
The Barbary Coast – that part of the North African coastline from the Straits of Gibraltar to Cape Bon – had been a centre for piracy, which spread far outside the Mediterranean. After the end of the Napoleonic War the British government resolved to deal with the problem. The Mediterranean Fleet, under the command of Lord Exmouth, and a Dutch squadron commanded by Vice-Admiral Baron von Theodorus van Capellan patrolled the coast, accompanied by troops, sappers and miners. Lord Exmouth offered treaties to the Beys of Tunis, Tripoli and Algiers if they would agree to prohibit the taking of Christian slaves. The Bey of Algiers rejected these entreaties, comforted by the fortress-like defences of Algiers.

But the well-defended port could not sustain the British and Dutch attack which reduced the town and harbour to near ruin. 1,200 slaves were released. The Bey surrendered his jewel-studded scimitar as a token of his complete capitulation.

Battle Honour:

Albion	*Beelzebub*	*Britomart*	*Cordelia*	*Fury*
Glasgow	*Granicus*	*Hebrus*	*Hecla**	*Heron**
*Impregnable**	*Informal**	*Leander**	*Minden**	*Mutine**
Prometheus	*Queen Charlotte*		*Severn*	*Superb**

AMBOINA 1810
17 February
Napoleonic War 1803–15
Amboina in the Moluccas was an important Dutch settlement defended by the formidable Victoria Castle, mounting, all-told, with its outlying batteries, 215 guns. Rear-Admiral William O'Brien Drury resolved to capture the town and harbour. His squadron comprised *Dover* (38), Captain Edward Tucker, *Cornwallis* (44), Captain William Montagu, *Samarang* (18), Commander Richard Spencer.

---

* These ships appeared on a supplementary list, which, together with a note of "some rocket boats", probably give a complete list.

Over 400 men from the Madras European Regiment and seamen and marines from the ships were "thrown ashore" in a gallant assault which gave them Victoria Castle and the whole island. They suffered only a handful of casualties. Three Dutch vessels were sunk. Neighbouring islands were captured and accepted British suzerainty.

Battle Honour: *Cornwallis* *Dover* *Samarang*

AMORHA 1858
5 March
Indian Mutiny 1857–58
Lucknow and Amorha became the two strategic targets for relief forces during the Indian Mutiny. (See LUCKNOW). Amorha lies 13 miles east of Faizabad (82° 23' E, 26°45' N) and close by Lucknow. A naval brigade of seamen and marines supported with howitzers and guns from *Pearl* marched on Amorha. The corvette's captain was Captain S. Sotheby. The march on Amorha included the destruction of forts and skirmishes with rebel forces, until, on 5 March, when the British forces had risen to about 1,800 men, they were assaulted by an army of rebels numbering perhaps 14,000. In a fierce battle that day the mutineers suffered enormous casualties at the hands of the professional Bengal Yeomanry, Gurkhas and Military Police. The mutineers were comprehensively defeated and put to flight.

Battle Honour: *Pearl*

ANZIO 1944
22 January
World War II 1939–45
Operation Shingle was the landing of substantial forces for an assault on Rome by the Allied forces, covered by a large concentration of ships, especially Royal Navy vessels. On the first day 36,034 troops and 3,069 vehicles were safely put ashore with fewer than 150 casualties. But it was to prove a miserable stalemate for four months before the final breakout from the bridgehead. Rome lay 37 miles north-west of Anzio. German forces were well

entrenched in natural defensive positions. They were aided by the weather: continual rain churned the bridgehead into a quagmire which bogged down the Allies and their transport. After ten days of bitter fighting the Allies had advanced a mere ten miles. Winston Churchill reported, "We have stranded a vast whale with its tail flopping about in the water."

Supplying the troops ashore was a grave problem, solved by trucks and DUKWs being pre-loaded in Naples, driven aboard LSTs, carried overnight to Anzio then driven ashore direct to supply dumps. Each week 15 LSTs made the run, carrying 3,750 tons of stores in 750 trucks.

When the troops broke through, Rome was theirs in two days. It had been an expensive campaign: 7,000 dead Allies and nearly 20,000 wounded. The Royal Navy came under attack and lost the cruisers *Penelope* and *Spartan* and the destroyers *Inglefield* and *Janus*. A dozen other ships were also lost.

Battle Honour:

Albacore	Barmond	Barndale	Beaufort	Boxer
Bruiser	Bude	Bulolo	Cadmus	Cava
Circe	Crete	Delhi	Dido	Espiègle
Faulknor	Glengyle	Grenville	Hornpipe	Inglefield
Janus	Jervis	Kempenfelt	Laforey	Loyal
Mauritius	Orion	Palomares	Penelope	
Prinses Beatrix		Rinaldo	Rothesay	
Royal Ulsterman		St Kilda	Sheppey	Spartan
Tetcott	Thruster	Two-step	Ulster Queen	Ultor
Urchin	Waterwitch			

MLs:

134,	295,	307	338,	443,
462,	554,	555,	558,	565,
567,	569,	575,	581	

ARCTIC 1941–45 (Russian Convoys)
World War II 1939–45

The area of operations for this honour has been defined as within the Arctic Circle except for the coastal waters of Norway to the south of Tromsö. Those eligible for the honour are defined as all ships and submarines including the covering forces which were employed as escort to or in support of the convoys running to and from North Russia, also those ships and submarines on patrol duty in the area which took part in a successful operation.

From the winter of 1941–42 the Royal Navy began escorting convoys to Russia, north-about Bear Island to Murmansk and Archangel. Although the convoys and some escorts were Allied the predominant content of the convoys and escorts was British. These convoys endured not only appalling weather and sea conditions but the threat of German U-boats, surface units and aircraft. One such convoy was PQ17.

Russian Convoy PQ17 2–13 July 1942

This convoy comprised thirty-five merchantmen, three rescue ships, two tankers and thirteen close escort vessels. A close support force of four cruisers and three destroyers accompanied the convoy. Long-range cover was provided by units of the Home Fleet under Admiral Sir John Tovey with two battleships, one carrier, two cruisers and fourteen destroyers. Several Allied submarines formed defensive patrol lines off the north Norwegian coast, in addition to all these other deployments.

The Germans had considerable forces at their disposal in these far northern waters. U-boats *U–334* and *U–456* were supported by six boats of the 'Eisteufel' Group (*U–251, U–335, U–657, U–88, U–457* and *U–376*). In Norwegian fjords lay the Trondheim Group of warships comprising the battleship *Tirpitz* (Admiral Schneiwind), heavy cruiser *Hipper*, destroyers *Hans Lody, Theodor Riedl, Karl Gulstar, Friedrich Ihn*; T boats *T 7* and *T 15*. Ships which had left Trondheim for Altenfjord were the pocket battleship *Admiral Scheer* (Vice Admiral Kummetz) heavy cruiser *Lützow*, destroyers *Friedrich Eckholt* and *Erich Steinbrinck*. The Narvik Group destroyers left Narvik for Trondheim: (*Z 24, Z 27, Z 28, Z 29, Z 30* and *Richard Beitzen*). An indication of the difficulty of piloting through these waters is given by the fact that the destroyers *Lody, Riedel* and *Karl Gustav* all ran aground but managed to return to base. *Lützow* also grounded and took no further part in the operations.

The Admiralty believed that the German North Sea Combat

Group – the combination of all these groups or squadrons – had put to sea in the direction of North Cape. With mounting anxiety for the safety of the convoy and its escorting forces, the Admiralty ordered the long-range group to retire to the west and to disperse the convoy – and later for it to scatter. The Home Fleet units turned about at Bear Island. At that time only three ships of the convoy had been lost, all to aircraft.

In the meantime the German North Sea Combat Group also turned back to base, judging the conditions and forces employed unlikely to prove rewarding. In the event the now unprotected and scattering convoy suffered terrible losses and casualties. All told, twenty-three of the merchant ships – two-thirds of those in the convoy – were sunk by either torpedo or bomb, plus one of the rescue ships, altogether totalling 144,000 tons. In addition, of course, all cargoes were lost. Five German aircraft were shot down.

This disastrous episode will long be debated in naval circles. What is not any longer disputed is the fact that the sailing of PQ 17 was an unsound operation of war, but political considerations made it paramount.

Summary of the losses: Of the 35 ships, 2 turned back, eight were sunk by U-boats, 7 damaged by aircraft then sunk by U-boats. Stores lost: 430 tanks, 210 aircraft, 3,350 vehicles, 99,316 tons of cargo. 153 merchant sailors were lost, 1,300 were rescued.

ABSTRACT OF STATISTICS RELATING TO RUSSIAN CONVOYS 1941–45

Number of convoys escorted to Russia = 40. Total ships = 720.
Number of convoys escorted from Russia = 35. Total ships = 680.

Goods delivered by Britain

3,830 tanks + 1,388 from Canada	4,338 radio sets
7,411 aircraft (including 3,129 USA)	9 MTBs
4,932 anti-tank guns	14 minesweepers
4,005 rifles and machine guns	4 submarines
1,800 radar sets	2,000 telephone sets

£120 millions-worth of raw materials, foodstuffs, industrial plant, medical and hospital supplies and equipment.

Allied Merchant Ship Losses:

British	35 ships
USA	47
Panama	7
USSR	9
Dutch	1
Norway	1
Total	100 ships = 605,837 Gross tons

Royal Navy Ships Lost:

Cruisers:	*Edinburgh, Trinidad*
Destroyers:	*Matabele, Punjabi, Somali, Achates, Hardy, Mahratta.*
Sloops:	*Kite, Lapwing.*
Frigate:	*Goodall.*
Corvettes:	*Denbigh Castle, Bluebell.*
Minesweepers:	*Gossamer, Niger, Leda, Bramble.*
Armed Whalers:	*Shera.*
Submarine:	*P551*

Battle Honour:

Acanthus	*Achates*	*Active*	*Activity*	*Airedale*
Algonquin	*Allington Castle*		*Alnwick Castle*	
Alynbank	*Amazon*	*Ambuscade*	*Angle*	*Anguilla*
Anson	*Arab*	*Argonaut*	*Argus*	*Ashanti*
Athabascan	*Avenger*	*Ayrshire*	*Badsworth*	*Bahamas*
Bamborough Castle		*Bazely*	*Beagle*	*Bedouin*
Belfast	*Bellona*	*Belvoir*	*Bentinck*	*Bergamot*
Bermuda	*Berwick*	*Beverley*	*Bickert*	*Blackfly*
Black Prince	*Blankney*	*Bluebell*	*Boadicea*	*Borage*
Bramble	*Branham*	*Brissendon*	*Britomart*	*Broke*
Bryony	*Bulldog*	*Burdock*	*Bute*	*Byron*
Caesar	*Cambrian*	*Camellia*	*Campania*	*Campanula*
Campbell	*Cape Argona*	*Cape Breton*	*Cape Mariato*	*Cape Palliser*
Caprice	*Cassandra*	*Cavalier*	*Celia*	*Charlock*
Chaser	*Chiltern*	*Cockatrice*	*Conn*	*Cowdray*
Cumberland	*Curacoa*	*Cygnet*	*Daneman*	*Dasher*
Deane	*Denbigh Castle*		*Devonshire*	*Diadem*

Dianella	Dido	Douglas	Dragon	Drury
Duckworth	Duke of York	Duncton	Echo	Eclipse
Edinburgh	Eglantine	Electra	Elm	Escapade
Eskdale	Eskimo	Essington	Farndale	
Farnham Castle		Faulknor	Fencer	Fitzroy
Foresight	Forester	Fury	Garland	Glasgow
Gleaner	Goodall	Graph	Grou	Grove
Haida	Halcyon	Hamlet	Hardy	Hazard
Heather	Hebe	Honeysuckle	Hound	Howe
Hugh Walpole		Huron	Hussar	Hyderabad
Hydra	Icarus	Impulsive	Inconstant	Indian Star
Inglefield	Intrepid	Iroquois	Jamaica	Jason
Javelin	Kent	Kenya	Keppel	
King George V		King Sol	Kite	La Malouine
Lady Madeleine		Lammerton	Lancaster	Lapwing
Lark	Leamington	Leda	Ledbury	Liverpool
Loch Alvie	Loch Dunvegan		Loch Insh	Loch Shin
London	Lookout	Lord Austin	Lord Middleton	
Lotus	Louis	Loyalty	Macbeth	Mackay
Magpie	Mahratta	Majesty	Malcolm	Manchester
Marne	Martin	Matabele	Matane	Matchless
Mermaid	Meteor	Meynell	Middleton	Milne
Monnow	Montrose	Mounsey	Musketeer	Myngs
Nairana	Nene	Newmarket	Newport	Niger
Nigeria	Norfolk	Northern Gem		
Northern Pride		Northern Spray		
Northern Wave		Notts County	Nubian	Oakley
Obdurate	Obedient	Offa	Onslaught	Onslow
Onyx	Ophelia	Opportune	Orestes	Oribi
Orwell	Outremont	Oxlip	P 45	P 54
P 212	P 221	P 247	P 614	P 615
Palomares	Pasley	Paynter	Peacock	Poppy
Port Colborne	Pozarica	Premier	Punjabi	Pytchley
Quadrant	Queen	Queenborough		
Raider	Rattlesnake	Ready	Redmill	Renown
Retriever	Rhododendron		Richmond	Rodney
Rupert	St Albans	St Elstan	St John	St Kehan
St Pierre	Saladin	Salamander	Sardonyx	Saumarez

Savage	Saxifrage	Scimitar	Scorpion	Scourge
Scylla	Seadog	Seagull	Sealion	Seanymph
Seawolf	Serapis	Sharpshooter	Sheffield	Shropshire
Shusa	Silja	Sioux	Sirius	Skate
Snowflake	Somali	Somaliland	Speedwell	Speedy
Starling	Starwort	Stella Capella	Stormont	Striker
Strule	Sturgeon	Suffolk	Sulla	Sumba
Sweetbriar	Swift	Tango	Tartar	Taurus
Tavy	Termagant	Tigris	Torbay	Tortola
Tracker	Tribune	Trident	Trinidad	Truculent
Trumpeter	Tuna	Tunsbergh Castle		Ulster Queen
Ulysses	Unique	Unruly	Ursula	Venomous
Venus	Verdun	Verulam	Victorious	Vigilant
Vindex	Virago	Vivacious	Viviana	Vizalma
Volage	Volunteer	Walker	Wallflower	Wanderer
Waskesui	Westwater	Watchman	Wells	Westcott
Wheatland	Whimbrel	Whitehall	Wild Goose	Wilton
Windsor	Woolston	Worcester	Wren	Wrestler
Zambesi	Zealous	Zebra	Zephyr	Zest
Zodiac				

FAA Squadrons: 802, 809, 811, 813, 816, 819, 822, 824, 825, 832, 833, 835, 842, 846, 853, 856, 882, 883, 893, 1832

ARMADA, THE SPANISH 1588
July/August
War with Spain 1588–96

The Spanish Armada comprised about 130 ships including thirty-three galleons and four galleasses. It was commanded by the Duke of Medina Sidonia. He sighted the Lizard on 19 July. It was his intention to sail the Armada up the Channel to link up with Parma's invasion force already assembled at Calais.

The English fleet, the main part of which was assembled at Plymouth, was commanded by Lord Howard of Effingham, with Francis Drake as his vice-admiral.

For nine days there followed a running battle as the Armada sailed slowly up Channel in a huge crescent formation with the

English ships engaging whenever the opportunity presented itself.

On 21 July the Spaniards lost the *Nuestra Senõra del Rosario* and the *San Salvador*. Two days later Frobisher's squadron got the better of a sharp engagement off Portland Bill. Another fierce scrap took place off Dunnose Head, Isle of Wight, on the 25th. But two days later, on the 27th, Sidonia came to a good anchorage at Calais.

The English fleet was not joined by a squadron from the Downs under Lord Henry Seymour and Sir William Wynter.

In order to prevent the embarkation of the Spanish and other forces invading England, the anchored Armada was attacked by fireships on the night of 28/29th – with remarkable results. Panic set in among the Spaniards: cables were cut and the ships fell into complete confusion as they attempted to avoid the fireships.

The decisive battle – off Gravelines – was fought the next day. Three or four Spanish galleons were lost and many others seriously damaged. The wind and current were driving the Spanish ships towards the lee shore of the Flemish shoals, but a sudden change of wind enabled the fleet to claw off the dangerous shoals.

Sidonia could not fight his way back down the Channel so he determined to return home to Spain north-about Scotland and Ireland, a voyage of tragic consequences with the west coast of Ireland littered with wrecks of his Armada.

Howard pursued the ships as far north as the Firth of Forth before calling off the pursuit.

Of the original 130 or so ships of Sidonia's Armada only about 70 finally reached home.

Battle Honour:

Achates	Advice	Aid	Antelope	Ark (Royal)
Bonavolia	Brigandine	Bull	Charles	Cygnet
Disdain	Dreadnought	Elizabeth Bonaventure		
Elizabeth Jonas	Fancy	Foresight	George	
(Golden) Lion	Hope	Mary Rose	Merlin	Moon
Nonpareil	Rainbow	Revenge	Scout	Spy
Sun	Swallow	Swiftsure	Tiger	Tramontana
Triumph	Vanguard	Victory	(White) Bear	White Lion

In addition, 158 merchant ships have also been awarded the honour.

ASHANTEE 1873–74
9 June – 4 February 1874
19th Century Colonial Wars

In 1867 the cession of territories on the Gold Coast of West Africa left the participants – the British, Dutch and local tribes – simmering with discontent. The Dutch were happy later to cede all their remaining Gold Coast territory, but the King of Ashantee embarked on an anti-European campaign. This stoked inter-tribal rivalry and the situation escalated into a full-blooded war with British troops, seamen and marines in defence of territories under nominal British protection.

On 11 April 1873 an indecisive battle was fought and 40,000 native rebels received a check. A fully-equipped British expeditionary force was mounted and despatched with a strong naval contingent. Detachments from the naval squadron took part in the widespread fighting up and down the coast. Sir Garnet Wolseley's expeditionary force finally won the day and peace was concluded on 13 February 1874.

<u>Campaign Honour:</u>

Active	*Amethyst*	*Argus*	*Barracouta*
Beacon	*Bittern*	*Coquette*	*Decoy*
Dromedary	*Druid*	*Encounter*	*Himalaya*
Merlin	*Rattlesnake (1873)*		*Seagull (1873)*
Simoon	*Tamar*	*Victor Emmanuel (1874)*	

The honour is dated 1873–74 except where indicated to the contrary.

ATLANTIC 1939–45
World War II 1939–45

The Atlantic Campaign honour has been awarded to all ships and submarines which were employed as escorts to ocean convoys in the North Atlantic – an area defined as the North Atlantic from the equator to the Arctic circle – and to those ships of support groups which took part in a successful action.

This battle was the longest-lasting, the most far-reaching one of World War II, one of the most bitterly fought campaigns of modern history. It is impossible to epitomize in a matter of a few paragraphs such a vast and complex battle, the fortunes of which swayed first one way then the other. A huge bibliography on the battle exists, which covers the drama and horror of the long-drawn-out battle in all its facets from both the British and the German viewpoints.

The barest outline is given here of four convoy battles in order to indicate the bitterness of the Atlantic battle. Perhaps the stark figures in the accompanying tables will also help give a glimpse of the horrors of this long campaign. "The Battle of the Atlantic," Churchill wrote, "was the dominating factor all through the war. Never for one moment could we ever forget that everything else-where depended upon its outcome."

ATLANTIC: CONVOY HX 79
October 1940

This convoy battle was one of the first fought by a Wolf Pack. It included U-boats commanded by the so called 'aces' Günther Prien, Heinrich Bleichrodt, Engelbert Endrass and Joachim Schepke. The home-bound convoy HX 79 was escorted by ten RN vessels led by the old destroyer *Whitehall*.

Some of these German commanders had finished attacking a slow convoy, SC 7: they had in company the most successful U-boat commander of all time, Otto Kretschmer, who had just increased his total of sinking by six ships totalling about 80,000 tons. Now they could hardly believe their luck when they came upon the hapless HX 79.

The convoy comprised 49 ships, ten escorts and the Dutch submarine *O–14*, which, incidentally, contributed nothing to the defence of the convoy.

In five hours of the night of 19–20 October 1940 these U-boat commanders ran alongside the columns of ships firing the remainder of their torpedoes to port and starboard, sinking 60,000 tons of shipping.

The significance of the mauling of these two convoys was the Prime Minister's and the government's immediate and positive re-action: destroyers were transferred from anti-invasion duties to supplement convoy escorts; radar for escorts became a top priority; a new and high-powered and independent command, C-in-C Western Approaches, was brought into being with a large operational HQ at Liverpool; a radical change in anti-submarine training and the setting up in Tobermory Bay of a rigorous course for escorts and their officers in convoy duties and A/S tactics. All of these contributed to the subsequent victory in the Atlantic battle.

ATLANTIC: CONVOY HG 76
December 1941
German Focke-Wulf Kondor long-range aircraft homing U-boats on to Gibraltar convoys in 1941 impelled the Admiralty to suspend sailings, especially after the loss of five merchant ships and the destroyer *Cossack* in HG 75. Two points in particular influenced this decision: firstly, Coastal Command was unable to give cover along the whole route of the convoys; secondly, agents in nearby Algeciras with powerful binoculars could give accurate intelligence of all Gibraltar shipping movements.

Convoy HG 76, comprising 31 ships, was a resumption of these suspended sailings. It departed from Gibraltar on 14 December 1941. Commander F.J. (Johnny) Walker, the Navy's leading A/S tactician, in his sloop *Stork*, commanded the 36th Escort Group. Sixteen escorts gave strong cover: two destroyers, four sloops, nine corvettes, the escort carrier *Audacity* and the CAM ship *Darwin*.

Dönitz deployed seven U-boats of his *Seeräuber* Group, and homed them on to the convoy by Kondors of 1KG 40 from Bordeaux. One of the U-boat commanders was Endrass in *U-567*.

It was dusk on the second evening when the most southerly U-boat first contacted the convoy, soon joined by a second. The following morning *U-131* was attacked by Martlets from *Audacity*, then attacked and sunk by destroyers. *U-434* was sunk the following day, soon after the destroyer *Stanley* had been torpedoed and blown up with a huge sheet of flame. Walker raced to counter-attack, forced *U-434* to surface, rammed and depth-charged her to destruction.

The U-boats scored their greatest success when they torpedoed and sank *Audacity*, a great loss to the defenders' firepower. Soon Walker's sloop was in collision with the *Deptford*, but both survived. Unknowingly *Deptford* had already destroyed Endrass's *U-567* in an earlier attack.

Despite the loss of *Audacity* and *Stanley*, the scales balanced strongly in favour of Walker and his escorts. Four out of seven U-boats were destroyed, against the loss of only one ship of the convoy.

ATLANTIC: CONVOY ONS 5
April/May 1943

The battle element of this convoy passage was fought over a period of six consecutive days between the B7 Escort Group commanded by Captain Peter Gretton assisted by the US Navy's 3rd Support Group, and a pack of U-boats numbering about forty. Twelve merchant ships were sunk for the loss of seven U-boats, five to enemy action and two to collision. But, most significantly, it was a decisive victory over wolf-pack tactics and the end of the wolf-pack's ascendancy over escorts.

The convoy was a slow one of about 6 knots, westbound, comprising 42 ships, with Gretton commanding the destroyer *Duncan*, a frigate and 4 corvettes. Seas were rough, weather bad and visibility poor – which grounded Iceland-based aircraft. Dönitz had organized a formidable concentration of forty U-boats which he named the *Fink* Group, comprising U-boats of the *Amsel* Group off Newfoundland, and of the *Star* and *Specht* Groups, to the north and east respectively.

Five attacks were repulsed before a sixth sank a freighter at dawn on 29 April. Shortage of fuel compelled Gretton to leave the convoy and hand over command to Lieutenant-Commander Sherbrooke in the frigate *Tay*. Other escorts were also detached but reinforcements came in the shape of the US 3rd Escort Group.

By 5 May the U-boats gained an advantage and sank five ships in two hours, but the escorts' counter-measures damaged at least four U-boats. RCAF Catalinas helped keep U-boats submerged, as did continuing storms, but these same storms scattered the convoy. Two more ships were picked off in the main body of the convoy, and another to stragglers. Yet another two were lost that night, when the storm worked more to the radar advantage of the escorts rather than the part-blinded U-boats.

Five U-boats were sunk during twenty-four attacks on the convoy. *Oribi* and *Sunflower* rammed one each: *Snowflake* destroyed one with depth-charges. *Loosestrife* forced another to the surface with depth-charges and she then blew up. And *Vidette* sank one with her hedgehog. Several more were damaged, and another two collided and sank.

May 1943 was the turning point in the Atlantic battle with U-boats being sunk at the rate of one a day.

ATLANTIC: CONVOYS HX 229/SC 122
March 1943

Forty-four U-boats were concentrated along patrol lines to intercept these convoys. Yet detection in the end came by chance. *U-653* was retiring from patrol to effect some repairs when ships of HX 229 were sighted. By nightfall five U-boats had concentrated and sunk eight vessels. The escorts were too few and had been hit by bad luck.

What followed has been described as "the greatest convoy battle of all time". SC 122 was a slow convoy from Sydney, Nova Scotia, bound for the UK, and comprised fifty ships in thirteen columns. It enjoyed a strong escort – B5 Escort Group, with Commander Boyle as Senior Officer in the destroyer *Havelock*, the frigate *Swale*, five corvettes, a US destroyer, a trawler and rescue ship (which collected 165 men during the battle).

Convoy HX 229 left New York four days later on 9 March. It comprised forty ships organized into eleven columns. Escort was provided by B4 Escort Group, with the Senior Officer Lieutenant-Commander G.J. Luther in the destroyer *Volunteer* – his first ever command of an escort group, and an unfamiliar one to him. His group was augmented during the battle by more destroyers and corvettes.

A third convoy intruded into the story: HX 229A. It comprised thirty-six ships with the 40th Escort Group of two frigates, two sloops and two cutters.

Thus three convoys were spread over a vast area of the Atlantic – perhaps 10,000 men of all nations with 100 ships flying a multitude of ensigns about to do battle with storms and the enemy.

On the night of 16/17 March 1943 the larger well-escorted HX 229 had caught up with the slower under-escorted SC 122 until both virtually coalesced into one huge convoy of enormous proportions. It was on this massive armada that about forty-four U-boats descended. The next two days were of Wagnerian proportions with ships sinking with remorseless regularity. Escorts simply could not cope with the overwhelming attacks in the mountainous seas, swept by icy winds and snow storms.

THE BATTLE ENDED WITH THESE LOSSES:

Convoy SC 122	9 ships	53,094 tons
Convoy HX 229	13 ships	93,502 tons
	22 ships	146,596 tons

In addition the 1,340 ton destroyer *Highlander* was lost. Further, HX 229 lost a vessel of 14,795 tons by collision with an iceberg, and another vessel, *Campobello*, was lost to bad weather. One U-boat, *U-384*, was sunk. The apparent victor of this convoy battle of March 1943 became the vanquished only two months later.

Campaign Honour:

Abelia	*Aberdeen*	*Acanthus*	*Acasta*	*Achates*
Active	*Activity*	*Acute*	*Affleck*	*Agassiz*
Ailsa Craig	*Aire*	*Alaunia*	*Albatross*	*Alberni*
Alca	*Alcantara*	*Aldenham*	*Algoma*	*Alisma*
Allington Castle		*Alnwick Castle*		*Alynbank*
Amaranthus	*Amazon*	*Amberley Castle*		*Ambuscade*
America	*Amethyst*	*Amherst*	*Anchusa*	*Anemone*
Angle	*Anguilla*	*Annan*	*Annapolis*	*Antares*
Antelope	*Anthony*	*Antigonish*	*Antwerp*	*Aquamarine*
Arab	*Arabis*	*Arawa*	*Arbiter*	*Arbutus*
Archer	*Arctic Explorer*		*Arctic Pioneer*	
Arctic Ranger	*Arcturus*	*Ardent*	*Argus*	*Ariguani*
Armeria	*Arnprior*	*Arran*	*Arrow*	*Arrowhead*
Arsenal	*Arvida*	*Asbestos*	*Ascania*	*Ascension*
Ashanti	*Asphodel*	*Assiniboine*	*Aster*	*Asturias*
Atherstone	*Atholl*	*Atmah*	*Attacker*	*Aubretia*
Auckland	*Audacity*	*Aurania*	*Auricula*	*Ausonia*
Avon	*Avon Vale*	*Awe*	*Aylmer*	*Ayrshire*
Azalea	*Bachaquero*	*Baddeck*	*Badsworth*	*Baffin*
Bahamas	*Balfour*	*Ballinderry*	*Balsam*	

Bamborough Castle		Banff	Barberry	Barcliff
Barle	Barnwell	Barrie	Barthorpe	Bartizan
Bath	Battleford	Battler	Bayfield	Bayntum
Bazely	Beacon Hill	Beagle	Beauharnois	Beaumaris
Beaver	Bedouin	Begonia	Belleville	Belmont
Bellwort	Bentinck	Bentley	Bergamot	
Berkeley Castle		Berkshire	Bermuda	Berry
Berwick	Betony	Beverley	Bickerton	Bideford
Birdlip	Biter	Bittersweet	Blackfly	Black Swan
Blackmore	Blackwood	Blairmore	Blankney	Bleasdale
Bligh	Bluebell	Boadicea	Bombadier	Borage
Border Cities	Boreas	Boston	Bowmanville	Bradford
Braithwaite	Brandon	Brantford	Brecon	Breda
Bredon	Bridgewater	Brilliant	Brimnes	Brissendon
Broadwater	Broadway	Brocklesby	Brockville	Broke
Bruiser	Bryony	Buckingham	Buctouche	Bude
Bugloss	Bulldog	Bullen	Bulolo	Burdock
Burges	Burke	Burlington	Burnham	Burra
Burwell	Bush	Bushwood	Bute	Butser
Buttercup	Buttermere	Buxton	Byard	Byron
Cachalot	Caicos	Cairo	Calder	Caldwell
Calendula	Calgary	California	Cam	Camellia
Camito	Campania	Campanula	Campbell	
Campbeltown	Campeador V	Campion	Camrose	Candytuft
Cans	Canton	Cap-de-la-Madeleine		Cape Argona
Cape Breton	Cape Clear	Cape Comorin		Cape Mariato
Cape Palliser	Cape Portland	Cape Warwick		Capel
Capilano	Caradoc	Carisbrook Castle		Caraquet
Carlplace	Carnarvon Castle		Carnation	Carnoustie
Carthage	Castleton	Cathay	Catherine	Cato
Cauvery	Cava	Cavina	Cayman	Celandine
Celia	Ceres	Chambly	Chamois	Chance
Chanticleer	Charlestown	Charlock	Charlottetown	Charybdis
Chaser	Chaudière	Chebogue	Chedabucto	Chelmer
Chelsea	Cheshire	Chesterfield	Chicoutimi	Chilliwack
Chitral	Churchill	Cilicia	Clare	Clarkia
Clayoquot	Clematis	Clevla	Cleveland	Clinton
Clover	Coaticook	Cobalt	Cobourg	

Coldstreamer Coll Collingwood Colombo Coltsfoot
Columbia Columbine Combatant Comorin Conn
Conqueror Convolvulus Cooke Copinsay Copper Cliff
Coreopsis Corfu Corinthian Cosby Cossack
Cotillion Cotton Coventry Coventry City Cowdray
Cowichan Cowslip Crane Crabstoun Crispin
Crocus Croome Cubitt Cuckmere Culver
Cumbrae Curacoa Cutty Sark Cyclamen Cygnet
Dacres Dahlia Dainty Daneman Dangay
Dart Dasher Dauntless Dauphin Davy
Dawson Deane Decoy Delhi Delphinium
Deptford Derby County Derbyshire Derwent Despatch
Deveron Devon City Dianella Dianthus Digby
Dittany Dochet Domett Dominica Dorade II
Dornoch Dorothy Gray Dorsetshire Douglas Dovey
Drumheller Drummondville Drury Duckworth
Dumbarton Castle Duncan Duncton Dundas
Dundee Dunedin Dunkery Dunnotar Castle Dunvegan
Dunvegan Castle Dunver Earl Kitchener East View
Ebor Wyke Echo Eclipse Eday Edinburgh
Edmunston Effingham Eglantine Eglinton Egret
Ekins Electra Ellesmere Elm Emerald
Emperor Empress Enchantress Encounter Engadine
Enterprise Erebus Erica Erin Eriksay
Erne Erraid Escapade Escort Esk
Esperance Bay Esquimalt Essington Ettrick
Evadne Evenlode Exe Exmoor Exmouth
Eyebright Fairfax Fal Fame Fandango
Fantome Farndale Faulknor Fearless Fencer
Fennel Fergus Fetlar Fidelity Findhorn
Firedrake Fishguard Fitzroy Flatholm Fleetwood
Fleur de Lys Flint Flint Castle Foley Folkestone
Foresight Forest Hill Forester Fort Francis Fort William
Fort York Fortune Fowey Foxhound Foxtrot
Fraser Fredericton Freesia Friendship Fritillary
Frontenac Fury Fusilier Gallant Galt
Gananoque Gardenia Gardiner Garland Garlies
Gateshead Gatineau Gavotte Gazelle Genista

Gentian Georgetown Georgian Geranium Giffard
Gipsy Glace Bay Gladiolus Gleaner Glenarm
Glowworm Gloxinia Goathland Godavari Goderich
Godetia Goodall Goodson Gore Gorleston
Gorgon Gossamer Gould Gozo Grafton
Granby Grandmère Great Admiral Grecian
Grenade Grenadier Grenville Greyhound Griffin
Grindall Gurkha Grou Grove Gruinard
Guardsman Guelph Guysborough Haarlem
Hadleigh Castle Halifax Hallowell Hamilton
Hamlet Hardy Hargood Hart Hartland
Harvester Hascosay Hastings Hasty Havant
Havelock Havock Hawkesbury Hazard Hazel
Heartsease Heather Helmsdale Heliotrope Hepatica
Hereward Hermes Heron Herschell
Hertfordshire Hespeler Hesperus Heythrop Hibiscus
Highlander Hilary Hollyhock Holmes Homeguard
Honesty Honeysuckle Hornpipe Hoste Hostile
Hotspur Huddersfield Town Hugh Walpole
Humberstone Hunter Huntsville Hurricane Hurst Castle
Hurworth Husky Hussar Hyderabad Hydrangea
Hyperion Ibis Icarus Ilex Ilfracombe
Imogen Imperial Imperialist Impulsive Inchkeith
Inchmarnock Inconstant Indian Star Inglefield Inglis
Ingonish Inkpen Inman Intrepid Inver
Iroquis Isis Itchen Ithuriel Ivanhoe
Jacinth Jackal Jaguar Janus Jaseur
Jasmine Jason Jasper Javelin Jed
Jervis Bay Joliette Jonquière Jonquil Juliet
Jumna Juno Kale Kamloops Kamsack
Kampuskasing Keats Keith Kelly
Kelvin Kempenfelt Kempthorne Kenilworth Castle
Kenogami Kenora Kent Kentville Kenya
Keppel Kerrera Khyber Kilbirnie Kilbridge
Killegray Kilmarnock Kilmartin Kilmington Kilmore
Kimelford Kincardine King George V King Sol
Kingcup Kingston Kingston Agate
Kingston Amber Kingston Beryl

Kingston Chrysolite Kipling Kirkella Kistna

Kitchener Kite Kiwi Knaresborough Castle

Kokanee Konkan Kootenay La Hulloise La Malbaie

La Malouine Lacencia Lachine Lachute Laconia

Lady Beryl Lady Elsa Lady Hogarth Lady Lilian

Lady Madeleine Lady Shirley Laforey Lagan

Lamerton Lanark Lancaster Lancer Landguard

Largs Larkspur Lasalle Lauderdale

Launceston Castle Lauzon Lavender Lawson

Leamington Leaside Leda Leeds Castle Leeds United

Legion Leith Lethbridge Letitia Levis

Leyland Liddesdale Lightfoot Linaria Lincoln

Lincoln City Lindsay Lively Lobelia Loch Achray

Loch Craggie Loch Eck Loch Fada Loch Fyne Loch Glendu

Loch Insh Loch Killin Loch More Loch Oskaig Loch Quoich

Loch Ruthven Loch Scavaig Loch Shin Loch Tulla Locheport

London Londonderry Long Branch Longueuil Loosestrife

Lord Hotham Lord Middleton Lord Nuffield

Lord Stanhope Loring Lossie Lotus

Louis Louisburg Lowestoft Ludlow Lulworth

Luneburg ML 170 ML 172 ML 175 MMS 80

MMS 81 MMS 303 MMS 1066 Macbeth Mackay

Magnolia Magpie Mahone Malaya Malcolm

Malines Mallow Maloja Malpeque Man-o-War

Manners Mansfield Maori Maplin Margaree

Marguerite Marigold Maron Marsdale Martin

Matane Matapedia Mauritius Mayflower Mazurka

Meadowsweet Medicine Hat Melbreak Melita Melville

Menestheus Meon Merceditta Merrittonia Meteor

Middlesex Middleton Midland Mignonette Mildenhall

Milford Milltown Milne Mimico Mimosa

Minas Minna Miscou Moa Moncton

Monkshood Monnow Montbretia Montclare Montgomery

Montreal Montrose Mooltan Moorsman Moorsom

Moosejaw Morden Moreton Bay Morpeth Castle

Morris Dance Mounsey Mourn Moyola Mulgrave

Musketeer Myosotis Myrmidon Nab Wyke Nairana

Nanaimo Napanee Narborough Narcissus Narwhal

Nasturtium	Nene	Neptune	Ness	Nestor
New Glasgow	New Waterford		New Westminster	
New York City		Newark	Newmarket	Newport
Niagara	Nigella	Niger	Nigeria	Nipigon
Noranda	Norfolk	Norsyd	North Bay	
Northern Dawn	Northern Foam	Northern Gem	Northern Gift	
Northern Pride	Northern Reward	Northern Sky	Northern Spray	
Northern Sun	Northern Wave	Norwich City	Notts County	
Nyasaland	Oakham Castle		Oakville	Oasis
Obdurate	Obedient	Odzani	Offa	Onslaught
Onslow	Ophelia	Opportune	Orangeville	Orchis
Orduna	Orfasy	Oribi	Orient Star	Orillia
Orion	Orissa	Orwell	Oshawa	Ottawa
Otway	Outremont	Owen Sound	Oxford Castle	Oxlip
Oxna	PC 74	Palomares	Panther	Papua
Parrett	Parrsboro	Parry Sound	Pasley	Pathfinder
Patroller	Paynter	Peacock	Pegasus	Pelican
Pelorus	Penetang	Penn	Pennywort	
Pentland Firth	Penstemon	Penzance	Peony	Perim
Periwinkle	Perth	Peterborough	Peterhead	Petronella
Petunia	Pevensey Castle		Pheasant	Philante
Picotee	Pict	Pictou	Pimpernel	Pincher
Pink	Pirouette	Plym	Polruan	Polyanthus
Poppy	Porcher	Porchester Castle		Porpoise
Port Arthur	Port Colborne	Port Hope	Portage	Portsdown
Postilion	Potentilla	Poundmaker	Pozarica	Premier
Prescott	Pretoria Castle		Primrose	Primula
Prince David	Prince Robert	Prince Rupert	Prodigal	Prompt
Prospect	Protea	Puffin	Puncher	Punjabi
Pursuer	Pylades	Qu'Appelle	Quadrille	Qualicum
Quantock	Queen	Queen Emma	Quentin	Quesnel
Quiberon	Quickmatch	Quinte	Racehorse	Rahah
Rajputana(AMC)		Rajputana(M/s)		Ramillies
Ramsey	Ranee	Ranpura	Rapid	Ravager
Reading	Reaper	Recruit	Reculver	Red Deer
Redmill	Redoubt	Redpole	Redshank	Regina
Registan	Reighton Wyke		Reindeer	Renown
Repulse	Resolution	Restigouche	Retalick	Retriever

Revenge	Rhododendron		Richmond	Rimouski
Ringdove	Ripley	Rivière de Loup		Rochester
Rockcliffe	Rockingham	Rockrose	Rockwood	Rodney
Rorqual	Rosaura	Rose	Rosemary	Rosthern
Rother	Rowley	Roxborough	Royal Marine	Royal Mount
Royal Scotsman		Royal Sovereign		Ruler
Runnymede	Rupert	Rushen Castle	Rutherford	Rye
Sabina	Sable	Sabre	Sackville	Sagitta
Saguenay	St Albans	St Apollo	St Boniface	St Cathan
St Catherines	St Clair	St Croix	St Elstan	St Francis
St John	St Kenan	St Kilda	St Lambert	St Laurent
St Loman	St Mary's	St Nectan	St Pierre	St Stephen
St Thomas	St Wistan	St Zeno	St Thérèse	Saladin
Salisbury	Salopian	Salvia	Samphire	Sanda
Sandwich	Saon	Sapper	Sarawak	Sardonyx
Sarnia	Saskatchewan	Saskatoon	Sault Sainte Marie	
Saxifrage	Scarba	Scarborough	Sceptre	Scimitar
Scottish	Scylla	Scythian	Sea Cliff	Seadog
Seaford	Seaham	Seal	Sealyham	Seanymph
Sea Rover	Searcher	Seascout	Selkirk	Sennen
Setter	Severn	Seychelles	Shakespeare	Shalimar
Sharpshooter	Shawinigan	Shediac	Sheffield	Sheldrake
Sherbrooke	Sherwood	Shiant	Shiel	Shikari
Shippigan	Shropshire	Sidon	Sikh	Sioux
Skagi	Skate	Skeena	Skomer	Smilax
Smiter	Smith's Falls	Snakefly	Snapper	Snowberry
Snowdrop	Snowflake	Somaliland	Sorel	
Southern Flower		Southern Gem	Southern Isle	
Southern Pride		Southern Prince		Southern Sea
Southern Shore		Spark	Spartan	Speaker
Spearhead	Speedwell	Spey	Sphene	Spikearn
Spiraea	Sportsman	Sposa	Staffa	Stafnes
Stalker	Stanley	Starling	Starwort	Statice
Steadfast	Stella Capella	Stella Carina	Stella Pegasi	Stellarton
Stoic	Stoke City	Stonecrop	Stonetown	Stora
Stork	Storm	Stormont	Stratford	Strathadam
Strathella	Strathroy	Striker	Stroma	Strongbow
Strule	Stuart Prince	Stubbor	Sturdy	Stygian

Sudbury	Summerside	Sunflower	Supreme	Surf
Surprise	Sussexvale	Swale	Swansea	Sweetbriar
Swift Current	Sybil	Symbol	Taciturn	Tadoussac
Tamarisk	Tanatside	Tango	Tantivy	Tarantella
Tattoo	Taurus	Tavy	Tay	Tedworth
Tees	Test	Texada	Thalassa	Thane
The Pas	Thetford Mines		Thirlmere	Thorlock
Thornborough		Thrasher	Three Rivers	Thule
Thunder	Thyme	Tillsonburg	Timmins	
Tintagel Castle		Tiree	Tobago	Torbay
Torrington	Tortola	Totland	Tourmaline	Towey
Tracker	Trail	Transcona	Trent	Trentonian
Trident	Trillium	Tritellier	Trondra	Trouncer
Truant	Truculent	Trumpeter	Truro	Tui
Tumult	Tunsberg Castle		Turcoman	Tweed
Tyler	Tyrian	Ullswater	Ulster Queen	Ultimatum
Ultor	Uganda	Universal	Unruly	Unsparing
Unst	Unswerving	Untiring	Upstart	Usk
Valentine	Valleyfield	Vancouver	Vanessa	Vanoc
Vanquisher	Vansittart	Varanga	Vascama	Vegreville
Veleta	Velox	Venetia	Vengeful	Venomous
Verbena	Verity	Veronica	Versatile	Vervain
Vesper	Vetch	Veteran	Victoriaville	Victrix
Vidette	Ville de Quebec		Vimy	Vindex
Violet	Viscount	Visenda	Visigoth	Viva II
Vivacious	Viviana	Vizalma	Voltaire	Volunteer
Voracious	Vortigern	Vulcan	Wakeful	Walker
Wallaceburg	Wallflower	Walney	Walpole	Wanderer
Warspite	Warwick	Wasaga	Waskesiu	Watchman
Waveney	Wear	Wedgeport	Wellard	Wellington
Wells	Wensleydale	Wentworth	Wessex	West York
Westcott	Westmount	Weston	Wetaskiwin	Weyburn
Whimbrel	Whirlwind	Whitaker	Whitby	Whitehall
Whitehaven	Whitehorn	Whitethroat	Whitshed	Wild Goose
Wild Swan	Wildflower	William Scoresby		Willowherb
Winchelsea	Winchester	Windermere	Windflower	Windsor
Windrush	Winnipeg	Wishart	Wisteria	With
Witherington	Wolborough	Wolfe	Wolsey	Wolverine

Woodcock	*Woodpecker*	*Woodruff*	*Woodstock*	*Woolston*
Worcester	*Worcestershire*		*Worthing*	*Wren*
Wrestler	*Wyvern*	*Yes Tor*	*York*	*York City*
Yorkshireman	*Zanzibar*	*Zetland*	*Zinnia*	*Zulu*

<u>FAA Squadrons:</u>   700, 802, 804, 807, 808, 810, 811, 813, 814, 816, 818, 819, 820, 825, 833, 834, 835, 836, 837, 838, 840, 846, 860, 881, 892, 896, 898, 1832.

AZORES 1591
31 August – 1 September
War with Spain 1588–96

Note: Various compelling sources have designated AZORES 1591 a Single-Ship Battle Honour and have placed it in that section. The definitive listing – the Battle Honour (blue file) in the Historical Branch Library – does just this in AFO 2565/54, Issue 98/54 dated October 1954, plus sundry later additions. However, the draft manuscript for the BR (Book of Reference) compiled for publication in 1957 (but not, in fact, published) placed the engagement in the main battle honour section rather than the single-ship section. This is perhaps a more appropriate placing, which we have followed here.

The action was fought between an English squadron of seven sail commanded by Lord Thomas Howard and a far superior Spanish squadron under the command of Don Alonso de Bazan. The seven English ships were *Revenge*, flagship of Sir Richard Grenville, *Defiance, Nonpareil, Bonaventure, Lion, Foresight* and *Crane*. They had waited weeks off Flores, in the north-west of the Azores, in the hopes of intercepting a Spanish treasure fleet. Then on 31 August they were surprised at anchor, caught unawares. Howard stood out to sea with his squadron and engaged the Spanish squadron in a running fight till darkness cloaked his escape – all except Grenville's *Revenge*. She remained to fight it out with the Spaniards. She was hopelessly outnumbered. She fought for a total of fifteen hours in the course of which she sank two Spanish ships. But by daylight on 1 September she had been totally dismasted, all upper works had been shot away and she had six feet of water in her hold. Forty of her crew lay dead and many more were severely wounded. *Revenge* struck. Two days later Grenville died of his many wounds, and *Revenge* foundered in a storm as if determined not to submit to captivity.

<u>Battle Honour:</u>   *Revenge*

B

BALTIC 1854–55
28 March – 20 September 1854
17 April – 10 December 1855
Crimean War 1853–56

Alarmed by Russian expansion in the Black Sea Britain and France joined forces and declared war. They resolved to despatch a fleet to the Baltic to protect their various interests, but France was too committed, so it was left to Britain to provide a fleet, which duly left Spithead.

A notable feature of the fleet was that never before had a large force composed exclusively of steam vessels (plus sails) departed from England on a hostile mission. The age of steam had arrived. Twelve screw-driven ships comprised this first fleet, led by the massive 131-gun *Duke of Wellington*, flagship of Vice-Admiral Sir Charles Napier, with a complement of 1,100 men.

The remainder of the force comprised:
Royal George (120) Captain Henry J. Codrington (990 crew)
St Jean d'Acre (101) Captain Hon Henry Keppel (900)
Princess Royal (91) Captain Lord Clarence Paget (850)
Edinburgh (60) Rear Admiral Henry D. Chads (660)
Hogue (60) Captain William Ramsay (660)
Ajax (60) Captain Frederick Warden (450)
Blenheim (60) Captain Hon Frederick T. Pelham (600)
Impérieuse (51) Captain Rundle B. Watson (530)
Arrogant (46) Captain Hastings R. Yelverton (450)
Amphion (31) Captain Astley C. Key (320)
Tribune (31) Captain Hon Swynfen T. Carnegie (300)

Napier was charged with blockading the Russian fleet in the Baltic: he was not to risk his fleet unnecessarily yet he was to afford protection to Swedish and Danish ships.

The Russians were, in fact, contained: the island of Bomarsund was assaulted and captured with over 2,000 prisoners. Apart from these modest achievements the Baltic campaign achieved virtually nothing.

Battle Honour:

1854:

Alban	Algiers	Boscawen	
Cumberland	Dauntless	Gladiator	Hannibal
Hecla	Janus	Leopard	Miranda
Monarch	Neptune	Odin	Penelope
Pigmy	Prince Regent	Princess Royal	Resistance
Rhadamanthus	Rosamund	Royal William	St George
St Jean d'Acre	St Vincent	Sphinx	Stromboli
Termagant	Tribune	Tyne	Valorous
Wrangler	Zephyr		

1854–55:

Ajax	Amphion	Archer	
Arrogant	Basilisk	Belleisle	Blenheim
Bulldog	Caesar	Conflict	Cressy
Cruizer	Cuckoo	Desperate	Dragon
Driver	Duke of Wellington		Edinburgh
Euryalus	Gorgon	Hogue	Impérieuse
James Watt	Lightning	Locust	Majestic
Magicienne	Nile	Otter	Porcupine
Royal George	Snap	Volcano	Vulture

1855:

Aeolus	Badger	Beacon	
Biter	Blazer	Calcutta	Carron
Centaur	Colossus	Cornwallis	Cossack
Dapper	Drake	Esk	Exmouth
Falcon	Firefly	Geyser	Gleaner
Grappler	Growler	Harrier	Hastings
Havock	Hawke	Hind	Jackdaw
Lark	Magpie	Manly	Mastiff
Merlin	Orion	Pelter	Pembroke
Pickle	Pincher	Porpoise	Princess Alice
Prompt	Pylades	Redbreast	Redwing
Retribution	Rocket	Ruby	Russell
Sinbad	Skylark	Snapper	Starling
Stork	Surly	Swinger	Tartar
Thistle	Volage	Weazle	

BANDA NEIRA 1810
9 August 1810
Napoleonic War 1803–15
Banda Neira is the most important of a dozen islands in the Banda Sea, Indonesia, situated about 50 miles south of Ceram (or Seram). Rear-Admiral William O'B Drury despatched a small force there in mid-1810. Captain Christopher Cole commanded *Caroline* (36), *Piedmontaise* (38), *Barracouta* (18) and *Mandarin* (12). En route from Madras to reinforce Amboina Cole received intelligence of a concentration of 700 regular Dutch troops stationed on Banda Neira. He elected to attack this force. He launched a determined and clever attack on the island using seamen, marines and troops of the Madras European Regiment, captured a fortress and accepted the surrender of no fewer than 1,500 Dutch troops.

<u>Battle Honour:</u>   *Barracouta*   *Caroline*   *Piedmontaise*

BARENTS SEA 1942
31 December 1942
World War II 1939–45
Captain R. St V. Sherbrooke earned a Victoria Cross for his gallantry in command of his destroyer flotilla in defence of Convoy JW 51B from Loch Ewe to northern Russia. Sherbrooke's own destroyer was the *Onslow* (1,540 tons, four 4.7").

Toward the end of 1942 the Admiralty adopted the plan of despatching smaller groups of ships as convoys to Russia. Thus JW 51A was the first half of a convoy which reached Kola Inlet on Christmas Day: it was quickly followed by the second half, JW 51B. The awful severity of the weather, it was generally agreed, would help reduce the danger of both air and U-boat attacks.

Sherbrooke led his six destroyers and five smaller warships from the anchorage with fourteen merchant ships. A severe gale part-scattered the convoy on the very day that Rear-Admiral R.L. Burnett, with the cruisers *Sheffield* (9,100 tons, 12 × 6") and *Jamaica* (8,000 tons, 12 × 6") left Kola to meet Sherbrooke halfway and give support.

Unluckily for them, *U-354* sighted the convoy on 30 December, despite the awful weather conditions. Vice-Admiral Kummetz with his flag in the heavy cruiser *Hipper* (12,500 tons, 8 × 8") led the Lützow (12,750 tons, 8 × 8") and six destroyers to intercept. This force split.

Burnett's cruisers had not established contact, and a day of utter confusion developed in atrocious conditions.

Hipper located the convoy and severely damaged the *Onslow*, blinding Sherbrooke in one eye and overwhelmed the minesweeper *Bramble*. Snow squalls prevented *Lützow* from annihilating the convoy and her protective escorts. *Hipper* attacked again, crippling the destroyer *Achates* (1,350 tons, 4 × 4.7") which continued to fight for another two hours before sinking.

Then fortune turned: Burnett came on the scene and promptly sank a destroyer and scored three hits on the *Hipper*. Kummetz turned about and headed back to Alten Fjord. *Lützow* fired from long range but the battle was over. The convoy reached Kola Inlet unharmed. The Germans suffered the price of hesitancy and the ignominy of failure to press home their attack, for the convoy had been at their mercy.

Battle Honour:

Achates	*Hyderabad*	*Jamaica*	*Northern Gem*	*Obdurate*
Obedient	*Onslow*	*Orwell*	*Rhododendron*	*Sheffield*

BARFLEUR 1692 followed by LA HOGUE 1692
19 – 22 May and 23 – 24 May
War of the English Succession 1689–97

Two years before Barfleur the French admiral, the Comte de Tourville had wrested superiority in the Channel from the English by his victory off Beachy Head. Now Barfleur, and its dramatic sequel at La Hogue a day or so later, regained not only the Channel superiority for the English but settled decisively the Anglo-French naval struggle during the War of the English Succession.

The exiled King James II was trying to regain his throne by invading England from a base in Cherbourg, where he concentrated an army of 30,000 men and 500 transports. Tourville waited for more reinforcements, but as these failed to materialize he weighed from Brest with forty-four of the line (a few authorities quote thirty-eight) entering the Channel on 17 May but without the Toulon fleet back-up.

Unknown to him, Admiral Sir Edward Russell (later Earl of Orford) had mustered a huge Anglo-Dutch fleet of just under one hundred ships of the line at Portsmouth. The two battle fleets sighted each other off Cap Barfleur on the Cotentin Peninsula. Russell wore his flag in the *Britannia* (100) and Tourville in his flag-ship, the *Soleil Royal* (104). The two battle lines engaged and fierce fighting ensued. Early in the afternoon a dense fog settled over the battle area, but Tourville skilfully extricated his fleet and slowly drew away to the west. Both fleets anchored at nightfall, neither having lost a ship.

The following morning Tourville continued sailing westward to the Channel Islands and Russell began a general chase. After the fleets had anchored again for the night the chase continued the following day (21st). Tourville then shifted his flag to the *Ambitieux* (96).

The *Soleil Royal* went aground near Cherbourg where she was trapped by Vice-Admiral Sir Ralph Delavall on the 22nd with the Red Squadron. *Soleil Royal, Triomphant* (76) and *Admirable* (90) were all destroyed by fire.

Some twenty-two ships were chased by Admiral Sir John Ashby (Blue Squadron) through the race at Alderney into St Malo, while others escaped towards the Bay of La Hogue, where the battle was fought to a bitter end.

The combined assembled fleets for the Battle of Barfleur comprised nearly 140 ships, with possibly the world's greatest clash at sea in prospect: three fleets waiting on a wind for fame and fortune – or crushing defeat.

Battle Honour: this award serves both Barfleur and La Hogue. Separate awards are not recognized:

Advise	Aetna	Albemarle	Berwick	Blaze
Bonaventure	Britannia	Burford	Cadiz Merchant	Cambridge
Captain	Centurion	Charles Galley	Chester	Crown
Defiance	Deptford	Dreadnought	Duchess	Duke
Eagle	Edgar	Elizabeth	Essex	Expedition
Extravagant	Falcon	Flame	Fox	Grafton

Greyhound	Griffin	Half Moon	Hampton Court	
Hawk	Hopewell	Hound	Hunter	Kent
Lemfox	Lightning	Lion	London	Mary Galley
Monck	Monmouth	Montagu	Neptune	
Northumberland		Ossory	Owner's Love	Oxford
Phaeton	Portsmouth	Resolution	Restoration	Roebuck
Royal Katherine		Royal William	Ruby	Rupert
St Albans	St Andrews	St Michael	Sandwich	Sovereign
Speedwell	Spy	Stirling Castle	Stromboli	Swiftsure
Thomas and Elizabeth		Tiger Prize	Vanguard	Vesuvius
Victory	Vulcan	Vulture	Warspite	
Windsor Castle		Wolf	Woolwich	

BARFLEUR: LA HOGUE 1692
23–24 May
War of the English Succession 1689–97

The battle of La Hogue was the continuation of the battle of Barfleur between an Anglo-Dutch fleet and a French fleet.

On 23 May Sir Cloudesley Shovel, Rear Admiral commanding the Red Squadron, was ordered to destroy the French ships left at anchor off La Hogue. But Shovel had been severely hurt by a large splinter wound in the thigh, so his place was taken by Vice-Admiral Sir George Rooke, commanding the Blue Squadron.

Fifteen French ships of the line had been caught by the flood tide and lay at anchor in the bays of La Hogue and Cherbourg. Three of them had already been dispatched – the flagship *Soleil Royal*, *Admirable* and *Triomphant*: the remaining twelve sailed deeper into the bay, among the scores of transports assembling for an attempted invasion of England by James II.

English and Dutch fireships, as well as the ships of the line, pursued the French ships and transports, wreaking dreadful destruction by fire and shot. Every one of the twelve ships of the line was destroyed. All told the French lost all fifteen of their ships in the combined Barfleur/La Hogue battles.

So close inshore was the battle fought that crowds watched from ashore, including, it is said, James II himself. The Allied boats and fireships operated in such shallow waters that French cavalry were despatched to attack them. We have the remarkable record of French troopers being pulled off their horses by seamen with boathooks.

The Allies gained a stunning victory, which proved decisive in the direction and outcome of the war.

BASQUE ROADS 1809 (Basque and Aix Roads, Oléron Roads)
11–16 April
Napoleonic War 1803–15

Rear-Admiral Willaumez sailed with ten of the line from Brest southward to join a smaller French squadron already in the anchorage at Basque and Aix Roads, but he was followed by Admiral Gambier's Channel Fleet and blockaded in the Roads.

The Admiralty determined to neutralize this French threat in the Bay of Biscay and despatched Lord Cochrane with a reinforcing squadron of fireships to join Gambier off Rochefort.

The fireships and explosion vessels, each loaded with several hundred barrels of gunpowder, were launched on the night of 11–12 April. In the confusion of cutting cables and avoiding the fireships, all but two of the French ships ran aground. However, the engagement lacked the success expected. Gambier declined to assist Cochrane till later the following day, when the *Varsovie* (80), *Aquilon* (74) and *Tonnere* (80) were taken or burnt. Sporadic actions over the next few days were inconclusive. A great opportunity for a crushing victory was squandered.

Cochrane opposed a parliamentary vote of thanks to Gambier, citing his excessive caution in battle. But he protested too much, continued to make a nuisance of himself, lost support and ruined his own career.

Battle Honour:

Aetna	Aigle	Beagle	Bellona	Caesar
Caledonian	Conflict	Contest	Donegal	Doteral
Emerald	Encounter	Fervent	Foxhound	Gibraltar
Growler	Hero	Illustrious	Impérieuse	Indefatigable
Insolent	King George	Lyra	Martial	Mediator
Nimrod	Pallas	Redpole	Resolution	Revenge
Theseus	Thunder	Unicorn	Valiant	Whiting

BAY OF BISCAY 1805 (Cape Ortegal, Strachan's Action)
4 November
Napoleonic War 1803–15

After their crushing defeat at Trafalgar the remnants of the thirty-three strong Franco-Spanish fleet dispersed and sought safety to seaward. Four of them – *Formidable* (80), *Mont Blanc* (74) *Scipion* (74) and *Duguay-Trouin* – appeared to have made good their escape and headed for the French ports. They were under the flag of Rear Admiral Dumanoir Le Pelley. But fourteen days after the battle this force encountered Captain Sir Richard Strachan in *Caesar* (80) with three 74s and four frigates off Cape Ortegal, the north-west shoulder of Spain.

The French declined battle and a long chase ensued before they were brought to action and compelled to fight. After a series of fierce engagements all the French ships struck. The successful commanding officers of the British ships were: Strachan in *Caesar*; Captain Alan Hyde Gardner in *Hero* (74); Captain Halstead in *Namur*; Captain Lee in *Courageux* (74); Captain Pater in *Bellona* (74).

The English casualties amounted to 24 killed and 111 wounded. The French casualties totalled 730.

Duguay-Trouin was eventually taken into Royal Navy service as a boys' training ship with the name *Implacable* at Devonport from 1858 until as recently as 1949.

Battle Honour:

Aeolus	Caesar	Courageux	Hero	Namur
Phoenix	Révolutionnaire		Santa Margarita	

BELGIAN COAST 1914–18
World War I

For four years the Belgian coast was the pivotal point of the left flank of the British army on the Western Front, and it threatened the flanks and rear of the German armies in France. Antwerp, in particular, became of strategic importance.

Winston Churchill, as First Lord of the Admiralty, wrote to the Prime Minister and to General Kitchener, giving his view that the sustained and effective defence of Antwerp was "a matter of high consequence".

The forts of Antwerp came under the fire of 17" howitzers. The British sent 2,000 marines, a RN division and tens of thousands of soldiers to defend the port. But Antwerp fell and the navy evacuated the defenders back to England.

Heavy demands were made on the navy. Ports throughout the land were scoured for ships able to bombard the German positions. Even old battleships and 40-year-old 250-ton gunnery tenders were brought into service. Bombardments were carried out week after week, month after month; these memorable series of naval operations continued for four years. The campaign culminated in 1918 with the assaults on Zeebrugge and Ostend.

Campaign Honour:

Afridi	Albyn	Amazon	Ariel	Attentive
Botha	Brighton Queen		Brilliant	Broke
Bustard	Cambridge	Carysfoot	Centaur	Cleopatra
Columbia	Cossack	Crane	Crusader	Curran
Devonia	Duchess of Montrose		Erebus	Excellent
Exmouth	Falcon	Faulknor	Fawn	Ferret
Flirt	Foresight	General Craufurd		
General Wolfe		Gipsy	Glen Avon	Gorgon
Gransha	Greyhound	Gurkha	Hazard	Humber
Iris	Irresistible	Jupiter II	Kangaroo	Kempton
Lady Ismay	Lance	Lapwing	Laurel	Leven
Lightfoot	Lizard	Lochinvar	Lord Clive	Lucifer
Lysander	Manly	Mansfield	Maori	Marmion II
Marshal Ney	Marshal Soult	Mastiff	Matchless	Medea
Melpomene	Menelaus	Mentor	Mermaid	Mersey
Milne	Miranda	Mohawk	Moorsom	Morris
Murray	Myrmidon	Nimrod	Nubian	Nugent
P11	Peary	Phoebe	Prince Eugene	
Prince Rupert	Queen Victoria		Racehorse	Radiant
Ravenswood	Recruit	Redoubtable	Retriever	Revenge
Rinaldo	Riviera	Russell	Sapphire	Saracen
Sargetta	Satyr	Sharpshooter	Sirius	
Sir John Moore		Skilful	Springbok	Starfish

Superman	Swift	Syren	Tartar	Taurus
Termagant	Terror	Thruster	Truculent	Undaunted
Ure	Venerable	Velox	Vestal	Viking
Westward Ho	Zulu			

<u>Monitors:</u>	M23	M24	M25	M26
	M27	TB4	TB24	
<u>MLs:</u>	103	105	110	239
	252	272	276	279
	280	282	283	532

<u>CMBs:</u> 1, 2, 3, 4, 5, 7, 8, 9, 10, 12, 13, 14A, 15A, 16A, 19A, 20A, 21B, 22B, 23B, 24A, 25BD, 64BD, 66BD, 68BD, 70A, 71A, 73BD, 74BD, 76A, 86BD, 89BD

BELLE ILE 1761 (Belle Isle)
7 June
Seven Years' War 1756–63

The island was captured by troops of the Royal Artillery, Light Dragoons, two Marine battalions and numerous foot soldiers supported in strength by ships, frigates, bombs and fireships under the command of the Hon Augustus Keppel in HMS *Valiant*.

<u>Battle Honour:</u>

Achilles	Actaeon	Adventure	Aetna
Aldborough	Blast	Buckingham	Burford
Chichester	Dragon	Druid	Escort
Essex	Firedrake	Flamborough	Fly
Furnace	Hampton Court	Hero	Infernal
Launceston	Lynn	Melampe	Monmouth
Prince of Orange	Sandwich	Southampton	Swiftsure
Temeraire	Torbay	Valiant	Vesuvius

BELLE ISLE 1795 – See CORNWALLIS'S RETREAT

BENIN 1897
8–28 February
19th Century Colonial Wars

A peaceful mission of officers of the Niger Coast Protectorate was massacred by an organized force of the King of Benin about twelve miles from Benin City.

Immediate reprisals were called for by the British to avenge the killings and to contain the lawlessness. Rear Admiral Rawson undertook to reduce the city and to capture the king, his generals and priest. He assembled an impressive squadron comprising his flagship *St George* and five other ships from the Cape Station, supplemented by two more from the Mediterranean Station.

A naval brigade was landed and marched on the city which was taken on 18 February. The greatest number of casualties suffered by the British were non-military. There were 2,290 cases of fever.

<u>Battle Honour:</u>

Alecto	*Barossa*	*Forte*	*Magpie*	*Philomel*
Phoebe	*St George*	*Theseus*	*Widgeon*	

BISCAY 1940–45
World War II

The qualifying area for this Second World War campaign award was defined as the waters between the latitudes of Ushant and Cape Ortegal from 12° W to the coast of France. Ships and submarines which were employed on patrol duty and took part in a successful action are honoured. The interception and sinking of an enemy blockade runner was not regarded as adequate qualification for the award.

Hitler's acquisition of Norway's extensive and complex coastline and the subsequent conquest of the Low Countries and France gave Admiral Dönitz the means of turning Britain's maritime flanks by judicious employment of his U-boat force. He promptly set about the construction of heavily fortified bases on the French Atlantic coast – at Brest, Lorient, St Nazaire, La Rochelle and Bordeaux. Possession of these French ports gave an incalculable advantage to Germany, including a reduction of over 50% in the transit time of U-boats to their Atlantic hunting grounds. The construction of massive concrete pens in these Biscay ports strengthened them almost to the point of invulnerability.

The toll of Allied shipping sunk mounted alarmingly.

By 1942–3 Coastal Command of the RAF, employing radar and other technical equipment, began the slaughter of the U-boats in the Bay.

Germany countered the radar with Metox, a radar receiver of great operating range. Early in 1943, however, the situation changed. Britain had developed a new Ultra High Frequency radar of 10-centimetre wavelength undetectable by Metox. Powerful searchlights named Leigh Lights also played their part. Dönitz ordered his U-boats to proceed submerged at night and to charge batteries during the day up top with AA guns alerted.

In July 1943 the RN 2nd Support Group and US and RAF aircraft sunk nine U-boats in one week, whereupon Dönitz suspended all Biscay departures. It was back to the traditional British blockade of centuries ago.

The war still had nearly two years to run, but the battle of the Bay of Biscay – and, indeed, the Atlantic – had virtually been won.

Campaign Honour:

Abdiel	Albrighton	Archer	Ashanti	Assiniboine
Bellona	Berry	Bideford	Borage	Brissendon
Cachalot	Calgary	Charybdis	Chaudière	Conqueror
Crane	Dahlia	Diadem	Dominica	Duckworth
Edmundston	Egret	Enterprise	Essington	Glasgow
Godetia	Graph	Haida	Hastings	Havelock
Hurricane	Iroquois	Kite	Kootenay	Landguard
Loch Killin	Louis	Mauritius	Monkshood	Nene
Onslow	Ottawa	Pimpernel	Qu'Appelle	Restigouche
Rockingham	Saskatchewan	Saxifrage	Sceptre	Scylla
Seanymph	Sheffield	Skeena	Snowberry	Starling
Stubborn	Tally Ho	Tanatside	Tartar	Thunderbolt
Tuna	Tweed	Unbeaten	Unique	Ursa
Victorious	Vimy	Viscount	Volunteer	Warspite
Warwick	Waveney	Wear	Wild Goose	Woodpecker
Wren				

FAA Squadron: 817

'BISMARCK' 1941
23–27 May
World War II

The pursuit and sinking of the German 45,000-ton battleship *Bismarck* is a text-book model of command of the seas.

Accompanied by the heavy cruiser *Prinz Eugen* (12,750 tons, 8 × 8") she broke out from her Gdynia base to attack North Atlantic convoys under the command of Vice Admiral Lütjens. Both ships were intercepted by the patrolling cruisers *Suffolk* (9,800 tons, 8 × 8") and *Norfolk* (9.925 tons, 8 × 8") in the Denmark Strait, near the Greenland ice-edge. Admiral Sir John Tovey, C-in-C Home Fleet, dispatched the battlecruiser *Hood*, the grandest symbol of British naval supremacy (42,100 tons, 8 × 15") commanded by Captain R. Kerr and wearing the flag of Vice Admiral L.E. Holland, and the newly-commissioned battleship *Prince of Wales* (Captain Leach, 35,000 tons, 10 × 14"), then 220 miles to the SE to intercept the German squadron.

Shortly before 6 am on 24 May battle was joined at 25,000 yards. After about 15 minutes when all three capital ships had been struck or straddled, *Bismarck's* fifth salvo penetrated one of *Hood's* magazines and she blew up. Out of more than 1,400 men, just three survived – a midshipman, an able seaman and an ordinary signalman.

Prince of Wales was also hit and seriously damaged: she managed to break off the engagement, but not until after having scored three hits on *Bismarck*, one of which created a serious oil leak. Small though it was, it became a significant influence on the choice of options opened to Lütjens. When the action was broken off the Admiral abandoned the Atlantic foray and headed for a French port.

Admiral Pound at the Admiralty and Tovey in his flagship marshalled considerable forces to try to intercept Lütjens. Tovey in *King George V* (35,000 tons, 10 × 14") sailed from Scapa with *Repulse* (32,000 tons, 6 × 15", 20 × 4.5"), the carrier *Victorious* (23,000 tons, 35 aircraft), five cruisers and six destroyers. From convoy escort duties *Rodney* (33,900, 9 × 16") and *Ramillies* (29,150 tons, 8 × 15") altered course to intercept, their convoys re-routed for security. Command of the seas was being exercised powerfully.

Lütjens detached Prinz Eugen and she reached Brest independently, while *Bismarck* managed to give the slip to the shadowing British cruisers. After intensive searching, a Catalina flying boat of Coastal Command sighted *Bismarck* only 700 miles from Brest. Tovey detached the cruiser *Sheffield* to make contact and shadow while *Ark Royal*, detached from Gibraltar's Force H, flew off a strike force of Swordfish aircraft, which mistook the cruiser for the *Bismarck* and launched an abortive attack. Late that evening another strike was launched and a torpedo from one of the fifteen attacking aircraft scored a crucial hit right aft which damaged *Bismarck's* propellors and jammed her rudder. This damage was to prove decisive. It gave Captain Vian, commanding the 4th Destroyer Flotilla in *Cossack* (1,870 tons, 8 × 4.7"), time to locate the battleship and launch torpedo attacks.

In the early hours of the following day, 17 May, Tovey in *KGV*, with *Rodney*, closed with *Bismarck* and awaited daylight rather than undertake a night action.

For two hours the British ships pounded the German guns to silence. The cruiser *Dorsetshire* (9,975 tons, 8 × 8") dispatched her with torpedos and *Bismarck* sank at 10.36 am 400 miles from Brest with her ensign still flying. Only 110 men from a crew of 2,400 were rescued by *Dorsetshire* and *Maori* (9,870 tons, 8 × 4.7").

Two incidents soured the victory. At Churchill's instigation Admiral Pound ordered *KGV* to remain on the scene even though running out of fuel: "She must do so even if it means subsequently towing her home." Had this been done, *Rodney* and *KGV*, towed at 6 – 8 knots would have been sacrificed to the *Luftwaffe* and Dönitz's U-boats. Pound later had the good grace to apologize to Tovey for having allowed the signal to be sent.

The second incident originated in the same way. Churchill persuaded Pound to require Tovey to charge Admiral Wake-Walker of *Norfolk* and Captain Leach of the *PoW* at a court martial for failing to engage the *Bismarck* during her run south. Tovey took unkindly to this injustice and threatened to haul down his flag so that he might stand as prisoner's friend to both these distinguished officers. That ended the matter.

The *Bismarck* had been hunted by a total of seven battleships or battlecruisers, two aircraft carriers, twelve cruisers and numerous destroyers. She had been in combat at one time or another with *Hood* and *Rodney*, the modern battleships *KGV* and *PoW*, with the heavy cruisers *Norfolk*, *Suffolk* and *Devonshire*, the two carriers *Victorious* and *Ark Royal*, and with Vian's five destroyers.

Battle Honour:

Achates	*Active*	*Antelope*	*Anthony*	*Ark Royal*
Aurora	*Cossack*	*Dorsetshire*	*Echo*	*Edinburgh*
Electra	*Galatea*	*Hermione*	*Hood*	*Icarus*
Inglefield	*Intrepid*	*Kenya*	*King George V*	*Maori*
Mashona	*Neptune*	*Nestor*	*Norfolk*	
Prince of Wales		*Punjabi*	*Renown*	*Repulse*
Rodney	*Sheffield*	*Sikh*	*Somali*	*Suffolk*
Tartar	*Victorious*	*Zulu*		

FAA Squadrons: *800, 808, 810, 818, 820, 825*

BRIDPORT'S ACTION 1795 – see *Groix Island*

BUGIA 1671
8 May
War Against Mediterranean Piracy

Vice Admiral Sir Edward Spragge's squadron of six ships attacked and set ablaze seven warships and three Algerine corsairs in Bugia Bay (now Port de Bougie) in a daring daylight attack. His squadron also bombarded the town and castle, killing, it was estimated, upward of 360 people. 'Old Treky', as Spragge was known, was wounded in the action.

See the entry for ALGIERS and notice how the problems of piracy in the Mediterranean were still active 135 years later.

Battle Honour:

Advice	*Dragon*	*Garland*	*Little Victory*
Mary	*Portsmouth*	*Revenge*	

BURMA 1824–26
5 March 1824 – 25 February 1826
19th Century Colonial Wars

The First Burma War was brought about by "irritation of the presence and growing power of the British in India". There was also a general hatred of the foreigner and an eye on the wealth to be had by the plunder of British factories. This was evidenced by the numerous attacks on British East India territories. The British decided to take decisive action. An expeditionary force was formed which comprised two divisions of men from Calcutta and Madras, a naval squadron commanded by Commodore Charles Grant in *Larne* (20) Commander F. Marryat; *Sophie* (18) Commander G.F.Ryves, and *Diana*, the first paddle steamer seen in India. Others joined, including *Liffey* (50), *Slaney* (20) and four company cruisers. The total strength amounted to 8,701 men, of whom 4,077 were British.

Landings were made up the River Irrawaddy to defend Rangoon; Prome was captured, as was Bassein. But cholera and other diseases decimated the troops and seamen. The British commander, Sir Archibald Campbell, died; an armistice was attempted but failed; a peace treaty was signed but not ratified by either side. This was followed by a fierce battle and the Burmese forces were slaughtered, compelling them to surrender.

Campaign Honour:
The files indicate that the list had been difficult to compile:

Alligator	*Arachne*	*Boadicea*	*Champion*	*Diane*
Tamar	*Tees*	*(List marked Incomplete)*		

Added later:

Larne	*Sophie*	*Diana (?)*	*Liffey*	*Slaney*

(List thought to be complete, but it may not be so.)

BURMA 1852–53
10 January 1852 – 30 June 1853
19th Century Colonial Wars

The First Burmese War, ending in 1826, was followed by an unhappy period at the diplomatic level, Burma refusing to accept a resident minister and repudiating the 1826 treaty. A crisis developed in 1851 when two British ship masters were detained at Rangoon on trumped-up charges and the masters were obliged to purchase their freedom.

Britain responded by sending *Fox* (42) with Commodore G.R. Lambert aboard to give support to the East India steamer *Tenasserim*. Both ships anchored at Rangoon. They were joined by *Serpent* (12) and the East India steamers *Prosperine* and *Phlegethon*. Then came the small ship *Hermes* (6).

This force now took possession of a Burmese warship and carried out a blockade of Rangoon, Bassein and Martaban. Calmness and a cool handling of the situation failed to stop outrages and the Burmese adopted an increasingly provocative stance. Finally an ultimatum was delivered: deal with the problems reasonably or be taken over and annexed to India.

On 30 December 1852, after a heavy battle at Pegu, a proclamation declared the Province of Pegu annexed to the Empire and any immediate intention of effecting further conquests in Burma was formally abandoned.

Relations with Burma remained unhappy: indeed, it was not until 1862 that normal relations were resumed between the courts of London and Ava (the old capital of Burma).

Campaign Honour:

Hastings	*Hermes*	*Rattler*	*Salamander*
Serpent			

1852–3:

Cleopatra	*Contest*	*Fox*	*Spartan*
Sphinx	*Winchester*		

1853:

Bittern	*Styx*

BURMA 1944–45
October 1944 – April 1945
May – August 1945
World War II 1939–45

This Campaign Honour dates from 1944, more than two years after the initial Japanese assault on the country. The occupation had been effected with the speed and brutality associated with Japan's entry into the war. British troops were driven back to the

55

Indian border and the Japanese rested on the Chindwin.

December 1943 saw a second Allied campaign launched on the Arakan, and the Japanese launched an assault on India, investing Kohima and Imphal and suffering horrendous casualties, estimated at 65,000.

The Arakan campaign down the coast was decisive. Ramree Island was assaulted in January 1945. The Royal Navy and Royal Indian Navy gave full support. Guns sited in caves overlooking the landing beaches were silenced by *Queen Elizabeth* (32,700 tons, 8 × 15") supported by the cruiser *Phoebe* (5,450 tons, 10 × 5.25") and the carrier *Ameer* (11,420 tons, 24 aircraft): the bombardment was the heaviest of the campaign. The battleship fired 69 15" rounds.

Ramree became a springboard for the advance on Rangoon which was captured in early May 1945, within days of peace being declared in Europe. As if to mark the occasion the monsoon rains flooded the country. In three months the Japanese in Burma were totally destroyed.

Campaign Honour:

1944–5:			
Ameer	*Barpeta*	*Barracuda*	
Cauvery	*Eskimo*	*Flamingo*	*Haitan*
Jumna	*Kathiawar*	*Kedah*	*Kenyo*
Kistna	*Konkan*	*Llanstephan Castle*	
Napier	*Narbada*	*Nepal*	*Newcastle*
Nguva	*Nigeria*	*Norman*	*Nubian*
Paladin	*Pathfinder*	*Phoebe*	*Queen Elizabeth*
Raider	*Rapid*	*Redpole*	*Rocket*
Roebuck	*Shoreham*	*Spey*	*Teviot*
White Bear			

FAA Squadron: *815*

1945:			
Agra	*Bann*	*Bengal*	
Bihar	*Bombay*	*Ceylon*	*Chameleon*
Cumberland	*Cyclone*	*Deveron*	*Emperor*
Empress	*Glenroy*	*Godavari*	*Halladale*
Hunter	*Jed*	*Khedive*	*Khyber*
Kumaon	*Lahore*	*Largs*	*Lulworth*
Nith	*Orissa*	*Pamela*	*Patna*
Penn	*Persimmon*	*Pickle*	*Plucky*

Poona	*Prins Albert*	*Racehorse*	*Rajputana*
Recruit	*Redoubt*	*Rifleman*	*Rohiekhand*
Rotherham	*Royalist*	*Sandray*	*Saumarez*
Scaravay	*Shah*	*Shiel*	*Silvio*
Stalker	*Suffolk*	*Sussex*	*Sutlej*
Taff	*Tartar*	*Test*	*Trent*
Una	*Venus*	*Verulam*	*Vestal*
Vigilant	*Virago*	*Virginia*	*Waveney*

<u>FAA Squadrons:</u> *800, 804, 807, 808, 809, 851, 896, 1700*

C

CABERETA POINT – see MARBELLA 1705

CABRITA ISLAND – see MARBELLA 1705

CADIZ 1596
21 June
War With Spain 1588–96

Until 1660 the town and port of Cadiz was known as Cales. It was one of the wealthiest places in Europe in the 15th and 16th centuries, largely because of its geographic position. It was to Cadiz that all the Spanish treasure ships from the Americas sailed. Thus it became a favourite target for Spain's enemies to attack. It was here that Drake "singed the King of Spain's beard" in 1587, burning all the shipping he could find.

In 1596 the Earl of Essex and Lord Howard of Effingham, victor of the Armada battles of 1588, replicated Drake's earlier attack when they commanded an English squadron that sacked Cadiz and captured most of the Spanish ships in harbour. It was valued at the time as twelve million ducats, probably equating to about £6 million.

Battle Honour:

This award, like that for the Armada, is distinguished by the fact it was awarded to merchant ships – 63 in the case of Cadiz. As they are not Royal Navy vessels they are not recorded here.

Ark Royal	*Charles*	*Crane*	*Dreadnought*
Lion	*Lion's Whelp*	*Mary Rose*	*Mere Honour*
Moon	*Nonpareil*	*Quittance*	*Rainbow*

Repulse	Swiftsure	Tramontana	Truelove
Vanguard	Warspite	Witness	

CALABRIA 1940
9 July
World War II 1939–45

The first capital-ship action of the Second World War in the Mediterranean took place off Calabria in the extreme south-west of Italy and established British ascendancy at sea over the Italians at the beginning of the war with Italy. It was an ascendancy never to be relinquished by the Royal Navy.

Admiral Sir Andrew B. Cunningham with the battleships *Warspite* (30,600 tons, 8 × 15"), *Malaya* (31,000 tons, 8 × 15") and *Royal Sovereign* (29,150 tons, 8 × 15"), the carrier *Eagle* (36,800 tons, 100 aircraft) with escorting cruisers and destroyers gave cover to two convoys from Malta to Alexandria.

The Italian Admiral Campioni's flagship, the battleship *Giulio Cesare* (23,622 tons, 10 × 12.6"), fought off an air strike from *Eagle's* aircraft, but when the cruiser *Bolzano* (10,000 tons, 8 × 8") and the flagship herself were struck by shells from *Warspite* Campioni broke off the engagement.

<u>Battle Honour:</u>

Dainty	Decoy	Defender	Eagle	Gloucester
Hasty	Hereward	Hero	Hostile	Hyperion
Ilex	Janus	Juno	Liverpool	Malaya
Mohawk	Neptune	Nubian	Orion	
Royal Sovereign		Stuart	Sydney	Vampire
Voyager	Warspite			

<u>FAA Squadrons:</u> 813, 824

CAMEROONS 1914
September 1914
World War I 1914–18

Cameroon was formerly a German colony on the west coast of Africa extending from the mouth of the Rio del Bey to a point slightly below latitude 3° N with boundaries agreed between

Germany, Britain and France. At the outbreak of war the Allies resolved to deprive Germany of her powerful wireless station by which she kept in touch with her warships at sea.

A force of British, French and Belgian troops numbering about 4,500 landed to attack Douala. The Germans retaliated by sinking eleven ships in the river to form a barrier but it was ineffective. The strategic target Douala was quickly taken and it was then decided to conquer the whole territory. Within a few weeks 1,200 German prisoners had been taken, but it took until February 1915 before all towns had been cleared of the enemy and the Allies firmly established. The naval operations were carried out by: *Astraea, Challenger, Cumberland, Dwarf*, the Niger Flotilla comprising: *Alligator, Balbus, Crocodile, Ivy, Molesley, Porpoise, Remus, Vampire, Vigilant* and *Walrus*.

Battle Honour:

| *Astraea* | *Challenger* | *Cumberland* | *Dwarf* |

CAMPERDOWN 1797
11 October
French Revolutionary War 1793–1803
A main plank of the Admiralty's strategy of war for centuries has been the maintenance of a continuous blockade of enemy ports. This confinement had the additional advantage of denying the enemy much sea time while ensuring tremendous sea experience for the British seamen and their ships.

Just such a blockade in the summer of 1797 by Admiral Adam Duncan herded the Dutch fleet into the Texel as if into a cattle pen. Even when Duncan's fleet retired for necessary refit or stores he left ships on patrol watching for any enemy ship movements. It was a late 18th century parallel of the 20th century blockading of *Tirpitz* and *Bismarck*.

In October 1797, when Duncan sailed for the Yarmouth Roads with the major part of his fleet, the Dutch ships made a move. Sixteen Dutch of the line and nine frigates, all under the command of Vice Admiral Jan de Winter, quit their anchorages. Their every move was watched by Captain Trollope in the *Russell* (74) and his accompanying small squadron. Duncan hastened back and joined Trollope on the morning of 11 October.

Battle was joined soon after noon about three miles north-west of Camperdown (Kamperduijn) on the Dutch coast. The fleets were fairly evenly matched: eighteen of the line and seven frigates under de Winter faced Duncan's fleet of sixteen of the line and eight frigates. Duncan had the advantage of somewhat heavier guns and the weather gage. He closed at once in two squadrons, his own comprising eight of the line in line abreast attacking the Dutch van and Vice-Admiral R. Onslow attacking the rear with ten ships.

A ferocious battle ensued over the next three and a half hours and Onslow's success was almost complete; Rear-Admiral Reyntjes in the Dutch *Jupiter* (74), *Haarlem* (68), *Alkmaar* (56), *Delft* (56) and *Monnikendam* (44) all struck.

Duncan sought out de Winter's *Vrijheid* (74) lying fifth in the line. After hours of fighting de Winter surrendered at 3.15 pm by which time he was the only unwounded man on the deck. By then, too, four more of his ships had struck: *Hercules* (64), *Gelijkheid* (68), *Admiral Tjerk Hiddes de Vries* (68) and *Wassenaer* (64).

So heavy had been the casualties on both sides and so severe the damage to ships that with the approach of darkness Duncan headed off for base, but so damaged were some of the prizes that two sank under tow to England and the others never saw sea service again. Details of ships engaged follow.

Battle Honour:

Isis (50) Captain W. Mitchell
Lancaster (64) Captain J. Wells
Belliqueux (64) Captain J. Inglis
Bedford (74) Captain Sir T. Byard
Ardent (64) Captain R. Burgess
Venerable (74) Admiral Duncan
Triumph (74) Captain W.H. Essington
Veteran (64) Captain G. Gregory
Monarch (74) Vice-Admiral R. Onslow
Powerful (74) Captain W. O'Bryen Drury
Director (64) Captain W. Bligh
Russell (74) Captain H. Trollope
Monmouth (64) Captain J. Walker
Montagu (74) Captain J. Knight

Adamant (50) Captain W. Hotham
Agincourt (64) Captain J. Williamson
Frigates:

| *Beaulieu* | *Rose* | *King George* | *Active* | *Diligent* |
| *Spectacular* | *Circe* | *Martin* | | |

CAPE BON 1941
13 December
World War II 1939–45

Four Allied destroyers fought a spirited action with Italian forces in a brilliant night action in the early hours of 13 December 1941 off Tunisia's Cape Bon. The destroyers comprised *Sikh* (1,870 tons, 8 × 4.7"), *Maori* (1,870 tons, 8 × 4.7"), *Legion* (1,920 tons, 6 × 4.7") and the Dutch *Isaac Sweers*, all under Commander G.H. Stokes. Two Italian light cruisers were sunk: *Alberto di Giussano* (5,069 tons, 8 × 6") and *Alberico da Barbiano* (5,069 tons, 8 × 6").

Battle Honour: *Legion*   *Maori*   *Sikh*

CAPE FRANÇOIS 1757
21 October
Seven Years' War 1756 –63

Captain Arthur Forrest commanded a small squadron comprising *Augusta* (60), *Edinburgh* (64) and *Dreadnought* (60) which fought gallantly against a more powerful French squadron off the north coast of San Domingo in the West Indies near the French naval base of Cape François. Forrest awaited a convoy but instead met Admiral de Kersaint's squadron of *Intrépide* (74), *Sceptre* (74), *Opiniâtre* (64), a 50 and three frigates. A fierce 2½ hour engagement followed and both sides suffered severe damage. De Kersaint retired to his base and Forrest to Port Royal in Jamaica where it took weeks to restore the ships to fighting fitness, by which time the French convoy had made good its departure.

Battle Honour: *Augusta*   *Dreadnought*   *Edinburgh*

CAPE MATAPAN – see MATAPAN 1941

CAPE OF GOOD HOPE 1795
16 September
French Revolutionary War 1793 – 1802
The hostility of Holland impelled Britain to despatch an expedition to the Dutch Cape Colony. The force, under the overall command of Vice-Admiral Sir George Elphinstone in his flagship *Monarch*, comprised the following:

  Monarch (74) Captain John Elphinstone
  Victorious (74) Captain William Clark
  Arrogant (74) Captain Richard Lucas
  America (64) Captain John Blankett
  Stately (64) Captain Billy Douglas
  Echo (16) Commander Temple Hardy
  Rattlesnake (16) Commander John William Spranger

The squadron anchored in Simon's Bay in early July 1795. One thousand seamen and hundreds more marines and soldiers landed and were put under the command of General Alfred Clark. The Dutch were hounded "from post to post" over a period of some weeks. On 3 September the sudden appearance of fourteen sail of British East Indiamen with large reinforcements prompted the Dutch governor to sue for peace and on 16 September the town, the colony and about 1,000 regular Dutch troops surrendered.

Battle Honour:

America	*Crescent*	*Echo*	*Hope*	*Jupiter*
Monarch	*Moselle*	*Rattlesnake*	*Ruby*	*Sceptre*
Sphinx	*Stately*	*Tremendous*	*Trident*	

CAPE OF GOOD HOPE 1806
8–18 January
Napoleonic War 1803–1815
An expedition to capture Cape Town from the Dutch was assembled under the command of Commodore Sir Home Riggs Popham

in *Diadem* (64), with *Raisonnable* (64), *Belliqueux* (64), *Diomède* (64), *Leda* (38), *Narcissus* (32), *Espoir* (18), *Encounter* (14) and later the brig *Protector*. This squadron covered the landing of an assault force of about 5,000 men under the command of Major-General Sir George Keith. Most of the ships engaged shore batteries. The Dutch burnt their ship *Bato* (68) in Simon's Bay to avoid her capture by the British. The British naval losses were nil and casualties were minimal.

Battle Honour:

Belliqueux	*Diadem*	*Diomède*	*Encounter*
Espoir	*Leda*	*Protector*	*Raisonnable*

CAPE ORTEGAL – see BAY OF BISCAY 1805

CAPE PASSERO – see *Passero* 1718

CAPE ST VINCENT – see ST VINCENT (THE MOONLIGHT BATTLE) 1780

CAPE SPADA – see SPADA 1940

CAPE TENEZ (or TENES) 1805
4 February
Napoleonic War 1803–15

A convoy of thirty-two ships was in a position about 30 miles north-west of Cape Tenez in Algeria on 4 February 1805 when it was attacked by a force of French ships. The convoy was escorted by two small vessels, *Arrow* (18) and *Acheron* (8). The two French ships were *Hortense* and *Incorruptible*, both more heavily armed than the British ships. After a spirited engagement three merchantmen were captured by the French and both British warships had been battered into submission. Immediately after being taken *Arrow* sank, and, soon after, *Acheron* was fired by the French.

Battle Honour: *Acheron*   *Arrow*

CATTARO 1814
5 January
Napoleonic War 1803 – 15
After ten days' cannonade Cattaro (Kotor in Yugoslavia) in the Adriatic surrendered to a British squadron comprising *Bacchante* (38), Captain William Hoste, and *Saracen* (18), Commander John Harper. This success was soon followed by the surrender of Ragusa (Dubrovnik) and of the island of Paxo.

Rear Admiral Thomas Fremantle was in overall control and by the beginning of March 1814 every remaining French possession in the Adriatic had been reduced.

Battle Honour: *Bacchante*   *Saracen*

CAYENNE 1809
14 January
Napoleonic War 1803–15
Cayenne, the capital of French Guiana, stands at the mouth of the River Cayenne. In 1809 the British resolved to attack it. Captain James Yeo in *Confiance* (20) with the support of two Portuguese brigs and sundry small craft gave cover to the assault force of some 250 men. After surviving the fierce ordeal of landing in a heavy surf the force stormed many forts in a number of spirited actions.

Cayenne was captured, 400 regular troops, 600 white militia and 200 native troops gave up their arms. The expedition was described by Sir William Clowes as "one of the most striking examples of the accomplishment of great ends with what were apparently inadequate materials".

Battle Honour: *Confiance*

CHESAPEAKE 1781
(a) 16 March 1781 (ACTION OFF CAPE HENRY)
(b) 5 September 1781 (VIRGINIA CAPES)
American War of Independence 1775 – 83

This first and unsatisfactory encounter at sea in the American War of Independence took place about 40 miles north-east of Cape Henry in Chesapeake Bay. It was fought between a French squadron commanded by Commodore Destouches who, on balance, won a tactical victory, and a British squadron commanded by Rear-Admiral Marriot Arbuthnot, who was left with temporary command of the bay.

The French flagship *Duc de Bourgogne* (80), with seven more of the line and two frigates, met Arbuthnot's eight of the line and four frigates in thick haze off Cape Henry. And thus began the first of two naval encounters in the bay in 1781 between French and British naval squadrons, both arising from British attempts to prevent French aid reaching America.

After an hour's exchange of gunfire the French line broke and the French ships stood out to sea to clear the battle area. Arbuthnot's leading ships were severely disabled, having borne the brunt of battle. As each squadron lost the other in the haze the encounter petered out. Neither commander could be overly pleased with his performance, but at least Arbuthnot stood in command of the bay. Nevertheless, because of his failure to achieve a conclusive victory, the battle was to have significant consequences.

<u>Battle Honour:</u>

Adamant	*America*	*Bedford*	*Europe*	*Guadeloupe*
Irish	*London*	*Pearl*	*Prudente*	*Robust*
Royal Oak				

The second Chesapeake battle was more crucial than the first. If ever an admiral helped to lose a land battle, then Rear-Admiral Thomas Graves was such a man. The pity of it was that the land commander was Cornwallis, his surrender was at Yorktown, and with it American independence from the British was assured.

By the time the battle was fought there had been a concentration of enemy land forces investing the British troops at Yorktown.

At sea the French Admiral de Grasse had brought his Caribbean fleet of twenty-four of the line to Chesapeake Bay. In response Admiral Rodney despatched his second-in-command, Rear-Admiral Samuel Hood, with fourteen of the line to reinforce Graves, who eventually assumed command of a force comprising nineteen of the line in the 98-gun *London*. Hood commanded the rear and Rear-Admiral Drake the van.

De Grasse's fleet was at anchor just inside the bay. Graves was well aware of the gravity of the battle in prospect. He may well have had in mind Byng's end after his tactical blunder at Minorca in 1756. Yet, despite having the advantage of weather, of formation and of surprise, he made a faulty approach, so that after 2½ hours of indecisive action Hood's division had not yet become engaged. The situation had called for a Jervis or Collingwood – the Nelson touch. It got instead indecision and lack of resolution, and it brought about a spasmodic battling over several days, in the course of which the badly damaged *Terrible* (74) had to be sunk.

De Grasse himself seemed reluctant to engage too closely, but his primary task was to reinforce the beseiged American armies. On 11 September he re-entered the bay. Graves held a Council of War on the 13th; in view of the poor state of the British ships, the lack of bread and water, it was resolved to return to New York to refit. Graves retired north and left de Grasse in command of Chesapeake Bay. The way was clear for Cornwallis's defeat and surrender in the following month – and the loss of the American colonies.

British ships engaged were nineteen ships of the line and nine frigates:

SHIPS OF THE LINE			FRIGATES	
Ajax	*Alcide*	*Alfred*	*Adamant*	*Fortunée*
America	*Barfleur*	*Bedford*	*Nymphe*	*Orpheus*
Belliqueux	*Centaur*	*Europe*	*Richmond*	*Salamander*
Intrepid	*Invincible*	*London*	*Santa Monica*	*Sibyl*
Monarch	*Montagu*	*Princess*	*Solebay*	
Resolution	*Royal Oak*	*Shrewsbury*		
Terrible				

<u>Battle Honour:</u> No award was made for this second battle in Chesapeake Bay on 5 September 1781.

CHINA 1841 – 42 (FIRST CHINA or OPIUM WAR)
7 January 1841 – 21 July 1842

Britain had traded in the Far East, through the East India Company, for two centuries, much of the trade being in the drug opium. So widespread was drug-taking that China resolved in 1837 to exterminate the trade. China clashed with Britain and other states over this policy with the result that war was declared. A punitive expedition was mounted by Britain which resulted in a series of naval and military operations against China. Chusan was captured and several other cities stormed. Nanking was threatened. At the subsequent peace treaty Hong Kong was ceded to Britain.

Campaign Honour:

Druid	Herald	Larne	Melville	Nimrod
Pylades	Samarang	Sulphur	Wellesley	

1841–2

Algerine	Blonde	Calliope	Columbine	Hyacinth
Jupiter	Modeste	Rattlesnake	Starling	

1842

Apollo	Belleisle	Childers	Clio	Cornwallis
Dido	Endymion	Harlequin	Hazard	North Star
Plover	Sapphire	Vixen	Wanderer	Young Hebe

CHINA 1856–60 (SECOND CHINA WAR)
1 October 1856 – 26 June 1858
1 August – 24 October 1860

The immediate cause of the Second China War was the capture by the Chinese of the cutter *Arrow* on charges of piracy. The charge was probably justified but she was a British registered vessel and her release was demanded. War broke out with the bombardment of Canton by the British and its capture in December 1857 by forces under the command of Admiral Sir Michael Seymour, C-in-C of the station. In May 1858 the Taku forts were taken. A large force of British and French troops, sailors and marines assaulted and captured Peking. The Treaty of Tientsin concluded the war and the treaty was ratified on 24 October 1860 allowing freedom of travel by Europeans in the interior, freedom to preach Christianity and legalizing the importation of opium.

<u>Campaign Honour:</u>

<u>1856 – 60:</u>

Acorn	Actaeon	Adventure	Algerine
Amethyst	Assistance	Auckland	Banterer	Barracouta
Beagle	Belleisle	Bittern	Bustard	Calcutta
Camilla	Clown	Comus	Cormorant	Coromandel
Cruiser	Drake	Elk	Encounter	Esk
Firm	Forester	Furious	Fury	Haughty
Hesper	Highflyer	Hong Kong	Hornet	Inflexible
Insolent	Janus	Kestrel	Lee	Leven
Nanking	Niger	Nimrod	Pioneer	Pique
Plover	Racehorse	Sampson	Sans Pareil	
Sir Charles Forbes	Slaney	Spartan	Starling
Staunch	Surprise	Sybille	Tribune	Volcano
Watchful	Winchester	Woodcock	

<u>1860:</u>

Bouncer	Cambrian	Centaur	Chesapeake
Cockchafer	Flamer	Grasshopper	Hardy	Havock
Impérieuse	Magicienne	Odin	Pearl	Retribution
Reynard	Ringdove	Roebuck	Scout	Simoon
Snake	Snap	Sparrowhawk	Sphinx	Urgent
Vulcan	Watchman	Weazle	

CHINA 1900 (BOXER RISING and TAKU FORTS)
10 June – 31 December 1900

Boxer was the name given to the secret society in China which practised boxing and callisthenic rituals, believing them to give protection against bandits. The Boxers attempted to drive all foreigners from China and by 1899 they were openly attacking Chinese Christians and western missionaries; by the following May they were roaming the countryside around the capital, Peking.

The European countries raised an international force of 2,100 men who were sent from the northern port of Tientsin to Peking where by now the Boxers were burning churches and foreign residences, and killing suspected Christians in what became known as the Boxer Rising or Rebellion. In June 1900 the international force commanded by Commander Christopher Cradock (*Alacrity*) bombarded and reduced the Taku Forts (also known as the Peiho Forts) in the Gulf of Pe-chi-li.

Peking was finally captured on 14 August 1900.

The following ships participated but did not land a naval brigade and therefore failed to qualify for the battle honour:

Arethusa	Bonaventure	Canning	Clive	Dalhousie
Daphne	Dido	Esk	Goliath	Hart
Hermione	Humber	Isis	Linnet	Marathon
Peacock	Pigmy	Pique	Plover	Protector
Redpole	Rosario	Snipe	Undaunted	Wallaroo
Waterwitch	Woodcock	Woodlark		

Taku Forts: These ships were engaged but not awarded an honour:

Algerine	Lion (French)	Iltis (German)
Bobr (Russian)	Giliak (Russian)	Koreytz (Russian)

HM Ships *Fame* and *Whitney* captured four Chinese torpedo boats in the Pei Ho below Tongku.

<u>Battle Honour:</u>

Alacrity	Algerine	Aurora	Barfleur
Centurion	Endymion	Fame	Orlando
Phoenix	Terrible	Whiting	

COPENHAGEN 1801
2 April
French Revolutionary War 1793–1803

The Baltic states of Russia, Sweden and Denmark deplored Britain's interruption of their trade with the continent to such an extent that the Tsar even confiscated British ships. Admiral Sir Hyde Parker, with Vice-Admiral Horatio Nelson, sailed with a substantial fleet on a sabre-rattling expedition to Denmark.

This celebrated British naval victory is largely attributable to Nelson's meticulous planning and tenacious execution, but it is also well known as the occasion of his blind eye gesture.

Admiral Sir Hyde Parker commanded a Baltic fleet comprising eighteen of the line and thirty-five smaller vessels. Parker and Nelson were ordered to attack the Danish fleet in the strongly defended harbour of Copenhagen. Parker deployed twelve of the line, five frigates, two sloops, five bomb vessels and two fire ships to Nelson, who would lead the attack.

On 1 April 1801 Nelson negotiated the Outer Channel and positioned his squadron just two miles from the formidable Danish line of eighteen warships, hulks and floating batteries: moored near the Trekroner fortress by the harbour entrance lay four line of battle ships and supporting vessels.

Nelson's plan was to lead ten of his ships and anchor the frigates in the narrow King's Deep Channel and anchor the *Edgar* (74) opposite the Danish fifth in the line while each succeeding ship passed her on the disengaged side to take up position.

The operation began on the morning of 2 April, but before *Edgar* was in position the plan had already gone awry, in part at least: *Bellona* (74) and *Russell* (74) were stranded in the Middle Ground Shoal and *Agamemnon* (74) was unable to occupy her position.

With the remaining ships in position a fierce bombardment of the Danish defences began. When the Danish flagship *Dannebrog* (Admiral Fischer) was set ablaze the Admiral shifted his flag to the *Holstein*. Hyde Parker was not happy with the progress of the battle and signalled "Discontinue the engagement". Nelson employed his blind eye ploy, though Captain Riou of the *Amazon* (38) obeyed and was withdrawing his frigate when he was killed.

Danish resistance began to falter; the burning flagship blew up; two more ships cut their cables and foundered. Sporadic fire came from various ships as English boats sought prizes, but a ceasefire was agreed and Nelson began a difficult extrication of his ships, two more of which ran aground.

Casualties on both sides were very heavy. A commander other than Nelson could well have withdrawn early with no discredit.

Battle Honour:

Agamemnon	Alcmene	Amazon	Ardent	Arrow
Bellona	Blanche	Cruizer	Dart	Defence*
Defiance	Désirée	Discovery	Edgar	Elephant
Explosion	Ganges	Glatton	Happy	Hecla
Isis	Jamaica	London*	Monarch	Otter
Polyphemus	Raisonnable*	Ramillies*	Russell	St George*

| Saturn* | Sulphur | Terror | Veteran* | Volcano |
| Warrior | Zebra | Zephyr | | |

Ships marked with an asterisk were not engaged: they were support ships, but were awarded the battle honour.

CORAL SEA 1942
4–8 May
World War II 1939–45

The Japanese Admiral Nagumo's devastating striking force of aircraft carriers had spectacular successes in the early months of the war in the Far East: the series of raids against Rabaul in New Guinea, the strike on Darwin, the broad sweep into the Indian Ocean to Ceylon and the Bay of Bengal, bombing Colombo and Trincomalee, sinking two British heavy cruisers and the small carrier *Hermes*. Admiral Somerville's makeshift fleet narrowly missed disaster. Nagumo's series of victories were brought to a halt in the Coral Sea. It may have been a tactical victory but for the first time he experienced a reversal with serious losses.

The Battle of the Coral Sea took place south of the Solomon Islands, waged by Task Force 17 under the command of Rear-Admiral F.J. Fletcher USN. It removed the threat of invasion of Australia. It was also the first major action in which only aircraft carriers were engaged and in which the heavy surface escorts never sighted each other. Two Australian cruisers were engaged.

Battle Honour: *Australia   Hobart*

CORNWALLIS'S RETREAT 1795 see BELLE ÎSLE
17 June
French Revolutionary War 1793–1803

Vice Admiral William Cornwallis displayed great skill in extricating his squadron from a superior enemy force without loss. He wore his flag in *Royal Sovereign* (100), had four 74s and had two frigates in company north of Belle Isle in the Bay of Biscay when he was surprised by a powerful French squadron of twelve of the line, two 50s and nine frigates under the command of Admiral Villaret de Joyeuse.

Cornwallis fled south under full sail, *Bellerophon* (74) and *Brunswick* (74) jettisoning gear to help speed their flight. Joyeuse's ships caught up, and a series of sporadic engagements ensued on 17 June in the course of which *Royal Sovereign* rescued the damaged *Mars* (74).

Captain Robert Stopford in the frigate *Phaeton* tricked Joyeuse by signalling to a non-existent British fleet. The French gave up the chase and Cornwallis escaped, having suffered no ship losses.

Battle Honour:

Bellerophon	*Brunswick*	*Mars*	*Pallas*	*Phaeton*
Royal Sovereign	*Triumph*			

CRETE 1941
20 May – 1 June
World War II 1939–45

The Royal Navy fought vicious battles against the German *Luftwaffe* during the evacuation of troops from Greece, the defence of the island of Crete and the subsequent evacuation of British and Commonwealth troops from the island. The battles were spread over many days and resulted in heavy losses and casualties to the Mediterranean Fleet, commanded by Admiral Sir Andrew B. Cunningham from the naval base at Alexandria.

The admirals most closely associated with these actions were Vice-Admiral Pridham-Wippell, Rear-Admiral King, Rear-Admiral Rawlings and Rear-Admiral Glennie. The destroyer flotillas most heavily engaged were: 5th (Mountbatten), 10th (Walker) and 14th (Mack).

The cost of the defence of the island of Crete and the evacuations from both Greece and Crete in terms of ships and personnel is as follows:

Warships sunk:

Cruisers:	*Calcutta* (4,200 tons),
	Gloucester (9,600 tons) – 750 men lost with her.
	Fiji (8,000 tons).

Destroyers: *Kashmir* (1,690 tons)
                 Hereward (1,340 tons)
                 Kelly (1,695 tons)
                 Greyhound (1,335 tons)
                 Juno (1,690 tons)
                 Diamond (1,370 tons)
                 Imperial (1,370 tons)
                 Wryneck (1,100 tons)

Ships damaged included the following:
   Warspite, Barham, Valiant, Formidable, Orion, Ajax, Perth, Dido, Naiad, Coventry, Carlisle and nine other destroyers.
   Killed and missing: 2,261 – with many more wounded.

Battle Honour:

Abdiel	*Ajax*	*Auckland*	*Barham*	*Calcutta*
Carlisle	*Coventry*	*Decoy*	*Defender*	*Dido*
Fiji	*Flamingo*	*Formidable*	*Glengyle*	*Glenroy*
Gloucester	*Greyhound*	*Griffin*	*Grimsby*	*Hasty*
Havock	*Hereward*	*Hero*	*Hotspur*	*Ilex*
Imperial	*Isis*	*Jackal*	*Janus*	*Jervis*
Juno	*Kandahar*	*Kashmir*	*Kelly*	*Kelvin*
Kimberley	*Kingston*	*Kipling*	*Kos 21*	*Kos 22*
Kos 23	*Lanner*	*Naiad*	*Napier*	*Nizam*
Nubian	*Orion*	*Perth*	*Phoebe*	
Queen Elizabeth		*Rorqual*	*Salvia*	*Stuart*
Syvern	*Valiant*	*Vampire*	*Vendetta*	*Voyager*
Warspite	*Waterhen*	*Widnes*		

MLS: *1011*   *1030*   *1032*

MTBs: *67*   *213*   *216*   *217*   *314*

FAA Squadron: *803, 805, 806, 826, 829*

CRIMEA 1854–55
17 September 1854 – 9 September 1855
(Sea of Azov until November 1855)
Following an action off the Black Sea port of Sinope in northern Turkey between Russian and Turkish fleets at the end of November 1853, Britain and France entered the war on the side

of Turkey. The main theatre of war was the Black Sea.

In September 1854 an Anglo-Franco-Turkish expeditionary force was landed near Sevastopol from a fleet of 400 ships and transports carrying about 60,000 men.

Sevastopol was invested and, when bombarded, it was demonstrated for the first time the superiority of the armoured steamship with explosive shells over the wooden walls and solid shot.

The Russians surrendered Sevastopol in September 1855 after scuttling their fleet. The resulting Peace of Paris marked the outlawing of piracy but the real landmark was the arrival of the prototype of a modern battleship.

Campaign Honour:

Apollo	Arethusa	Bellerophon	Brenda	Britannia
Circassia	Fury	Minna	Modeste	Pigmy
Retribution	Sampson	Sans Pareil	Shark	Trafalgar
Varna	Vengeance			

1854–55:

	Agamemnon	Albion	Algiers	Ardent
Arrow	Banshee	Beagle	Caradoc	Curlew
Cyclops	Danube	Dauntless	Diamond	Firebrand
Furious	Gladiator	Harpy	Highflyer	Industry
Inflexible	Leander	London	Lynx	Medaera
Medina	Miranda	Niger	Queen	Rodney
Royal Albert	Simoon	Sphinx	Spitfire	Stromboli
Swallow	Terrible	Tribune	Valorous	Viper
Vulcan	Wasp			

1855:

	Boxer	Camel	Clinker	Cracker
Curacoa	Fancy	Firm	Flamer	Glatton
Grinder	Hannibal	Hardy	Jasper	Leopard
Magnet	Meteor	Moslem	Oberon	Odin
Oneida	Princess Royal		Raven	
St Jean d'Acre	Snake	Sulina	Weser	Wrangler

CURACOA 1807
1 January
Napoleonic war 1803–15

The Curacoa incident was described by a leading naval historian as "By far the most brilliant exploit of the year 1807". It occurred in the West Indies where Vice-Admiral James R.Dacres commanded the Jamaica Station. He received intelligence of the island of Curacoa reportedly anxious for an alliance with Britain and despatched a small squadron to investigate: *Arethusa* (38) Captain Charles Brisbane; *Latona* (38) Captain James A.Wood; *Anson* (44) Captain Charles Lydiard and *Fisgard* (38) Captain William Bolton.

Dacres was an officer of great bravery. He decided to enter Curacoa Harbour to negotiate only when the town lay under the guns of his squadron. The harbour was defended by a number of forts, by a 38-gun frigate and a 22-gun corvette. Dacres gave the defenders a five-minute offer to surrender or "I shall immediately storm your batteries". When the time elapsed he was as good as his word.

The harbour was battered to pieces and by noon on 1 January the whole island was in his hands.

The enterprise earned Dacres a knighthood.

Battle Honour:

Anson	*Arethusa*	*Fisgard*	*Latona*
Morne Fortunée			

D

DARDANELLES 1915–16
19 February 1915 – 8 January 1916
World War I 1914–18

The Dardanelles is the narrow strait which separates European Turkey from Asian Turkey and gives an exit from the Sea of Marmara to the Mediterranean. In the First World War it became the scene of a bitter campaign both ashore on the Gallipoli peninsula and at sea when capital ships of the Royal Navy attempted to force the passage to Constantinople after silencing the Turkish forts guarding the entrance to the strait with heavy naval ordnance.

The navy duly bombed these forts, but not into submission. Further, the Turks had laid minefields across the narrows and the British losses in capital ships became serious. The battlecruiser *Inflexible* struck a mine and withdrew to Malta. The pre-dreadnought battleship *Irresistible* and the *Ocean* were both mined and sank.

The campaign degenerated into an amphibious battle involving large numbers of ANZAC forces ashore. Turkish opposition was fierce and the losses appalling on the Gallipoli peninsula.

Further naval losses cost the navy dear. The pre-dreadnought *Goliath* was sunk by a Turkish torpedo boat. the pre-dreadnought *Triumph* was torpedoed and sunk by the German U-boat *U-21*, and two days later the same U-boat had the distinction of sinking the pre-dreadnought *Majestic*.

Early in January 1916 the British positions were evacuated and the campaign aborted, but not before the pre-dreadnought battleship *Russell* sank off Malta after being mined. A final casualty was Winston Churchill whose stout-hearted defence of the venture as First Lord of the Admiralty left him with little alternative but to resign.

<u>Campaign Honour:</u>

Anemone	Ark Royal	Arno	Aster	Bacchante
Basilisk	Beagle	Ben-My-Chree		Blenheim
Bulldog	Canning	Canopus	Chatham	Chelmer
Colne	Cornwall	Cornwallis	Dartmouth	Doris
Dublin	Earl of Peterborough		Edgar	Endymion
Euryalus	Exmouth	Foresight	Foxhound	Fury
Gazelle	Glory	Goliath	Grafton	Grampus
Grasshopper	Harpy	Havelock	Hector	Heliotrope
Hibernia	Honeysuckle	Humber	Hussar	Implacable
Inflexible	Irresistible	Jed	Jonquil	Kennet
Laforey	Lawford	London	Lord Nelson	Louis
Lydiard	Magnificent	Majestic	Manica	Mars
Minerva	Mosquito	Ocean	Osiris II	Peony
Prince of Wales		Prince Edward		
Prince George		Queen	Queen Elizabeth	
Queen Victoria		Racoon	Raglan	Rattlesnake
Renard	Ribble	River Clyde	Roberts	Russell
Sapphire	Scorpion	Scourge	Sir Thomas Picton	
Staunch	Swiftsure	Talbot	Theseus	Triad
Triumph	Usk	Venerable	Vengeance	Wear
Welland	Wolverine			

<u>Monitors:</u> M 15, M 16, M 17, M 18, M 19, M 21, M 29, M 31, M 32, M 33

<u>Submarines:</u> AE2, B6, B11, E2, E7, E11, E12, E14, E15, E20

<u>Torpedo Boat:</u> 064

DENMARK STRAIT – see 'BISMARCK' ACTION 1941

**DIEGO SUAREZ (MADAGASCAR or
OPERATION IRONCLAD) 1942
5 – 7 May
World War II 1939–45**

Madagascar was occupied by Vichy French forces. It lay vulnerable to Japanese attack. The island would act as an excellent base for them to command the Indian Ocean, threatening all routes to and from East Africa and the Middle East.

A direct frontal attack on the island was launched by British forces on 5 May 1942. The enemy were taken completely by surprise. The destroyer *Anthony* (1,350 tons, 4 × 4.7") took a party of fifty marines from the battleship *Ramillies* (29,150 tons, 8 × 15") in under the eastern coastal defences in a heavy sea. She became embarrassed by the large number of prisoners taken. Aircraft from *Illustrious* and *Indomitable* attacked the harbour and airfield. *Devonshire* (9,850 tons, 8 × 8") and four destroyers covered landings from seventeen ships on the west coast. By 0300 on the 7th the town and its defences were captured.

The attack demonstrated the ability of the three services to act together, the navy transporting large forces of soldiers over thousands of miles of sea and putting them ashore under carrier-borne aircraft.

Rear-Admiral E.N. Syfret commanded the operation from his flagship *Ramillies*. Major-General R.G. Sturges commanded the troops and Marines. The only British loss was the corvette *Auricula*, sunk by a mine.

Battle Honour:

Active	Anthony	Auricula	Bachaquero
Cromarty	Cromer	Cyclamen	Devonshire
Duncan	Freesia	Fritillary	Genista
Hermione	Illustrious	Inconstant	Indomitable
Jasmine	Javelin	Karanja	Keren
Laforey	Lightning	Lookout	Nigella
Pakenham	Paladin	Panther	Poole
Ramillies	Romney	Royal Ulsterman	Thyne
Winchester Castle			

FAA Squadrons: 800, 810, 827, 829, 831, 880, 881, 882

DIEPPE 1942
19 August
World War II 1939–45
The assault by sea-borne forces on the beaches and installations of Dieppe in France was a rehearsal for the Second Front – the landings in Normandy. The operation was commanded by Captain

J. Hughes-Hallett aboard *Calpe* and Major-General J.H. Roberts (Canadian Division).

Operation Jubilee was mounted specially to give battle experience to Canadian troops and to test techniques and weaponry. 237 naval vessels were engaged. 4,961 Canadian troops plus 1,057 Commandos and some US Rangers were used. Sixty-seven squadrons of aircraft were also employed in the battle.

Fighting was fierce and casualties on the British side were very heavy indeed. The Hunt class destroyer *Berkeley* (907 tons, 4 × 4") was so badly damaged she had to be sunk. Thirty-three landing craft were lost. 3,363 Canadians and 607 Commandos became casualties and 106 British aircraft were lost. By comparison the German losses were relatively slight: forty-eight aircraft were lost and all other casualties amounted to about 600.

It had been a disastrous operation, but on the credit side the British learned many important lessons which bore fruit in the planning and execution of Operation Overlord – the Normandy landings two years later, probably saving thousands of lives.

Battle Honour:

Albrighton	*Alresford*	*Bangor*	*Berkeley*
Blackpool	*Bleakdale*	*Blyth*	*Bridlington*
Bridport	*Brocklesby*	*Calpe*	*Clacton*
Duke of Wellington		*Eastbourne*	*Felixstowe*
Fernie	*Garth*	*Glengyle*	*Ilfracombe*
Invicta	*Locust*	*Polruan*	*Prince Charles*
Prince Leopold	*Prins Albert*	*Prinses Astrid*	*Prinses Beatrix*
Queen Emma	*Rhyl*	*Sidmouth*	*Stornoway*
Tenby			

MLs: *114, 120, 123, 171, 187, 189, 190, 191, 193, 194, 208, 214, 230, 246, 291, 292, 309, 343, 344, 346*

MGBs: *50, 51, 312, 315, 316, 317, 320, 321, 323, 326*

SGBs: *5, 6, 8, 9*

DOGGER BANK 1781
5 August
American War of Independence 1775–83
A bitterly fought action off the Dogger Bank about 60 miles east of

Northumberland, between Captain (later Admiral Sir) Hyde Parker and the traditional enemy, the Dutch, in the form of Rear-Admiral Zoutman, each admiral escorting a convoy of merchantmen, the British one comprising some 200 vessels.

They were evenly matched antagonists: *Fortitude* (74) and six more of the line against *Admirel de Ruijter* (68) and six of the line, plus smaller vessels. Each convoy managed to disperse clear of the battle area, the British to England and the Dutch to the Texel. Parker had the wind advantage and bore down on Zoutman; battle began when the squadrons were within half a musket shot of each other. "For three hours and forty minutes [they] tore at each other until, mutually shattered, they fell apart." The battle saw neither side gain an advantage, and though the losses were small each exhausted squadron was relieved to break off the action. The Dutch *Hollandie* (64) suffered so severely that she failed to make port.

Battle Honour:

Artois	*Belle Poule*	*Berwick*	*Bienfaisant*
Buffalo	*Cleopatra*	*Dolphin*	*Fortitude*
Latona	*Preston*	*Princess Amelia*	*Surprise*

DOGGER BANK 1915
24 January
World War I 1914–18

Although this was a British naval victory, a tactical error saved the German squadron from suffering a severe mauling.

Rear-Admiral Franz von Hipper sailed from Wilhelmshaven with the object of attacking British patrols in the seas around the Dogger Bank in the North Sea. He took with him a formidable force of battlecruisers: the First Scouting Group, *Seydlitz* (flag: 25,000 tons 10 × 11"), *Moltke* (23,000 tons, 10 × 11"), *Derfflinger* (28,000 tons, 8 × 12"), together with the armoured cruiser *Blücher* (15,500 tons, 12 × 8.2"), accompanied by four light cruisers and two destroyer flotillas.

Acting Vice-Admiral Sir David Beatty's battlecruiser force was despatched from Rosyth, augmented by the Harwich Force commanded by Commodore R.Y. Tyrwhitt. It was Beatty's purpose to position his force between Hipper and his base. Beatty had the battlecruisers *Lion* (26,350 tons, 8 × 13.5"), *Tiger* (27,000 tons, 8 × 13.5"), *Princess Royal* (same class as *Lion*), *New Zealand* (18,800 tons, 8 × 12") and *Indomitable* (17,250 tons, 8 × 12") escorted by the 1st Light Cruiser Squadron and torpedo boats.

Hipper's force was sighted early on 24 January and a high-speed action ensued in the course of which the *Seydlitz* was struck by a 13.5" shell from *Lion*, silencing her X and Y turrets and killing 160 men. *Blücher* was also hit and began to lose way. The German force seemed to be in grave danger.

Then three shells struck *Lion* and she rapidly fell astern. Rear-Admiral Arthur Moore in *New Zealand* assumed command of the pursuit, but concentrated the fire of his whole squadron on the _crippled *Blücher* instead of pursuing the remainder of Hipper's force. *Blücher* capsized and sank after three hours of indescribable punishment; only 189 of her crew were rescued. By then the opportunity of destroying the rest of the squadron had gone.

Lion was towed back to harbour. The total British casualties were fifteen killed and eighty wounded. Hipper lost 954 killed and hundreds more wounded. Germany learned a lesson from the battle, the need to prevent flash from bursting shells reaching magazines: their capital ships were thereafter rendered safe from such danger. Not so the British, and it cost the Royal Navy five major capital ships at Jutland sixteen months later.

Battle Honour:

Acheron	Arethusa	Ariel	Attack	Aurora
Birmingham	Defender	Druid	Ferret	Forester
Goshawk	Hornet	Hydra	Indomitable	Laertes
Laforey	Landrail	Lapwing	Lark	Laurel
Lawford	Legion	Liberty	Lion	Lookout
Louis	Lowestoft	Lucifer	Lydiard	Lysander
Mastiff	Mentor	Meteor	Milne	Minos
Miranda	Morris	New Zealand	Nottingham	Phoenix
Princess Royal		Sandfly	Southampton	Tiger
Tigress	Undaunted			

DONEGAL 1798 (WARREN'S ACTION)
12 October
French Revolutionary War 1793–1802
In this splendid action Commodore Sir John Warren defeated a French invasion force trying to take advantage of unrest in Ireland during the Revolutionary War.

The invasion force comprised the French ship of the line *Hoche*, commanded by Commodore Bompard, leading eight frigates packed with 3,000 troops. Warren displayed greater power: three ships of the line and eight frigates.

The two squadrons met in foul weather – the gale force winds had already removed *Hoche's* main topmast – at 11 am on 11 October. Warren ordered "General Chase" and overhauled the French ships the following morning when both forces were in a straggling order. By 11 am the flagship *Hoche* had struck and by early afternoon three frigates had also struck and prize crews were put aboard them. Three more were captured a few days later, and only two managed to reach France.

Battle Honour:

Amelia	*Anson*	*Canada*	*Ethalion*
Foudroyant	*Magnanime*	*Melampus*	*Robust*

DOVER 1652
19 May
First Dutch War 1652–54
This battle was fought between an English fleet commanded by General-at-sea Robert Blake and a Dutch fleet commanded by Marten Tromp. It was a battle brought about by "the honour of the flag": the English demanded that all foreign ships in English waters should lower topsails and dip flags to English ships. It was a provocative demand, especially to the Dutch, who were loath to conform. Relationships between the two seafaring nations were, to use a modern phrase, trigger-happy.

By the time of the outbreak of the First Dutch War in 1652 the English were losing the race for maritime power. The Dutch fishing and merchant fleets far outnumbered the English. In essence the war began when the Dutchman Tromp refused to salute Blake off

Dover. On coming within hail the Dutch ships started lowering topsails but were slow in dipping flags. Blake, perhaps precipitately, opened fire, even though it was a full month before official hostilities began. A general action between forty Dutch ships and twenty-five English ensued. Two Dutch ships struck, though one was recovered later when abandoned by her prize crew. England won the day and accelerated the outbreak of war.

Battle Honour:

Adventure	Andrew	Assurance	Centurion
Fairfax	Garland	Greyhound	Happy Entrance
James	Martin	Mermaid	Portsmouth
Reuben (?)	Ruby	Sapphire	Seven Brothers
Speaker	Triumph	Victory	Worcester (?)

DOVER 1917
20 – 21 April
World War I 1914–18

A brilliant night action between six British and twelve German destroyers took place in the English Channel. Admiral Reginald Bacon made his usual dispositions unaware of an impending German attack.

Commanders Evans and Peck of the flotilla leaders, *Broke* (1,704 tons, 6 × 4") and *Swift* (2,170 tons, 4 × 4") respectively, distinguished themselves in the ensuing violent high-speed action in which the German Commodore lost two of his ships – *G 42* and *G 85*.

Broke suffered serious damage and forty casualties in an action which typified the dashing destroyer work of the Navy, and which earned the commander renown as Evans of the *Broke*.

Battle Honour: *Broke*   *Swift*

DUNKIRK (OPERATION DYNAMO) 1940
28 May–4 June
World War II 1939–45

The evacuation of troops of the British Expeditionary Force at the Fall of France from Dunkirk and other French coastal locations across the Channel while under heavy air attacks from the German *Luftwaffe* was effected at heavy cost to the Royal Navy.

In a period of eight days 338,266 men were lifted in 848 craft of all types, some naval, most non-military. Almost all equipment and arms were abandoned in France, but the rescued troops formed the basis of new armies which returned to France during Operation Overlord in Normandy, four years later almost to the day.

Naval vessels played a large and vital part in the evacuation. More than fifty destroyers were involved in the operation; nine were sunk and nineteen damaged. Destroyers lifted a total of 102,843 men. Destroyers sunk during the operation were:

Valentine	(1,190 tons)	Lost 15 May.	Later salved.
Whitley	(1,120 tons)	Lost 19 May.	
Wessex	(1,100 tons)	Lost 24 May.	
Wakeful	(1,100 tons)	Lost 29 May.	
Grafton	(1,335 tons)	Lost 29 May.	
Grenade	(1,335 tons)	Lost 29 May.	
Basilisk	(1,360 tons)	Lost 1 June.	
Keith	(1,400 tons)	Lost 1 June.	
Havant	(1,335 tons)	Lost 1 June.	

<u>Battle Honour:</u>

Albury	*Amulree*	*Anthony*	*Argyllshire*
Arley	*Basilisk*	*Bideford*	*Brock*
Blackburn Rovers	*Boy Roy*	*Brighton Belle*	*Brighton Queen*
Calcutta	*Calvi*	*Cape Argona*	*Cayton Wyke*
Chico	*Codrington*	*Comfort*	*Conidaw*
Crested Eagle	*Devonia*	*Duchess of Fife*	*Dundalk*
Eileen Emma	*Emperor of India*	*Esk*	*Express*
Fidget	*Fisher Boy*	*Fitzroy*	*Fyldea*
Forecast	*Gallant*	*Gervais Rentoul*	*Girl Gladys*
Girl Pamela	*Glen Avon*	*Glen Gower*	*Golden Eagle*
Golden Gift	*Golden Sunbeam*	*Gossamer*	*Gracie Fields*
Grafton	*Grenade*	*Greyhound*	*Grive*
Grimsby Town	*Guillemot*	*Gulzar*	*Halcyon*
Harvester	*Havant*	*Hebe*	*Icarus*
Impulsive	*Intrepid*	*Inverforth*	*Ivanhoe*
Jacketa	*Jaguar*	*Javelin*	*John Cattling*

Keith	Kellett	King Orry	Kingfisher
Kingston Alalite	Kingston Andalusite		Kingston Olivine
Lady Philomena	Leda	Llanthony	Locust
Lord Cavan	Lord Howard	Lord Howe	Lord Inchcape
Lydd	Mackay	Malcolm	Marmion
Medway Queen	Midas	Mona's Isle	Montrose
Mosquito	Nautilus	Nesukis	Niger Olvina
Oriole	Our Bairns	Pangbourne	Paxton
Plinlimmon	Polly Johnson	Princess Elizabeth	
Queen of Thanet	Ross	Royal Eagle	Sabre
Saladin	Salamander	Saltash	Sandown
Saon	Sargasso	Scimitar	Sharpshooter
Shikari	Shipmates	Silver Dawn	Skipjack
Snaefell	Speedwell	Spurs	Stella Dorado
Sutton	The Boys	Thomas Bartlett	Thuringia
Torbay II	Ut Prosim	Vanquisher	Venomous
Verity	Vimy	Vivacious	Wakeful
Waverley	Westella	Westward Ho	Whitehall
Whitshed	Wild Swan	Winchelsea	Windsor
Wolfhound	Wolsey	Wolves	Worcester
Yorkshire Lass	Young Mun		

FAA Squadrons: 801, 806, 825, 826.

Numerous other 'Red Ensign' ships such as personnel ships, hospital carriers and so on, took part in the operation but have not been awarded the Battle Honour.

E

EGYPT 1801
8 March
French Revolutionary War 1793–1803
Napoleon Bonaparte was well aware of the strategic importance of Egypt not only as a gateway to the East but also as a bargaining counter when the time came for making peace. The British, too, were aware of these military, naval and diplomatic considerations. Consequently Bonaparte resolved to reinforce his naval and military presence in Egypt. The British followed suit. Once again, apart from some minor support from the Turks, the British stood alone against the French Alliance.

By 1801 Napoleon stood astride Europe, seemingly invincible, confident in conquering, superior in military skills and victories. But at sea the British were daring and superior – and they knew it.

In 1801 the British conducted the first successful amphibious expedition of the war, landing at Aboukir, employing overwhelming force, as is indicated by the list of ships engaged.

The Royal Navy forces were commanded by the C-in-C of the Mediterranean, Admiral George Elphinstone (1st Viscount Keith), and the military forces by General Sir Ralph Abercromby. Abercromby became a casualty and died of his wounds. Cairo was captured and isolated groups of Bonaparte's troops were rounded up and evicted by Turks and Mamelukes.

<u>Campaign Honour:</u>

Active	Agincourt	Ajax	Alexander	Alligator
Asp	Astraea	Athenian	Bebelmandel	Ballahou
Blonde	Bonne Citoyenne		Braakel	Cameleon
Ceres	Charon	Chichester	Cruelle	Cyclops
Cynthia	Dangereuse	Delft	Déterminée	Diadem

Diane	Dictator	Dido	Dolphin	Dover
Dragon	Druid	El Carmen	Entreprenante	
Espiègle	Europa	Eurus	Expedition	Experiment
Flora	Florentina	Foudroyant	Fox	Fulminante
Fury	Gibraltar	Good Design	Gorgon	Gozo
Greyhound	Haarlem	Hebe	Hector	Heroine
Inconstant	Inflexible	Iphigenia	Janissary	Kangaroo
Kent	Leda	Leopard	Madras	Minerve
Monmouth	Négresse	Niger	Northumberland	
Pallas	Pearl	Pegasus	Penelope	Peterel
Phoenix	Pigmy	Pique	Port Mahon	Regulus
Renommée	Renown	Resource	Roebuck	Romney
Romulus	Rosa	Salamine	Santa Dorothea	
Santa Teresa	Scampavia	Sensible	Sheerness	
Sir Sidney Smith		Spider	Stately	Sultana
Swiftsure	Tartarus	Termagant	Thetis	Thisbe
Tigre	Tourterelle	Transfer	Trusty	Ulysses
Urchin	Vestal	Victor	Victorieuse	Vincejo
Wilhelmina	Winchelsea	Woolwich		

ENGLISH CHANNEL 1939–45
World War II 1939–45

The limits of this area are defined as the English Channel and all waters from Southend right round to Bristol, the western limit being a line drawn from Ushant to the Scilly Isles and thence to the north coast of Cornwall. All ships which were employed as escorts to Channel coastal convoys qualify. All ships and submarines which were employed on patrol duty in the area and took part in a successful action or success achieved in connection with Operation Neptune – the naval element of the Normandy Landings – also qualify for the award.

The early years of the war, 1939, 1940 and 1941 in particular, were specially hazardous. Defensively the area was sown with the huge Dover Barrage of mines. The Germans laid their own mine-fields and introduced the magnetic mine which temporarily foxed the Navy until an unexploded mine with its parachute was discovered on the mud flats of the Thames estuary. A counter measure –

degaussing – was swiftly devised to solve the problem.* The threat of E-boat (MTB) attack was ever-present; German aircraft bombed, strafed and dive-bombed convoys. After the invasion summer of 1940 the thunderous shore guns of Cap Gris Nez added further ordeals for merchantmen and their escorts to cope with.

There was an absolute necessity to maintain the flow of shipping up and down the East Coast and the English Channel. For example, 40,000 tons of coal had to be shipped from the Thames to Bristol every week.

The Channel became a theatre of war of ever-changing complexity. High-speed E-boat actions flared; minesweepers plodded through the narrow seas towing their gear like dogs on a leash, the new Hunt Class destroyers strengthened the escort forces.

Captain S.W. Roskill, the official naval historian, describes a July 1940 convoy, CW 8, originally of twenty-one ships, passing westwards through the Straits of Dover with only modest air support. It suffered at least four dive-bombing attacks. Five merchant ships were sunk, two destroyers and four more ships damaged. E-boats sank three more ships. Only eleven of the original twenty-one managed to pass Dungeness. Fortunately mines failed to find a target.

When barrage balloons were towed aloft for added safety kites had to be substituted, for the balloons became too easy to shoot down.

In time it became common, in Roskill's words, for a convoy "to be preceded by minesweeping trawlers and closely escorted by perhaps two destroyers, three or four anti-submarine trawlers, half-a-dozen Motor Anti-Submarine Boats or Motor Launches and surrounded by six or eight balloon vessels. Overhead flew the Hurricanes and Spitfires of Fighter Command . . . British resolution in facing new perils . . . thus defeated the enemy's attempt to close the English Channel to our coastal traffic."

Campaign Honour:

Abelia	Acacia	Acanthus	Affleck
Albrighton	Algoma	Alisma	Amarose
Ambroise Paré	Anchusa	Anthony	Aristocrat

---

* A heavy electrical cable secured around a ship countered the magnetic impulse feature of the mine. It was simple but effective.

Armana	Armeria	Ashanti	Assiniboine
Atalanta	Athabaskan	Atherstone	Avon Vale
Azalea	Bachaquero	Baddeck	Balfour
Balsam	Bangor	Barrie	Bay
Beagle	Ben Urie	Berkeley	Berkshire
Bickerton	Bideford	Bilsdean	Birch
Blackpool	Black Prince	Blackthorn	Blackwood
Bleasdale	Blencathra	Bligh	Blyth
Borage	Boreas	Boston	Bradford
Brazen	Brecon	Brilliant	Brissendon
Brocklesby	Bude	Bulldog	Burdock
Burges	Burke	Byron	Calgary
Calpe	Cambridgeshire	Campanula	Campbell
Camrose	Canalside	Cape Comorin	Capel
Capstone	Caton Wyke	Cattistock	Celandine
Charles Henri	Charybdis	Chelmer	Chiddingfold
Clarkia	Clematis	Cleveland	Clyne Castle
Commander Evans		Conn	Conqueror
Convolvulus	Cooke	Corinthian	Coriolanus
Cornelian	Cosby	Cotswold	Cottesmore
Cowdray	Crane	Cranstoun	Curzon
Cyclamen	Daffodil	Dahlia	Dakins
Daneman	Deane	Delphinium	Deodar
Deptford	Deveron	Dianella	Dianthus
Domett	Dominica	Doon	Dornoch
Drumheller	Duckworth	Duff	Eastbourne
Easton	Egilsay	Eglinton	Ekins
Elgin	Ellesmere	Ennerdale	Ensay
Erebus	Eskdale	Eskimo	Essington
Felixstowe	Fernie	Fidelity	Fir
Fitzroy	Fleetwood	Fluellen	Forester
Ganilly	Garth	Gaston Rivière	Gentian
Geranium	Glaisdale	Gloxinia	Goathland
Godetia	Good Hope	Goodson	Grenville
Grey Fox	Grey Goose	Grey Owl	Grey Seal
Grey Shark	Grey Wolf	Griffin	Grimsby Town
Grimstead	Gweal	Haida	Halstead
Hambledon	Hart	Hartland	Hatsuse

Havelock	Heather	Herschell	Hesperus
Holmes	Honeysuckle	Horatio	Hornbeam
Huron	Hyderabad	Hydrangea	Icarus
Ideshire	Ijuin	Ilfracombe	Impulsive
Inchgower	Inconstant	Iris	Istria
Jackal	Jasper	Javelin	Juliet
Kalan	Keppel	Kingcup	Kingsmill
Kingston Andalusite		Kingston Chrysoberyl	
Kitchener	Kittiwake	Kootenay	Labuan
Lark	Lavender	Leeds United	Leith
Lerwick	Limbourne	Lincolnshire	Lindsay
Lioness	Loch Achanalt	Loch Alvie	Loch Fasa
Loch Fyne	Loch Killin	Loch Ruthven	Locust
Londonderry	Longa	Loosestrife	Lord Essendon
Lord Hailsham	Lord Howe	Lord Plender	Lord Snowden
Lord Stanhope	Lord Stonehaven	Lord Wakefield	Louisburg
Lundy	Luneburg	Mackay	Malaya
Malcolm	Mangrove	Manor	Mayflower
Melbreak	Mendip	Meon	Meynell
Middleton	Mignonette	Milford Duchess	Mimico
Montrose	Moosejaw	Morris Dance	Mourne
Mousa	Myosotis	Narbarda	Narborough
Nasturtium	Ness	Newport	Night Hawk
Northward Ho	Notre Dame de France		Ocean View
Offa	Olive	Olvina	Ommering
Orchis	Ottawa	P 511	PC 74
Pangbourne	Parrsboro	Patti	Pearl
Pelican	Penylan	Perim	Peterhead
Petunia	Pine	Pink	Pointer
Poppy	Port Arthur	Port Colbourne	Prescott
Primrose	Prince Charles	Prince Leopold	Prince Robert
Princess Iris	Prins Albert	Prospect	Puckeridge
Puffin	Pytchley	Quadrille	Qualicum
Quickmatch	Quorn	Radnor Castle	Reboundo
Redmill	Redwood	Regina	Retalick
Revenge	Rhododendron	Rhyl	Righto
Rimouski	Rocket	Rockwood	Rodney
Romsey	Rosevean	Rothesay	Rousay

Rowan	Rowley	Royal Eagle	Ruby
Rupert	Ruskholm	Rutherford	St Albans
St Helena	St John	St Kilda	Saladin
Sasebo	Scalpay	Scarborough	Scarron
Scimitar	Shakespeare	Shippigan	Skate
Snowberry	Spragge	Staffa	Star of India
Starwort	Stata	Statice	Stayner
Stevenstone	Stockham	Stonecrop	Stormont
Stratagem	Stronsay	Sulist	Summerside
Sunflower	Sussexvale	Sutton	Swansea
Swansea Castle	Swordfish	Talybont	Tanatside
Tartar	Tavy	Thornborough	Torbay
Torrington	Towy	Tretonian	Trollope
Tyler	Tynedale	Ullswater	Ulster
Ulster Monarch	United Boys	Unseen	Vanity
Vanoc	Vanquisher	Vatersay	Versatile
Vesper	Victrix	Vidette	Ville de Quebec
Vimy	Vivacious	Volunteer	Waldegrave
Walker	Walpole	Wanderer	Warspite
Watchman	Waterfly	Wedgeport	Wensleydale
Westcott	Westminster	Weston	Whalsey
Whimbrel	Whitaker	Whitehall	Whitshed
Wild Goose	Winchester	Windsor	Witherington
Wolsey	Woodcock	Woodstock	Worcester
Wrestler	Zanzibar		

MLs: 163, 291, 1231

MGBs: 608, 615

MTBs: 15, 17, 22, 31, 32, 49, 52, 55, 56, 69, 84, 86, 95, 229, 236

SGBs: 6, 9

FAA Squadrons: 811, 812, 819, 825, 841

F

FALKLANDS 1914
8 December
World War I 1914 – 18
Only days after the defeat at Coronel (see page 250) the First Lord
of the Admiralty, Winston Churchill, and Admiral Fisher, the First
Sea Lord, despatched with all haste from Plymouth the two
powerful battlecruisers *Invincible* and *Inflexible* (both 17,250 tons,
8 × 12") to the South Atlantic. Vice-Admiral Sir Doveton Sturdee
was given command.

Sturdee rendezvoused with Rear-Admiral Stoddart, who had
assembled all available warships at Montevideo, and the force
proceeded southwards to the Falklands, arriving at Port Stanley on
7 December 1914.

Meanwhile the victorious German Admiral Graf von Spee made
a crucial decision: to attack and destroy the base installations at the
Falklands which he believed to be undefended, before breaking out
into the Atlantic, through the British blockade and back to
Germany.

He detached *Gneisenau* (11,420 tons, 8 × 8") and *Nürnberg*
(3,350 tons, 10 × 4.1") to reconnoitre Port Stanley ahead of the
squadron, and the gunnery officer of *Gneisenau* saw with horror
the distinctive tripod masts of two British battlecruisers in the outer
anchorage. Von Spee turned and sped south-east as fast as he could.

Sturdee had also been unprepared for the sighting. Several of his
ships were coaling, but within two hours all ships had steam up and
set off on a long pursuit. Both von Spee and the British knew that
the battlecruisers' superior fire power (a total of 16 × 12" guns) and
speed (they had been designed for just such an eventuality) would
be decisive, and that probably only darkness would save the
German squadron.

But by 1 pm on the same day, 8 December, the flagging *Leipzig* (3,544 tons, 12 × 4.1") was coming under British fire. Von Spee ordered his light cruisers to disperse, while his heavier ships, *Scharnhorst* and *Gneisenau* (both with 8 × 8" guns), engaged the powerful British battlecruisers. The outcome was inevitable. The German flagship sank with all hands at 4.15 pm. and *Gneisenau* followed at 6 pm.

The pursuit of the light cruisers was equally devastating. *Glasgow* (4,800 tons, 2 × 6" and 10 × 4") and *Cornwall* (9,800 tons, 14 × 6") sank *Leipzig*. *Kent* (9,800 tons) sank the *Nürnberg* with her 12 6" guns after a tremendous chase. Only the *Dresden* (3,544 tons, 12 × 4.1") escaped destruction but the search for her continued and three months later she was found in the island of Mas a Fuera, west of Chile. On the approach of *Kent* and *Glasgow* the light cruiser scuttled herself.

Thus the whole of von Spee's squadron had been eliminated in one of the most striking episodes of revenge at sea and demonstrated the extent of British seapower.

Battle Honour:

Bristol	*Carnarvon*	*Cornwall*	*Glasgow*
Inflexible	*Invincible*	*Kent*	*Macedonia*

FALKLAND ISLANDS 1982
2 April – 14 June
Falkland Islands War 1982

Britain's first missile war started when 2,500 Argentinians invaded the Falkland Islands, claiming sovereignty over what they called 'the Malvinas'. The islands were defended by a token force of eighty-four Royal Marines. Within a few days twenty ships left Portsmouth, including the carriers *Invincible* and *Hermes*, under the command of Rear-Admiral J.F. Woodward, to undertake the biggest British naval/military operation since the end of the Second World War.

The British forces fought a sharp, skilful and speedy action and recovered the islands. The P & O cruise liner *Canberra* (48,000 gross registered tonnage) and the *Queen Elizabeth II* (64,863 grt) were requisitioned for trooping/accommodation duties.

The Navy was subjected to bomb and missile attacks and suffered serious losses, including the sinking of the following: *Sheffield, Ardent, Antelope, Coventry, Atlantic Conveyor, Sir Tristram, Sir Galahad. Plymouth* and *Glamorgan* were both damaged. SSN *Conqueror* torpedoed and sank the Argentinian cruiser *General Belgrano*, and the submarine *Santa Fe* was abandoned and wrecked.

At midnight on 14 June Brigadier General Menendez surrendered all Argentinian forces on the islands.

Battle Honour:

Active	*Alacrity*	*Ambuscade*	*Andromeda*
Antelope	*Antrim*	*Ardent*	*Argonaut*
Arrow	*Avenger*	*Brilliant*	*Bristol*
Broadsword	*Cardiff*	*Conqueror*	*Cordelia*
Courageous	*Coventry*	*Dumbarton Castle*	
Endurance	*Exeter*	*Farnella*	*Fearless*
Glamorgan	*Glasgow*	*Hecla*	*Herald*
Hermes	*Hydra*	*Intrepid*	*Invincible*
Junella	*Leeds Castle*	*Minerva*	*Northella*
Onyx	*Penelope*	*Pict*	*Plymouth*
Sheffield	*Spartan*	*Splendid*	*Valiant*
Yarmouth			

Royal Fleet Auxiliaries:

Appleleaf	*Bayleaf*	*Blue Rover*	*Brambleleaf*
Engadine	*Fort Austin*	*Fort Grange*	*Olmeda*
Olna	*Pearleaf*	*Plumleaf*	*Regent*
Resource	*Sir Bedivere*	*Sir Galahad*	*Sir Geraint*
Sir Lancelot	*Sir Percivale*	*Sir Tristram*	*Stromness*
Tidepool	*Tidespring*	*Typhoon*	

FAA Squadrons: 737, 800, 801, 809, 815, 820, 824, 825, 826, 829, 845, 846, 847, 848, 899.

Merchant ships taken up from trade were awarded the Battle Honour:

Anco Charger	*Atlantic Causeway*	*Atlantic Conveyor*
Baltic Ferry	*British Dart*	*British Esk*
British Tay	*British Test*	*British Trent*
British Wye	*Canberra*	*Contender Bezant*
Elk	*Europic Ferry*	*Fort Toranto*
Geestport	*Iris*	*Irishman*

Lycaon	Nordic Ferry	Norland
Queen Elizabeth II	Saint Edmund	Salvageman
Saxonia	Scottish Eagle	Shell Eburna
Stena Seaspread	Tor Caledonia	Uganda
Wimpey Seahorse	Yorkshireman	

FINISTERRE 1747
3 May
War of the Austrian Succession 1739–48*

Cape Finisterre lies about 50 miles NNW of Vigo; it is the most north-westerly cape of Spain, and is not to be confused with Finisterre or Finistère, the NW Department of France. This naval battle was fought about 70 miles north by west of the Cape in the Bay of Biscay in May 1747 between a French and a British fleet.

Rear Admiral Sir George Anson, later Admiral Lord Anson, wore his flag in *Royal George* (90). He had with him twelve ships of the line, cruising in search of French convoys. On 3 May a large concentration of French ships was encountered. It comprised two convoys, one bound for India and the other for Canada, all of them under the protection of Admiral de la Jonquière with a totally inadequate escort which he bravely formed into line of battle. The two convoys had not yet parted for their separate destinations. There were thirty-eight French ships in all. The story is told briefly in *The Oxford Companion to Ships and the Sea*:*

> "The French fleet was sighted at 9.30 am and at noon nine of the French ships were seen to be forming a line of battle while the rest made all sail away. At 3 pm Anson hoisted the signal for a general chase and by 4 o'clock the first British ship was up with the rearmost of the French. A running fight then ensued, the other British ships joining in as they got up. By 7 pm all the ships that had remained in the French line had struck their colours. The main body of the British fleet then brought-to, and three ships were detached

---

* Also known as the War with Spain. On the one hand were Austria, Great Britain and Holland, on the other Spain, France, Bavaria and the Prussians.

* Edited by Peter Kemp and published 1976 by Oxford University Press.

to pursue the convoy, of which about six were captured as well as two small vessels of the escort. Night saved the rest."

It was for this substantial naval victory that Anson was raised to the peerage.

Battle Honour:

Ambuscade	*Bristol*	*Centurion*	*Defiance*
Devonshire	*Falcon*	*Falkland*	*Monmouth*
Namur	*Nottingham*	*Prince Frederick*	*Prince George*
Princess Louisa	*Vulcan*	*Windsor*	*Yarmouth*

FIRST TEXEL – see SCHEVENINGEN 1653

FIRST OF JUNE, THE GLORIOUS, 1794
1 June (and 28–29 May)
French Revolutionary War 1793–1802

This battle in the North Atlantic between Admiral Lord Howe and the French Admiral Villaret de Joyeuse was the first major encounter at sea between the warring countries. The outcome is not easy to assess: on the face of it Howe triumphed – as is implied in the name given to the battle, which had no geographic location other than a chart reference – by taking six valuable prizes and sinking a seventh ship of the line. But Joyeuse's objective was to give cover to a large convoy of grain ships from America to starving France. Despite Howe's victory, every merchantman reached France safely.

The battle was the culmination of several weeks of patient patrolling in the Western Approaches by Howe's fleet of thirty-four of the line. Reward came on 28 May in heavy seas when his flagship *Queen Charlotte* (100) sighted Joyeuse's fleet of twenty-six of the line. Joyeuse had the weather gage and for three days fended off Howe's attempts to reach the grain convoy away to the south. Skirmishing occurred during these days, with casualties, damage and losses to both sides, but the Frenchman was unexpectedly reinforced by another four of the line under Rear-Admiral Neilly.

97

1 June dawned clear, the opposing fleets were about four miles apart. Howe, having gained the windward position, bore down on the French line, intending to break through at all points and attack from leeward. *Queen Charlotte, Marlborough, Defence, Royal George* and *Queen* did just that, but other admirals and captains either misunderstood the intentions or baulked the issue and failed to break through. The result was a mêlée.

Six French of the line struck, two of them 80s, and *Le Vengeur du Peuple* (74) foundered after a monumental duel with *Brunswick*. Joyeuse's flagship *Montagne* (120) was heavily damaged and suffered 300 men killed.

Weeks of patrolling and days of battling took their toll. Howe, at sixty-eight, was exhausted. Had he had the stamina of a younger man he might well have captured the convoy too. It is the view of many that he should have done so anyway.

The King visited the fleet at Spithead at the end of June, and the occasion is captured by Sir William Dillon, then a midshipman:[*]

"To the noble and gallant Lord Howe, His Majesty presented a diamond-hilted sword of the value of 3,000 guineas; also a gold chain to be worn round the neck . . . The two next senior admirals, Graves and Hood, were created Irish peers: the four rear-admirals baronets. All the flag officers received gold chains similar to that given to Lord Howe, and the captains received medals – at least a certain number of them.[**] Pensions were settled on all that were wounded. All the Senior Lieutenants of the ships of the line that were in action received the rank of Commander. The Master of the *Queen Charlotte*, Mr Bowen, was made a Lieutenant."[***]

The French suffered 7,000 men killed, wounded and taken prisoner. Howe had eight ships badly damaged and 1,150 casualties.

[*]   *Dillon's Narrative*, Navy Records Society, 1953, Vol 1, p. 150.
[**]   Strangest omission was that of Captain Cuthbert Collingwood. But he was awarded one later. This medal is of historical interest: it was the first of all naval medals.
[***] Bowen became a Commissioner and a Rear-Admiral, a rare achievement for a warrant officer in those days.

Battle Honour:

Alfred	*Aquilon*	*Audacious*	*Barfleur*
Bellerophon	*Brunswick*	*Caesar*	*Charon*
Comet	*Culloden*	*Defence*	*Gibraltar*
Glory	*Impregnable*	*Incendiary*	*Invincible*
Latona	*Leviathan*	*Majestic*	*Marlborough*
Montagu	*Niger*	*Orion*	*Pegasus*
Queen	*Queen Charlotte*	*Ramillies*	*Ranger*
Rattler	*Royal George*	*Royal Sovereign*	*Russell*
Southampton	*Thunderer*	*Tremendous*	*Valiant*
Venus			

FOUR DAYS' BATTLE 1666
1–4 June
Second Dutch War 1665–67

A prolonged and fierce battle, one of the classics of naval history, was fought in the southern North Sea between an English fleet of fifty-six ships under the command of the Duke of Albemarle and a massive Dutch fleet of eighty-five ships commanded by Admiral de Ruyter. The Duke of Albemarle was to be joined later by Prince Rupert and his twenty ships, but they were to be detached to intercept a French force mistakenly believed to be coming to the aid of the Dutch.

Despite his inferiority in numbers Albemarle attacked the Dutch soon after noon on 1 June in thick weather off the North Foreland, with light winds in his favour. A running battle ensued. Cornelis Tromp's southern squadron was chased close to the French coast.

De Ruyter joined action later in the afternoon and soon Albemarle's flagship was badly mauled. Admiral Sir William Berkeley was killed and his *Swiftsure* (64) surrendered. Rear-Admiral Sir John Harman's flagship *Henry* (64) had a narrow escape from Evertsen's division of ships, but repelled several Dutch ships of the line and fireships and killed Evertsen with his last cannonade.

At the end of the first day Albemarle stood off to the west to repair damage. The second day found him with only about forty ships seaworthy against de Ruyter's eighty-odd. Nevertheless battle was again joined, the fleets engaging on opposite tacks, but the

English were unable to take advantage of confusion in the Dutch line. By the end of the second day Albemarle was in full retreat.

The retreat continued throughout the third day when three disabled ships were burnt to avoid capture. Then disaster struck when Admiral Sir George Ayscue's flagship *Royal Prince* (90) ran aground on the Galloper Sands, was captured and torched. That night Prince Rupert joined Albemarle, which enabled the English to muster about sixty ships against seventy-eight Dutch sail on the fourth day of battle.

Another day of bitter fighting ensued. Rupert's *Royal James* (82) and Albemarle's *Royal Charles* (80) were both seriously damaged, and Admiral Sir Christopher Myngs was killed aboard *Victory*. Both fleets became exhausted. As the day wore on Albemarle gained the weather advantage and thus a degree of safety. The battle was over. De Ruyter retired that evening. The losses were horrific. The English lost seventeen ships (including two flagships) and about 8,000 men. The Dutch had about 2,000 casualties and lost six ships.

The English, however, had remarkable powers of recovery. Only seven weeks later they fought another battle of major proportions at Orfordness.

Battle Honour:

Amity	Antelope	Assurance	Black Bull
Black Spread Eagle		Bonaventure	Breda
Bristol	Clove Tree	Convertine	Diamond
Dragon	Dreadnought	Essex	Expedition
Gloucester	Greyhound	Happy Entrance	Henrietta
Henry	Hound	House de Swyte	Leopard
Lilly	Little Katherine	Little Unicorn	Loyal George
Mary Rose	Plymouth	Portland	Portsmouth
Princess	Rainbow	Reserve	Revenge
Richard	Royal Charles	Royal James	Royal Katherine
Royal Prince	St George	St Paul	Sevenoaks
Spread Eagle	Swallow	Swiftsure	Triumph
Vanguard	Victorious	Young Prince	

G

GABBARD (North Foreland) 1653
2–3 June
First Dutch War 1652–54

The name of this battle is taken from the Gabbard Sands off Orfordness, Suffolk. The English fleet comprised about 115 ships including five fireships all under the command of Generals-at-sea George Monck and Richard Deane. All told these ships were manned by 16,300 men and carried 3,840 guns. The Dutch fleet was equally formidable. Admiral Marten Tromp commanded a fleet of 104 ships which included six fireships. Tromp's vice-admirals were de Ruyter and de With.

The fleets sighted each other at dawn on 2 June 1653 but light winds delayed action being joined till 11 o'clock. The first broadside killed Richard Deane. The first day of battle found the Dutch hard pressed and they suffered losses of three or four ships.

On the following day Blake arrived on the scene with 18 sail and the Dutch were routed. They withdrew to the Flanders Shallows where the larger English ships would be unable to follow. Thus the Dutch became blockaded. Both fleets settled down to undertake extensive repairing and refitting.

The Dutch losses had been enormous. Eleven ships had been captured by the English, six more had been sunk and three more blown up. The English lost no vessels, although 126 men were killed and 236 wounded. 1,360 Dutchmen were taken prisoner.

Battle Honour:

Adventure	Advice	Andrew	Arms of Holland
Amity	Ann and Joyce	Anne Piercey	Assistance
Assurance	Bear	Benjamin	Blossom
Brazil	Centurion	Convert	Convertine
Crescent	Crown	Culpeper	Diamond
Dolphin	Dragon	Dragoneare	Duchess
Eagle	Eastland Merchant		Employment

Essex	Exchange	Expedition	Fair Sisters
Falcon	Falmouth	Foresight	Fortune
Fox	George	Gift	Gilli Flower
Globe	Golden Fleece	Guinea	
Hamburg Merchant		Hampshire	Hannibal
Happy Entrance	Heart's Ease	Hopeful Luke	Hound
Hunter	Industry	James	John and Abigail
Jonathan	Kentish	King Ferdinando	Laurel
Lion	Lisbon Merchant	London	Loyalty
Malaga Merchant	Marmaduke	Martin	Mary
Merlin	Mermaid	Middlesborough	Nicodemus
Nonsuch	Oak	Paul	Pearl
Pelican	Peter	Phoenix	Portsmouth
President	Princess Maria	Prosperous	Providence
Prudent Mary	Rainbow	Raven	Reformation
Renown	Resolution	Richard and Maria	
Roebuck	Ruby	Samaritan	Samuel Talbot
Sapphire	Sarah	Society	Sophia
Speaker	Stork	Success	Sussex
Swan	Tenth Whelp	Thomas and Lucy	
Thomas and William		Tiger	Triumph
Tulip	Vanguard	Victory	Violet
Waterhound	Welcome	William	William and John
Worcester			

GENOA (HOTHAM'S FIRST ACTION) 1795
13–14 March
French Revolutionary War 1793–1803

This was an unsatisfactory action between a French squadron commanded by Rear-Admiral Martin with fifteen ships of the line and Vice-Admiral William Hotham with fourteen of the line from his Mediterranean fleet.

Martin was escorting an assault force from Toulon to recapture Corsica when he encountered Hotham's squadron cruising in the Gulf of Genoa about 20 miles south-west of Genoa. Two days of manoeuvring like shadow boxers followed, with Hotham showing little inclination to close.

On 13 March the French 84 *Ça Ira* rammed her next ahead, the *Victoire*, losing her fore and main topmasts. The British frigate *Inconstant* quickly closed and engaged her, swiftly followed by Captain Nelson in *Agamemnon* (60) who meted out great punishment to her bigger adversary. Nelson was no stranger to Corsica – in the previous year he had lost an eye there.

The following day's action was indecisive. Pierre Martin stood away to the west under full sail, and Hotham let him go, satisfied, it seems, with capturing *Ça Ira* and the *Centaur* (74) which had her in tow.

Battle Honour:

Agamemnon	Bedford	Blenheim	Boreas
Britannia	Captain	Centurion	Courageux
Diadem	Egmont	Fortitude	Fox
Illustrious	Inconstant	Lowestoffe	Meleager
Moselle	Poulette	Princess Royal	Romulus
St George	Tarleton	Terrible	Windsor Castle

GIBRALTAR 1704
24 July
War of the Spanish Succession 1702–13

After a period of lean naval pickings – apart from the buccaneering achievement at Vigo which stood alone as an exploit of any brilliance – the British resolved to make an attempt on the Spanish-held Gibraltar. Though Admiral Sir George Rooke only acted under pressure and was slow and very cautious, at least he was resolute and exacting, and for this he was chosen to lead the attack.

He commanded a naval force with his flag in *Royal Katherine*. In command of the soldiery and marines ashore was the Prince of Hesse-Darmstadt.

Rooke stood on guard with the bulk of his squadron against the French fleet at Toulon. He sent in a squadron under the command of George Byng to bombard the town while a body of marines led by the Prince landed on the neck of the peninsula, to isolate the town and garrison from relief. One hundred guns defended Gibraltar. But the mole was swept by cannon fire from the ships, then stormed by the sailors. At one stage a giant explosion caused near panic and a great number of casualties. After a prolonged bombardment during which the British losses were sixty killed and 217 wounded the governor surrendered the town on the 25th.

Battle Honour:

Bedford	*Berwick*	*Dorsetshire*	*Eagle*	*Essex*
Grafton	*Kingston*	*Lenox*	*Monck*	*Monmouth*
Montagu	*Nassau*	*Nottingham*	*Ranelagh*	
Royal Katherine		*Suffolk*	*Yarmouth*	

GLÜCKSTADT 1814
5 January
Napoleonic War 1803–15

In October 1813 Captain Arthur Farquhar of the Royal Navy arrived off Heligoland in his ship *Désirée* (36) to take up duty as Senior Officer. On 30 November, with a small squadron, he co-operated with a Russian force in an attack on the gun batteries protecting Cuxhaven. He crossed the Elbe and pushed up to Glückstadt in Holstein where he helped the Crown Prince of Sweden in bombarding Glückstadt's fortress. After six days of bombardment the fortress was captured on 5 January 1814. Farquhar's squadron comprised: *Désirée* (36), *Shamrock* (10), Commander John Marshall, *Hearty* (14) Commander James Rose, *Blazer* (14) Lieutenant Francis Banks, *Piercer* (14) Lieutenant Joshua Kneeshaw, *Redbreast* (14) Lieutenant Sir George Mouat Keith plus eight gunboats.

Battle Honour:

Only two vessels of the squadron were awarded the honour:

Blazer	*Désirée*

'GRAF SPEE' ACTION – see RIVER PLATE – 1939

GRAVELINES – see ARMADA – 1588

GREECE 1941
April
World War II 1939–45

Greece was attacked in strength on 6 April 1941 by German troops, armour and aircraft, and that night the port of Piraeus was put out of action when the ammunition ship *Clan Fraser* was struck by a bomb; the resulting massive explosion sank another ten ships.

A fortnight later the decision was taken to mount Operation Demon, the evacuation of Greece by British troops. The operation started on 24/25 April. Only minor ports and beaches could be used, and the round trip to the safety of Egypt was about 1,000 miles. Germany enjoyed almost complete air supremacy. During seven nights of evacuation 50,732 troops were saved for the loss of four transports and two destroyers.

<u>Battle Honour:</u>

Ajax	Auckland	Calcutta	Carlisle	Coventry
Decoy	Defender	Diamond	Flamingo	Gleanearn
Glengyle	Griffin	Grimsby	Hasty	Havock
Hereward	Hero	Hotspur	Hyacinth	Isis
Kandahar	Kimberley	Kingston	Muroto	Nubian
Orion	Perth	Phoebe	Salvia	Stuart
Ulster Prince	Vampire	Vendetta	Voyager	Waterhen
Wryneck				

GROIX, ÎLE DE (BRIDPORT'S ACTION) 1795
23 June
French Revolutionary War 1793–1803

Île de Groix was the name given to the battle fought between Admiral Bridport's Channel Fleet and a French squadron under Admiral Villaret de Joyeuse off Quiberon Bay in 1795. Bridport was one of the famous Hood family of admirals and captains. Alexander Hood, Viscount Bridport, was the younger brother of Samuel, Viscount Hood, of greater naval fame.

Bridport's fleet had been giving distant cover to the landing of French royalist exiles in Brittany. On 22 June Bridport sighted nine French ships of the line which immediately turned and headed for Lorient when they sighted the British ships. Bridport gave chase and overhauled the French squadron engaging the ships early the next morning off the Île de Groix.

In a spirited action three of the rear Frenchmen struck: *Alexandre* (74) was an English ship – *Alexander* – captured by the French the previous year: she was a poor sailer and evidently had not improved under French ownership. *Tigre* (74) struck, as did *Formidable* (74). The latter was renamed *Belle Isle* instead of the usual practice of a ship retaining her foreign name on being captured.

Bridport was content with the outcome of his action and made off with his prizes. Joyeuse considered himself lucky to have avoided further destruction or loss and made for Lorient.

Battle Honour:

Aquilon	Argus	Astraea	Babet
Barfleur	Charon	Colossus	Dolly
Galatea	Incendiary	Irresistible	London
Megara	Nymphe	Orion	Prince of Wales
Prince George	Revolutionnaire	Royal George	Russia (Russell?)
Sanspareil	Thalia	Valiant	

GUADALCANAL 1942–43
World War II 1939–45

Guadalcanal lies in the chain of islands known as the Solomons. It was the scene of one of the most prolonged and fiercely contested naval battles of the Second World War.

The islands had been captured by the Japanese in 1941 – 42. They marked the southern limit of the Japanese advance. Retribution came in August 1942: on the 7th the shores of Guadalcanal were assaulted by 10,000 American troops. It was the beginning of a bitterly fought campaign predominantly US in character and content, resulting in the following naval battles:

SAVO ISLAND (see page 206)	EASTERN SOLOMONS
CAPE ESPERANCE	SANTA CRUZ ISLAND
GUADALCANAL	TASSAFARONGA

As the Americans regained command of the Solomons in 1943 there occurred these additional battles:

RENNELL ISLAND	KULA GULF (see page 120)

KOLOMBANGARA	VELLA GULF
(see page 268)	
VELLA LAVELLA	EMPRESS AUGUSTA BAY
CAPE ST GEORGE	

(see page 268)

During this campaign the main Japanese naval base was at Rabaul, whence resolute naval forces sailed regularly between the eastern and western Solomons, a route known as The Slot. So regular was the traffic that it too earned a nickname – The Tokyo Express. And so many naval ships were sunk between Guadalcanal and Florida Island that a third name was coined – Iron Bottom Sound – to mark the ships' graves.

There was a fearsome struggle before US forces could claim the ascendancy in February 1943. The British support was confined to a small Australian and New Zealand input.

Battle Honour:

Achilles	*Arunta*	*Australia*	*Canberra*
Hobart	*Kiwi*	*Moa*	*Tui*

GUADELOUPE 1810
5 February
Napoleonic War 1803–15

Guadeloupe is a West Indian island lying in the Lesser Antilles. In 1810 it was the scene of a naval/military battle with the military forces commanded by Lieutenant-General Sir George Beckwith and the naval support commanded by Vice-Admiral the Hon Alexander Forrester Inglis Cochrane in *Pompée*.

Cochrane received intelligence of sickness raging on the island and that the colonial militia was disaffected and morale low. The island seemed ripe for attack.

On 27 January his fleet and military forces appeared off the island. On the following morning landings were effected with virtually no opposition. The two main landings were under the command of Commodore William C. Fahie in *Abercrombie* (74), and the other that of Commodore Samuel J. Ballard of *Sceptre* (74).

After some days' fighting surrender terms were proposed and the island finally capitulated on 5 February. Between that date and 22

February the Dutch islands of St Martin, St Eustatius and Saba were "peaceably" taken by the same forces.

<u>Battle Honour:</u>

Abercrombie	*Achates*	*Alcmene*	*Alfred*	*Amaranthe*
Asp	*Attentive*	*Aurora*	*Bacchus*	*Ballattou*
Belleisle	*Blonde*	*Castor*	*Cherub*	*Cygnet*
Elizabeth	*Fawn*	*Forester*	*Freija*	*Frolic*
Gloire	*Grenada*	*Guadeloupe*	*Hazard*	*Laura*
Loire	*Melampus*	*Morne Fortunée*		*Perlen*
Plumper	*Pompée*	*Pultusk*	*Ringdove*	*Rosamund*
Savage	*Sceptre*	*Scorpion*	*Snap*	*Star*
Statira	*Surinam*	*Thetis*	*Vimiera*	*Wanderer*

GULF OF GENOA – see GENOA 1795

GUT OF GIBRALTAR 1801 (Algeciras and the Straits, Saumarez's Action)
6 and 12–13 July
French Revolutionary War 1793–1802

In July 1801 Rear-Admiral Sir James Saumarez fought two separate actions within a week off Gibraltar against a squadron of French and Spanish ships of the line. The first action had an unhappy outcome for Saumarez. He wore his flag in *Caesar* (80) and had five 74s in company.

On the morning of 6 July he encountered an inferior Spanish squadron commanded by Rear-Admiral Durand-Linois, comprising three of the line and a frigate lying at anchor in Algeciras Bay. Linois was forced to run his ships ashore to avoid destruction and gain the sanctuary of shore guns.

One of Saumarez's 74s, the *Hannibal*, got too close inshore and ran aground where she was pounded into submission by the shore batteries. The British squadron retired to Gibraltar to lick its wounds. It secured its revenge six days later.

Patched and repaired, the British ships sailed and met a combined Franco-Spanish force at dusk on 12 July. It comprised eight of the line and three frigates. At midnight the two Spanish first rates – both of 112 guns, the *Real Carlos* and *San Hermenegildo* – caught fire and collided. They both foundered with heavy loss of life. Soon after this disaster the French 74 *St Antoine* was taken. Several of the British ships were damaged, especially the third rate *Venerable*, but all reached Gibraltar safely.

The battle became known as the Gut of Gibraltar. When the news reached England Saumarez became a national hero.

<u>Battle Honour:</u>

Audacious	*Caesar*	*Calpe*	*Louisa*	*Spencer*
Superb	*Thames*	*Venerable*		

H

HAVANA 1762
13 August
Seven Years' War 1756 – 63
The Seven Years' War was fought in Europe, North America and India. On the one side were the French, Austrians and Russians. Opposing them were Frederick the Great of Prussia, with some assistance from Britain, already engaged in a colonial war with France. The Royal Navy's role was all-important and led to Britain becoming the world's chief colonial power. Wolfe would have gained no victory without the Navy to bring the men and supplies to the battlefield; nor would India have been added to the British Crown without the naval supremacy established round the coasts of India.

In the West Indies Havana was captured after two months' investment by Admiral Sir George Pocock in his flagship *Namur*, supported by Captain Keppel* and his brother the Earl of Albemarle.

The British squadron comprised twenty-two ships of the line, thirty other ships and 100 transports. British troops landed on the island of Cuba in June 1762 and two months later Havana fell. Of the twelve ships of the Spanish squadron in the harbour nine ships of the line were captured and another three sunk.

The war ended with the Treaty of Paris in 1763 by which Britain gained Canada, Louisiana and Florida. And by this treaty North America became Anglo-Saxon.

Battle Honour:

Alarm	*Alcide*	*Basilisk*	*Belleisle*
Bonetta	*Cambridge*	*Centaur*	*Cerberus*

*Later Admiral. His share of the prize money is quoted as £25,000.

Cygnet	*Defiance*	*Devonshire*	*Dover*
Dragon	*Echo*	*Edgar*	*Enterprise*
Ferret	*Glasgow*	*Grenado*	*Hampton Court*
Intrepid	*Lizard*	*Lurcher*	*Marlborough*
Mercury	*Namur*	*Pembroke*	*Porcupine*
Richmond	*Stirling Castle*	*Sutherland*	*Temple*
Thunderer	*Trent*	*Valiant*	*Viper*

HELIGOLAND 1914
28 August
World War I 1914–18

Fought off Heligoland Bight between British and German light forces within three weeks of the outbreak of war.

The Admiralty planned a raid on German patrols to entice German forces into action and to bring them within range of Vice-Admiral Beatty's capital ships' guns. The British force comprised the Harwich Force: the light cruisers *Arethusa* (3,500 tons, 2 × 6" and 6 × 4") and *Fearless* (3,300 tons, 10 × 4"), leading twenty-one destroyers in two flotillas, commanded by Commodore R.T. Trywhitt. He was covered by the 1st Battle Cruiser Squadron (Vice-Admiral David Beatty) and the 1st Light Cruiser Squadron (Commodore W.E. Goodenough).

The battle started when Tyrwhitt entered the Bight at dawn and sighted two patrolling destroyers, one of which was promptly sunk. German light cruisers appeared on the scene and Tyrwhitt found himself embroiled in several high-speed actions, opposed by no less than six light cruisers: *Stettin* (3,350 tons, 10 × 4.1"), *Frauenlob* (2,715 tons, 10 × 4.1"), *Mainz* (4,350 tons, 12 × 4.1"), *Köln* (as Mainz), *Stralsund* (4,450 tons, 12 × 4.1") and *Ariadne* (2,660 tons, 10 × 4.1"). Rear-Admiral Maas's flag was in *Köln*.

Beatty's response to a call for assistance and his force's appearance was timely and decisive. His force comprised the battlecruisers *Lion* and *Princess Royal* (both 26,350 tons, 8 × 13.5"), *Invincible* (17,250 tons, 8 × 12"), *Queen Mary* (26,500 tons, 8 × 13.5") and *New Zealand* (18,800 tons, 8 × 12"). This squadron was covered by eight cruisers and a number of destroyers.

The three German cruisers *Köln*, *Ariadne* and *Mainz* were sunk.

The remainder scattered into the mist and escaped.

British casualties amounted to thirty-five killed and forty wounded. The Germans lost over 1,200 men killed and taken prisoner.

Battle Honour:

Aboukir	Acheron	Amethyst	Archer	Arethusa
Ariel	Attack	Bacchante	Badger	Beaver
Birmingham	Cressy	Defender	Druid	Euryalus
Falmouth	Fearless	Ferret	Firedrake	Forester
Goshawk	Hind	Hogue	Invincible	Jackal
Laertes	Laforey	Lance	Landrail	Lapwing
Lark	Laurel	Lawford	Legion	Lenox
Leonides	Liberty	Linnet	Lion	Liverpool
Lizard	Llewellyn	Lookout	Louis	Lowestoft
Lucifer	Lurcher	Lydiard	Lysander	New Zealand
Nottingham	Phoenix	Princess Royal		Queen Mary
Sandfly	Southampton			

Submarines: D2, D8, E4, E5, E6, E7, E8, E9

LA HOGUE – see BARFLEUR 1692

HOTHAM'S FIRST ACTION – see GENOA, GULF OF GENOA 1795

J

JAPAN 1945
16 July – 11 August
World War II 1939–45
The areas relating to this campaign award cover the mainland of Japan, and it will be seen that the time scale for the campaign covers less than one month at the very end of the Second World War in the Far East.

Those awarded the campaign honour were the Royal Navy fleet carriers and their FAA squadrons which took part in the final air assault on Japanese warships and shore positions. Attacks were carried out remorselessly, even to the day of final surrender. The magnitude of the forces marshalled for the final assault is expressed in the following statistics: at the surrender the Fleet Air Arm of the Royal Navy comprised no fewer than 59 carriers, 3,700 aircraft and more than 72,000 men. Of this force of carriers 34 were operational in the Far East on VJ day, but, as can be seen, only four fleet carriers were awarded the JAPAN 1945 honour.

<u>Battle Honour:</u>

| *Formidable* | *Implacable* | *Indefatigable* | *Victorious* |

<u>FAA Squadrons:</u>   *801, 820, 828, 848, 849, 880, 887, 1771, 1772, 1834, 1836, 1841, 1842.*

JAVA 1811
July – 18 September
Napoleonic War 1803–15
The reduction of Java in 1811 was accomplished by troops under the command of Lieutenant-General Sir Samuel Auchmuty and naval forces commanded by Rear-Admiral the Hon (later Sir) Robert Stopford with his flag in *Scipion*.

Stopford had been sent in the autumn of the previous year as C-in-C of the Cape of Good Hope with orders to reduce Mauritius, which had fallen before he got there.

In August 1811 Stopford received orders from Vice-Admiral Drury on his death bed to take command of an expedition to Java. He entrusted the preliminary direction of the operation to Captain Christopher Cole of *Caroline* (36), which entailed the transportation of an army from India.

The expedition was a complete success, after which Stopford returned to his own station and in 1812 he was promoted Vice-Admiral.

Battle Honour:

Akbar	*Barracouta*	*Bucephalus*	*Cornelia*	*Caroline*
Dasher	*Doris*	*Harpy*	*Hecate*	*Hesper*
Hussar	*Illustrious*	*Leda*	*Lion*	*Minden*
Modeste	*Nisus*	*Phaeton*	*Phoebe*	*President*
Procris	*Psyche*	*Samarang*	*Scipio*	
Sir Francis Drake				

JUTLAND (Skagerrak) 1916
31 May
World War I 1914–18

The greatest battle at sea of the First World War was fought between the main fleets of the Royal Navy and the Imperial German Navy. Both opposing fleets were divided into two distinct advance forces consisting on the one hand of battlecruisers, cruisers and destroyers under the command of Vice-Admiral David Beatty and Vice-Admiral Franz von Hipper, and on the other hand the main fleets of battleships, cruisers and destroyers commanded by Admiral Sir John Jellicoe and Vice-Admiral Reinhard Scheer.

The German plan was to lure the British Grand Fleet to sea from its bases over carefully positioned U-boats which could then launch torpedo attacks. But this ill-conceived plan suffered many defects and failed in many respects. Yet Jutland (or Skagerrak as the Germans call it) was a contest between mighty Britain and the newcomer, a battle where, curiously, the most modern weapons – submarines and aircraft – were not employed. This clash of the capital ships was to be the first major battle of its kind, and the last. Jutland was unique, and will ever remain so.

It was also a chapter of might-have-beens, but one thing is certain. The German High Seas Fleet should never have escaped the annihilation that faced it in the murky wastes of the North Sea in 1916.

Hipper put to sea with his scouting force, followed by Scheer's main Battle Fleet about 60 miles astern. Intelligence of these moves became known to the Admiralty and the Grand Fleet (always ready at short notice for sea) sailed. Beatty's force left harbour ahead of Jellicoe, and was, like Scheer, followed by the Main Fleet about 60 miles astern.

On that day, 31 May 1916, most of the world's capital ships were at sea, seeking battle, none of them knowing the strength of the opposition or their exact whereabouts.

Action started almost by accident. *Galatea* (3,520 tons, 2 × 6") and 6 × 4") on the port wing of the advanced cruiser screen turned to investigate a Swedish merchant ship almost at the same time as a German warship on the port wing of their advance screen did the same. In a few minutes "Enemy in sight" was being flashed to the battlefleets.

Beatty's Battlecruiser Force (less the battleships) and Hipper's Battlecruiser Scouting Force were soon engaged, the latter trying to lure Beatty to the south towards Scheer's battleships. In this phase of the engagement six British and five German battlecruisers were exchanging shots.

Within a short time the *Indefatigable* (18,750 tons, 8 × 12") had been pounded to destruction by the accurate shelling of *Von der Tann* (21,000 tons, 8 × 11"). The *Queen Mary* (27,000, 8 × 13.5"), battered by the *Seydlitz* (25,000 tons, 10 × 11") and the *Derfflinger* (28,000 tons, 8 × 12"), blew up with frightening suddenness. Beatty then found himself confronted with Scheer's battle force.

He turned his battlecruisers away to the northward, hoping to draw Scheer towards Jellicoe's main Battle Fleet. Hipper and Scheer, neither aware that Jellicoe was at sea, complied: they expected to destroy Beatty's battlecruisers.

At 6 pm about 80 miles west of the Jutland peninsula the two main fleets clashed. Soon the cruiser *Wiesbaden* sank. Minutes later the armoured cruiser *Defence* (14,600 tons, 4 × 9.2" and 10 × 7.5") exploded and sank. *Derfflinger*, assisted this time by *Lützow* (28,000 tons, 8 × 12"), again demonstrated her accurate gunnery by inflicting terrible damage on *Invincible* (17,250 tons, 8 × 12"), which soon blew up. However, *Lützow* was so seriously pummelled in this phase that she sank the following day. Jellicoe deployed his fleet into line of battle on the port wing column, a masterly move which put his fleet across Hipper's line of retreat and crossed the German's T. The scene was all set for a resounding British victory. But it was not to be.

The battle continued in a confused fashion throughout the night. During this night phase Hipper avoided being trapped by Jellicoe and managed to extricate his forces, only encountering light British opposition. The old pre-dreadnought *Pommern* (13,200 tons, 14 × 6.7") suffered much damage in the night and finally sank at 4.10 am.

The light cruiser *Frauenlob* (2,715 tons, 10 × 4.7") took a lot of punishment and she sank. The German destroyer *Elbing* was rammed and sunk by a German battleship, and the light crusier *Rostock* (4,900 tons, 12 × 4.1") sank after a fierce duel with British destroyers. *Black Prince* (13,550 tons, 6 × 9.2" and 10 × 6") had to be abandoned when fires gained control and she sank.

When daylight came on 1 June the German fleet had reached the safety of its own minefield in the Heligoland Bight. Jellicoe and the British found themselves gazing at an empty sea.

The losses sustained were as follows:

BRITISH	GERMAN
3 Battlecruisers	1 Pre-Dreadnought
3 Armoured cruisers	1 Battlecruiser
8 Destroyers	4 Light Cruisers
	5 Destroyers
6,090 men killed	2,550 men killed

The place of Jutland in the war is debated to this day, more than eighty years later. Tactically and in material terms the rewards went to Scheer and Hipper. Strategically the British retained command of the sea and the German High Seas Fleet never again came out to dispute control. As one journalist put it "The German fleet had assaulted its gaoler, but is still in prison."

Battle Honour:

Abdiel	Acasta	Achates	Acheron	Active
Agincourt	Ajax	Ambuscade	Ardent	Ariel
Attack	Badger	Barham	Bellerophon	Bellona
Benbow	Birkenhead	Birmingham	Black Prince	Blanche
Boadicea	Broke	Calliope	Canada	Canterbury
Caroline	Castor	Centurion	Champion	Chester
Christopher	Cochrane	Collingwood	Colossus	Comus
Conqueror	Constance	Contest	Cordelia	Defence
Defender	Dublin	Duke of Edinburgh		Engadine
Erin	Falmouth	Faulknor	Fearless	Fortune
Galatea	Garland	Gloucester	Goshawk	Hampshire
Hardy	Hercules	Hydra	Inconstant	Indefatigable
Indomitable	Inflexible	Invincible	Iron Duke	Kempenfelt
King George V		Landrail	Lapwing	Laurel
Liberty	Lion	Lizard	Lydiard	Maenad
Magic	Malaya	Mandate	Manners	Marksman
Marlborough	Marne	Martial	Marvel	Mary Rose
Menace	Michael	Midge	Milbrook	Mindful
Minion	Minotaur	Mischief	Monarch	Mons
Moon	Moorsom	Moresby	Morning Star	Morris
Mounsey	Munster	Mystic	Narborough	Narwhal
Neptune	Narissa	Nessus	Nestor	
New Zealand	Nicator	Noble	Nomad	Nonsuch
Nottingham	Oak	Obdurate	Obedient	Onslaught
Onslow	Opal	Ophelia	Orion	Ossory
Owl	Pelican	Petard	Phaeton	Porpoise
Princess Royal		Queen Mary	Revenge	Royalist
St Vincent	Shannon	Shark	Southampton	
Sparrowhawk	Spitfire	Superb	Temeraire	Termagant
Thunderer	Tiger	Tipperary	Turbulent	Unity
Valiant	Vanguard	Warren	Warspite	Yarmouth

K

KENTISH KNOCK 1652
28 September
First Dutch War 1652–54

The battle was named after the sandbank of that name in the southern North Sea. The English fleet comprised sixty-eight ships commanded by General-at-Sea Robert Blake. He defeated a Dutch fleet of fifty-nine ships commanded by Admiral Witte de With.

The Dutch fleet was sighted by Blake's ships at about noon on 28 September 18 miles east of North Foreland. Action was joined at 5 pm at the Kentish Knock, a shallow in the Thames Estuary. Blake and his vice-admiral, William Penn, engaged the van and centre divisions of de With's ships, followed by the rear. The action broke up into a series of small irregular engagements with many ships running aground. English aggression proved compelling and put the Dutch to flight. The onset of darkness brought an end to the battle. The Dutch had lost two ships and many others suffered heavy damage and casualties.

Battle Honour:

Andrew	Diamond	Garland	Greyhound	Guinea
James	London	Nightingale	Nonsuch	Pelican
Resolution	Ruby	Sovereign	Speaker (List incomplete)	

KOREA 1950 – 51
Korean War 1950–53

The area covered by this campaign award is the whole of the Korean coast.

North Korean forces launched an assault on South Korean positions at the end of June 1950, precipitating a frustrating three-year war. The attack was condemned by the United Nations, and fifteen member states, led by the USA and including units of the Royal Navy, went to South Korea's aid. The Commonwealth Task Force included RAN, RNZN and Canadian units as well as RN: four store ships, twelve fleet oilers and the hospital ship *Maine* were included.

In a near-perfect amphibious operation at Inchon an invasion force was thrown ashore covered by four carriers, two escort carriers, seven cruisers, thirty-four destroyers and a great number of frigates and minesweepers. North Korea had no navy and was thus vulnerable to sea-borne attacks.

These landings and subsequently the Inchon evacuation were the two main features of the naval war. The objective of the landings was to capture the capital, Seoul, and cut lines of supply. In 1950 70,000 men of the US 10th Corps were landed from 550 landing craft. British naval support was given by the cruisers *Jamaica* and *Kenya* (both 8,000 tons, 12 × 6"). During the operation *Jamaica* fired 1,290 rounds of 6" and 393 rounds of 4": *Kenya* fired 1,242 rounds of 6" and 205 rounds of 4". *Jamaica* also has the distinction of being the first UN ship to shoot down an enemy aircraft.

Red China's involvement in the Korea War took place on 31 December 1950 and the war dragged on till an armistice was signed on 27 July 1953. British ships took part in the evacuation – *Kenya* and *Ceylon* and the two Australian destroyers *Bataan* and *Warramunga*.

Battle Honour:

Alacrity	Alert	Amethyst	Anzac
Athabaskan	Bataan	Belfast	Birmingham
Black Swan	Cardigan Bay	Cayuga	Ceylon
Charity	Cockade	Comus	Concord
Condamine	Consort	Constance	Cossack
Crane	Crusader	Culgoa	Glory
Haida	Hart	Hawea	Huron
Iroquois	Jamaica	Kaniere	Kenya
Modeste	Morecambe Bay	Mounts Bay	Murchison
Newcastle	Nootka	Ocean	Opossum
Putaki	St Bride's Bay	Shoalhaven	Sioux
Sparrow	Sydney	Taupo	Telemachus
Theseus	Tobruk	Triumph	Tutira
Tyne	Unicorn	Warramunga	Whitesand Bay

Royal Fleet Auxiliaries: *Wave Premier   Wave Prince*
FAA Squadrons: *800, 801, 802, 804, 805, 807, 808, 810, 812, 817, 821, 825, 827, 898.*

KUA KUM 1849
20 October
19th Century: Chinese Piracy

The Kua Kum, variously Cua Keum and Cua Cam, is one of the three mouths of the Red River, the boundary between China and Indo China. Commander John C.D. Hay in *Columbine* (16) led *Fury* (6), the Bengal Marine steamer *Phlegethon* and a party of seamen from *Hastings* in flushing out dozens of pirate junks trapped inshore of the banks and shoals and islands, destroying fifty-eight in the Kua Kum over a period of two days.

Battle Honour: *Columbine   Fury   Hastings*

KULA GULF 1943
13 July
World War II 1939–45

This was an almost identical battle with that of Kolombangara a week later. Both were in the series of naval battles during the Guadalcanal campaign. Both employed similar tactics, with almost identical results. Rear-Admiral Walden L. Ainsworth USN commanded at both battles.

The Japanese force was engaged in a routine inter-island service. Ainsworth deployed his force in the favoured night formation: destroyers in the van and rear and cruisers in the centre. He had four destroyers and three cruisers. On sighting the enemy ships in Kula Gulf the cruisers closed the seven destroyers acting as transports, plus another three acting as escorts. Fire was opened with almost machine-gun rapidity and torpedoes fired at will. In the confused action one Japanese destroyer was sunk, but the US cruiser *Helena* was struck by no less than five torpedoes and sank with heavy loss of life.

The British cruiser *Leander* participated in the battle. She suffered no damage nor losses.

Battle Honour: *Leander*

KUWAIT 1991

The Gulf War 1990–91

President Saddam Hussein's Iraqi forces launched an invasion of neighbouring Kuwait on 1 August 1990 and in 48 hours overran the country and designated Kuwait an Iraqi province. The United Nations condemned the invasion and large and powerful UN forces were marshalled, including strong contingents from America and Britain.

Britain already had naval forces in the area. The Armilla Patrol had been set up to protect merchant ships during the years-long Iran/Iraq war. This was now to be supplemented by the two US carriers *Eisenhower* and *Independence*. The United Nations ordered a strict naval blockade of Iraq and Kuwait and during the next eight months nearly 30,000 ships were challenged and more than 1,200 were boarded and searched.

The land war began on 17 January on the expiry of a deadline. The operation codenamed Desert Shield, became Desert Storm. Iraq launched ninety-five Scud missiles against Kuwait and Saudi Arabia.

At sea the coalition forces were busy. Missiles from carrier-borne aircraft and Cruise missiles from battleships, cruisers and submarines rapidly subdued the Iraqis. British naval aircraft and helicopters systematically destroyed the light Iraqi naval force. The Gulf waters had to be cleared of mines and the Royal Navy's plastic-hulled minehunters proved ideal for the task.

On 3 March 1991 a ceasefire became effective after the almost total destruction of Hussein's military, air and naval forces.

The Honour was awarded to Royal Navy units in the Gulf War: to HM Ships, RN Air Squadrons and RFAs which were: either actively engaged in operations against Iraqi forces or engaged in logistic support duties in the Central and Northern Gulf to the west of the meridian 51° E at any time between 17 January and 28 February 1991.

<u>Battle Honour:</u>

Atherstone	Brave	Brazen	Brilliant	Cardiff
Cattistock	Dulverton	Exeter	Gloucester	Hecla
Herald	Hurworth	Ledbury	London	Manchester

<u>Royal Fleet Auxiliaries:</u>

| Argus | Bayleaf | Diligence | Fort Grange | Olna |
| Resource | Sir Bedivere | Sir Galahad | Sir Percivale | Sir Tristram |

1. The first *Ark Royal*, which saw distinguished service in the Armada campaign, 1588. (*National Maritime Museum*).

2. This sailing plan of the Armada's crescent formation was sketched by the Grand Duke of Tuscany's ambassador to Lisbon on 18 May, 1588. It records the Spanish captains' names and their ships' position in the formation. It proved highly effective against the English attacks, 1588. (*Archivo di Stato di Firenze*).

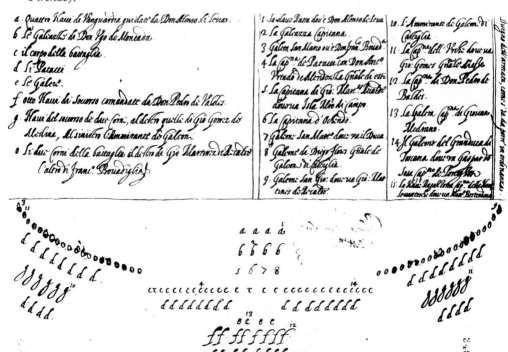

3. HMS *Vanguard*, Sir William Wynter's flagship at the decisive Battle of Gravelines, 1588. The painting is by Sir Oswald Brierly (1817-94) (*National Maritime Museum*).

4. Martin Frobisher, the tough Yorkshireman who commanded a squadron against the Armada in his flagship *Triumph*, 1588 (*Curator of the Bodleian Library, Oxford*).

5. This picture shows the Spanish Armada off the Scottish coast when the Spaniards were preparing their ships for the forthcoming Atlantic experience, even to the extent of casting overboard the horses and ponies originally intended to draw the land artillery on English soil (*Rijksmuseum*).

6. James, Duke of York, saw several of his friends die alongside him aboard his flagship in the Battle of Lowestoft, 1665. The Duke's ship is closely engaged with the Dutch flagship, shortly to blow up after a hit in her powder room. Battle of Lowestoft, 1665 (*National Maritime Museum*).

7. The Royal Navy takes great pride in family names such as Hood, Savage, Wallace, Saumarez and Inglefield, but the Evertsens of the Dutch Navy outstrip them all. Lieutenant-Admiral Jan Evertsen (1600-66) took command of the fleet at Lowestoft when Lord Obdan was killed. Although he extricated many ships to safety, townsfolk threw him into the harbour in disgust at the Dutch defeat. He died at the Battle of Orfordness, having had both his legs shot off. (*National Maritime Museum*).

DEN E.MANHAFTEN ZEE-HELD IAN EVERTSZ. RIDDER, VICE ADMIR'.VAN ZEELANDT.&.

9. James, Duke of York and Albany (1633-1701) later became James II of England. He was the younger brother of Charles II. James showed great enterprise and personal courage as a naval commander and was rewarded with a resounding victory over the Dutch at the Battle of Lowestoft in 1665 (*National Portrait Gallery*).

8. Samuel Pepys (1633-1703), diarist, was also a brilliant administrator, reformer, Secretary of Affairs for the Navy and, with royal approval, set up a Commission to re-establish the navy and restore the spirit and discipline of the men (*National Maritime Museum*).

10. Vice-Admiral M.A. de Ruyter (1607-76) was the Nelson of the Netherlands. A giant among the famous band of Dutch 17th century admirals, he was the Duke of York's chief adversary. His striking success in the Medway humiliated England (*Rijksmuseum*).

11. In June, 1667, a Dutch squadron led by de Ruyter sailed up the Thames estuary and into the River Medway, severed the chain guarding the entrance and surprised the English fleet at anchor. Many ships were burned and the *Royal Charles*, one-time flagship of King James, was towed off in triumph. Her heavily decorated stern is still preserved in the Rijksmuseum (*Rijksmuseum*).

12. The Four Days Battle, 1666 (*National Maritime Museum*).

13. The Battle of La Hogue, 1692 (*National Maritime Museum*).

14. The Battle of Vigo Bay, 1702 (*National Maritime Museum*).

15. The Battle of Flamborough Head, 1779 (*National Maritime Museum*).

16. Portsmouth Dockyard and the Common Hard in the late 18th century showing the ship-of-the-line HMS *Victory* some years before her 1805 victory at Trafalgar (*National Maritime Museum*).

17. HMS *London*, the eighth of twelve bearing that name. She fought at the Battles of Chesapeake (1781), Groix (1795) and Copenhagen (1801) (*National Maritime Museum*).

18. Vice-Admiral Adam Duncan, 1st Viscount Duncan (1731-1804) served in the Moonlight Battle (1780) and won a striking victory over the Dutch at Camperdown in 1797. A Scot of towering build and great personal courage and bravery (*David A Thomas*).

19. Admiral Sir Edward Codrington (1770-1851) earned the distinction of being the last commander of a fleet to fight a major action wholly under sail - at Navarino Bay in 1827. Commanded the *Orion* (74) at Trafalgar in 1805 (*David A Thomas*).

20. HMS *Alexandra* in 1882 during the bombardment of Alexandria. She was the fastest battleship afloat at that time (*National Maritime Museum*).

21. HMS *Dreadnought*, the 17,900-ton brainchild of Admiral Fisher, was launched in 1906. She was the first big-gun turbine-driven capital ship and made every other battleship in the world obsolete (*National Maritime Museum*).

22. Admiral Sir John Jellicoe commanded the British forces at the Battle of Jutland, 1916 (*David A Thomas*).

23. HMS *Lion* and battlecruisers under heavy fire during the Battle of Jutland, 1916 (*MOD/N*).

24. The Battle of the River Plate, 1939 (*National Maritime Museum*).

25. HMS *Kelly*, one-time command of Admiral of the Fleet Lord Mountbatten, holder of the Crete 1941 battle honour (*Imperial War Museum*).

26. The Australian destroyer HMAS *Nizam* returns to Alexandria crowded with troops evacuated from Crete. She survived the Mediterranean battles, then earned the Pacific honour of Okinawa, 1945 (*Australian War Memorial*).

27. HMS *Nelson* won the Second World War honours of Malta Convoys 1941-2, North Africa 1942-3, Mediterranean 1943, Sicily 1943, Salerno 1943, Normandy 1944. She and *Rodney* were the first RN ships to mount 16" guns, all nine grouped for'ard (*National Maritime Museum*).

28. Japanese Admiral Nagumo's Striking Force sank the two heavy cruisers *Dorsetshire* and *Cornwall* in the Indian Ocean in April, 1942. *Dorsetshire*, in particular, displayed a proud list of battle honours. This picture shows hundreds of survivors being rescued.

29. HM Battleship *Warspite*, flagship of Admiral Sir Andrew B. Cunningham, Commander-in-Chief Mediterranean, and perhaps the most honoured ship in RN history. She is seen here in the Mediterranean in 1941 (*National Maritime Museum*).

30. Admiral Sir Tom Phillips (right) and his Chief-of-Staff, Rear Admiral Palliser, in Singapore, December, 1941. A few days later Japanese aircraft sank HMS *Prince of Wales* and HMS *Repulse*. 47 officers and 793 men lost their lives (*Imperial War Museum*).

31. The Battle of the North Cape, 1943. The sinking of the German battleship *Scharnhorst* (*National Maritime Museum*).

32. HMS *Invincible* has the distinction of bearing the battle honours Falklands 1914 and Falkland Islands 1982 among her list of honours dating back to 1780.

L

LAGOS 1759
18–19 August
Seven Years' War 1756–63

An important naval battle was fought off Lagos in southern Portugal between a British squadron under the command of Admiral the Hon Edward Boscawen and a French squadron under Commodore De La Clue.

Boscawen had been blockading De La Clue's ships in Toulon for some time, but he managed to give Boscawen the slip and set off for the Straits en route to Brest. His squadron comprised ten of the line, two 50s and three frigates. He wore his flag in *Namur* (90).

As soon as Boscawen received intelligence of De La Clue's escape he sailed westward from Gibraltar with fourteen of the line and several frigates.

Early on 18 August seven of De La Clue's ships were sighted off the Portuguese coast, the remainder of the French force having made for Cadiz without orders. Action began in the the afternoon. The French *Centaure* (74) was taken and the *Namur* much disabled aloft. Boscawen transferred his flag to the *Newark* (80). The boat in which he transferred was hit by a round shot and the Admiral plugged the hole with his wig. The chase continued through the night until four of the Frenchmen found sanctuary in Lagos Bay while the other two escaped in the darkness. So hurried was the flight of the flagship, the *Océan* (80), that she ran aground in the bay under full sail, her three masts going by the board. She struck her colours, her crew fled ashore and she was set ablaze.

The other three Frenchmen in the bay anchored under the protection of the Portuguese shore batteries. Boscawen adopted the principle of "hot chase" and pursued the enemy into the bay. The next morning he captured the *Temeraire* (74) and *Modeste* (64) while the 74 *Redoubtable* was wrecked and burnt by her crew.

De La Clue was carried ashore during the battle, with a leg shot off, and died the following day. Boscawen enjoyed the fruits of a splendid and incredibly well-conducted victory. In summary the French losses amounted to:

Captured	Burnt
Centaure	*Ocean*
Modeste	*Redoubtable*
Temeraire	

Battle Honour:

Active	*Ambuscade*	*America*	*Conqueror*
Culloden	*Edgar*	*Etna*	*Favourite*
Gibraltar	*Glasgow*	*Gramont*	*Guernsey*
Intrepid	*Jersey*	*Lyme*	*Namur*
Newark	*Portland*	*Prince*	*Rainbow*
St Albans	*Salamander*	*Shannon*	*Sheerness*
Swiftsure	*Tartar's Prize*	*Thetis*	*Warspite*

LAKE CHAMPLAIN 1776
11 and 13 October
American War of Independence 1775–83

Lake Champlain is a large lake in the northern USA between the States of New York and Vermont. In 1776 it was the scene of two naval battles. A third battle took place there in 1814 but was not awarded a Battle Honour.

The first battle, or more properly, phase, was fought for the control of communications on the lake. The American colonists had established themselves with a flotilla of small craft under the command of Benedict Arnold. The first phase of the encounter began on the 11th and finished with the second phase on the 13th, ending in complete British victory.

The ships were all built on the lake, the largest being the brig/sloop *Inflexible* (18). Commander Thomas Pringle commanded her.

The second phase was fought off Crown Point and all the American ships were sunk or captured except four which made good their escape to Ticonderoga.

Another battle took place on the lake in 1814 for which no honour was awarded. It took place on 11 September between a squadron of British ships commanded by Commodore Downie with his flag in *Confiance* (37), a brig of 16 guns, two sloops (11) and twelve small gunboats. The American squadron, commanded by Commodore Thomas Macdonough, comprised the USS *Saratoga* (26), three vessels carrying a total of 44 guns and ten rowed galleys. Two hours of heavy fighting left the American ships in command of the lake.

Battle Honour:

Carleton	*Inflexible*	*Loyal Convert*	*Maria*	*Thunderer*

LEAKE'S SECOND RELIEF OF GIBRALTAR – see MARBELLA 1705

LEYTE GULF 1944
20 – 27 October
World War II 1939–45

This great naval battle, the Trafalgar of the Second World War, was fought over several days in October 1944 in the seas around Leyte Gulf in the Philippines between the Japanese main fleet and the 3rd and 7th Fleets of the USA. In terms of the size of the opposing forces and the sea area over which it was fought it was the biggest naval battle in history. The British involvement was relatively insignificant and was restricted to a few RAN cruisers and smaller vessels.

The three main battle areas were fought at:

Surgigao Strait   Samar   Cape Engaño

The USN commanders were Admiral William Halsey (3rd Fleet) and Admiral Thomas Kinkaid (7th Fleet). Their joint victory ended the effectiveness of the Imperial Japanese Navy; it had virtually been swept from the seas. Ultimate defeat for Japan was assured. The total losses at Leyte amounted to:

JAPANESE LOSSES	USA LOSSES
3 battleships	1 light carrier
4 aircraft carriers	2 escort carriers
6 heavy cruisers	2 destroyers
4 light cruisers	1 destroyer escort
9 destroyers	

Nearly every other ship engaged was damaged to some extent.

Battle Honour:

Ariadne   Arunta   Australia   Gascoyne   Shropshire
Warramunga

LIBYA 1940–42
September 1940–June 1942
World War II 1939–45
The area relating to this Campaign Honour is defined as inshore between Port Said and Benghazi. All ships and vessels of the Inshore Squadron (Force W) were entitled to the award, excluding the heavier covering forces which were employed in maintaining Tobruk (then under siege) and other places on the coast and generally in supplying the army of the Western Desert. FAA Squadrons, both carrier-borne and shore-based, are also eligible.

Campaign Honour:

1940:   *Hereward   Hyperion   Janus   Juno*
             Mohawk   Nubian

FAA Squadron: *819.*

1940–41:

Chakla	*Dainty*	*Fiona*	*Ladybird*
Protector	*Stuart*	*Terror*	*Vampire*
Vendetta	*Voyager*	*Waterhen*	

FAA Squadrons: *803, 806, 813, 815, 824.*

1940–42:   *Aphis   Jervis*

1941:

Abdiel	*Arthur Cavenagh*		*Auckland*	*Aurora II*
Bagshot	*Calcutta*	*Calm*	*Chakdina*	*Chantala*

Coventry	Cricket	Defender	Encounter	Fareham
Flamingo	Glenearn	Glengyle	Glenroy	Gnat
Greyhound	Grimsby	Hailstorm	Huntley	Kai
Kandahar	Kingston	Kos 21	Latona	May
Milford Countess		Muroto	Napier	Nebb
Nizam	Ouse	Paramatta	Rosaura	Salvia
Sikh	Sindonia	Skudd III	Skudd IV	Soira
Southern Floe	Stoke	Svana	Thorbryn	Thorgrim
Wryneck	Yama	Yarra		

MLs: 1012, 1023

MTBs: 68, 215

1941 – 42:

Aberdare	Avon Vale	Burgonet	Carlisle
Cocker (ex Kos 19)		Decoy	Eridge
Falk	Farndale	Gloxinia	Griffin
Hasty	Havock	Hero	Heythrop
Hotspur	Hyacinth	Jackal	Jaguar
Kimberley	Kipling	Klo	Legion
Moy	Peony	Protea	Skudd V
Soika	Sotra	Southern Isle	Southern Maid
Southern Sea	Toneline	Wolborough	

MLs: 1048, 1051

FAA Squadrons: 805, 826

1942:

Airedale	Aldenham	Antwerp	Arrow
Beaufort	Beves	Boksburg	Croome
Delphinium	Dulverton	Erica	Exmoor
Farnham	Firmament	Gribb	Grove
Hurworth	Imhoff	Kingston Coral	Kingston Crystal
Langlaate	Lively	Malines	Parktown
Primula	Seksern	Snapdragon	Southwold
Treern	Victoria I	Vulcan	Zulu

MLs: 266, 267, 348, 355, 1004, 1005, 1039, 1046, 1069.

MTBs: 61, 259, 260, 261, 262, 263, 266, 267, 309, 311, 312.

FAA Squadron: 821

LINGAYEN GULF 1945
5–9 January
World War II 1939–45

The campaign for the recovery of the Philippines from the Japanese invaders in 1945 included the naval battle of Lingayen Gulf where the US assault forces were spearheaded by a support force of 164 ships including six old battleships, twelve escort carriers, ten destroyer/transports and sixty-three minesweepers. The Fleet Commander was Vice-Admiral Oldendorf. A small number of HM Australian ships took part in the battle.

Australia encountered bitter fighting against suicide pilots and was struck no less than five times – and still survived.

It took weeks of bitter fighting before the whole of the Philippines were liberated.

Battle Honour:

Arunta *Australia* *Gascoyne* *Shropshire* *Warramunga*
Warrego

LISSA 1811
13 March
Napoleonic War 1803–15

A most creditable victory for a small British squadron of four frigates over a stronger force of three French frigates (each with 44 guns), three Venetian frigates and four or five smaller vessels took place off Lissa Island on the Dalmatian coast.

Captain William Hoste with the *Amphion, Active* and *Cerberus* (all 5th rates*) and the 6th rate *Volage* were using Lissa as a base.

The French Commodore Dubourdieu was despatched from Ancona with his mixed squadron, plus 500 troops, to occupy Lissa. The squadrons sighted each other north of the island at dawn on the 13th. Dubourdieu, having the weather gage, bore down on the British ships in two divisions. Hoste was one of Nelson's protégés

---

* 5th rates carried between 32 and 44 guns with a weight of broadside between 636 and 350 lb (288 to 158 kg). A 6th rate carried between 20 and 28 guns with a broadside between 250 and 180 lb (113 to 81 kg). See detailed explanation in the Introduction.

and rallied his squadron with the signal "Remember Nelson"; a spirited battle ensued. After three hours the French flagship had been driven ashore and blown up, killing the Commodore. Three other frigates were taken and the remainder of the force fled.

Battle Honour:

Active	*Amphion*	*Cerberus*	*Volage*

LOUISBURG 1758
8 June–26 July
Seven Years' War 1775–83

Louisburg was a French naval base near the mouth of the St Lawrence. In 1758 an operation was planned for the capture of Quebec from the French. In the early months of that year a huge armada of 150 transports was assembled to carry 13,000 men from Spithead to Louisburg. The naval command was in the capable hands of Admiral the Hon Edward Boscawen in his flagship *Namur* (90). The land forces were commanded by General Jeffrey Amherst. It was they who would deliver a great blow to the French dominion in North America.

At Halifax this fleet of transports met its escort of twenty-three sail of the line and eighteen frigates. The French opposition was ineffectual. On 2 June the fleet landed a strong force on the south-east coast of Cape Breton Island and fighting continued for several weeks.

There was little opposition at sea. The navy landed and sustained all the forces ashore, bombarded the French and by the end of July the defenders were ready to consider surrender. The final straw came on 24 July. After the steady bombardment of Louisburg from land and sea the French warships had been greatly reduced, but two ships, *Prudent* (74) and *Bienfaisant* (64), were still capable of resistance. Boscawen resolved to cut them out. Boats from the fleet assembled, then set off with muffled oars in fog. The two prizes were boarded. *Prudent* was aground and had to be set on fire. *Bienfaisant* was successfully towed away under constant fire from the shore batteries.

The total French losses amounted to four of the line burnt and one taken, four vessels sunk in the harbour as blockships and a frigate taken. Louisburg and the whole of Cape Breton Island surrendered to the British.

Battle Honour:

Active	Beaver	Bedford	Boreas
Burford	Captain	Centurion	Defiance
Devonshire	Diana	Dublin	Gramont
Halifax	Hawke	Hunter	Juno
Kennington	Kingston	Lancaster	Lightning
Namur	Nightingale	Northumberland	Nottingham
Orford	Pembroke	Port Mahon	Prince Frederick
Prince of Orange	Princess Amelia	Royal William	Scarborough
Shannon	Somerset	Squirrel	Sutherland
Terrible	Trent	Vanguard	York

LOWESTOFT 1665
3 June
Second Dutch War 1665–67

Lowestoft was one of the classic battles of sail, fought on an enormous scale between an English fleet of 109 ships commanded by James, Duke of York (the King's brother) and 103 ships of a Dutch fleet commanded by Admiral Opdam (or Obdam) Jacob van Wassenaer, off the Suffolk coast about 40 miles south-east of Lowestoft.

The Dutch fleet was marauding near the Dogger Bank at the end of May, capturing a convoy of twenty English merchant ships, when James, Duke of York received intelligence of the enemy activity. James, in his flagship the *Royal Charles* (80), led the English fleet in weighing anchor from the Gunfleet and proceeding to Southwold Bay. James had with him, commanding two of the enormous squadrons, the Earl of Sandwich (Montagu) and Prince Rupert, two of the famous generals-at-sea.

Two days of manoeuvring these vast fleets preceded the battle, which was joined at 4 am on 3 June, each fleet passing the other on opposite tacks, each ship engaging as the enemy ships came into range. Soon the battle had degenerated into a mêlée on a grand scale.

In the centre the two flagships *Royal Charles* and *Eendracht* (76), fought a bitter battle, the latter just failing in an attempt to board

James's ship. At one stage a chain shot killed many officers and men alongside James, who was spattered with their blood. A chronicler (probably James's flag captain Sir William Penn) wrote: "At 12 came A shot from Opdam yt killed ye Earl of Falmouth [Charles Berkeley] Lord Musgrave [Muskerry] and Mr Boyle [younger son of the Earl of Burlington]."

Eendracht then received a shot in her powder room and exploded with devastating force. Only five of her complement of many hundreds were rescued. With the death of Wassenaer, Vice-Admiral Jan Evertsen took command. Another demoralizing blow to the Dutch was the death of Vice-Admiral Kortenaer aboard the *Groot Hollandia*.

The English gradually gained the upper hand and the Dutch began to give way. Ships fouled each other, and no fewer than seven Dutch ships were lost by fire in this way.

With great skill Evertsen and Cornelis Tromp marshalled the Dutch fleet into a controlled withdrawal towards the Texel and Maas estuary, which was reached by the late evening. They had lost thirty-two ships, only nine of which were taken as prizes; their casualties amounted to about 4,000 killed and 2,000 taken prisoner.

The English losses were amazingly light by comparison. The *Charity*, captured early in the battle, was the only ship lost. In terms of seamen, 283 were killed and 440 wounded.

Battle Honour:

Adventure	Amity	Anne	Antelope
Assistance	Assurance	Bear	Bendish
Blackamore Merchant		Bonaventure	Breda
Briar	Bristol	Castle Frigate	Colchester
Constant Katherine		Convertine	Diamond
Dolphin	Dover	Dragon	Drake
Dreadnought	Dunkirk	Eagle	Fame
Forester	Fountain	Garland	George
Gloucester	Golden Lion	Guernsey	Guinea
Hambro' Merchant		Hampshire	Happy Return
Henrietta	Henry	Horseman	Hound
Jersey	John and Abigail	John and Katherine	
John and Thomas	Katherine	Kent	King
King Ferdinando	Leopard	Lion	London

Loyal George	Loyal Merchant	Maderas	Marmaduke
Martin	Mary	Maryland Merchant	
Mary Rose	Milford	Monck	Montagu
Newcastle	Nightingale (?)	Old James	Oxford
Pembroke	Plymouth	Portland	Portsmouth
Providence	Princess	Prudent Mary	Rainbow
Reserve	Resolution	Return	Revenge
Royal Charles	Royal Exchange	Royal James	Royal Katherine
Royal Prince	St Andrew	St George	Sapphire
Satisfaction	Society	Success	Swallow
Swiftsure	Tiger	Triumph	Uniform
Vanguard	Yarmouth	York	Young Lion

LUCKNOW 1858
16 March
Indian Mutiny 1857–58

By the mid-19th century the East India Company had enjoyed a century-long rule in India supported by a small force of British troops and a naval presence. The Crimean War and unrest in Burma, China and Persia spread to India where native troops became increasingly disaffected and fearful of native religions being suppressed.

The last straw came with the introduction of the Enfield rifle (replacing the musket). To load the new rifle a greased patch in the cartridge had to be removed by the teeth. Rumour spread that the grease came from the fat of a sacred (to Hindus) cow, or of a pig – unclean to a Muslim. Lord Anson, C-in-C India, ordered the cartridges to be used ungreased, but this remedy came too late. The Indian mutiny erupted. It started at Meerut on 10 May 1857. The next day Europeans in Delhi were massacred. 3,000 troops were ordered to besiege Delhi. Lucknow, about 250 miles south-east of Delhi, was also besieged. The garrison at Cawnpore was massacred. A relief force for Lucknow was formed.

The Navy was called to assist at Lucknow and Gwalior. Three ships – *Sanspareil* (70), *Shannon* (51) and *Pearl* – were despatched under the command of Rear-Admiral Sir Michael Seymour to

Calcutta from Hong Kong to help quell the mutiny. (For *Pearl*'s actions see AMORHA, p. 16).

Shannon, the largest steam frigate afloat, sailed up the River Hoogly with 560 men aboard to join the Lucknow relief force. Her commanding officer, Captain Peel VC, was wounded and died aged 34, "perhaps the most brilliant officer of his day".

The mutiny collapsed after a brilliant operation at Gwalior in June 1858. It had cost 2,000 British lives: another 9,000 died of disease and sunstroke. The government of India was transferred to the British Crown later in the year.

<u>Battle Honour:</u>   *Shannon*

M

MADAGASCAR – see DIEGO SUAREZ 1942

MALAGA – see *Velez Malaga* 1704

MALAYA 1942–45
World War II 1939–45
The Malaya Battle Honour relates to the Malacca Straits and waters
adjacent to the Malay peninsula and Sumatra between 7° N to 7° S
and 95° E to 108° E. The award was won by ships and submarines
which took part in a successful action in the area. The destroyers of
the 26th Flotilla, *Saumarez, Venus, Virago, Verulam* and *Vigilant*
for example, receive the award Malaya 1945 for their successful
exploit in sinking the Japanese heavy cruiser *Haguro*.
<u>Campaign Honour:</u>

Emperor	*Jupiter*	*Saumarez*	*Scythian*	*Seascout*
Selene	*Sturdy*	*Subtle*	*Taciturn*	*Tally Ho*
Taurus	*Telemachus*	*Thorough*	*Thule*	*Tiptoe*
Tradewind	*Trenchant*	*Trespasser*	*Trump*	*Tudor*
Venus	*Verulam*	*Vigilant*	*Virago*	

<u>FAA Squadron:</u>   *851*

MALTA CONVOYS 1941–42
World War II 1939–45
On 10 January 1940 Italy declared war on Britain and France,
creating the burden of an unwanted theatre of war in the
Mediterranean whose resources from all the Services were already

stretched almost beyond endurance. The extra responsibility on the Fleet and in particular upon Admiral Sir Andrew B. Cunningham, C-in-C of the Mediterranean Fleet, was a heavy burden. The main fleet was stationed at Alexandria guarding the eastern basin. A small but effective Force operated from Gibraltar under the command of Vice-Admiral Sir James Somerville.

It became clear after the fall of France that the French Navy would have to be marginalized to deny its use by the Germans or Italians, and it became the Royal Navy's melancholy duty to immobilize, capture or sink the French Fleet. (See DAKAR p. 252 and ORAN p. 277–8).

The Italian Navy enjoyed considerable superiority over the British on paper. It comprised six battleships, seven heavy cruisers, fourteen light cruisers, fifty-nine destroyers and 108 submarines. This substantial fleet lacked the fighting spirit of the Royal Navy, whose aggression and resolution found no match in Mussolini's navy. The impressive Italian fleet of submarines achieved little in comparison with German U-boats. It is a matter of fact that the two greatest achievements in terms of Axis submarine warfare in the Mediterranean, the sinking of the carrier *Ark Royal* and the destruction of the battleship *Barham*, were both German achievements.

The greatest danger to the Royal Navy in the Mediterranean came from the bombers of the Luftwaffe, and the damage and losses sustained by the Navy were considerable. The sustenance of besieged Malta became a major duty for the Royal Navy, and it is to the Fleet's credit that the names of the operations it undertook have become emblazoned in the annals of the Navy – Excess, Substance, Harpoon, Halberd, Pedestal. And between these brutal convoy operations the Navy managed to engage in sea engagements, in air strikes, in army support, in the springboard of Operation Torch, and the Axis attempt to escape from North Africa: SINK BURN DESTROY, Cunningham signalled the Fleet in time-honoured style: LET NOTHING PASS.

Convoys from Gibraltar and Alexandria to beleaguered Malta took on the role of a fleet operation: capital ships to defend the convoy from marauding Italian capital ships; aircraft carriers to provide fighter protection against high-level bombers of the Italian air force and the dive bombers of the Luftwaffe; cruisers and AA cruisers to give AA protection to the capital ships and merchantmen; destroyers for escort and AA duties.

To illustrate the ferocity of some of these battles three such convoy operations are described here.

MALTA: OPERATION EXCESS
10–11 JANUARY 1941
This operation was a convoy battle fought between Force H from Gibraltar under the command of Vice-Admiral Sir James Somerville, units of the Mediterranean Fleet under the command of the C-in-C, Admiral Sir Andrew Cunningham, and the German Fliegerkorps X based in Sicily.

The action arose over the passage of four merchantmen in a convoy, one ship destined for Malta and the other three for the Piraeus. Force H covered the passage as far as the Straits of Sicily; there the cruisers *Southampton* (9,100 tons, 12 × 5"), *Gloucester* (9,400 tons, 12 × 5") and *Bonaventure* (5,450 tons, 10 × 5.25") and five destroyers took over responsibility. Long-range cover was given by the battleships *Valiant* (32,700 tons, 8 × 15") and *Warspite* (30,600 tons, 8 × 15"), the carrier *Illustrious* (23,000 tons, 36 aircraft) and accompanying cruisers and destroyers.

Aircraft from Fliegerkorps X struck on 10 January. *Illustrious* was hit six times and her armoured deck failed to prevent serious damage. An eye witness reported seeing a bomb "bounce like a ball" along the flight deck. The carrier limped into the questionable safety of Malta for repairs. *Warspite* was also hit. The following day *Southampton* and *Gloucester* were heavily bombed and *Southampton* had to be abandoned.

The four merchantmen reached their destinations.

MALTA: OPERATION HARPOON
12–16 June 1942
Operation Harpoon was the name given to a particularly complex and difficult joint convoy operation, attempting to fight through to Malta a convoy from Gibraltar simultaneously with another from Alexandria.

After heavy fighting with Axis light surface units, U-boats and

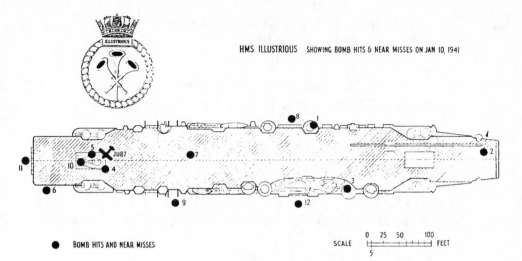

● BOMB HITS AND NEAR MISSES

SCALE

0   25   50   100
FEET
5

aircraft, the Alexandria convoy was aborted with the loss of two of the freighters. Although heavy units of the Italian fleet were at sea, they were not committed to the battle.

The Gibraltar element of the operation suffered even more heavily. Four out of six freighters were sunk during the attacks, together with the light cruiser *Hermione* (5,450 tons, 10 × 5.25"). Furthermore, five destroyers and a cruiser were damaged. The Italians lost the cruiser *Trento* (10,000, 8 × 8") while the flagship, the battleship *Littorio* (35,000 tons, 9 × 15") suffered damage from bomb hits and a torpedo.

MALTA: OPERATION PEDESTAL
10–15 August 1942
A bitter battle developed over several days when the Royal Navy tried to fight through a convoy of fourteen freighters from Gibraltar to Malta, just two months after the fierce experience of the Harpoon convoy. Central to the whole saga was the British-manned US oil tanker *Ohio*, laden with fuel oil desperately needed by the defending aircraft at Malta. Vice-Admiral Sir Neville Syfret commanded the British force which consisted of:

Carriers:
Indomitable (Rear-Admiral D.W. Boyd) 50 aircraft

Victorious (Rear-Admiral Sir A.L. St A.Lister) 34 aircraft
Furious 42 Spitfire aircraft for Malta. 4 aircraft

Battleships:
Nelson (Vice-Admiral Sir Neville Syfret) 33,950 tons.
Rodney (33,900 tons: both ships 9 × 16" and 12 ×6")

Cruisers:
Nigeria (Rear-Admiral H.M. Burroughs) 8,000 tons, 12 × 6"
Kenya (8,000 tons, 12 × 6")
Manchester (9,400 tons, 12 × 6")
Cairo (4,290 tons, 8 × 4")
Phoebe (5,450 tons, 10 × 5.25")
Sirius (5,450 tons, 10 × 5.25")
Charybdis (5,450 tons, 10 × 5.25")

Destroyers: 28
Submarines: 9

The bulk of the Italian fleet remained in harbour due to lack of oil supplies, but heavy and sustained air attacks were launched by Italian and German aircraft operating from Sardinia and Sicily in the course of which *Indomitable* was damaged and the *Victorious* was struck by two bombs which bounced along the armoured flight deck. The convoy and escorts were also subjected to submarine and E-boat attacks. The carrier *Eagle* was sunk by *U-73*. The Italian submarine *Axum* fired a spread of four torpedoes which struck the *Nigeria, Cairo* and the tanker *Ohio*. The *Cairo* had to be sunk by torpedo and gunfire from HM ships. In a daring night attack Italian E-boats torpedoed the *Manchester* and she had to be scuttled later. A stray aircraft torpedo struck the destroyer *Foresight* and she was subsequently sunk by the *Tartar*.

Nine of the fourteen merchant ships were sunk and most of the remainder were damaged. Despite *Ohio's* extensive damage she made an epic arrival at Valetta, barely afloat, lashed to rescue vessels either side of her to give buoyancy and steerage way.

Operation Pedestal had been a desperate encounter, but the Royal Navy, at great sacrifice, had begun to raise the siege of Malta.

Battle Honour:

Ajax — Amazon — Antelope — Arethusa
Ark Royal — Argus — Arrow — Avon Vale
Ashanti — Aurora — Badsworth — Beaufort
Bedouin — Beverley — Bicester — Blankney
Bonaventure — Boston — Bramham — Breconshire
Cachalot — Cairo — Calcutta — Carlisle
Charybdis — Cleopatra — Clyde — Coltsfoot
Cossack — Dainty — Decoy — Defence
Derwent — Diamond — Dido — Dulverton
Duncan — Eagle — Echo — Edinburgh
Encounter — Eridge — Escapade — Eskimo
Euryalus — Farndale — Faulknor — Fearless
Firedrake — Fleur de Lys — Foresight — Forester
Fortune — Foxhound — Furious — Fury
Gallant — Geranium — Gloucester — Gloxinia
Greyhound — Griffin — Gurkha — Hasty
Havock — Hebe — Hereward — Hermione
Hero — Heythrop — Hurworth — Hyacinth
Hythe — Icarus — Ilex — Illustrious
Indomitable — Inglefield — Intrepid — Ithuriel
Jaguar — Janus — Jervis — Jonquil
Juno — Kandahar — Kelvin — Kenya
Keppel — Kimberley — Kingston — Kipling
Laforey — Lance — Ledbury — Legion
Lightning — Lively — Liverpool — Lookout
Malaya — Malcolm — Manchester — Manxman
Maori — Marne — Matchless — Mohawk
Naiad — Nelson — Neptune — Nestor
Nigeria — Nizam — Nubian — Olympus
Onslow — Oribi — Orion — Osiris
Otus — P31 — P32 — P34
P36 — P42 — P43 — P44
P221 — P222 — Pandora — Parthian
Partridge — Pathfinder — Penelope — Penn
Peony — Perth — Phoebe — Porpoise
Prince of Wales — Proteus — Quentin — Renown

Rodney	Rorqual	Rye	Salvia
Sheffield	Sikh	Sirius	Somali
Southampton	Southwold	Speedy	Spiraea
Talisman	Tartar	Thunderbolt	Triumph
Trusty	Unbeaten	Unique	Upholder
Upright	Urge	Ursula	Utmost
Valiant	Vansittart	Venomous	Victorious
Vidette	Warspite	Welshman	Westcott
Wilton	Wishart	Wolverine	Wrestler
York	Zetland	Zulu	

MLs: 121, 134, 135, 168, 459, 462.

FAA Squadrons: 800, 801, 806, 807, 808, 809, 812, 813, 816, 820, 824, 825, 827, 831, 832, 884, 885.

MARBELLA 1705 (ACTION OFF CABRITA, CABARETA POINT, LEAKE'S SECOND RELIEF OF GIBRALTAR)

10 March

War of the Spanish Succession 1702–13

This action resulted from a French attempt to land troops for the recapture of Gibraltar. It was fought between a squadron of French ships of the line under the command of Commodore Baron de Pointis, and a similar squadron commanded by Vice-Admiral Sir John Leake.

The French squadron arrived in Gibraltar Bay, but a rising gale drove the French force to leeward towards Marbella.

The British squadron lay off Cabrita Point 9 miles south-west of Marbella. Leake had with him five ships of the line. At daybreak on 10 March Leake surprised de Pointis. The British Admiral had every advantage and he pressed home his attack with speed and vigour. In a swift and skilful action the British took the 66-gun *Ardent*, the *Marquis* (66) and *Arrogant* (60). Two more of the line, the flagship *Magnanime* (74) and *Lys* (66), were driven ashore and burnt by their crews to avoid capture.

Leake had not only scored a remarkable victory but had saved Gibraltar from attack and had enhanced his already high reputation.

Antelope	Bedford	Canterbury	Expedition
Greenwich (?)	Hampton Court	Lark	Leopard
Newcastle	Nottingham	Pembroke	Revenge
Swallow	Tiger	Warspite (List incomplete.)	

MARTINIQUE 1762
16 February
Seven Years' War 1756–63

This French-occupied island in the West Indies was captured by British naval forces commanded by Rear-Admiral George Brydges Rodney with his flag in *Marlborough*, and military forces under the command of Major-General the Hon Robert Monckton.

When Rodney left Plymouth in October 1761 to take command of the West Indies Fleet he carried with him plans to attack and occupy Martinique, for it held a dominating and strategic position in the islands.

Monckton's force of soldiers, marines and seamen were given powerful support by the navy.

On 10 February the important citadel of the capital, Fort Royal, surrendered and gave Rodney "possession of the noblest and best harbour in these parts".

Rodney had also destroyed fourteen of the best French privateers, with more "to be delivered under the terms of the surrender".

He went on to conquer other islands: St Lucia, St Vincent and Grenada fell to him in quick succession.

Battle Honour:

Alcide	Amazon	Antigua	Barbados
Basilisk	Crescent	Crown	Culloden
Devonshire	Dover	Dragon	Dublin
Echo	Falkland	Foudroyant	Grenado
Greyhound	Levant	Lizard	Marlborough
Modeste	Nightingale	Norwich	Nottingham
Raisonnable	Repulse	Rochester	Rose
Stag	Stirling Castle	Sutherland	Temple
Temeraire	Thunder	Vanguard	Virgin
Woolwich	Zephyr		

MARTINIQUE 1794
5–22 March
French Revolutionary War 1793–1802

In 1794 Vice-Admiral Sir John Jervis arrived in Jamaica with four sail of the line escorting ships carrying 7,000 men, the invasion force under the command of Sir C. Grey to capture Martinique.

The expedition proved easier than at first thought. It was found that the island was defended by just 700 men. The French *Bienvenue* was taken in Fort Royal's harbour.

Having conquered Martinique Jervis went on to occupy St Lucia and Guadeloupe.

Battle Honour:

Asia	Assurance	Avenger	Beaulieu
Blonde	Boyne	Dromedary	Experiment
Irresistible	Nautilus	Quebec	Rattlesnake
Roebuck	Rose	Santa Marguerita	Sea Flower
Spiteful	Tormentor	Ulysses	Vengeance
Venom	Vesuvius	Veteran	Winchelsea
Woolwich	Zebra		

MARTINIQUE 1809
24 February
Napoleonic War 1803–15

In the summer of 1808 intelligence received by the British made it clear that the strategic island of Martinique was in need of provisions and her garrison had been reduced. It was decided to take advantage of this situation.

More than forty ships of war were prepared for the assault on the island and all preparations were complete by the end of January 1809. The operation was under the command of Rear-Admiral the Hon Alexander Cochrane with his flag in *Neptune* (98). A fleet of transports was necessary to convey the 10,000 troops, marines and seamen forming the landing forces. They were under the command of Lieutenant-General Beckwith.

To illustrate how enormous was the operation the list of ships awarded the Battle Honour gives the commanding officers' names and the ships' armament.

This powerful armada of ships arrived off Martinique on 30 January. It was garrisoned with 2,400 regular troops, 2,500 militia and 290 guns. In the harbour lay *Amphitrite* (40). Nearby lay *Diligente* (18) and *Carnation* (18), both recently taken from the British.

After assaulting the island in several places, reducing forts and destroying ships over a period of about three weeks, the opposition had been overcome and Martinique surrendered.

<u>Battle Honour:</u>

Neptune (98) Captain Charles Dilkes
Pompée (74) Commodore George Cockburn
York (74) Captain Robert Barton
Belleisle (74) Captain William Fahie
Captain (74) Captain James Wood
Intrepid (64) Captain Christopher Nesham
Ulysses (44) Captain Edward Woollcombe
Acasta (40) Captain Philip Beaver
Penelope (36) Captain John Dick
Ethalion (38) Captain Thomas Cochrane
Aeolus (32) Captain Lord William Fitzroy
Circe (32) Captain Hugh Pigot
Cleopatra (38) Captain Samuel Petchell
Eurydice (24) Captain James Bradshaw
Cherub (18) Commander Thomas Tucker
Gorée (18) Commander Joseph Spear
Star (18) Commander Francis Collier
Stork (18) Commander George Le Geyt
Amaranthe (18) Commander Edward Brenton
Eclair (12) No name
Forester (18) Commander John Richards
Frolic (18) Commander Thomas Whinyate
Recruit (18) Commander Charles Napier
Wolverine (18) Commander John Simpson
Express (6) Lieutenant William Malone
Haughty (14) Lieutenant John Mitchell
Swinger (14) No name
Pelorus (?14) No name
Fawn (18) Commander the Hon George Crofton

Gloire (36) Captain James Carthew

Hazard (18) Commander Hugh Cameron

Mozambique (14) Lieutenant James Atkins

Port Espagne (16) Commander Alexander Kennedy

Surinam (18) Commander John Lake

Ring Dove (16) Commander William Ferrie

Supérieure (16) Commander George Sanders

Bellette (18) Commander George Andrews

Snap Commander James Stewart

Demarara (16) Commander William Dowers

Pultusk (20) Commander George Pringle

Liberty (14) Lieutenant John Codd

Subtle (10) Lieutenant Brown

Bacchus (10) Lieutenant Charles Jermy

Cuttle (Schooner) Lieutenant Thomas Bury

St Pierre No name

Dominica No name

MATAPAN 1941
28–29 March
World War II 1939–45

The Battle of Matapan was a night action off the cape of that name fought between the British Mediterranean Fleet commanded by Admiral Sir Andrew Cunningham and units of the Italian Fleet under the overall command of Admiral Iachino.

Intelligence of an intended sortie by Italian naval forces against British convoys to Greece prompted Cunningham to despatch four cruisers and four destroyers under Vice-Admiral Pridham-Wippell to rendezvous with five more destroyers south of Crete.

Meanwhile Cunningham sailed from Alexandria with his flag in *Warspite* (30,600 tons, 8 × 15"), *Barham* (31,100 tons, 8 × 15") and *Valiant* (32,700 tons, 8 × 15"), the carrier *Formidable* (23,000 tons, 36 aircraft), and nine escorting destroyers to give distant cover to Pridham-Wippell.

Air reconnaissance located an enemy force but it was not until after noon on 28 March that Cunningham knew this to be the battleship *Vittorio Veneto* (35,000 tons, 9 × 15"), nine cruisers and fourteen destroyers. Iachino realized he had lost the element of surprise, and, being without air cover, he altered course and headed for base.

Formidable flew off a strike of torpedo aircraft to try to slow down the battleship, but it was the second strike at 3.15 which scored a hit on her port quarter and reduced her speed to 19 knots. A third strike failed to hit the enemy flagship. However, the heavy cruiser *Pola* (10,000 tons, 8 × 8") was struck by a torpedo which brought her to a stop. Iachino detached the 8" heavy cruisers *Fiume* and *Zara* and a division of destroyers to stand by the stricken ship while he continued his westerly flight.

At 9 pm the British cruisers in the van of the fleet reported a darkened ship as they sped past. It was the *Pola*.

Cunningham prepared his ships to open fire when two more cruisers suddenly appeared crossing the flagship's bows. He turned to starboard and the British battleships opened fire with their 15" broadsides at a point-blank range of 3,500 yards. Searchlights exposed the *Fiume* and *Zara* with their guns trained fore and aft, totally unprepared for action. Both ships were reduced to blazing hulks and sank. An Italian destroyer, the *Vittorio Alfieri*, attempted a brave torpedo attack but was overwhelmed by gunfire from *Barham*. Another destroyer, the *Giosue Carducci*, was also sunk. Both were ships of 1,709 tons and 4 × 4.7" guns.

Later the crippled *Pola* was located and sunk, many of her crew being rescued.

Battle Honour:

Ajax	Barham	Defender	Formidable	Gloucester
Greyhound	Griffin	Hasty	Havock	Hereward
Hotspur	Ilex	Jaguar	Janus	Jervis
Juno	Mohawk	Nubian	Orion	Perth
Stuart	Valiant	Vendetta	Warspite	

FAA Squadrons: *700, 803, 806, 815, 826, 829.*

MEDITERRANEAN 1940–45
World War II 1939–45

The area covered by this Battle Honour was the whole of the Mediterranean, the western limit being a line joining Cape Spartel and Cape Trafalgar. It includes all ships and submarines not covered by any of the named Battle Honours for the area: that is to say the destruction of an enemy ship or submarine which was effected during and in connection with a recognized campaign, e.g. Sicily 1943, is regarded as an incidental item of a campaign and not as qualifying for a separate Battle Honour award. If, however, the success was unconnected with any named operation for which a Battle Honour is granted then it will qualify for the general award Mediterranean with the qualifying year. It was during this campaign that Admiral Sir Andrew Cunningham made his momentous signal to the Admiralty: BE PLEASED TO INFORM THEIR LORDSHIPS THAT THE ITALIAN BATTLEFLEET LIES AT ANCHOR UNDER THE GUNS OF THE FORTRESS OF MALTA

Battle Honour:

Abercrombie	Ajax	Alynbank	Aphis	Argonaut
Ark Royal	Atherstone	Aubretia	Aurora	Barham
Beaufort	Bicester	Blackfly	Blankney	Blencathra
Bluebell	Brecon	Calcutta	Caledon	Calpe
Cape Town	Clyde	Cockchafer	Coventry	Croome
Cuckmere	Dainty	Decoy	Deptford	Diamond
Dido	Dulverton	Duncan	Eagle	Easton
Enchantress	Encounter	Erebus	Eridge	Euryalus
Exmoor	Farndale	Faulknor	Fearless	Firedrake
Fleetwood	Foresight	Formidable	Foxhound	Galatea
Gallant	Garland	Glenearn	Glengyle	Gloucester
Gloxinia	Gnat	Grenville	Greyhound	Griffin
Gurkha	Haarlem	Hambledon	Hasty	Havock
Hereward	Hermione	Hero	Hobart	Holcombe
Hotspur	Hursley	Hurworth	Hyacinth	Hyperion
Ilex	Illustrious	Imperial	Inglefield	Isis
Islay	Jackal	Jade	Jaguar	Janus
Javelin	Jersey	Jervis	Juno	Jupiter
Kandahar	Kashmir	Kelly	Kelvin	Kent
Kilmarnock	Kipling	Ladybird	Laforey	Lamerton
Lance	Largs	Lauderdale	Legion	Liddesdale
Lively	Liverpool	Lookout	Lotus	Loyal
Malaya	Marigold	Mauritius	Mendip	Meteor
Miosa	Mohawk	Mull	Naiad	Nelson

Neptune	Newfoundland		Nubian	Offa
Orion	Osiris	P31	P33	P34
P37	P42	P46	P228	P247
Pakenham	Paladin	Pandora	Panther	Parthian
Penelope	Penn	Petard	Phoebe	Poppy
Porpoise	Port Arthur	Prinses Beatrix		Protea
Proteus	Quail	Queenborough		
Queen Emma	Quentin	Quiberon	Quilliam	Raider
Ramillies	Regent	Regina	Renown	Restigouche
Roberts	Rodney	Rorqual	Rover	
Royal Ulsterman		Rysa	Safari	Sahib (P212)
Saltarelo	Saracen (P247)		Saxifrage	Scarab
Seraph	Shakespeare	Sheffield	Shoreham	Sickle
Sikh	Simoon	Sirius	Southern Isle	
Southern Maid		Southern Sea	Tetcott	Thorn
Thrasher	Thunderbolt	Tigris	Torbay	Triad
Trident	Triton	Triumph	Trooper	Troubridge
Truant	Tumult	Turbulent	Tyrian	Uganda
Ulster	Ultimatum (P34)		Ultor	Umbra (P35)
Unbeaten	Unbending (P37)		Undine	Unique
United	Universal	Unrivalled	Unseen	Unshaken
Untiring	Upholder	Upright	Uproar	Upstart
Urchin	Urge	Ursula	Utmost	Valiant
Vendetta	Vetch	Ville de Quebec		Voyager
Warspite	Whaddon	Wilton	Wishart	Woolongong
Wrestler	Wryneck	York	Zetland	Zulu

MTBs: 311, 633, 634, 635, 637, 639, 656

FAA Squadrons: 700, 767, 800, 803, 806, 810, 812, 813, 815, 816, 818, 819, 820, 821, 824, 826, 828, 829, 830

MESOPOTAMIA 1914–17
World War I 1914–18

The long duration of this campaign was "riddled with indecision and foolhardy orders". The campaign cost over 80,000 British and Indian casualties, including nearly 13,000 men who died of disease.

Britain landed Indian troops on 23 October 1914 and a month later had captured Basra in Iraq, defeating the Turks.

With the addition of reinforcements in the early part of 1915 plans were made to advance north to Baghdad with a force commanded by General Charles Townshend. River gunboats and other vessels won a victory at Ctesiphon, Mesopotamia.

The Turks were defeated again at Kut-el-Amara, assisted by gun crews from naval brigades. The attempt to advance further was repulsed. Townshend fell back upon Kut where the force was invested and after some months surrendered with 8,000 British and Indian troops.

In 1916 General Sir Frederick Maude's expedition force moved north and recaptured Kut on 22–23 February 1917. He then captured Baghdad, employing naval brigades for the crews of seven river gunboats. Before he could capture the Mosul oilfields he died of cholera. His successor brought the campaign to an end.

Battle Honour:

Bahrein	*Bee*	*Blackfly*	*Butterfly*
Caddisfly	*Clio*	*Comet*	*Cranefly*
Dragonfly	*Espiègle*	*Firefly*	*Flycatcher*
Gadfly	*Greenfly*	*Hoverfly*	*Julnar*
Lawrence	*Lewis Pelly*	*Mantis*	*Massoudieh*
Mayfly	*Miner*	*Moth*	*Muzaffri*
Ocean Odin	*Saafly*	*Scarab*	*Sedgefly*
Shaitan	*Shushan*	*Snakefly*	*Stonefly*
Sumana	*Tarantula*	*Waterfly*	

MINORCA 1798
15 November
French Revolutionary War 1793 – 1803

While the bulk of the Mediterranean Fleet, under the command of Lord St Vincent, remained outside the Straits of Gibraltar blockading Cadiz, he detached a squadron of seven ships under Rear-Admiral Sir John Duckworth with his flag in *Leviathan* to attack the island of Minorca. The military force was commanded by General the Hon Charles Stuart. Seamen and marines were landed in force from all seven of Duckworth's ships. In the face of such overwhelming force the island capitulated.

Argo	*Aurora*	*Centaur*	*Constitution*
Cormorant	*Leviathan*	*Petrel*	

MONTECRISTO 1652
28 August
First Dutch War 1652 – 54

Captain Richard Badiley commanded a small squadron of four ships escorting a convoy of four sail south of Leghorn near the island of Montecristo when he was attacked by a small Dutch squadron commanded by Captain Johan van Galen.

Tactical skirmishing took place on 27 August, but battle was joined on the 28th. The convoy was safely protected and made good its escape. In the engagement Badiley got the upper hand and one Dutch ship struck. Curiously she bore the same name as one of Badiley's squadron – *Phoenix*.

Battle Honour:

Constant Warwick	*Elizabeth*	*Paragon*
Phoenix		

MOONLIGHT BATTLE 1780 – see ST VINCENT

N

NARVIK 1940
10 and 13 April
World War II 1939–45

Narvik is a seaport of northern Norway and was the scene of two naval battles among its fjords during the Second World War.

At the time of the German invasion of Norway in 1940 a force of ten German destroyers was despatched to capture the town and seaport. Commodore Bronte commanded the operation.

In the first action on 10 April the British 2nd Destroyer Flotilla under Captain (D) B.A.W. Warburton-Lee in the 1,505 tons *Hardy* (5 × 4.7") , with *Havock, Hunter, Hostile* and *Hotspur* (all 1,350 tons, 4 × 4.7"), entered the fjord leading to Narvik at dawn and engaged and sank two German destroyers, the *Wilhelm Heidkamp* (2,411 tons, 5 × 5") and *Anton Schmidt* (2,411 tons, 5 × 5"), killing the commodore.

Several supply ships were also sunk and damage was inflicted on other destroyers.

On the return journey down Ofot Fjord five more modern destroyers were encountered and, in a high-speed action, *Hunter* and *Hardy* were so badly damaged that they were beached. Warburton-Lee was fatally wounded when a shell struck the bridge and wheelhouse of *Hardy*. He was awarded a posthumous VC. The rest of the flotilla made good its escape.

The second battle was fought three days later when the veteran battleship *Warspite* (30,600 tons, 8 × 15"), wearing the flag of Vice-Admiral Whitworth, entered the approaches to Narvik with an escort of destroyers. The eight remaining German destroyers known to be hiding in the various inlets in the fjords of Narvik were sought out with the aid of reconnaissance aircraft from *Warspite* and the carrier *Furious* and brought to action. All were either sunk or otherwise destroyed at no loss to the Royal Navy. Furthermore, a U-boat which had taken shelter at the head of a fjord was also sunk. She was *U-64*.

While both battles were a conspicuous success for the Royal Navy, they failed to prevent the Germans from capturing the seaport and town of Narvik, and eventually the whole of Norway.

The German losses were as follows:

Wilhelm Heidkamp	(2,411 tons,	5 × 5")
Hermann Kunne	"	"
Hans Ludemann	"	"
Diether von Roeder	"	"
Anton von Schmidt	"	"
Bernd von Arnim	(2,230 tons	")
Erich Giese	"	"
Erich Koeliner	"	"
Georg Thiele	"	"
Wolfgang Zenker	"	"
U-64	"	"

<u>Battle Honour:</u>

Bedouin	*Cossack*	*Eskimo*	*Forester*
Foxhound	*Furious*	*Hardy*	*Havock*
Hero	*Hostile*	*Hotspur*	*Hunter*
Icarus	*Kimberley*	*Punjabi*	*Warspite*

NAVARINO 1827
20 October
Greek War of Independence 1821–29

The Battle of Navarino was fought between a combined British, French and Russian fleet commanded by Vice-Admiral Sir Edward Codrington and a Turco-Egyptian fleet under Ibrahim Pasha, who was trying to restore Turkish rule over Greece. The Allied fleet comprised:*

---

* Sources differ surprisingly in figures of ships comprising both the Allied and the Turco-Egyptian fleets. These are taken from Kemp's *Oxford Companion*.

SHIPS OF THE LINE		FRIGATES	OTHERS	COMMANDER
British	4	3	4	Codrington
French	4	1	2	De Rigney
Russian	4	4		Heyden
Total	12	8	6	

The Turco-Egyptian fleet comprised seven ships of the line, fifteen frigates, twenty-six corvettes and seventeen others. It lay at anchor in Navarino Bay on the south-west coast of the Peloponnese in a roughly horseshoe formation.

Codrington had Admiralty instructions to use force only as a last resort because of the political sensitivity of the situation. But the impression one gets is that the provocation on both sides was more than a saint could bear. Codrington, it is clear, wanted action. He ordered his fleet to anchor right inside the bay, almost within the horseshoe of ships, and started parleying.

There was much to-ing and fro-ing of boats. One such was fired upon by Turkish musketeers who believed it to be a boarding party; a British ship replied with a shot which echoed round the bay. Soon other shots followed, action broke out everywhere and a battle ensued which lasted about four hours.

The Pasha's fleet was decisively punished, losing one ship of the line, twelve frigates and twenty-two corvettes; casualties amounted to about 4,000 men. No Allied ships were sunk, though many suffered extensive damage.

Codrington was recalled to London and was lucky to be cleared of charges for disobeying orders.

The battle was the last major battle of sail-of-the-line. The next major clash at sea was to be Jutland, eighty-nine years later, but aeons ahead in terms of technological and scientific advances.

Battle Honour:

Albion	Asia	Brisk	Cambrian	Dartmouth
Genoa	Glasgow	Mosquito	Philomel	Rose
Talbot	Hind (List probably complete.)			

NEGAPATAM 1758

3 August

Seven Years' War 1756–63

Three months after the indecisive encounter off Cuddalore in SE India (see SADRAS 1758 p. 194), another inconclusive action occurred between a British squadron commanded by Vice-Admiral George Pocock and a French squadron commanded by Admiral Comte D'Aché off nearby Negapatam. It could well have been named Pocock's Pursuit.

Pocock, in his flagship *Yarmouth* (64), and with another six of the line, chased the Comte's nine of the line for several days before the Frenchmen were finally brought to action at noon on 3 August.

A shot from *Yarmouth* carried away *Zodiaque's* (74) wheel which caused the French flagship to collide with the *Duc d'Orléans*. Both survived the experience. D'Aché managed to disentangle, and later to disengage his ships. Under cover of darkness he thereupon retired to the north.

No ships had been sunk, but casualties on both sides were heavy.

Battle Honour:

Cumberland	*Elizabeth*	*Newcastle*	*Protector*
Queensborough	*Salisbury*	*Tiger*	*Weymouth*
Yarmouth			

NEGAPATAM 1782

6 July

American War of Independence 1775–83

This battle was the third encounter between Admiral Sir Edward Hughes's British squadron and Admiral Suffren's French squadron off south-east India in 1782. (See SADRAS 1782 and PROVIDIEN 1782, pp. 194 and 186)

The battle arose from Suffren's preparations to capture the British base at Negapatam. Hughes received intelligence of these plans and sailed from Trincomalee on Ceylon's east coast to frustrate the French assault.

When the two squadrons, each comprising eleven of the line, clashed a battle royal was in prospect, but, although it was fiercely fought and the casualties were heavy, no ship was taken or sunk.

At one time Captain Cillart of the French *Sévère* (64) struck to the British *Sultan* (74) but his men refused to surrender, won the day and rejoined their squadron.

In the evening both squadrons lay inshore and anchored as if for a well-earned breathing space. Suffren then retired north to Cuddalore, thwarted in his attempted assault.

Battle Honour:

Burford	Eagle	Exeter	Hero Isis
Magnanime	Monarch	Monmouth	Seahorse
Sultan	Superb	Worcester	

NEW GUINEA 1942–44
World War II 1939–45

By the spring of 1942 Japan had conquered the Philippines, the Netherland East Indies, Burma and Malaya. This was months ahead of their schedule. It had also been achieved at a cost of a few thousand casualties and the Japanese had lost no ship larger than a destroyer. Japan's future strategy had to be re-appraised. The Naval General Staff proposed a plan for isolating Australia by moving from Rabaul into Eastern New Guinea, down the New Hebrides and Solomons to the Fijis and Samoa.

Lae and Solomanua were taken in early March. The battle of Port Moresby intervened and the Japanese were repulsed for the first time; it marked the limit of their Pacific onslaught and area of conquest.

The Allied – American and Australian – expedition along the north coast of New Guinea was supported by Allied naval units during the long and bitter campaign, notorious as much for its malarial jungle as the ferocious enemy.

In June 1943 the Allies, having achieved air superiority, mounted an offensive against Japanese-held islands off New Guinea, culminating in the capture of Finchhafen in October 1943. Huge Japanese forces became isolated. The New Guinea campaign gave support and strength to the left hook of the two-handed thrust leading to the recapture of the Philippines.

At sea the Battle of the Bismarck Sea was fought: the Japanese attempted to fight through a convoy to relieve their forces ashore, and in doing so lost all eight transports, four destroyers and 3,000 troops. They never made the attempt again.

Campaign Honours

1942:	Warrego			
1942 – 44:				
Arunta	Australia	Ballarat	Bendigo	Broome
Colac	Deloraine	Katoomba	Latrobe	Lithgow
Shropshire	Stuart	Swan	Whyalla	
1943:	Ararat			
1943 – 44:				
Benalla	Bunbury	Bundaburg	Echuca	Gladstone
Glenelg	Kapunda	Pirie	Reserve	Shepparton
Stawell	Vendetta	Wagga	Warramunga	
1944:				
Cootamunga	Cowra	Gascoyne	Geelong	Goneburn
Gympie	Hawkesbury	Kiama	Mildura	Parkes
Rockhampton	Stahan	Townsville		

NEW ZEALAND 1845–47
19th Century Wars

New Zealand came within the orbit of the East Indies Station. Thus, when a rebellion of natives, aggrieved at having been swindled over sales of their land, upset the peaceful settlement of the colony, it was a small squadron of ships and a brigade of marines from the East Indies which was despatched to deal with the situation.

In December 1845 Captain Charles Graham, commanding *Castor* (36), landed with 340 officers, marines and seamen. He had in company: *Racehorse* (18), Commander George Hay; *North Star*; *Calliope* (28), Captain Edward Stanley (who "quietened and cleared North Island"), and the Honourable East Indies Company ship *Elphinstone*.

There was desultory fighting with tribal chiefs until 1847 by which time the British reinforcements were powerful, the natives suffered greatly and they gladly accepted the terms offered by the British.

Campiagn Honour:

Calliope	*Castor*	*Driver*	*Elphinstone*
Hazard	*Inflexible*	*North Star*	*Racehorse*
Rattler	*Salamander*		

1852 – 53:

Cleopatra	*Contest*	*Fox*	*Spartan*
Sphinx	*Winchester*		

1853:

Bittern	*Styx*

NEW ZEALAND 1860–66
19th Century Wars

At the end of the previous New Zealand campaign in 1852 the mother country granted the island self-government, and after much wrangling and hesitation a full parliamentary system was achieved by 1856. Now came another costly and wasteful campaign with seemingly endless squabbling and struggling between settlers and Maoris. For ten years the British tried to find a peaceful solution. British regiments and colonial riflemen finally proved too much for the Maoris. The natives became worn out, the colonist agonized by the cost of the war. No shots were fired after 1871.

Battle Honour:

1860 – 61:

Cordelia	*Iris*	*Niger*	*Pelorus*	

1863 – 66:

Curacoa	*Eclipse*	*Esk*	*Falcon*	*Harrier*
Himalaya	*Miranda*			

1865:

Brisk

NILE 1798 (Aboukir Bay)
1 August
French Revolutionary War 1793–1803

This classic sea battle was fought between the well-ordered fleet commanded by Rear-Admiral Sir Horatio Nelson on the one hand

and the French Admiral Brueys with his much less well-ordered squadron.* Nelson won a splendid victory due primarily to his audacious and brilliant handling of a squadron disciplined and exercised in the skills of war at sea.

Nelson had scoured the Mediterranean for weeks for the French Toulon fleet and its convoy of transports for the invasion of Egypt, which carried with it none other than Napoleon Bonaparte.

The French Expeditionary Force eluded Nelson's squadron and landed at Aboukir Bay 15 miles east of Alexandria, while the fleet anchored in the bay, close inshore. Nelson's force arrived off Alexandria on 1 August and was rewarded with the sight of the French fleet at anchor.

Nelson was in command of what many consider to have been the finest squadron of its size ever assembled in the age of sail. These magnificent 74s were commanded by skilled professionals, a "band of brothers" who knew Nelson's mind, his unswerving adherence "to use your utmost endeavours to take, burn, sink or destroy".

Admiral Brueys sighted Nelson's ships, but was not unduly worried. True, while he was at anchor he must be at a tactical disadvantage – and further handicapped with watering and stores parties ashore. But he had carefully selected the anchorages for his ships, anchorages which even the most critical eye might deem impregnable: they were protected on two sides by shoals and breakers, flanked by frigates and a land battery on Aboukir Island. In guns, he had a heavier weight in metal than Nelson. Furthermore, even the time of day was advantageous to him, for sunset was not many hours away.

Nelson thought otherwise. He resolved to attack at once, not to wait for the morrow. He also detected an opening, small, but an opening nonetheless, allowing penetration of the enemy's line on his blind side – between the ships at anchor and the shoals.

Captain Foley's *Goliath* led the squadron with the NNW breeze at his back, passed along the centre and van of the French line,

---

* Brueys had no confidence in his revolutionary captains: he thought them ignorant boors. His ships were badly undermanned, some lacking a third or quarter of their complement. Discipline was poor. Brueys knew his squadron was unequal to a British squadron of the same strength.

crossed the van and attacked from the leeward side. Within two hours the first five French ships had been carronaded and shot into submission, and had struck.

In the centre there was a terrible struggle. Brueys' giant 120 gun flagship *L'Orient* blasted Captain Darby's *Bellerophon* with a thunderous broadside which dismasted and almost wrecked his ship, killing 200. The *Majestic*, too, suffered cruelly and Captain Westcott was killed.

Brueys was struck and killed by a shot from *Swiftsure*. Later the flagship *L'Orient* was seen to be ablaze. This magnificent ship blew up at 10 pm and this seemed to signal a significant moment in the battle. Although the *Tonnant* and *Franklin* continued to fight gallantly, the French were beaten. With the collapse of the French centre, the British ships passed down the line to engage the enemy rear, but by then the British were exhausted. Even so, three more 74s were taken or burnt.

All told the French lost eleven of the line and two frigates. The intrepid Rear-Admiral Villeneuve in *Guillaume Tell* (80) and the *Généreux* (74) and two frigates managed to escape destruction. Within eighteen months even these two ships of the line had met their end in the Mediterranean.

Nelson's brilliant victory established British naval supremacy in the Mediterranean and effectively stranded Napoleon's Expeditionary Force in Egypt. Gone were his dreams of conquering India. Napoleon's political standing also suffered a severe check. For the first time he was shown to be vulnerable and not the invincible conqueror all Europe believed him to be.

<u>Battle Honour:</u> the ships, their guns and commanding officers are listed:

Alexander	(74)	Captain Alex J. Ball
Audacious	(74)	Captain D. Gould
Bellerophon	(74)	Captain H.D.E. Darby
Culloden	(74)	Captain T. Troubridge
Defence	(74)	Captain J. Peyton
Goliath	(74)	Captain T. Foley
Leander	(50)	Captain T.B. Thompson
Majestic	(74)	Captain G.B. Westcott
Minotaur	(74)	Captain T. Louis

Orion	(74)	Captain J. Saumarez
Swiftsure	(74)	Captain B. Hallowell
Theseus	(74)	Captain R.W. Miller
Vanguard	(74)	Admiral H. Nelson
		Captain E.Berry
Zealous	(74)	Captain S.Hood

Statistics:	Total Guns	1,012	(French) 1,190
	Total Men	8,068	11,230
	Casualties	218 k 678 w	1,451 k 1,479 w

NORMANDY 1944
6 June
World War II 1939–45

Because of the enormity of the operations comprising the Normandy Landings or the Battle for Normandy this entry tells the story in statistics. The overall Commander-in-Chief of all the armed forces was General Dwight Eisenhower. The Commander of all the naval forces was Admiral Sir Bertram Ramsay, and the name given to the naval element of the battle was "Operation Neptune". It comprised:

Warships	1,212
Landing Ships and Craft	4,026
Ancillaries	731
Merchant Vessels	864
Total	6,833

78% were British; 17% were USA; 5% were French, Norwegian, Dutch, Polish and Greek. Over 10,000 marines took part. They manned no less than two-thirds of the landing craft.

In a period of about three months (from D-Day to the capture of Le Havre in September) 750 bombardments had been carried out by cruisers and larger ships. The expenditure of ammunition by destroyers and larger ships was:

16" and 15" rounds	3,371
7.5" to 5.25"	31,250
4.7" to 4"	24,000
Total	58,621#

Further: 609 mines were swept and 28 surface actions took place. During this same three-month period the following were landed in Normandy:

352,570 men
1,410,600 tons of stores
152,000 vehicles

Commenting on the naval element of the Normandy Landings Potter and Nimitz* put it in these terms: "Operation Neptune" was predominantly British. They [the British] bore the responsibility for the success of the invasion:

> They had to transport the assault troops to the beaches and land them with their equipment. They had to provide shipping to handle the enormous flow of supplies across the Channel – 600 – 700 tons a day per division, in addition to mechanised equipment. They had to act as floating artillery until the guns could be put ashore. They had to provide for the orderly and timely arrival of reinforcement troops and their supplies and equipment and they had to make provision for the evacuation of casualties. They had to keep German naval units out of the Channel. They had to sweep lanes through the minefields and clear the beaches of obstacles that would impede the landing of troops ashore . . . Intricate timing was required to bring all the component parts of the invasion to the beaches on schedule; any disruption could prove disastrous."

<u>Battle Honour:</u>

Abelia	Adventure	Affleck	Ajax	Albatross
Alberni	Albrighton	Albury	Algonquin	Apollo
Ardrossan	Arethusa	Argonaut	Aristocrat	Armeria
Ashanti	Aylmer	Azalea	Bachaquero	Baddeck
Balfour	Balsam	Bangor	Beagle	Beaumaris
Belfast	Bellona	Bentley	Bickerton	Blackpool
Black Prince	Blackwood	Blairmore	Blankney	Bleasdale
Blencathra	Bligh	Bluebell	Boadicea	Bootle
Borage	Boston	Braithwaite	Bridlington	Bridport

---

* *Sea Power*, Editors E.B.Potter and Chester W.Nimitz, Prentice Hall, 1960.

Brigadier · Brissendon · Britomart · Bulolo · Burdock

Buttercup · Calgary · Cam · Camellia · Campanula

Campbell · Camrose · Cape Breton · Capel · Cape Town

Caraquet · Catherine · Cato · Cattistock · Celandine

Ceres · Charlock · Chaudière · Chelmer · Clarkia

Clematis · Clover · Cockatrice · Cooke · Cotswold

Cottesmore · Cowichan · Crane · Dacres · Dahlia

Dakins · Danae · Despatch · Deveren · Diadem

Dianella · Dianthus · Domett · Dominica · Dornoch

Douwe Aukes · Drumheller · Duckworth · Duff

Duke of Wellington · Dunbar · Eastbourne · Eglinton

Elgin · Emerald · Emperor · Enterprise · Erebus

Eskimo · Essington · Fame · Fancy · Faulknor

Fernie · Forester · Fort William · Fort York · Fraserburgh

Friendship · Frobisher · Fury · Garlies · Garth

Gatineau · Gazelle · Gentian · Geranium · Glasgow

Gleaner · Glenearn · Glenroy · Goatfell · Goatland

Godetia · Golden Eagle · Goodson · Gore · Gorgon

Gozo · Grecian · Grenville · Grey Fox · Grey Goose

Grey Owl · Grey Seal · Grey Shark · Grey Wolf · Grou

Guysborough · Haida · Halcyon · Halstead · Hambledon

Hargood · Harrier · Hart · Havelock · Hawkins

Heather · Hilary · Hind · Holmes · Honeysuckle

Hotham · Hotspur · Hound · Huron · Hussar

Hydra · Icarus · Ilfracombe · Impulsive · Inconstant

Inglis · Invicta · Isis · Jason · Javelin

Jervis · Keats · Kellett · Kelvin · Kempenfelt

Kenora · Keppel · Kingcup · Kingsmill · Kitchener

Kite · Kootenay · Lapwing · Largs · Lark

Larne · Lavender · Lawford · Lawson · Lennox

Lightfoot · Lindsay · Llandudno · Loch Fada · Loch Killin

Lochy · Locust · Londonderry · Loosestrife · Louisburg

Loyalty · Luneburg · Lydd · Lyme Regis · Mackay

Magpie · Malpeque · Matane · Mauritius · Mayflower

Melbreak · Melita · Mendip · Meon · Meynell

Middleton · Mignonette · Milltown · Mimico · Minas

Misoa · Montrose · Moorsom · Moosejaw · Mounsey

Mourne · Narborough · Narcissus · Nasturtium · Nelson

Nith	Northway	Obedient	Offa	Onslaught
Onslow	Onyx	Opportune	Orchis	Orestes
Oribi	Orion	Orwell	Ottawa	Outremont
Oxlip	Pangbourne	Parrboro	Pelican	Pelorus
Pennywort	Persian	Petunia	Pickle	Pincher
Pink	Pique	Plover	Plucky	Poole
Poppy	Port Arthur	Port Colbourne		Postillion
Potentilla	Prescott	Primrose	Prince Baudouin	
Prince Charles	Prince David	Prince Leopold		Prins Albert
Prinses Astrid	Prinses Josephine Charlotte		Pursuer	Pytchley
Qu'Appelle	Qualicum	Queen Emma	Quorn	Ramillies
Rattlesnake	Ready	Recruit	Redpole	Regina
Restigouche	Retalick	Rhododendron		Rifleman
Rimouski	Riou	Roberts	Rochester	Rodney
Romney	Ross	Rowley	Royal Ulsterman	Rupert
Ryde	Rye	St Helier	St John	St Laurent
Salamander	Saltash	Sandown	Saskatchewan	Saumarez
Savage	Scarborough	Scawfell	Scorpion	Scott
Scourge	Scylla	Seagull	Seaham	Selkirk
Serapis	Seymour	Shippigan	Sidmouth	Sioux
Sirius	Skeena	Southdown	Southern Prince	Speedwell
Spragge	Starling	Starwort	Statice	Stayner
Steadfast	Stevenstone	Stockham	Stork	Stormont
Strule	Summerside	Sunflower	Sutton	Swansea
Sweetbriar	Swift	Tadoussac	Talybont	Tanatside
Tartar	Tasajera	Tavy	Teme	Tenby
Thames Queen		Thornborough		Torrington
Tracker	Trentonian	Trollope	Tyler	
Ulster Monarch		Undaunted	Undine	Urania
Urchin	Ursa	Vanquisher	Venus	Vegreville
Versatile	Verulam	Vervain	Vesper	Vestal
Vidette	Vigilant	Vimy	Virago	Vivacious
Volunteer	Waldegrave	Walker	Wallflower	Walpole
Wanderer	Warspite	Wasaga	Waskesiu	Watchman
Waveney	Wedgeport	Wensleydale	Westcott	Whimbrel
Whippingham	Whitaker	Whitehall	Whitehaven	Whitshed
Wild Goose	Windsor	Woodstock	Worthing	Wren
Wrestler	X20	X23		

FAA Squadrons: *808, 885, 886, 897.*

In the following entries the figures in brackets denote the number of vessels:

MTB Flotillas:

1st (8), 5th (7), 13th (8), 14th (12), 21st (7), 22nd (7), 29th (8), 35th (10), 51st (7), 52nd (9), 53rd (7), 55th (12), 59th (8), 63rd (8), 64th (7), 65th (19).

MLs:

1st (8), 2nd (9), 4th (4), 5th (12) 7th (4), 10th (10), 11th (13), 13th (8), 14th (13), 15th (6), 19th (4), 20th (14), 21st (9), 23rd (8), 33rd (7), 50th (5), 51st (4), 103rd (8), 150th (9), 151st (9).

MGBs: 1st (6).

MMSs:

101st, 102nd, 104th, 115th, 132nd, 143rd – all of ten boats, and 250th (11).

BYMs:

150th, 159th, 165th and 167th all of ten vessels.

SGBs: 1st (6).

Note: for reasons of space, names of the following have been omitted: Small Craft and Auxiliaries comprising: A/S Trawlers, other trawlers, surveying vessels, Danlayers, Mulberries, Pluto ships and Blockships.

   Acknowledgements: Many of these statistics have been taken from *The Royal Navy Day By Day*, ed: R.E.A. Shrubb and A.B. Sainsbury (1979), to whom grateful thanks are due.

NORTH AFRICA 1942–43 (OPERATION TORCH)
8 November 1942–20 February 1943
World War II 1939–45

The struggle to seize North Africa in November 1942 (known by the code name Operation Torch) was waged between formidable Allied forces and the Vichy French forces, supported by units of the French fleet operating from its colonial empire. The Operation was not simply a military battle, it was an enterprise hedged about by political and diplomatic intrigue, even to the extent of trying to satisfy Russia by providing a species of second front, something for which Russia had been clamouring in order to relieve the pressure on their beleaguered armies on the Eastern Front. Some critics claim

CLASS OF SHIP	Western Naval Task Force (Morocco) Rear Admiral Hewitt USN	Central Naval Task Force (Oran) Commodore Troubridge	Eastern Naval Task Force (Algiers) V/Admiral Burrough	Force H & Fuelling Force V/Admiral Syfret
HQ Ship			Largs	Bulolo
Aircraft Carriers	Ranger	Argus		Victorious Formidable Furious
Escort Carriers	Santee, Cheneango Sangamon, Suwanee	Biter Dasher	Avenger	
Battleships and Battle-cruisers	Massachusetts Texas New York			Duke of York Renown Rodney
Cruisers	Augusta, Wichita Tuscaloosa Philadelphia Savannah, Brooklyn, Cleveland	Aurora Jamaica	Sheffield Scylla Charybdis	Bermuda Argonaut Sirius
Destroyers	38	13	13	17
Submarines	4	2	3	
Corvettes		6	4	1
Sloops		2	3	
Minesweepers	11	8	7	
Landing Ships Tanks		3		
Landing Ships Infantry		15	11	
Combat Loaders	23		4	

that the whole Operation was an unnecessary enterprise, that these colonial nonentities would have fallen like ripe fruit had the energies and forces used to displace them been properly employed elsewhere.

The armed forces employed in the assaults are listed in the accompanying table.

In addition, there were 109 other vessels such as trawlers, tankers etc. About 65,000 men, not counting follow-up forces, were landed on beaches. In addition to the more than 300 warships which are tabled, about 370 merchant ships were employed. Air support initially came from carriers, but by D-Day + 3 160 fighters were ashore at Casablanca, another 180 at Oran and ninety at Algiers.

Opposition from French forces was not strong or prolonged, although the sinking of two ex-US Coast Guard cutters (escort vessels) *Walney* and *Hartland* in Oran harbour was a fierce engagement. Within a few days all French forces under the command of Admiral Darlan had surrendered.

Only Tunisia, defended by German forces, resisted stoutly, and it was to be six months before the North Africa campaign was brought to an end on 12 May 1943.

Battle Honour:

1942:

Abbeydale	Aberdeen	Achates	Algerine	Alynbank
Argonaut	Argus	Avenger	Beagle	Bermuda
Bideford	Biter	Blean	Boadicea	Bradford
Bramham	Broke	Brown Ranger		Bulldog
Bulolo	Burke	Charybdis	Clyne Castle	Coltsfoot
Coreopsis	Cowdray	Cumberland	Dasher	Delhi
Deptford	Derwentdale	Dianella	Duke of York	Eastbourne
Empyrean	Emmerdale	Erne	Exe	Fluellen
Gardenia	Geranium	Glengyle	Hartland	Horatio
Hoy	Ibis	Ilfracombe	Imperialist	Ithuriel
Jamaica	Jonquil	Karenja	Keren	
Kingston Chrysolite		Landguard	Largs	Laurel
Leith	Leyland	Lord Hotham	Lulworth	Malcolm
Marigold	Martin	Meteor	Milne	Misoe
Nasprite	Norfolk	Onslow	Opportune	Oribi
Othello	P45	P48	P54	P221

P222	P228	Palomares	Partridge	Pelican
Philante	Poppy	Porcupine	Quentin	Renown
Returno	Rhododendron		Roberts	Rochester
Ronaldshay	Ronsay	Rysa	St Nectar	Sandwich
Scarborough	Scottish	Scylla	Sheffield	Spiraea
Starwort	Stork	Swale	Tribune	Tynwald
Ulster Monarch		Ursula	Vansittart	Victoria
Walney	Wrestler			

FAA Squadrons: 804, 809, 817, 832, 880, 882, 883, 884, 891.

1942 – 43:

Acute	Alarm	Albacore	Amazon	Antelope
Arctic Ranger	Ashanti	Aubretia	Aurora	Avon Vale
Bachequero	Banff	Bicester	Boreas	Brilliant
Brixham	Bude	Cadmus	Calpe	Cava
Clacton	Clare	Convolvulus	Coriolanus	Dewdale
Dingledale	Easton	Eday	Egret	Elbury
Enchantress	Eskimo	Farndale	Felixstowe	Filey Bay
Fleetwood	Formidable	Foula	Furious	Goth
Hengist	Hunda	Hussar	Inchcolm	Jaunty
Jura	Kerrera	Kintyre	Lammerton	Linnet
Loch Oskaig	Londonderry	Lookout	Lord Nuffield	Lotus
Luneburg	Maidstone	Mull	Negro	Nelson
Offa	P51	P217	P219 (Seraph)	Panther
Pathfinder	Penn	Penstemon	Polruan	Pozarica
Prescott	Prinses Beatrix		Puckerridge	Quality
Queen Emma	Quiberon	Restive	Rhyl	Rodney
Rother	Rothesay	Royal Scotsman		
Royal Ulsterman		Ruskholm	St Day	St Mellons
Samphire	Sennen	Shiant	Sirius	Speedwell
Spey	Stornaway	Stroma	Strongsay	Sturgeon
Tartar	Tasajera	Vanoc	Velox	Venomous
Verity	Vetch	Vienna	Violet	Westcott
Westray	Wheatland	Wilton	Wishart	Wyvern
Woodstock				

FAA Squadrons: 700, 800, 807, 820, 822, 885, 893.

MLs: 238, 273, 280, 283, 295, 307, 336, 338, 433, 444, 458, 463, 469, 471, 480, 483.

HDMLs: 1127, 1128, 1139.

NORTH CAPE 1943 ('*Scharnhorst*' Action)
26 December
World War II 1939–45

This engagement was in the time-honoured naval style, with British forces defending an important convoy from attacks by a marauding force of German ships, aircraft and submarines. The antagonists comprised a squadron of the Home Fleet under the command of Admiral Sir Bruce Fraser with a detached cruiser force under Rear-Admiral R. Burnett, and a battle group of the German Navy commanded by Rear-Admiral Erich Bey.

On 20 December 1943 Convoy JW55B, comprising nineteen ships, sailed from Loch Ewe for Russia via the North Cape. Two days later Convoy RA55A of twenty-two ships left Kola Inlet in North Russia homeward-bound. Both convoys had heavy close destroyer escorts.

A covering force of the 10th Cruiser Squadron consisted of *Belfast* (11,500 tons, 12 × 6"), *Norfolk* (9,925 tons, 8 × 8") and *Sheffield* (9,400 tons, 12 × 6"). Distant cover was given by the Home Fleet squadron comprising the battleship and flagship *Duke of York* (35,000 tons, 10 × 14"), the cruiser *Jamaica* (8,000 tons, 12 × 6") and four destroyers.

The battlecruiser *Scharnhorst* (32,800 tons, 9 × 11") was known to be in Alten Fjord at the northern extremity of Norway. Rear-Admiral Bey (Flag Officer Destroyers) was deputizing for Vice-Admiral Kummetz (FOC Battle Group). On Boxing Day at 4 am *Scharnhorst* and five destroyers left harbour and headed for the convoys in bitter weather and atrocious sea conditions. Convoy JW55B was being trailed by *U-601*. Burnett's cruiser squadron was 150 miles east of the enemy and Fraser's battle group was about 220 miles to the south-west of the convoy. *Scharnhorst* was about 100 miles south-east of the convoy.

That morning Burnett picked up *Scharnhorst* by radar, closed at full speed and opened fire at 13,500 yards. The first salvoes struck home and among other damage, destroyed the battlecruiser's forward radar installation. Bey was taken completely by surprise, turned away and escaped in the appalling sea and weather conditions; so bad were they that Bey detached his destroyers to base and operated alone. This needs no comment other than to record that not only did the British destroyers remain at sea, but they participated fully in the battle that followed.

Burnett guessed that Bey would work round and head for the convoy, and he acted accordingly. Sure enough, when *Scharnhorst* spotted the convoy it was Burnett's cruisers which emerged from the gloom and engaged him for twenty minutes, inflicting more damage. Bey broke off the action and headed south-east – unwittingly directly towards Fraser's battle group.

Duke of York's radar picked up *Scharnhorst* four hours later at the extreme range of 44,000 yards. She and *Jamaica* closed the range to 12,000 yards before *Belfast* illuminated the target with starshell and opened fire.

For the second time that day Bey was totally surprised. His guns were seen to be trained fore and aft. There began a systematic battering of this fine ship by a display of accurate gunfire rarely matched in battle: of fifty-two broadsides fired by *Duke of York* thirty-one scored straddles, with enough hits to put turrets A and B out of action and rupture steam pipes to reduce her speed. Altogether she was struck by about thirty 14" shells, plus a good number of 6" and 8" shells. She was also hit by eleven of the fifty-five torpedoes fired at her. As an eye-witness recorded, "She must have been a hell on earth".

A feature of the early evening battle was the destroyer attack launched by *Savage, Saumarez, Scorpion* and the Norwegian *Stord*, which closed as near as 3,000 yards under heavy secondary armament fire to launch their torpedoes.

A little later the other destroyer division comprising *Musketeer, Opportune, Virago* and *Matchless* attacked from even shorter ranges. The target was now a dull red glow in a black pall of smoke. At 7.45 pm she blew up and sank. Only thirty-six men from a crew of 1,986 were rescued from the icy Arctic sea.

Battle Honour:

Belfast	Duke of York	Jamaica	Matchless	Musketeer
Norfolk	Opportune	Savage	Scorpion	Sheffield
Saumarez	Virago			

NORTH SEA 1939–45
World War II 1939–45
See also ENGLISH CHANNEL 1939–45 pp. 88–9

The waters qualifying for this campaign honour embraced all the North Sea to the eastward between Southend and the Shetland Isles except the coastal waters of Norway. All ships employed as escorts to coastal convoys on the east coast of the UK qualified for the award, as did any ships and submarines employed on patrol duty which took part in a successful action. The following list of ships indicates the great activity in the area and the susceptibility of convoys to air attacks.

During the early months of the Second World War the Germans had sown mines extensively in the English Channel, the North Sea, especially harbour entrances, estuaries and shallows, but particularly the Thames estuary, where five minefields were laid. In the early weeks of the war the port of London was almost brought to a halt: twenty-seven ships and the destroyer *Blanche* were mined and sunk in the estuary, and many others were mined but survived, including HMS *Belfast*, the Imperial War Museum cruiser moored in the Pool of London.

In the first four months of the war seventy-nine merchant ships of over 260,000 tons had been sunk, and the flow of shipping disrupted considerably.

But the Royal Navy and Coastal Command of the RAF gained the ascendancy, protecting convoys from air and sea attacks.

In these same early four months the effectiveness of adopting convoys was brought home to everyone. During this period in the North Sea

Ships escorted in convoy = 5,756	Ships lost	= 12
Ships independently routed and lost		= 102

Throughout the nearly six years of war in the North Sea the loss rate of all ships was one tenth of one per cent.

Something approaching 400 ships were awarded the campaign honour.

Campaign Honour:

Acute	Adonis	Aiglon	Ailsa Craig	Alarm
Alberni	Albrighton	Ampulla	Angle	Annan
Anquilla	Arab	Ardrossan	Arrow	Ascension
Aster	Atherstone	Atmah	Ayrshire	Baluchistan
Bassett	Bayntun	Begonia	Berkeley	Berkshire
Betony	Black Swan	Blean	Bleasdale	Blencathra
Blyth	Bonito	Borage	Bournemouth Queen	
Bressay	Braithwaite	Bridgewater	Broadway	Broke
Brontes	Burges	Bute	Byron	Cadmus
Caistor Castle	Calgary	Camellia	Campbell	Camrose
Cape Comorin		Cape Palliser	Cape Portland	Cape Sable
Carnatic	Castlenau	Cattistock	Charlestown	Charlock
Chelmer	Cleveland	Clover	Coll	Congre
Conn	Conqueror	Copper Cliff	Corinthian	Cosby
Cotillion	Cotswold	Cottesmore	Coverley	Cranstoun
Cubitt	Culver	Curacoa	Curzon	Daffodil
Dahlia	Dakins	Damsay	Daniel Clowden	Davy
Deane	Doon	Dudgeon	Dunavon	Dunbar
Duncton	Dunkery	Easton	Ebor Wyke	Eglinton
Ekins	Else Rykens	Eroican	Erebus	Escort
Estrella D'Alva		Estrella Do Norte		Evelyn Rose
Exmoor	Farndale	Fencer	Fernie	Filla
Fitzroy	Flamingo	Flores	Fortune	Foxtrot
Garth	Gavotte	Gleaner	Goatfell	Goathland
Godetia	Goldcock	Goodwin	Gossamer	Graph
Grayling	Greenfly	Grenadier	Guillemot	Gunner
Gurkha	H49	Halstead	Hambledon	Haydon
Holderness	Holmes	Hornbeam	Hornpipe	Hyderabad
Hydra	Icarus	Imogen	Indian Star	Inglefield
Invercauld	Jason	Jasper	Jura	Kashmir
Kellett	Kenilworth Castle		Kennet	Killegray
Kingcup	King's Grey	Kingston	Kingston Agate	
Kingston Amber		Kingston Olivina		Kintyre
Kittiwake	Lacerta	Lady Estella	Lady Madeleine	Lancaster
Lapwing	Lark	Lauderdale	Leeds	
Leicester City	Lewes	Liddesdale	Limbourne	Lincoln
Loch Dunvegan		Loch Eck	Londonderry	Loosestrife

Lord Austin	Lord Howe	Lord Plender	Lowestoft	Ludlow
Lydd	Lynton	Macbeth	Mackay	Magnolia
Malcolm	Mallard	Mallow	Man-o-War	Maron
Mazurka	Melbreak	Mendip	Meynell	Middleton
Mignonette	Millet	Minster	Minuet	Mona's Isle
Monnow	Montrose	Moorsom	Narwhal	Neil Mackay
Nene	Newark	Northern Foam		
Northern Sun	Oakley	Ocean Brine	Ogano	Olive
Onyx	Ophelia	Orchis	Oresay	Orkney
Othello	P247	Pearl	Pennywort	
Pentland Firth	Peterhead	Phrontis	Pink	Pintail
Pirouette	Pitstruan	Polka	Polo Norte	Poppy
Port Colbourne		Portsdown	Potentilla	
Preston North End		Primrose	Prince Charles	Puffin
Pytchley	Quadrille	Qualicum	Quantock	Quorn
Rattlesnake	Rayon	Redmill	Regardo	
Reighton Wyke		Restigouche	Retako	Retalick
Retriever	Rinaldo	Ringwood	Riou	Rosalind
Ross	Rousay	Rowena	Ruskholm	Rupert
Rutherford	St Albans	St Elstan	St John	St Kilda
St Mary's	Saint Thérèse	Salmon	Saltarelo	Sapphire
Scalpay	Scarborough	Sealion	Selkirk	Seymour
Shark	Shearwater	Sheldon	Sheldrake	Sheppey
Sherwood	Shippigan	Sir Galahad	Sir Geraint	Snowflake
Sorrel	Southdown	Southern Gem	Spearfish	Speedy
Spiraea	Spurs	Staffa	Starwort	Stayner
Stella	Stella Canopus		Stella Polaris	Stella Rigel
Stevenstone	Stoke City	Stork	Stornoway	Sturgeon
Sturton	Sunfish	Sunflower	Surface	Switha
Sword Dance	Tadoussac	Talybont	Tango	Tarantella
Tartan	Thames Queen		Thetford Mines	Thirlmere
Thornborough		Thyme	Tirce	Torrington
Trident	Tumby	Turquoise	Typhoon	Ursula
Valorous	Valse	Vanity	Vascama	Vega
Veleta	Verdun	Verity	Versatile	Vesper
Veteran	Viceroy	Vimiera	Vimy	Violet
Visenda	Vivacious	Vivien	Vizalma	Volunteer
Vortigern	Wakeful	Wallace	Wallflower	Walpole

Wedgeport	Wellard	Wells	Wensleydale	Westminster
Weston	Westray	Whaddon	Whiting	Whitshed
Widgeon	Wilton	Winchelsea	Winchester	Windsor
Witch	Wolfhound	Wolsey	Wolves	Woolston
Worcester	Worcestershire		Worthing	Wyvern
Urge	Yes Tor			

FAA Squadrons: 803, 811, 812, 825.

MGBs: 17, 20, 21, 38, 39, 59, 61, 64, 67, 74, 75, 86, 87, 89, 111, 112.

MTBs: 32, 34, 69, 70, 88, 93, 224, 230, 233, 234, 241, 617, 622, 624, 628.

NORWAY 1940–45
World War II 1939–45

The area of waters qualifying for this Battle Honour were the coastal waters of Norway as far north as the latitude of Tromsö. The area also includes the North Sea in the Norway operations from 8 April to June 1940. Recognition of FAA attacks such as those on *Tirpitz* is normally restricted to the carriers and squadrons concerned. The covering escorts on these occasions are not eligible for the award.

A significant battle at sea almost developed early in the Norwegian campaign of 1940 when the battlecruiser *Renown* with her escort of nine destroyers strove hard to bring to action the modern battlecruisers *Gneisenau* and *Scharnhorst*. At 0405 on 9 April the enemy ships were sighted and *Renown* opened fire at a range of nine miles. *Gneisenau* was struck and her main armament put out of action. The German ships broke off the action. *Renown* increased speed to 29 knots but her destroyers were unable to keep up in the rising sea and snow squalls. During this phase *Renown* again hit *Gneisenau* on her fore turret and again aft, but the faster, more modern enemy ships made good their escape and the chase was called off.

The campaign area remained important throughout the rest of the war for its effect on the U-boat war, the *Bismarck* escape, the *Scharnhorst* sinking, the *Tirpitz* threat and the Russian convoys.

Battle Honour:

Acanthus, Acasta, Acheron, Afridi, Algonquin, Amazon, Angle, Arab, Ardent, Arethusa, Ark Royal, Arrow, Ashanti, Aston Villa, Auckland, Aurora, Basilisk, Beagle, Bedouin, Bellona, Berwick, Birmingham, Bittern, Black Swan, Bradman, Brazen, Cachalot, Cairo, Calcutta, Campania, Campbell, Cape Chelyuskin, Cape Passero, Cape Siretoka, Carlisle, Chiddingfold, Clyde, Codrington, Cossack, Coventry, Curacoa, Curlew, Delight, Devonshire, Diadem, Diana, Echo, Eclipse, Edinburgh, Effingham, Eglantine, Electra, Ellesmere, Emperor, Encounter, Enterprise, Escapade, Esk, Eskimo, Fame, Faulknor, Fearless, Fencer, Firedrake, Flamingo, Fleetwood, Forester, Foxhound, Furious, Galatea, Gaul, Glasgow, Glorious, Glowworm, Grenade, Greyhound, Griffin, Guardian, Gurkha, Hammond, Hasty, Havelock, Hero, Hesperus, Highlander, Hostile, Icarus, Imperial, Implacable, Impulsive, Inglefield, Intrepid, Iroquois, Isis, Ivanhoe, Jackal, Janus, Jardine, Javelin, Juniper, Kelly, Kent, Kenya, Kimberley, Kipling, Larwood, Legion, Loch Shin, Manchester, Mansfield, Maori, Margaret, Mashona, Matabele, Mauritius, Melbourne, Mohawk, Myngs, Nairana, Nigeria, Norfolk, Northern Gem, Nubian, Offa, Onslaught, Oribi, Orwell, Pelican, Penelope, Porpoise, Premier, Prince Charles, Prince Leopold, Prins Albert, Prinses Beatrix, Protector, Punjabi, Pursuer, Queen, Queen Emma, Ranen, Renown, Repulse, Resolution, Rhine, Rodney, Rutlandshire, St Goran, St Magnus, St Sunniva, Satyr, Sceptre, Scott, Sealion, Searcher, Seawolf, Severn, Sheffield, Sikh, Snapper, Somali, Southampton, Spearfish, Stork, Striker, Stubborn, Suffolk, Sunfish, Sussex, Taku, Tapir, Tarpon, Tartar, Terrapin, Tetrarch, Thirlmere

Thistle	Tigris	Triad	Trident	Triton
Truant	Trumpeter	Tuna	Ursula	Valiant
Vandyck	Vanoc	Vansittart	Venturer	Verulam
Veteran	Victorious	Vindictive	Walker	Wanderer
Warspite	Warwickshire	Westcott	Whirlwind	Wistaria
Witch	Witherington	Wren	Wolverine	X24
York	Zambesi	Zealous	Zest	Zulu

MTBs: 711, 722

FAA Squadrons: 700, 701, 800, 801, 802, 803, 804, 806, 810, 816, 817, 818, 820, 821, 823, 825, 827, 828, 829, 830, 831, 841, 842, 846, 852, 853, 856, 880, 881, 882, 887, 894, 896, 898*, 1770, 1771, 1832, 1834, 1836, 1840, 1841, 1842.

---

* 898 Squadron appears in the AFO but not in the Admiralty Definitive List.

O

OKINAWA 1945
24 March – 21 June 1945
World War II 1939–45

The sea area relating to this award is simply defined as the Far East, and the ships and submarines and Fleet Air Arm squadrons qualifying for this honour are defined as those ships which are mentioned in the published Despatch as having taken part in Operation Iceberg.

The last great naval/military battle in the Pacific (before the planned assault on the islands of Japan itself) was the Battle of Okinawa. It was preceded by the attack on Sakishima, the group of islands immediately south-east of Okinawa. Bombardments and air strikes on this small group began on 4 March by Task Force 57 and lasted almost the whole of the month. Task Force 57 was commanded by Vice-Admiral Sir Bernard Rawlings. Aircraft from this Force dropped 1,000 tons of bombs on the airfields of Myako and Ishigaki islands. 1,000 rockets were fired and no fewer than 5,335 sorties were flown by aircraft from *Illustrious*, *Indomitable*, *Indefatigable* and *Victorious*. The battleships *Howe* and *KGV* were accompanied by five cruisers, eleven destroyers, with another three with the fleet train. Fifty-seven enemy aircraft were destroyed in combat and about the same number destroyed on the ground.

The British Task Force reinforced Vice-Admiral Mitscher's TF 58, the USN carrier force which comprised the main element in Admiral Spruance's 5th Fleet. The landing fleet (TF 51) comprised 430 transports and large landing ships, ten battleships, thirteen cruisers, eighteen escort carriers with 540 aircraft. Landings were made on 1 April. Five days later the Japanese began a six-week-long series of kamikaze attacks involving 2,000 aircraft. Twenty-six ships were sunk (none of them larger than a destroyer) and 164 damaged, including three carriers and three battleships.

Eventually American power dominated and organized Japanese resistance ceased. Ships of the Royal Navy, including the carriers *Indefatigable*, *Formidable* and *Victorious*, suffered serious damage, but the cost to the American troops amounted to 48,000 men dead and wounded.

Campaign Honour:

Achilles	*Argonaut*	*Avon*	*Ballarat*
Bendigo	*Black Prince*	*Cairns*	*Chaser*
Crane	*Euryalus*	*Findhorn*	*Formidable*
Gambia	*Grenville*	*Howe*	*Illustrious*
Indefatigable	*Indomitable*	*Kempenfelt*	*King George V*
Napier	*Nepal*	*Nizam*	*Norman*
Parret	*Pheasant*	*Quadrant*	*Quality*
Queenborough	*Quiberon*	*Quickmatch*	*Quilliam*
Ruler	*Sliner*	*Speaker*	*Striker*
Swiftsure	*Tenacious*	*Termagant*	*Troubridge*
Uganda	*Ulder*	*Undaunted*	*Undine*
Unicorn	*Urania*	*Urchin*	*Ursa*
Victorious	*Wager*	*Wessex*	*Whelp*
Whimbrel	*Whirlwind*	*Whyalla*	*Woodcock*

FAA Squadrons: 820, 848, 849, 854, 857, 885, 887, 894, 1770, 1830, 1833, 1834, 1836, 1839, 1840, 1841, 1842, 1844, 1845.

OLÉRON ROADS – see BASQUE ROADS 1809

OPERATION DYNAMO – see DUNKIRK 1940

OPERATION ICEBERG – see OKINAWA 1945

OPERATION OVERLORD – see NORMANDY 1944

OPERATION TORCH – see NORTH AFRICA 1942 – 43

ORFORDNESS 1666 (North Foreland)
25–26 July
Second Dutch War 1665–67

This battle was fought between an English fleet of eighty-nine ships and seventeen fireships jointly commanded by Prince Rupert and the Duke of Albemarle, and a smaller Dutch fleet of eighty-five ships, twenty fireships and ten smaller vessels, all under the command of Admiral De Ruyter – the Dutch Nelson. The result was a brilliant victory for the English, particularly important because it came so soon after the defeat in the Four Days' Battle.

The long-drawn-out battle began at about 10 am on St James's Day, 26 July, in the North Sea about 40 miles south-east of Orfordness in Suffolk. After two hours' battling Admiral Cornelis Tromp's rear squadron sailed out of line, broke through the English line and became locked in combat with the English Blue Squadron, the rear squadron, under Admiral Sir Jeremy Smythe in *Resolution* (74). Smythe gained the upper hand and this battle-within-a-battle became a pursuit of De Ruyter, progressing westward in a confused mêlée, while the main battle between the opposing vans and centres headed nearly due east. The Dutch van was in full flight by 3 pm and an hour later the centre gave way too, three flag officers, including Jan Evertsen, being killed. But by then the English were too exhausted to take advantage.

Although retreating, De Ruyter handled the situation in a disciplined and masterly fashion, even after his own flagship had been severely damaged.

Sporadic skirmishing occurred throughout the night and action flared up briskly in the early daylight hours, but the Dutch continued their retreat to the shoals of their coastline. The battle and pursuit were over.

The Dutch losses were considerable: twenty ships were lost, with 4,000 men killed or drowned and 3,000 wounded. The only English ship lost was Smythe's *Resolution*, and the casualties in men killed and wounded were considerably lighter than the enemy's.

Battle Honour:

Abigail	*Adventure*	*Advice*	*Aleppine*	*Amity*
Anne	*Antelope*	*Assistance*	*Assurance*	**Baltimore*
Blessing	*Bonaventure*	*Breda*	*Briar*	*Bristol*

Cambridge	*Castle	Centurion	Charles	
Charles Merchant		Coronation	Crown	Defiance
Delph	Diamond	Dover	Dragon	Dreadnought
Dunkirk	Eagle	*East India London		
*East India Merchant		Elizabeth	Expedition	Fairfax
Fanfan	Foresight	Fortune	Fox	*George
Gloucester	Golden Phoenix		Great Gift	Greenwich
Guilder de Ruyter		Guinea	Hampshire	
Happy Return	Helverson	Henrietta	Henry	
House of Sweeds		Jersey	*John and Thomas	
*Katherine	Kent	Land of Promise		Leopard
Lion	Lizard	*London Merchant		
Loyal London	*Loyal Merchant		Marmaduke	Mary
Mary Rose	Mathius	Monck	Montagu	Newcastle
Old James	Paul	Plymouth	Portland	Portsmouth
Princess	Providence	Rainbow	Resolution	Revenge
Richard	Richard and Martha		Royal Charles	Royal James
Royal Katherine		Royal Oak	(Royal) Sovereign	
Ruby	Rupert	St Andrew	St George	St Jacob
Samuel	Sancta Maria	Slothany	Swallow	Tiger
Triumph	Turkey	*Turkey Merchant		Unicorn
Unity	Vanguard	Victory	Virgin	Warspite
Welcome	Yarmouth	York	Zealand	

*Denotes that these ships were hired for war service.

ORTEGAL – see BAY OF BISCAY 1805

OSTEND 1918
10 May
World War I 1914–18
The Ostend element of the combined attack on Zeebrugge and Ostend on 22–23 April 1918 was, by contrast with the success of the Zeebrugge raid, a failure. This first attempt on Ostend seemed dogged with bad luck. The difficulties of navigation of the ships

intended as blockships for the harbour were accentuated by the change of wind which brought the artificial smoke screen back to seaward. The consequent obscuring of the harbour made it necessary to place some dependence on a buoy which by the merest coincidence had been moved the previous day by a mile or so to the eastward. Despite the most gallant efforts by Commander A.E. Godsal (*Brilliant*) and Lieutenant-Commander H.N.M. Hardy (*Sirius*) the blocking attempt "had not achieved success".

Both these commanding officers begged Vice-Admiral Keyes to give them a second chance and gave Keyes no peace until he consented. The battered old *Vindictive*, survivor of the Zeebrugge attempt, was hurriedly patched and made ready for the second attempt at Ostend. Success would mean denial of Ostend as a base for the 40 – 50 U-boats resting and refitting there. Such a reward was worth the effort.

The problems began when *Sappho* developed an engineering fault and fell behind. *Vindictive* went on ahead, found difficulty in locating the entrance, obscured by fog and intense gunfire. Godsal was killed on his bridge by a shellburst and never seen again. Lieutenant-Commander Crutchley assumed command. He sank the blockship in a poor position under intense fire. The crew were evacuated to waiting MLs. Crutchley then transferred to *Warwick* wearing Keyes's flag. She struck a mine before reaching Dover with another destroyer lashed alongside to keep her afloat. It was a sad end to a glorious attempt. The VC was awarded to Crutchley and to the two ML commanding officers Lieutenant Bourke RNVR and Lieutenant Drummond RNVR.

Battle Honour:

Faulknor	*Prince Eugene*	*Trident*	*Velox*	*Vindictive*
Warwick	*Whirlwind*			

CMBs: 22B, 23B, 24A, 25BD, 26B, 30B.
MLs: 254, 276.

P

PACIFIC 1939–45
World War II 1939–45
The Pacific theatre of operations in the Second World War was
predominantly American, with only a minor British, Australian and
New Zealand contribution, except for the British Pacific Fleet's
participation in the 82-day Okinawa campaign in 1945 when the
ships engaged included four aircraft carriers, two battleships, four
cruisers, eleven destroyers and a large fleet train. (See OKINAWA
1945, p. 175)

See, in addition, the entries for Battle Honours for British ships
serving in the Pacific:

CORAL SEA 1942   (p. 72)
GUADALCANAL 1942–43   (pp. 106–7)
SAVO ISLAND 1942   (p. 206)
NEW GUINEA 1942–44   (pp. 154–5)
KULA GULF 1943   (pp. 120–1)
LEYTE GULF 1944   (pp. 125–6)
LINGAYEN GULF 1945   (p. 128)
OKINAWA 1945   (pp. 176–7)
JAPAN 1945   (p. 113)

While America concentrated on forming massive fleets and armies
of men for their strategy of island-hopping through the Pacific until
the dropping of the atom bombs brought the war to an end in
August 1945, the British still had the responsibility for escorting
Russian convoys, for patrolling the Atlantic, for the Burma front
and the building of an East Indies fleet and other commitments.
Campaign Honour:
1942:
Armidale   *Deloraine*   *Kalgoorlie*   *Voyager*
Warrnambool

1942–45:	*Arunta*		
1945:			
Barco	*Burdekin*	*Colac*	*Diamantha*
Dubbo	*Gascoyne*	*Hawkesbury*	*Hobart*
Kiama	*Lachlan*	*Latrobe*	*Lithgow*
Shropshire	*Stawell*	*Warramunga*	*Warrego*

Note: the BR (Book of Reference) intended for publication in 1957 omitted this Pacific entry.

PALEMBANG 1945
24 and 29 January
World War II 1939–45

This attack on Japanese oil installations in Sumatra was carried out by a British fleet designated Force 63, commanded by Vice-Admiral Philip Vian. It was opposed by four fighter squadrons of the 9th Air Division of the Japanese 7th Area Army and by heavy AA batteries. The fleet comprised virtually the whole of the British Pacific Fleet except the battleship *Howe*.

1st Aircraft Carrier Squadron: *Indomitable* (flag), *Illustrious*, *Victorious* and *Indefatigable*. Battleship: *King George V*.

4th Cruiser Squadron: *Argonaut, Black Prince, Euryalus, Ceylon*.

25th Destroyer Flotilla: *Grenville* (D), *Undine, Ursa, Undaunted*. 27th Destroyer Flotilla: *Kempenfelt* (D), *Wakeful, Whirlwind, Wager, Wessex, Whelp*.

This force carried 239 aircraft and was supported by an oiling group, Force 69: *Urchin, Echodale, Wave King, Empire Salvage* and, later, *Arndale*.

Meridian One was the codename for the strike at the Royal Dutch Oil Refinery at Pladjoe (24 January), the largest and most important oil refinery in the Far East.

Meridian Two was the codename for the second strike, on 29 January, on the second largest refinery at the Standard Oil Refinery at Soengi Gerong. These strikes were the two largest undertaken by the Fleet Air Arm during the Second World War. Enormous damage was inflicted, the effects of which lasted for months. Sixty-eight Japanese aircraft were destroyed. British losses amounted to: sixteen aircraft lost in battle, eleven ditched, fourteen destroyed in deck crashes: a total of forty-one aircraft from 378 sorties. Personnel losses amounted to thirty aircrew.

Battle Honour:

Illustrious   *Indefatigable*   *Indomitable*   *Victorious*

FAA Squadron: *820, 849, 854, 857, 887, 894, 1770, 1830, 1833, 1834, 1836, 1839, 1844.*

PASSERO 1718 (Cape Passero)
11 August
War for Sicily 1718–20

This war is sometimes called The War of the Quadruple Alliance.

Admiral Sir George Byng, later Viscount Torrington, won a significant sea victory over the Spanish even though the two countries were not at war.

The battle followed the Spanish invasion of Sicily and the foundation of the Quadruple Alliance in 1718. A large British fleet was despatched to the Mediterranean with Byng wearing his flag in *Barfleur* (90) – altogether nineteen ships of the line.

The force arrived at Messina on 9 August 1718 and contact was made on the following day, over four months before a declaration of war, with a Spanish squadron off Cape Passero on the southern tip of Sicily. Vice-Admiral Castañete's force comprised twelve of the line and several smaller ships. He wore his flag in the *Real San Felipe* (74).

As there was little wind the Spanish ships were towed by their galleys throughout the night, but the British ships caught up with them. The small craft were ordered inshore. Byng sent in eight frigates to chase them out. In the ensuing chase the British caught the Spanish ships and by nightfall the Spaniards were in full flight and heavily mauled. Spanish losses are difficult to assess – sources vary – but it appears that something like seven ships of the line and nine frigates were captured or burnt, as well as many more smaller vessels. The Spanish Admiral was killed. Byng was rewarded with the title Viscount Torrington.

Battle Honour:

Argyll	*Barfleur*	*Breda*	*Burford*
Canterbury	*Captain*	*Dorsetshire*	*Dreadnought*

Dunkirk	*Essex*	*Garland*	*Grafton*
Griffin	*Kent*	*Lenox*	*Loo*
Montagu	*Orford*	*Ripon*	*Roebuck*
Royal Oak	*Rupert*	*Shrewsbury*	*Superb*

PELAGOSA 1811
29 November
Napoleonic War 1803–15

This was a spirited action between two small squadrons of British and French ships in the Adriatic near Lissa where Captain Murray Maxwell commanded the *Alceste* (38), the *Active* (48: Captain James A. Gordon), *Unité* (36: Captain Edwin H. Chamberlayne) and *Acorn* (20: Captain George M. Bligh).

The French squadron was commanded by Commodore Montfort in *Pauline* (40), accompanied by *Pomone* (40) and *Persanne* (26). *Acorn* had been detached to remain in Lissa harbour to defend the area. Action at sea began at 11 am and continued till late afternoon. *Unité* chased *Persanne*, which failed to keep up with her consorts and stood away to the north-east. *Persanne* was overtaken and, when badly damaged, struck.

Active and *Alceste* engaged the other two ships fiercely. After *Pomone* had lost two of her masts (the third was to come down later) she struck; she had fifty killed and wounded out of a crew of 332. But the two British ships were themselves too badly damaged to follow *Pauline* and she made good her escape. *Active* lost seven killed and thirteen wounded from 218 men aboard, and *Alceste* suffered eight killed and twenty-seven wounded.

<u>Battle Honour:</u>   *Active*   *Alceste*   *Unité*

PORTLAND 1653 (The Three Days' Battle)
18–20 February
First Dutch War 1652–54

This was fought between a fleet of eighty English ships under the command of General-at-Sea Robert Blake, supported by Monck, Deane and William Penn, and a Dutch fleet of equal size escorting a fleet of about 150 merchantmen, all under the command of

Tromp. The English ships assembled at Portsmouth as the Dutch approached the Channel and sighted the Dutch convoy off Cap Le Havre. Tromp ordered the convoy to turn away while he attacked the English fleet.

Action was joined on the 18th off Portland and it soon developed into a long-running battle. Tromp was supported by De Ruyter and Evertsen, but they were all hampered by having to protect the convoy. Tromp displayed great skill and seamanship in keeping his losses to a minimum and reaching the safety of Gravelines.

Blake gave up the chase after many ships ran out of ammunition during the three-day chase.

Tromp lost eleven warships, thirty merchantmen and nearly 2,000 men killed or drowned. Blake lost one ship and nearly 1,000 killed. His was a decisive victory and it represented a turning point in the war with the Netherlands.

Battle Honour:

Advantage	Adventure	Advice	Amity
Angel	Ann and Joyce	Ann Piercey	Assistance
Assurance	Brazil (?)	Centurion (?)	Charles
Chase	Convert	Convertine	Cullen (?)
Cygnet	Diamond	Discovery	Dolphin
Dragon	Duchess	Eagle	Elizabeth and Ann
Exchange	Expedition	Fairfax	Falmouth
Foresight	Fortune	Gift	Gilliflower
Guinea	Hannibal	Happy Entrance	Katherine
Kentish	Laurel	Lion	
Lisbon Merchant(?)		Martin	Mary
Merlin	Nicodemus	Nightingale	Nonsuch
Oak	Old Warwick	Paradox	Paul
Pearl	Pelican	Plover	President
Princess Maria	Prosperous	Providence	Rainbow
Raven	Reformation	Richard and Martha	Roebuck
Ruby	Ruth	Sampson	Sapphire
Satisfaction	Speaker	Speaker's Prize	Success
Sussex	Tenth Whelp (?)	Thomas and Lucy	
Thomas and William		Tiger	Triumph
Tulip	Vanguard	Victory	Waterhound
William and John	Worcester		

PORTO BELLO 1739 – see PUERTO BELLO

PORTO FARINA 1655
4 April
17th Century Mediterranean Piracy

Porto Farina, on the Tunisian coast of Africa, was the scene of this battle in 1655. An English fleet of twenty-four ships under the command of General-at-Sea Robert Blake wearing his flag in the *George* was despatched to the Mediterranean to conduct reprisals against Barbary pirates for their attacks on English shipping.

The Bey of Tunis rejected Blake's demands for redress. Blake replied by bombarding the Bey's forts before locating nine Algerian ships in nearby Porto Farina. He led a force of fifteen ships, forced the entrance to the harbour, silenced more batteries and destroyed all nine Algerian ships before withdrawing.

Battle Honour:

Amity	*Andrew*	*Bridgewater*	*Foresight*	*George*
Kent	*Merlin*	*Mermaid*	*Newcastle*	*Pearl*
Success	*Unicorn*	*Worcester*		

PORTO NOVO 1759
10 September
Seven Years' War 1756–63

The scene of this battle was 25 miles south-east of Porto Novo on the Coromandel coast of India near Cuddalore in a position 11° 03' N 79° 45' E. It was fought between a squadron of ten British ships commanded by Vice-Admiral George Pocock with his flag in *Yarmouth* and the French Commodore D'Aché in *Zodiaque* with eleven ships.

This was the third battle in these waters and was in itself inconclusive, but the final outcome was to Britain's advantage. The nine ships of the line and *Queenborough*, the single frigate, were awarded the battle honour.

Battle Honour:

Cumberland	*Elizabeth*	*Grafton*	*Newcastle*

| Queenborough | Salisbury | | Sunderland | Tiger |
| Weymouth | Yarmouth | | | |

PROVIDIEN 1782
12 April
American War of Independence 1775–83
This battle was the second clash in the Hughes/Suffren series of battles for the supremacy of the Indian Ocean in 1782 – 83. Vice-Admiral Sir Edward Hughes commanded eleven of the line and was reinforcing Trincomalee in Ceylon, which he had captured earlier in the year.

Admiral Pierre Suffren, destined to be remembered as one of France's greatest admirals – commanded twelve ships. It was his good fortune to encounter Hughes's squadron on a lee shore 12 miles NE by E of Providien Rock off Ceylon's eastern coast, with little searoom with which to play.

A bitter struggle developed between the French *Héros* (flag: 74), *L'Orient* (74), and *Brilliant* (64) and British *Superb* (flag: 74) and *Monmouth* (64). The latter was carronaded almost to a wreck but refused to strike; each side suffered about 500 casualties. Fighting continued until exhaustion set in. Both sides anchored for the night but neither resumed action the following morning. They licked their wounds in sight of each other for a week, then Suffren sailed north and Hughes south for Trincomalee.

Battle Honour:

Burford	*Combustion*	*Eagle*	*Exeter*	*Hero*
Isis	*Magnanime*	*Monarch*	*Monmouth*	*Seahorse*
Sultan	*Superb*	*Worcester*		

PUERTO BELLO 1739
22 November
War with Spain and France 1739–48
The scene of the first action of the War of Jenkins's Ear which developed into what came to be known as the War of Austrian Succession and the Spanish War.

Vice-Admiral Edward Vernon*, with his flag hoisted in the *Burford*, was despatched to the West Indies to act against Spain with instructions to intercept the annual assembly of Spanish treasure ships before the convoy left Mexico for Spain.

Intelligence directed Vernon to intercept the treasure at Puerto Bello, Panama. He led a squadron of six ships there, overwhelmed the defenders of the port, captured the valuable hoard of treasure and made off. The fortifications were blown up by the defenders' own gunpowder. Vernon's casualties only amounted to six killed and thirteen wounded.

<u>Battle Honour:</u>

Burford	*Hampton Court*	*Norwich*
Princess Louisa	*Strafford*	*Worcester*

PUNTO STILO 1940 – see CALABRIA

---

* He was the son of a Secretary of State and owed his promotion largely to influence.

Q

QUEBEC 1759
July – September
Seven Years' War 1756–63
The Seven Years' War started with French settlers in Canada forti-fying a number of posts against the advance of English settlers. As the war developed it was clear that the French city of Quebec "was the key to the conquest of upper Canada". Quebec lay 300 miles up the St Lawrence River. It was not until 1759 that an attack was launched to capture the city. 1759 was the *annus mirabilis* of the Seven Years' War, a year of extraordinary events and changes of fortune, and specifically the year of the Navy. The fleet, from first to last, was Britain's main weapon.

The attempt on the city was a brilliant exploit by Major-General James Wolfe and Vice-Admiral Charles Saunders in *Neptune*. The British fleet under Saunders carried an army up the St Lawrence, brilliantly navigated by Master (later Captain) James Cook. The fleet came to anchor on 26 June. It dominated the river and landed 17,000 men below the Plains of Abraham. The French troops under Montcalm greatly outnumbered the British but their morale was low and resistance modest.

All British attacks failed until Wolfe found a means of climbing the cliffs and hoisting guns to the Heights. The French Governor finally offered surrender and the capitulation was signed on 18 September. By then both British army commanders had been killed. The new army commander, Brigadier-General George Townshend, paid handsome credit to every aspect of the naval activity in support of the troops in his Despatch: "It is my duty . . .

to acknowledge . . . how great a share the Navy has had in this successful campaign."

Battle Honour:

Alcide	Baltimore	Bedford	Boscawen	Captain
Centurion	Cormorant	Crown	Devonshire	Diana
Dublin	Echo	Euros	Fowey	Halifax
Hind	Hunter	Lizard	Lowestoffe	Medway
Neptune	Nightingale	Northumberland		Orford
Pelican	Pembroke	Porcupine	Prince Frederick	
Prince of Orange		Princess Amelia		Racehorse
Richmond	Rodney	Royal William	Scarborough	Scorpion
Seahorse	Shrewsbury	Somerset	Squirrel	
Stirling Castle	Strombolo	Sutherland	Terrible	Trent
Trident	Vanguard	Vesuvius	Zephyr	

QUIBERON BAY 1759
20 November
Seven Years' War 1756–63

One of the most celebrated naval battles in the Royal Navy's history was fought between a British force – the Western Squadron – under Admiral Sir Edward Hawke commanding twenty-three of the line with his flag in the *Royal George* (100) and Admiral the Comte de Conflans with twenty-one French of the line including his flagship *Soleil Royal* (80), and three frigates. Hawke's force was augmented by a squadron of ten small ships commanded by Commodore Duff.

The French were planning an invasion of Ireland. Conflans evaded the British blockade of Brest and took his squadron to strengthen the invasion forces. In a rising westerly gale he sought sanctuary in Quiberon Bay, where the squadron hove to west of Belle Isle.

Admiral Hawke learnt of Conflans' escape from Brest and set off in pursuit. He located the Frenchman's ships in the treacherous, rock-strewn shoal waters of the bay. The master of Hawke's flagship dared to warn the Admiral of the dangerous shallows, but the latter replied, "You have done your duty in pointing out to me the danger. Now lay me alongside the enemy's flagship."

Conflans believed Hawke would not hazard his ships and attempt to force a battle in such confined water, and dreadful weather. He was wrong.

In bitter fighting the British van mauled the French rear, and during the afternoon and evening the French *Formidable* (80) struck, the battered *Superbe* (74) capsized, the badly damaged *Héros* struck, and when the *Thésée* was practically wrecked by the *Torbay* she foundered with the loss of about 700 men.

When darkness fell the British anchored, but some of the French beat out of the bay and escaped south. Others broke their backs on the bar in attempting to shelter in the Vilaine estuary, or became trapped after lightening ship by jettisoning their cannons.

The *Soleil Royal*, flagship, got under way early the following day, but grounded on the Rouelle Shoal and was burnt by her crew to prevent capture. Later the *Juste* (70) foundered in the Loire estuary. Eight French ships managed to escape to Rochefort.

Conflans lost a total of seven ships of the line and 2,500 men killed or drowned. Of those ships which survived many were unfit for further sea service. The British lost two ships, *Resolution* (74) and *Essex* (64), both of which ran aground early in the battle and were wrecked in the continuing storm.

Hawke's was a brilliant victory achieved by skilled seamanship, daring and resolution under most adverse conditions, and off an enemy shore. In achieving this victory he also dispelled the threat of invasion. Further, the British could now turn their attention to the naval scene in the far seas.

Battle Honour: all ships which participated in the battle, listed in the following table, were awarded the Battle Honour.

HAWKE'S FLEET

Royal George	(100)	Sir E. Hawke	*Hero*	(74)	Hon G. Edgecumbe
		Capt Campbell	*Swiftsure*	(70)	Sir T. Stanhope
Union	(90)	Sir C. Hardy	*Dorsetshire*	(70)	P. Denis
		Capt J. Evans	*Burford*	(70)	J. Gambier
Duke	(90)	T. Graves	*Chichester*	(70)	E.S. Willet
Namur	(90)	M. Buckle	*Temple*	(70)	Hon W. Shirley
Mars	(74)	Commodore	*Revenge*	(64)	J. Storr
		Jas. Young	*Essex*	(64)	L. O'Brien
Warspight	(74)	Sir J. Bentley	*Kingston*	(60)	T. Shirley
Hercules	(74)	E. Fortesque	*Intrepide*	(60)	J. Maplesden
Torbay	(74)	Hon A. Keppel	*Montagu*	(60)	J. Rowley
Magnanime	(74)	Lord Hawke	*Dunkirk*	(60)	R. Digby
Resolution	(74)	H. Speke	*Defiance*	(60)	P. Baird

DUFF'S SQUADRON

Rochester	(50)	R. Duff	*Venus*	(36)	T. Harrison
Portland	(50)	M. Arbuthnot	*Vengeance*	(28)	G. Nightingale
Falkland	(50)	Fr S. Drake	*Coventry*	(28)	F. Burslem
Chatham	(50)	J. Lockhart	*Maidstone*	(28)	D. Diggs
Minerva	(32)	A. Hood	*Sapphire*	(32)	J. Strachan

R

RIVER PLATE ('*Graf Spee*' Action)
13 December 1939
World War II 1939–45

The first naval battle of the Second World War took place in the estuary of the River Plate on the east coast of South America. It was fought between a small cruiser force commanded by Commodore H. Harwood and the German pocket-battleship *Admiral Graf Spee* (12,100 tons, 6 × 11" and 8 × 5.9") commanded by Captain H. Langsdorff.

Harwood's cruiser force was one of many searching for the *Graf Spee*, which was on a marauding expedition against Allied merchant shipping in southern waters. Harwood thought that the busy shipping lanes of the Plate (Montevideo – Buenos Aires – La Plata) would attract Langsdorff, and he was proved right when on 13 December he sighted the *Graf Spee*.

Harwood wore his broad pennant in *Ajax* (6,985 tons, 8 × 6") and had in company *Exeter* (8,390 tons, 6 × 8") and HMNZS *Achilles* (7,030 tons, 8 × 6").

Langdorff closed the British squadron at full speed. Harwood divided his force, *Exeter* to one side and the two light cruisers to the other, compelling Langdorff to split his main armament between two forces, or concentrate on one, to the advantage of the other.

Within half an hour *Exeter* was in dire trouble. The heavy 11" shells had silenced all but one of her main guns. *Ajax* and *Achilles* also suffered hits, but they had also struck *Graf Spee* with their 6" shells. *Ajax* came in for special attention and when she was badly damaged Harwood called off the action and retired behind a smokescreen.

Curiously, *Graf Spee* did not pursue and force an outright

victory, or even head away to the broad expanse of the South Atlantic. Instead she set course for Montevideo, a neutral port.

British ships began to head for the River Plate while the damaged German ship remained secured alongside, trapped into believing that a strong force already lay in wait in the estuary.

On 17 December Langsdorff took *Graf Spee* out of harbour to the three-mile limit and scuttled her in shallow waters. A few days later he committed suicide.

Battle Honour: *Achilles*   *Ajax*   *Exeter*

FAA Squadron: *700*

RUSSIAN CONVOYS – see ARCTIC 1941–45

S

SABANG 1944
25 July
World War II 1939–45
This was an air strike and naval bombardment of Japanese-occupied installations at Sabang, Sumatra. Surface ships of the Eastern Fleet engaged Japanese shore batteries. Operation Crimson was under the command of Admiral Sir James Somerville in the battleship *Queen Elizabeth* (32,700 tons, 8 × 15") in company with the battlecruiser *Renown* (32,000 tons, 6 × 15") and the carriers *Illustrious* and *Victorious*.

Battle Honour:

Ceylon	*Cumberland*	*Gambia*	*Illustrious*
Kenya	*Nigeria*	*Phoebe*	*Quality*
Queen Elizabeth	*Quickmatch*	*Quilliam*	*Racehorse*
Raider	*Rapid*	*Relentless*	*Renown*
Rocket	*Roebuck*	*Rotherham*	*Tantalus*
Templar	*Victorious*		

FAA Squadron: *831, 1830, 1833, 1834, 1836, 1837, 1838.*

SADRAS 1758
29 April
Seven Years' War 1756–63
This was hardly a battle, more like a scrappy indecisive encounter, with some damage to both sides.

The French had a naval base at Pondicherry on the Coromandel coast of SE India, and the British had one at nearby Cuddalore, south of Madras fronting on to the Bay of Bengal. The French Admiral Comte D'Aché in his flagship *Zodiaque* (74) and Vice-

Admiral Pocock in his flagship *Yarmouth* (64) commanded the respective light squadrons.

Each sighted the other at about 9 am as Pocock was preparing to leave Port St David Roads. It was afternoon when contact was made and each squadron of ships were in line. Seven British and nine French (one was a 36 gun frigate) opposed each other. Away to leeward the French had another 74 and a frigate.

Pocock opened fire at a range of "half a musket shot" of the flagship. The British rear failed to give good support and later three captains were court-martialled. The French line gave way but Pocock's ships were unable to catch the fleeing ships.

The inconclusive nature of this encounter was attributed to the strict adherence to the Fighting Instructions.

Battle Honour:

Cumberland	*Elizabeth*	*Newcastle*
Protector	*Queensborough*	*Salisbury*
Tiger	*Weymouth*	*Yarmouth*

SADRAS 1782
17 February
American War of Independence 1775–83

This battle was the first of a series of five engagements fought between Vice-Admiral Sir Edward Hughes and the French Commodore Pierre André de Suffren during 1782–83. (See PROVIDIEN, NEGAPATAM, TRINCOMALEE and CUDDALORE.)

This first meeting took place off Madras, 9 miles SE of Sadras. Suffren had with him a small convoy of transports and he was not anxious to join battle. Hughes weighed anchor and set off in pursuit. He managed to capture six of the transports. On the 17th the two squadrons engaged. Suffren had eleven of the line and Hughes nine. The Frenchman had the wind advantage and concentrated his attack on the last five in Hughes's line.

Exeter (64) suffered seriously and was almost taken, and Hughes's own flagship, *Superb*, was also badly damaged. The wind suddenly changed and allowed the British van to come up and rescue the flagship. The battle petered out and Suffren was content to get clear of the British. His captains showed little resolution during the fight and failed to turn advantage to victory.

Battle Honour:

Burford	Combustion (fireship)	Eagle	Exeter
Hero	Isis	Minorca	Monarch (?Monmouth)
Seahorse (frigate)		Superb	Worcester

ST KITTS 1782
25–26 January
American War of Independence 1775–83

This was a remarkable battle between a British fleet commanded by Rear-Admiral Sir Samuel Hood, commanding twenty-two ships of the line, and the French Admiral Comte de Grasse with twenty-four of the line and a large number of transports which had landed 8,000 troops and captured St Kitts in the West Indies. The troops had been landed at the Basseterre anchorage. When de Grasse left the anchorage to do battle with Hood, the latter determined to avoid battle and to seize the anchorage itself. This he did. In a masterly move he took his fleet into the anchorage and, despite the rear being harassed by de Grasse and shore batteries engaging his ships, he had them anchor in succession so that attacking ships would receive full broadsides from the British ships. Hood beat off two or more such attacks and de Grasse lost heart and withdrew, but as the British troops ashore had surrendered Hood found an opportunity to slip away unnoticed and reached safety.

Battle Honour:

Ajax	Alcide	Alfred	America
Barfleur	Bedford	Belliqueux	Canada
Centaur	Champion	Eurydisis	Expedition
Gros Inlet	Intrepid	Invincible	Monarch
Montagu	Nymphe	Prince George	Prince William
Princessa	Prudent	Resolution	Russell
St Albans	Shrewsbury	Sibyl	Solebay

ST LUCIA 1778
15 December
American War of Independence 1775–83

St Lucia is one of the smaller islands of the Windward group in the West Indies. In November 1778 Rear-Admiral Samuel Barrington, commander of the much weakened naval forces in the area, was reinforced by ships from the North American station, but almost simultaneously the French naval strength in the area was also increased by about twelve of the line under Admiral D'Estaing.

On 14 December Barrington's small squadron gave support to a British expeditionary force landing troops to capture St Lucia when intelligence was received of the approach of the French squadron. But Barrington's force was protected by a good anchorage – the bay of Grand Cul de Sac – and his guns covered the entrance.

D'Estaing in the *Languedoc* (90), leading a transport fleet of 7,000 troops to re-take the island, was repulsed at Carenage by shore batteries, and then twice more at Barrington's anchorage. He withdrew and landed the troops further north at an unprotected anchorage, but it was an abortive operation. Within a month the French Governor ashore had surrendered and the British occupation was complete.

Battle Honour:

Ariadne	*Aurora*	*Barbados*	*Boyne*	*Carcass*	*Centurion*
Ceres	*Isis*	*Pelican*	*Preston*	*Prince of Wales*	
St Albans	*Snake*	*Venus*	*Weazle*		

ST LUCIA 1796
24 March
French Revolutionary War 1793–1803

Rear-Admiral Sir Hugh Cloberry Christian with his flag in the *Thunderer* sailed for the West Indies with a small squadron. After setting up his command at Martinique he tackled his first objective – St Lucia. He collected a large body of troops under Lieutenant-General Sir Ralph Abercromby. Three landings of assault troops secured the island on the first day and the whole island surrendered. Christian went on to capture St Vincent and Grenada on a flowing tide of success.

Battle Honour:

Alfred	Arethusa	Astraea	Beaulieu	Bulldog
Fury	Ganges	Hebe	Medias	Pelican
Thunderer	Vengeance	Victorieuse	Woolwich	

ST NAZAIRE 1942
28 March
World War II 1939–45

Much of the humiliation heaped upon Britain by the Channel Dash was cast aside in the following month by the prestige gained at the Raid on St Nazaire at the mouth of the River Loire. St Nazaire was important for the Germans for two main reasons: primarily it served as a crucial base for their North Atlantic U-boat operations, saving the U-boats the long haul north-about the British Isles to and from a German base or through the Channel, which simply was not a proposition; secondly it contained the massive *Normandie* dock, large enough to accommodate the 42,900-ton battleship *Tirpitz*. The purpose of the Raid on St Nazaire was to destroy the U-boat and port installations, and secondly to destroy the lock to the dock.

HMS *Campbeltown* (the one-time USN destroyer *Buchanan*), commanded by Lieutenant-Commander S.H. Beattie, was strengthened and modified, and packed with explosives with the intention of ramming the dock caisson.

The operation was under the command of Commander R.E.D. Ryder from aboard MGB *314*. Commandos were under the military control of Lieutenant-Colonel A.C. Newman.

Ryder's MGB, an MTB and sixteen MLs were used to land the commandos, but the German defences were alerted to the attack. The explosives did considerable damage and the raid was rated a success, but only four MLs returned home safely. Five VCs were awarded for valour in this, Operation Chariot.

Battle Honour:	*Atherstone*	*Campbeltown*	*Tynedale*
MLs:	*156, 160, 177, 192, 262, 267, 268, 270, 298, 306,*		
	307, 443, 446, 457		
MGB:	*314*		
MTB:	*74*		

SAINTS – see THE SAINTS 1782

ST VINCENT 1780 (The Moonlight Battle)
16 January
American War of Independence 1775–83
Admiral Sir George Rodney left Plymouth on 29 January 1780 with a powerful fleet of twenty-two of the line and nine frigates. This force escorted a convoy of reinforcements for besieged Gibraltar and the trade for the West Indies, where Rodney was to take command of the Leeward Islands station.

An enemy force known as the Caracca Fleet, commanded by Commodore Don Juan de Yardi, comprised the *Guipuscoana* (64), six frigates and a merchant convoy of sixteen (some reports say seventeen merchant ships and five warships) bound for Cadiz with wheat and naval stores. On 8 January Rodney's fleet intercepted this force and captured it intact.

Rodney continued heading southward and eight days later when 12 miles south of Cape Finisterre he encountered a Spanish fleet commanded by Admiral Don Juan de Langara of eleven of the line and two frigates. Rodney immediately gave chase before a strong westerly wind and his van engaged the Spanish rear at about 4 pm. An hour later the 70-gun Spanish *San Domingo* blew up with what must have been a shattering blow, as vivid as the loss of *Hood* in 1941. Only one man survived from the crew of 600 men.

Though darkness fell the battle continued, the blustery weather allowing a fine clear moon. Rodney exercised his two-to-one superiority and by dawn six Spanish of the line had been taken: *Fenix* (80), Langara's flagship, the *San Julian* (70), *San Eugenio* (70), *Monarca* (70), *Princessa* (70) and *Diligente* (70).

The weather worsened and two of the prizes had to be abandoned on running aground; only good seamanship extricated the British from the dangerous lee shore. The Spanish also suffered ten ships badly damaged, and 5,000 men killed, wounded or captured. Five British ships were severely damaged and 300 men were lost.

Battle Honour:

Ajax	Alcide	Alfred	Apollo	Bedford
Bienfaisant	Culloden	Cumberland	Edgar	Hyena

Invincible	*Marlborough*	*Monarch*	*Montagu*	*Pegasus*
Prince George	*Resolution*	*Sandwich*	*Terrible*	*Triton*

ST VINCENT 1797
14 February
French Revolutionary War 1793–1802

Admiral Sir John Jervis's naval victory at St Vincent was a classic. The enemy fleet was twice the size of his own. The number of guns marshalled by the Spanish ships of the line totalled 2,308, including the incredible 136 of the massive *Santissima Trinidad*. Jervis could muster 1,232.

But he could also muster a 'band of brothers' of incomparable courage and tactical skills. Commodore Nelson in his *Captain* (74) twice excelled himself in the battle, ensuring victory; Troubridge in *Culloden*; Parker in *Prince George* (98); James Saumarez in *Orion* (74); Collingwood in *Excellent* (74).

A large but undermanned Spanish fleet under Admiral de Cordova left Cartagena for Cadiz. He commanded twenty-seven of the line, including his massive flagship and six 112s, plus twenty frigates.

Jervis weighed from Lisbon's Tagus on 18 January in the *Victory* (100), plus fourteen of the line and four frigates, and sailed to cruise off Cape St Vincent and intercept Cordova. On 13 February he was joined by Nelson from Gibraltar.

When the fog lifted off Cape St Vincent the following morning the Spanish fleet was seen to be straggling in two divisions and *Culloden* led to attack the weather division. Confusion spread along the line of Spanish ships, but, led by the *Santissima Trinidad*, they threatened to escape astern of the British column.

Nelson in *Captain*, third ship from the British rear, saw the threat, pulled out of line across *Excellent*'s bows and at great risk of being blown to smithereens, crossed the line of advance of Cordova's flagship and 112s. Perhaps more importantly, Nelson's tactic was totally contrary to the *Fighting Instructions*. No signal had yet been broken out that ships might act independently, however obvious the need. Nelson had the courage to do so. The *Captain* had her wheel and foremast shot away, but Nelson managed to place her alongside the *San Nicolas* (84) which had fouled herself with the 112 *Josef*. Both were heavily engaged with *Prince George*. Nelson boarded and captured the *San Nicolas*, then, using her as his "patent bridge for capturing enemies", boarded and captured the *San Josef* too.

This brilliant action increased the enemy confusion and Jervis took advantage of it. After an hour of battle the *Salvador del Mundo* (112) and *San Ysidro* (74) struck. At one time the *Santissima Trinidad* was threatened with capture but managed to extricate herself. Cordova managed to make good his escape to Cadiz and Jervis was happy enough with his four great prizes and returned home in triumph.

<u>Battle Honour:</u>
all the following ships were engaged and all were awarded the battle honour:

Victory	(100)	Admiral Sir John Jervis
		Captain R. Calder
Captain	(74)	Commodore H. Nelson
		Captain R.W. Miller
Blenheim	(90)	T.L. Frederick
Culloden	(74)	T. Troubridge
Excellent	(74)	C. Collingwood
Irresistible	(74)	G. Martin
Prince George	(98)	Rear-Admiral Parker
		Captain T.V. Irwin
Orion	(74)	Sir J. Saumarez
Goliath	(74)	Sir C.H. Knowles
Namur	(90)	J.H. Whitshed
Barfleur	(98)	Vice-Admiral Waldegrave
		Captain J.R. Dacres
Colossus	(74)	G. Murray
Diadem	(64)	G.H. Towry
Egmont	(74)	J. Sutton
Britannia	(100)	Vice-Admiral Thompson
		Captain T. Foley
Lively	(32)	Lord Garlies
La Minerve	(38)	G. Cockburn
Niger	(32)	E.J. Foote

Southampton	(32)	J. McNamara	
La Bonne			
Citoyenne	(18)	C. Lindsay	
Raven, brig	(18)	W. Prowse	
Fox, cutter	(12)	Lieutenant Gibson	

SALERNO 1943
9 September–6 October
World War II 1939–45

An amphibious assault was launched against the Germans in Italy in the area of Salerno as a first step towards capturing Naples. For four days after landing on the 9th 41 Commando were heavily engaged against experienced German divisions. A powerful naval presence was judged necessary and proved to be so. *Nelson, Rodney, Warspite, Valiant* and the carriers *Formidable* and *Illustrious* all made a contribution to the eventual success. *Warspite* and *Valiant* in particular helped restore the Allied situation by heavy bombardment. The Naval Commander wrote, "The margin of success in the landings was carried by the naval guns." The Germans attributed their failure to achieve a breakthrough to the beaches to the devastating effects of the battleships' gunfire. Sixty-two rounds of 15" shells were fired, thirty-five hitting their targets and ten more scoring near misses. *Warspite* was crippled by a radio-controlled bomb which exploded in No 4 boiler room and passed through the ship's bottom. A second one exploded close alongside and blew a hole on the waterline. She was towed to Gibraltar where large coffer dams were built on her bottom to effect repairs.

Battle Honour:

Abercrombie	*Acute*	*Albacore*	*Alynbank*	*Antwerp*
Atherstone	*Attacker*	*Aurora*	*Battler*	*Beaufort*
Belvoir	*Blackmore*	*Blankney*	*Blencathra*	*Boxer*
Brecon	*Brittany*	*Brixham*	*Brocklesby*	*Bruiser*
Bude	*Cadmus*	*Calpe*	*Catterick*	*Charybdis*
Circe	*Clacton*	*Cleveland*	*Coverley*	*Delhi*
Derwentdale	*Dido*	*Dulverton*	*Echo*	*Eclipse*
Eggesford	*Ensay*	*Espiègle*	*Euryalus*	*Exmoor*

Farndale	Faulknor	Felixstowe	Fly	Formidable
Fury	Gavotte	Glengyle	Hambledon	Haydon
Hengist	Hilary	Holcombe	Hunter	Ilex
Illustrious	Inglefield	Intrepid	Jervis	Laforey
Lamerton	Ledbury	Liddesdale	Lookout	Loyal
Mauritius	Mendip	Minuet	Mousa	Mutine
Nelson	Nubian	Offa	Orion	Palomares
Panther	Pathfinder	Penelope	Penn	Petard
Pirouette	Polruan	Prince Charles	Prince Leopold	
Prinses Astrid	Prinses Beatrix		Prinses Josephine Charlotte	
Quail	Quantock	Queenborough		Quilliam
Raider	Reighton Wyke		Rhyl	Roberts
Rodney	Rothesay	Royal Scotsman		
Royal Ulsterman		St Kilda	Scylla	Shakespeare
Sheffield	Sheppey	Sirius	Stalker	Stella Carina
Stornoway	Tango	Tartar	Tetcott	Thruster
Troubridge	Tumult	Tyrian	Uganda	
Ulster Monarch		Ulster Queen	Unicorn	Valiant
Visenda	Warspite	Whaddon	Wheatland	

MLs: 238, 273, 280, 283, 336, 554, 555, 556, 557, 559,
                  560, 561, 562, 564, 566

HDMLs: 1242, 1246, 1247, 1253, 1254, 1258, 1270, 1271,
                  1297, 1301

BYMs: 11, 14, 24, 209

MMSs: 5, 133, 134

MSMLSs: 121, 126, 134, 135

FAA Squadrons: 807, 808, 809, 810, 820, 834, 878, 879, 880, 886,
                  887, 888, 893, 897, 899

SAN DOMINGO 1806
6 February
Napoleonic War 1803–15

This was a spirited action between a squadron of six ships of the
line and two frigates commanded by Vice-Admiral Sir John
Duckworth and a French squadron comprising the *Impérial* (120),
Alexandre (80), *Jupiter* (74), *Diomede* (74) and one other (? *Brave*),
plus two frigates, commanded by Rear-Admiral Leissègues.

Leissègues had escaped the Brest blockade and fled to the West Indies. He was followed from Cadiz by Duckworth who eventually caught up with him in Occa Bay at the eastern end of San Domingo.

After only one and a half hours of furious action Duckworth had routed the French squadron which had been caught provisioning. The huge *Impérial* and the *Diomede* were driven ashore and burnt to avoid capture. The remaining three of the line were captured. Only the two frigates escaped.

Battle Honour:

Acasta	Agamemnon	Atlas	Canopus
Donegal	Epervier	Kingfisher	Magicienne
Northumberland	Spencer	Superb	

SAN SEBASTIAN 1813
August – 8 September
Napoleonic War 1803–15

During the French peninsular campaign of August to September 1813 a British squadron of ships worked closely with the Spanish patriots against the French.

San Sebastian lay in a pretty bay with a stark fortress dominating the entrance and the town. The French border lay a few miles to the east and close by the west was Guernica. Further along the coast was Santander.

A naval squadron under the command of Sir George Collier of the *Surveillante* (38) employed his ships to bring off a hard-pressed British garrison of 1,150 men and convey them to the safety of Castro Urdiales, a few miles from Santander.

Collier's squadron co-operated with General Graham in the reduction of San Sebastian and blockaded the town for several weeks until the French surrendered early in September.

Battle Honour:

Ajax	Andromache	Arrow	Beagle	Challenger
Constant	Despatch	Freija	Holly	Juniper
Lyra	Magicienne	President	Revolutionnaire	Sparrow
Surveillante				

It is unclear what contribution was made during this campaign by the following:

Royalist, Nimble, Stork, Racer, Trio, Reindeer, Goldfinch and Gunboats *14, 16, 19, 20* and *22*.

SANTA CRUZ 1657
20 April
War With Spain 1655–60

Santa Cruz de Tenerife in the Canary Islands was Robert Blake's swan song. He was the General-at-Sea commanding a powerful squadron of ships which was blockading the port of Cadiz when he received intelligence of the Spanish treasure fleet from the West Indies having arrived at Santa Cruz. His ships weighed anchor and twenty-three men-of-war set sail for the Canaries. On 20 April the fleet arrived off Santa Cruz, a strongly fortified harbour where sixteen galleons carrying Spanish treasure could be counted.

Blake forced an entry into the harbour, under the well-positioned guns of the fortress and the galleons, in a finely executed operation. He then destroyed the Spanish fleet in a fierce battle, before extricating his own fleet in a fine display of seamanship. Sixty men had been killed, and the 64-gun *Speaker* was severely damaged and had to be towed home. Five Spanish ships had been taken and eleven more burnt or blown up. Rear-Admiral Richard Stayner who had led the offensive into the harbour received a knighthood.

Battle Honour:

Bridgewater	*Bristol*	*Centurion*	*Colchester*
Convert	*Fairfax*	*Foresight*	*George*
Hampshire	*Jersey*	*Langport*	*Lyme*
Maidstone	*Nantwich*	*Newbury*	*Newcastle*
Plymouth	*Speaker*	*Swiftsure*	*Unicorn*
Winsby	*Worcester*		

SAUMAREZ'S ACTION – see GUT OF GIBRALTAR 1801

SAVO ISLAND 1942
9 August
World War II 1939–45

This was a disastrous battle for the Allied heavy cruiser squadron giving cover to the Guadalcanal landings when the Japanese Admiral Mikawa's heavy cruiser squadron, comprising five heavy cruisers, two light cruisers and a destroyer, surprised them at Savo Island.

The Allied squadron was caught unprepared at 2 am. Illuminated by starshell, their guns shown to be trained fore and aft, they were blasted to destruction like the Italian cruisers at Cape Matapan. In half an hour the US cruisers, all over 9,000 tons with 9 × 8" guns, *Astoria*, *Quincy*, *Vincennes* and *Canberra* were sunk or so crippled that they foundered later. The Allied cruisers had been formed into three divisions to give cover to the amphibious forces which had landed two days earlier, each guarding one of the three seaward approaches on either side of Savo Island. The Japanese force from Rabaul struck first at the southern division, sank the *Canberra* and torpedoed the *Chicago*.

Mikawa then fell upon the northern group and sank the three cruisers *Vincennes*, *Quincy* and *Astoria*. A destroyer was also severely damaged.

The Allied casualties amounted to 1,023 men killed and 709 wounded. The Japanese losses were negligible. Only the flagship *Chokai* received any damage. Some honour was redeemed by the US submarine *S44* which sank the cruiser *Kako* on its return to Rabaul.

The Allied expenditure of ammunition was:

107 × 8", 385 × 5" and 8 torpedoes.

The Japanese expenditure was:

1,020 × 8", 176 × 5.5" and 61 torpedoes.

Battle Honour:

HMAS Australia	*HMAS Canberra*	*HMAS Hobart*

SCANDINAVIAN CONVOYS 1917
17 October and 12 December
World War I 1914–18

British convoys to Scandinavia came under attack in late 1917. In one naval encounter in October in a position 60° 06' N 1° 06' E the two gunboats *Mary Rose* (1,025 tons) and *Strongbow* (900 tons) each mounting 3 × 4" guns fought two German gunboats.

The *Bremse* and *Brummer* were both 866 tons and each mounted a massive single 8.2" gun. Both the British ships were sunk in this unequal contest.

The second encounter came two months later on 12 December when four German destroyers, *G101*, *G103*, *G104* and *V100* attacked and sank *Partridge* (1,025 tons) and *Pellew* (1,025 tons), each mounting 3 × 4" guns, while escorting a Scandinavian convoy, in a position 59° 48' N 3° 53' E, off the Norwegian coast about 120 miles from Stavanger.

Battle Honour:

Mary Rose	*Partridge*	*Pellew*	*Strongbow*

'SCHARNHORST' ACTION – see NORTH CAPE 1943

SCHEVENINGEN (First Texel) 1653
31 July
First Dutch War 1652–54

This was the last naval battle of this war. An English fleet commanded by General-at-Sea George Monck (Robert Blake was recovering from wounds) fought a bitter battle with a Dutch fleet commanded by Marten Tromp.

Both fleets were at sea around the Texel, and both numbered about one hundred ships. Admiral De With, with about twenty-seven ships and ten fireships, was blockaded by Monck. The two main fleets sighted each other at about noon on 29 July. Tromp cleverly lured Monck from his blockading area. Monck's fleet chased Tromp's and his leading ships engaged the last in Tromp's line. Only about thirty ships altogether became engaged.

De With managed to slip out of harbour with his force and in a rising gale sped to join Tromp.

At about 7 am on the 31st the fleets came to close action off the tiny harbour of Scheveningen. The battle raged for six hours. Tromp was killed by a musket shot to the heart. Jan Evertsen assumed command.

After hours of desperately hard fighting, the English gained ascendancy and by 8 pm the Dutch were in full flight and the battle was over.

The English lost about 250 killed, including a vice-admiral, a rear-admiral and five captains. Another 700 men were wounded and two ships were lost.

The Dutch lost at least fourteen ships, though Monck claimed to have taken or destroyed twenty to thirty Dutch ships; they also lost eight captains and 1,300 prisoners. It was a disastrous outcome for the Dutch. their one crumb of comfort was the raising of the siege of the Hague.

Battle Honour:

Advantage	Andrew	Assurance	Crescent
Diamond	Dragon	Duchess	Exeter Merchant
Expedition	Foresight	Gift	Golden Cock
Hannibal	Hound	Hunter	James
John and Katherine		Laurel	London
Malaga Merchant	Mary Prize	Mayflower	Merlin
Norwich	Oak	Phoenix	Portland
Portsmouth	President	Prosperous	Rainbow
Raven	Recovery	Renown	Resolution
Seven Brothers	Sophia	Tiger	Triumph
Tulip	Vanguard	Victory	William
Worcester			

SCHOONEVELD 1673
28 May
Third Dutch War 1672–74

The Schooneveld is (or was) a long basin guarding the entrance to the Scheldt estuary. Two battles were fought here: the first between an Anglo-French fleet commanded by Prince Rupert, with Admiral

Sir Edward Spragge as second-in-command, and a Dutch fleet commanded by the redoubtable Dutch Admiral De Ruyter. The composition of these two fleets was as set out:

	ANGLO-FRENCH	NETHERLANDS
Ships of the line	54 British	52
	27 French	
Frigates	11	12
Fireships	35	25
Flags	Prince Rupert (van)	Tromp (van)
	d'Estrées (centre)	De Ruyter (centre)
	Spragge (rear)	Banckerts (rear)

After days of reconnoitring and manoeuvring Prince Rupert determined to attack De Ruyter's fleet on 28 May, but the Dutchman emerged from the shoals with a favourable wind to meet the Allied combined fleet approaching in line abreast. For nine hours a fierce battle ensued, in the course of which De Ruyter broke the French line but had to fall back to help the hard-pressed Banckerts. Tromp (junior) also got into difficulties with the English van and was obliged to transfer his flag three times during the day.

The fleets disengaged during the evening and anchored within sight of each other. It was largely an inconclusive battle. The French lost two ships during the day, while the Dutch *Deventer* (70) was so badly damaged that she foundered during the night. But strategically few would argue with the Dutch who claimed it as a victory.

<u>Battle Honour:</u>

Advice	*Anne*	*Assurance*	*Bonaventure*	*Cambridge*
Charles	*Constant Warwick*		*Crown*	*Diamond*
Dreadnought	*Dunkirk*	*Edgar*	*Falcon*	*Foresight*
French Ruby	*Gloucester*	*Greenwich*	*Hampshire*	
Happy Return	*Henrietta*	*Henry*	*Lion*	*London*
Mary	*Mary Rose*	*Monck*	*Newcastle*	*Old Hames*
Prince	*Princess*	*Providence*	*Rachel*	*Rainbow*
Resolution	*Revenge*	*Royal Charles*	*Royal Katherine*	*Ruby*
Rupert	*St Andrew*	*St George*	*St Michael*	
Samuel and Anne		*Sovereign*	*Stavoreen*	*Sweepstakes*

| *Swiftsure* | *Triumph* | *Truelove* | *Unicorn* | *Victory* |
| *Warspite* | *Welcome* | *York* | | |

SFAX 1941
15–16 April
World War II 1939–45

Captain (D) P.J. Mack commanded the 14th Destroyer Flotilla in the Mediterranean, comprising the *Jervis*, *Janus*, *Nubian* and *Mohawk*. The flotilla intercepted an Italian convoy off the Tunisian coast heading for Tripoli at about 2 am on 16 April 1941. It comprised five merchant ships with a close escort of one large and two small destroyers.

Fire was opened at about 2.20 am and within minutes there was a general mêlée and high-speed destroyer night action in which all enemy ships were hit, damaged, sinking or ablaze.

Then *Mohawk* took two torpedo hits. The second, under her bridge, sank her in seven fathoms, leaving her forepart out of the sea. After an hour's action *Jervis*'s log read: "One destroyer sunk. two destroyers, four merchantmen burning furiously. The fifth merchantman (ammunition ship) sunk. *Mohawk* sunk . . ."

In fact, all of the convoy and its escorts were annihilated. Mack returned to Malta in triumph.

<u>Battle Honour:</u>

| *Janus* | *Jervis* | *Nubian* | *Mohawk* |

SICILY 1943
10 July–17 August
World War II 1939–45

Operation Husky was the name given to the invasion of Sicily, the first major step from North Africa to the Italian mainland. It was a major operation during which 115,000 British troops and 66,000 American troops were landed, together with all their paraphernalia. The ships involved were as follows:

	BRITISH	US	OTHERS
Warships	199	68	12
Landing and coastal craft	1,260	811	3
Merchant and troop ships	155	66	16

Losses were not heavy. In the first three weeks of the short campaign they were:

German losses: 3 U-boats and 8 Italian submarines sunk.

British losses: 4 merchant ships and 2 LSTs sunk by U-boats.
2 merchant ships and 2 cruisers damaged.
13 ships sunk by air attack and many more damaged.

<u>Battle Honour:</u>

Abdiel	*Abercrombie*	*Acute*	*Albacore*	*Aldenham*
Alynbank	*Antwerp*	*Aphis*	*Arrow*	*Atherstone*
Aurora	*Banff*	*Bann*	*Beaufort*	*Belvoir*
Bergamot	*Blankney*	*Blencathra*	*Bluebell*	*Bonito*
Boston	*Boxer*	*Brecon*	*Brissendon*	*Brittany*
Brixham	*Brocklesby*	*Bruiser*	*Bryony*	*Bulolo*
Burra	*Cadmus*	*Calpe*	*Camellia*	*Carlisle*
Cava	*Cedardale*	*Cessnock*	*Chanticleer*	*Circe*
Clacton	*Clare*	*Cleopatra*	*Cleveland*	*Cockchafer*
Colombo	*Convolvulus*	*Coriolanus*	*Crane*	*Cromarty*
Cygnet	*Dart*	*Delhi*	*Delphinium*	*Derwentdale*
Dianella	*Dido*	*Dulverton*	*Easton*	*Echo*
Eclipse	*Eday*	*Eggesford*	*Emmerdale*	*Erebus*
Erne	*Eskimo*	*Espiègle*	*Euryalus*	*Exmoor*
Farndale	*Faulknor*	*Felixstowe*	*Fishguard*	*Fly*
Formidable	*Foxtrot*	*Fury*	*Gavotte*	*Gawler*
Geraldton	*Glengyle*	*Grayling*	*Guardian*	*Hambledon*
Haydon	*Hazard*	*Hebe*	*Hilary*	*Holcombe*
Honeysuckle	*Howe*	*Hursley*	*Hurworth*	*Hyacinth*
Hyderabad	*Hythe*	*Ilex*	*Inchmarnock*	*Inconstant*
Indomitable	*Inglefield*	*Intrepid*	*Ipswich*	*Isis*
Islay	*Jervis*	*Juliet*	*Jumna*	*Keren*
Kerrera	*King George V*		*King Sol*	*Laforey*

Lammerton	Largs	Lauderdale	Ledbury	Liddlesdale
Lismore	Lookout	Lotus	Loyal	Man-o-War
Maryborough	Mauritius	Mendip	Mullet	Mutine
Nelson	Newfoundland		Nubian	Oakley
Offa Orion	Osiris	Oxlip	Paladin	Panther
Parthian	Pathfinder	Pearleaf	Penelope	Penn
Penstemon	Petard	Pheasant	Pirouette	Plym
Polruan	Poole	Poppy	Primula	
Prince Charles		Prince Leopold		Prins Albert
Prinses Astrid	Prinses Beatrix		Prinses Josephine Charlotte	
Protea	Puckeridge	Quail	Quantock	
Queenborough		Queen Emma	Quilliam	Raider
Reighton Wyke		Rhododendron		Rhyl
Roberts	Rockwood	Rodney	Romeo	Romney
Rorqual	Rothesay	Royal Scotsman		
Royal Ulsterman		Rye	Safari	Saracen
Scarab	Seaham	Seraph	Shakespeare	Sharpshooter
Shiant	Shoreham	Sibyl	Simoon	Sirius
Southern Isle	Southern Sea	Sportsman	Starwort	Stella Carina
Stornoway	Stroma	Sutlej	Tactician	Tango
Tartar	Taurus	Templar	Test	Tetcott
Teviot	Thruster	Torbay	Trent	Trespasser
Tribune	Trident	Trooper	Troubridge	Tumult
Tynedale	Tyrian	Uganda	Ulster Monarch	Ulster Queen
Ultor	Unbroken	Unison	United	Universal
Unrivalled	Unruffled	Unruly	Unseen	Unshaken
Unsparing	Uproar	Usurper	Valiant	Venomous
Vetch	Viceroy	Visenda	Wallace	Wanderer
Warspite	Whaddon	Wheatland	Whinbrel	Whitehaven
Whiting	Wilton	Wishart	Wolborough	Woolongong
Woolston	Wrestler			

MLs: 125, 126, 565, 1158, 1252

MGBs: 641, 657, 659, 660

MTBs: 57, 62, 63, 75, 77, 81, 82, 84, 85, 260, 265, 288, 289, 290, 295, 313, 633, 640, 665, 670

FAA Squadrons: 807, 817, 820, 880, 885, 888, 893, 899

SIRTE 1942
22 March
World War II 1939–45

Rear Admiral Philip Vian fought a battle which Admiral Cunningham, C-in-C of the Mediterranean, described as "one of the most brilliant actions of the war". The Battle of Sirte was fought on 22 March 1942. Vian displayed his pugnacious and formidable skills in defending an important convoy of four merchant ships from Alexandria to Malta.

Vian was commanding a squadron of four light cruisers and ten destroyers, augmented by a cruiser and a destroyer from Malta. They were joined later by a 'Hunt' class destroyer of an A/S sweeping patrol.

The Italian Admiral Iachino commanded a battle force: he wore his flag in the battleship *Littorio* (35,000 tons) which mounted 9 × 15" and 12 x 6" guns. In company were cruisers and ten destroyers. Vian detached the four freighters with a small escort away from the battle area. Vian's force then made an effective smoke-screen through which it launched a series of determined torpedo attacks. The Italians showed a marked reluctance to face the torpedo attacks through the screen.

Iachino tried to outflank Vian's force and the smoke but after three hours of skirmishing the Italian commander called it a day.

The destroyers *Havock*, *Kingston* and *Lively* (1,340, 1,690 and 1,920 tons respectively) all took 15" shell hits yet survived.

Two of the four freighters were sunk by air attack later and the other two reached Malta safely, though both were bombed and sunk at their moorings.

Battle Honour:

(The Admiralty appears to have omitted the active presence of *Havock* in this battle.)

Avon Vale	*Beaufort*	*Breconshire*	*Carlisle*	*Cleopatra*
Dido	*Dulverton*	*Eridge*	*Euryalus*	*Hero*
Hurworth	*Jervis*	*Kelvin*	*Kingston*	*Legion*
Lively	*Penelope*	*Sikh*	*Southwold*	

SKAGERRAK – see JUTLAND 1916

SOLEBAY (Southwold Bay) 1672
28 May
Third Dutch War 1672–74

This battle was fought between a combined Anglo-French fleet and a huge Dutch fleet in the North Sea. The result was both a tactical and a strategic victory for the redoubtable Dutch Admiral De Ruyter, who frustrated a planned invasion of the Netherlands.

Solebay, off the coast of Suffolk, was then a large curved bay, ideal as a fleet anchorage. At the end of May 1672 James, Duke of York, with his flag in the *Princess Royal* (120), commanded a vast fleet of English and French warships – over seventy ships of the line, and more than this number of frigates, fireships, transports and smaller vessels. The Earl of Sandwich, commanding the rear, wore his flag in the *Royal James* (100), and Admiral D'Estrées aboard the *St Philippe* (78) commanded the van. This huge assembly of ships lay at anchor provisioning in Solebay.

The Dutch fleet under De Ruyter in his flagship *Zeven Provincien* (82) discovered the combined fleet and, running before the stiff north-easterly wind, bore down on the anchorage with his fleet and with fireships.

The English centre division cut cables and stood to the north – with difficulty in face of the wind. The Frenchman, D'Estrées, managed to get away and fled south-east. De Ruyter, the Dutch admiral, detached Banckerts with about twenty ships to contain him, evening the odds for the rest of the fleet. These two divisions, D'Estrées' and Banckerts', fought a battle of their own and took no further part in the main action.

The main Dutch fleet, De Ruyter in the centre, Van Ghent in the rear, included heroes of the Medway (see MEDWAY, pp. 272–3): Van Brakel who took the *Royal Charles*; Jan Van Rijn who broke the chain boom, 'Devil' Evertsen, and his cousin, Cornelis the Younger.

Sandwich and Van Ghent engaged first. Brakel in his *Groot Hollandia* (60) also found himself obliged to engage Sandwich's *Royal James* in a fierce duel. Van Ghent was killed, then, as if in retribution, Jan Van Rijn's fireships set the mighty *Royal James* ablaze and she had to be abandoned. Sandwich and his son-in-law, Sir Phillip Carteret, got away in a boat which became so overloaded with survivors that it overturned, everyone aboard being drowned. Sandwich's body was recovered later.

The Duke of York experienced much action too, compelling him to shift his flag three times during the day.

By the evening the Allied fleet was content to disengage and allow the Dutch divisions to withdraw to the Maas. The English losses were four ships and 2,500 men. The Dutch lost two ships, *Jozua* (60) and *Stavoren* (48), and another which blew up in the night. De Ruyter had disabled the English fleet for about a month, had wrested command in the Channel and thwarted an invasion of the Netherlands. Small reason the Dutch regard him as their Nelson.

Battle Honour:

Adventure	*Advice*	*Alice and Francis*		
Ann and Judith		*Anne*	*Antelope*	*Bantam*
Bonaventure	*Bristol*	*Cambridge*	*Charles*	*Crown*
Dartmouth	*Diamond*	*Dover*	*Dreadnought*	*Dunkirk*
Edgar	*Fairfax*	*Forester*	*Fountain*	*French Ruby*
Gloucester	*Greenwich*	*Henry*	*Katherine*	*Leopard*
London	*Mary*	*Mary Anne*	*Monck*	*Monmouth*
Montagu	*Old James*	*Phoenix*	*Plymouth*	*Prince*
Princess	*Rachel*	*Rainbow*	*Resolution*	*Robert*
Royal James	*Royal Katherine*		*Ruby*	*Rupert*
St Andrew	*St Michael*	*Sovereign*	*Success*	*Sweepstakes*
Thomas and Edward		*Tiger*	*Triumph*	*Unicorn*
Victory	*Warspite*	*Yarmouth*	*York*	

SOUTH AFRICA 1899–1900
Boer War 1899–1902

The 1st Boer War was fought between the British Army and the Boers of the Transvaal in 1880–81. Peace came after the Boers gained a victory at Majuba Hill in 1881. Britain accepted the independence of the South Africa Republic under British sovereignty. Paul Kruger became president.

Some years later, in 1886, gold was discovered on the Rand and Uitlanders swept in to the Transvaal. These foreigners, denied citizenship by Kruger, appealed to Britain. But strained relations, worsened since the abortive Jameson Raid in 1885, festered until 1899 when Kruger gave Britain an ultimatum to keep clear of South African borders. War began on 11 October.

British naval brigades played a significant part in the subsequent fighting, mainly as gunners, their guns usually being of a heavier calibre than the army's artillery. A brigade from *Powerful* saved the day for Ladysmith when two 4.7" guns arrived.

It was 31 May before peace was signed, by which time Britain had suffered nearly 6,000 killed and 23,000 wounded. The Boers lost nearly 4,000 men.

Campaign Honour:

Barossa	*Doris*	*Forte*	*Monarch*
Philomel	*Powerful*	*Tartar*	*Terrible*

SOUTH FRANCE 1944
15–27 August
World War II 1939–45

The invasion of southern France in June 1944 by the Allies was given the codename Operation Dragoon. The assault forces were given cover by five battleships: *Arkansas*, *Nevada*, *Texas*, *Ramilles* (29,150 tons, 8 × 15") and the Free French *Lorraine*, with more than a dozen cruisers and numerous destroyers. The force was under the command of Vice-Admiral Kent Hewitt USN.

Three American and two French army divisions made the landings on seven selected sites along a thirty-mile stretch of coast between Hyères and Cannes. The objectives were to secure bridgeheads, capture neighbouring ports, especially Marseilles, then, with a force of twenty-one divisions, to strike up the Rhône Valley, link up with Patton's 3rd Army and form the western flank of the force invading Germany.

Opposition all along the invasion front was slight.

Campaign Honour:

Ailsa Craig	*Ajax*	*Aldenham*	*Antares*
Antwerp	*Aphis*	*Arcturus*	*Argonaut*
Aries	*Atherstone*	*Attacker*	*Aubretia*
Aurora	*Bardolf*	*Barford*	*Barholm*
Barmond	*Beaufort*	*Belvoir*	*Bicester*
Black Prince	*Blackmore*	*Borealis*	*Brave*

Brecon	*Brixham*	*Bruiser*	*Bude*
Caledon	*Calm*	*Calpe*	*Catterick*
Cleveland	*Clinton*	*Colombo*	*Columbine*
Crowlin	*Delhi*	*Dido*	*Eastway*
Eggesford	*Emperor*	*Farndale*	*Foula*
Haydon	*Highway*	*Hunter*	*Keren*
Khedive	*Kintyre*	*Larne*	*Lauderdale*
Liddesdale	*Lookout*	*Mewstone*	*Nebb*
Oakley	*Octavia*	*Orion*	*Polruan*
Prince Baudouin	*Prince David*	*Prince Henry*	*Prins Albert*
Prinses Beatrix	*Product*	*Pursuer*	*Ramillies*
Rhyl	*Rinaldo*	*Rosario*	*Rothesay*
Royalist	*Satsa*	*Scarab*	*Searcher*
Sirius	*Skokolm*	*Spanker*	*Stalker*
Stormcloud	*Stornoway*	*Stuart Prince*	*Teazer*
Tenacious	*Termagant*	*Terpsichore*	*Thruster*
Troubridge	*Tumult*	*Tuscan*	*Tyrian*
Ulster Queen	*Welfare*	*Whaddon*	*Zetland*

FAA Squadrons: 800, 807, 809, 879, 881, 882, 899

MLs: 273, 299, 336, 337, 338, 451, 456, 458, 461, 462, 463, 469, 471, 555, 556, 557, 559, 560, 562, 563, 564, 567, 576, 581

BYMSs: 2009, 2022, 2026, 2027, 2171, 2172

SOUTHWOLD BAY – see SOLEBAY 1672

SPADA 1940
19 July
World War II 1939–45
An engagement between the 6" gun cruiser HMAS *Sydney* (Captain J.A. Collins) with the 1,340 tons, 4 × 4.7" destroyers *Hasty*, *Havock*, *Hero* and *Hyperion* and the *Ilex* (1,370 tons) and the two Italian cruisers *Bartolomeo Colleoni* and the *Giovanni delle Bande Nere*, both of 5,069 tons and 8 × 6" guns.

In a spirited action off Cape Spada on the north coast of Crete, the 6,830 tons *Sydney* (8 × 6") sank the *Bartolomeo Colleoni*. The other cruiser was damaged but managed to escape destruction and reached Benghazi in safety.

<u>Battle Honour:</u>

Hasty	*Havock*	*Hero*	*Hyperion*
Ilex	*Sydney*		

SPANISH ARMADA – see ARMADA 1588

SPARTIVENTO 1940
27 November
World War II 1939–45

Admiral Sir James Somerville, commanding Force H in the Mediterranean, was entrusted with the passage of a convoy of three important merchant ships carrying tanks and other mechanical transport to the Middle East. With his flag in *Renown* (32,000 tons, 6 × 15") he had in company *Ark Royal* (22,000 tons, 36 aircraft), two cruisers and nine destroyers. Four corvettes gave close escort to the merchantmen.

Off Cape Spartivento an Italian squadron commanded by Admiral Campioni was encountered. It comprised the two battleships *Vittorio Veneto* (35,000 tons, 9 × 15") and *Guilio Cesare* (23,622 tons, 10 × 12.6"), seven heavy cruisers and sixteen destroyers.

An hour's engagement in which the heavy cruiser *Berwick* (9,750 tons, 8 × 8") and the Italian destroyer *Lanciere* (1,620 tons, 4 × 4.7") were damaged proved inconclusive on both sides and Campioni broke away. Because Somerville failed to pursue, a Board of Enquiry arrived in Gibraltar even before Somerville had returned to port to question the correctness of putting the safety of the convoy as the prime consideration. Cunningham, C-in-C of the Mediterranean Fleet, objected at this iniquitous action by the Admiralty. The Board's finding was totally in favour of Somerville.

<u>Battle Honour:</u>

Ark Royal	*Berwick*	*Coventry*	*Defender*	*Despatch*
Diamond	*Duncan*	*Encounter*	*Faulknor*	*Firedrake*

Forester	Fury	Gallant	Gloxinia	Greyhound
Hereward	Hotspur	Hyacinth	Jaguar	Kelvin
Manchester	Newcastle	Peony	Ramillies	Renown
Salvia	Sheffield	Southampton	Vidette	Wishart

FAA Squadrons: 700, 800, 808, 810, 818, 820

STRACHAN'S ACTION – see BAY OF BISCAY 1805

SUEZ CANAL 1915
2–4 February
World War I 1914–18
A Turkish attack on the Suez Canal was launched in February 1915.
It was strongly repulsed by British troops, assisted by naval units of
the Royal Navy and some small French ships.
Battle Honour:

Clio	Dufferin	Hardinge	Himalaya	Minerva
Ocean	Proserpine	Swiftsure	TB 043	

Armed Tugs:

Fanny	Lübeck	Mainstay	Mansoura	Prompt
Virginia				

SUNDA STRAIT 1942
28 February–1 March
World War II 1939–45
The surviving allied warships of the Battle of the Java Sea (see JAVA
SEA p. 267) all perished in a series of actions within a day or two
of the Java Sea battle.

The heavy cruiser USS *Houston* (9,050 tons, 9 × 8"), but with
one turret out of action, and HMAS *Perth* (6,830 tons, 8 × 6") sailed
from Batavia and endeavoured to clear the zone via the Sunda Strait
to the west of Java, but the area was swarming with Japanese
warships and the two cruisers were overwhelmed by a Japanese
squadron of Admiral Kurita's heavy cruisers, both ships being sunk
with heavy losses of men.

The damaged cruiser *Exeter* (8,390 tons, 6 × 8"), the destroyer *Encounter* (1,375 tons, 4 × 4.7") and the old USS *Pope* (1,190 tons, 4 × 4") left Sourabaya to try to escape, but were all overwhelmed by dive bombers and sunk with heavy loss of life. The defeat of the fragmented Allied forces in the Java Sea area was complete. The island of Java fell to the Japanese. It was an irony of the confused times that the two allied cruisers had inadvertently blundered into the Japanese invasion forces.

Battle Honour: HMAS *Perth*

SYRIA 1840
4 November
War Between Egypt and Turkey 1840

In 1837 the C-in-C Mediterranean was Admiral Sir Robert Stopford and he was still there in 1840 when war broke out between Egypt and Turkey. Matters deteriorated when the British government and the French took sides, the latter supporting the rebellious Mehemet Ali.

In August/September 1840 Sir Robert Stopford was reinforced by Commodore Charles Napier in *Princess Charlotte* with a small squadron; in addition there was support from Austrian and Turkish forces. The operations against Mehemet Ali were carried out "with celerity and vigour". Sidon and Beirut were occupied on 3 November, and Acre was reduced after a few hours' bombardment. Mehemet Ali evacuated Syria, France proved more amenable and the British officers were richly rewarded and honoured.

Battle Honour:

Asia	*Bellerophon*	*Benbow*	*Cambridge*
Carysfoot	*Castor*	*Cyclops*	*Daphne*
Dido	*Edinburgh*	*Ganges*	*Gorgon*
Hastings	*Hazard*	*Hydra*	*Implacable*
Magicienne	*Phoenix*	*Pique*	*Powerful*
Princess Charlotte		*Revenge*	*Rodney*
Stromboli	*Talbot*	*Thunderer*	*Vanguard*
Vesuvius	*Wasp*	*Zebra*	

There was some dispute about *Hecate*: she was denied the award.

T

TAMATAVE 1811
20 May
Napoleonic War 1803–15
This was a dashing frigate action between three 40-gun French frigates commanded by Commodore Roquebert, and three 36-gun frigates and a sloop commanded by Captain Charles Schomberg.

Schomberg's squadron comprised the *Astraea, Phoebe, Galatea* and the sloop *Racehorse*. Roquebert's ships were the *Renommée, Clorinde* and *Néreide*.

They clashed off Foul Point, north of Tamatave in Madagascar. The *Galatea* suffered serious damage, but when Roquebert was killed the *Renommée* struck. The *Néreide* escaped into Tamatave, then surrendered a few days later. The *Clorinde* got clear away and managed to reach Brest safely.

Battle Honour:

Astraea	*Galatea*	*Phoebe*	*Racehorse*

TARANTO 1940
11 November
World War II 1939–45
The Fleet Air Arm executed an attack on the Italian battle fleet in an action which helped in one night to redress the balance of naval power in the Mediterranean. The action was fought between aircraft of the Royal Navy carriers *Illustrious* (23,000 tons, 36 aircraft) and *Eagle* (36,800 tons, 100 aircraft) of the Mediterranean Fleet under Admiral Sir Andrew Cunnunghan and the Italian battle fleet at anchor in Taranto harbour.

Air reconnaissance over Taranto showed five of the six Italian battleships in commission lying at anchor. Cunningham resolved on an immediate strike. The *Eagle* herself was not available for the attack, so *Illustrious* was the lone carrier employed, her aircraft augmented by some from *Eagle*.

Twenty-one aircraft flew off from a position 180 miles south-east of Taranto starting at 8.40 pm, the first arriving over the target area two hours later. Complete surprise was achieved.

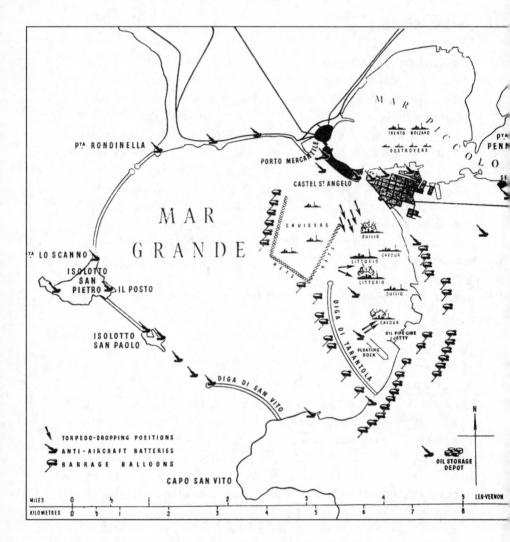

The Italian view of the Taranto strike.

Aircraft from Squadrons *813* and *824* (from *Eagle*) and *815* and *819* (from *Illustrious*) armed with torpedoes and bombs carried out Operation Judgement with great determination. Three battleships were sunk at their moorings, though all were subsequently salvaged: the new *Littorio* (35,000 tons) and the older *Conte de Cavour* (28,700 tons) and *Caio Duilio* (28,700 tons). Two aircraft were lost.

It was at such small cost that this successful operation re-established British command of the Mediterranean.

Battle Honour: *Illustrious*
FAA Squadrons: *813, 815, 819, 824*

TERNATE 1810
29 August
Napoleonic War 1803–15

Ternate lies in the Moluccas. It was captured by the British in 1810 with detachments of the Madras European Regiment and Madras Coastal Artillery, all of them under the command of Captain Tucker RN aboard *Dover*.

The fall of Amboina was speedily followed by the bloodless acquisitions of the neighbouring Dutch islands of Harouka, Naso-Laut, Bouru, Manipa and Saparov, and by the acceptance by the Sultan of Gorontale, in the Celebes, of British instead of Dutch suzereinty.

Captain Tucker proceeded later to Menado, another important post in the Celebes, and received its surrender, together with that of several dependent posts. At the end of August Tucker reduced Ternate after some sharp fighting.

Battle Honour: *Dover*

TEXEL 1673
11 August
Third Dutch War 1672–74

The Texel was the scene of the last battle of the Third Dutch War with the same adversaries: Prince Rupert, Admiral De Ruyter, the Frenchman D'Estrées, Banckerts, Sir Edward Spragge, Tromp –

they had all fought each other a couple of times earlier that summer of 1673. Once again the brilliant De Ruyter thwarted an Anglo-French invasion of the Netherlands.

The Allied fleet was commanded by Prince Rupert. It numbered ninety-two ships (the numbers are difficult to establish with certainty), plus thirty fireships. De Ruyter marshalled a fleet of about seventy-five ships of the line and frigates, plus about thirty fireships.

On the Allied side Prince Rupert commanded the centre, D'Estrées the van and Spragge the rear division.

On the Dutch side, De Ruyter commanded the centre, Banckerts the van and Tromp the rear.

Action was joined on 11 August when De Ruyter, having the weather gage, attacked the superior Allied force. The whole of D'Estrées's van division was separated from the main fleet by Banckerts' van and thrown into confusion, so that it gave no support to the English.

Thus the brunt of De Ruyter's attack fell upon the English centre and rear divisions; both suffered hours of fierce fighting and dreadful damage.

Spragge and Tromp had a desperate duel. Each shifted his flag three times during the day. Sadly, Spragge was drowned when the boat in which he was transferring took a shot and sank.

Eventually the two exhausted fleets drew apart, the English abandoning the attempt to land troops, and licking serious wounds. No ships had been lost but the damage suffered was enormous and the loss in men about 2,000.

De Ruyter's fleet also suffered serious damage, but no ships were lost and his casualties were about half the English.

Prince Rupert was quick to give as the reason for defeat the lack of French participation, but the real reason was the brilliance of De Ruyter's tactics and his skilful handling of huge fleets in action.

Battle Honour:

Advice	Anne	Assurance	Blessing
Bonaventure	Bristol	Cambridge	Charles
Crown	Diamond	Dolphin	Dreadnought
Dunkirk	Edgar	Fairfax	Falcon
Foresight	French Ruby	Friendship	Gloucester

Guernsey	Hampshire	Happy Return	Hard Bargain
Henrietta	Henry	Katherine	Leopard
Lion	Lizard	London	Mary
Mary Anne	Monck	Monmouth	Newcastle
Nonsuch (?)	Old James	Pearl	Plymouth
Portland	Portsmouth	Prince	Princess
Prudent Mary	Rainbow	Resolution	Roe
Rose	Royal Charles	Royal Katherine	Ruby
Rupert	St Andrew	St George	St Michael
Society	Sovereign	Stavoreen	Success
Supply	Swallow	Sweepstakes	Swiftsure
Triumph	Truelove	Unicorn	Victory
Warspite	Yarmouth	York	

THE SAINTS (The Saintes) 1782
12 April
American War of Independence 1775–83

This great naval battle was fought between a British fleet under Admiral Sir George Rodney, commanding thirty-six of the line, and a French fleet under the command of Vice-Admiral the Comte de Grasse comprising thirty-two ships of the line. The battle settled once and for all the naval dominance of the West Indies. It also added a chapter to the tactics of naval warfare in *Fighting Instructions* by introducing the tactic of breaking the line of battle, sailing through the gap in the line, carronading the enemy as the ship passed through the gap in the line, and even forcing the enemy to engage on both sides of his ship. The traditional and stereotyped line of battle, with both sides' line passing along the other and engaging ships as they came within range of shot, had hitherto been sacrosanct.

A curtain-raiser to the battle was an encounter four days before the Saints battle when de Grasse missed a fine opportunity at Dominica (see DOMINICA) to destroy Admiral Hood's van division of Rodney's fleet. Now he found himself lacking the superiority he had enjoyed in the earlier encounter. A long three-day pursuit of Rodney followed.

On 12 April at about 7 am the French fleet, with de Grasse in

Ville de Paris (104), hampered by a large convoy in its charge, was brought to action near a small group of islands in the channel between Guadeloupe and Dominica. The islands are The Saints or Saintes. The opposing lines of battle passed each other slowly on opposite courses, exchanging broadsides.

At 9.15 am the wind veered suddenly four points, the French line grew ragged in the lee of Dominica and developed gaps in the line. Rodney in *Formidable* (90), then the *Duke* (90) and the *Bedford* (74), snatched the opportunity to sail through the breaks in the French line. At the rear of the fleet second-in-command Admiral Sir Samuel Hood followed suit, with all twelve of his division following the *Bedford*. The British thus gained the weather gage and the French tried desperately hard to reform their line on their leeward-most ships. But they lost the 74s *Glorieux*, *César* and *Hector*, all of which struck their colours. By late afternoon *Ardent* had also been taken and the French flagship was surrounded.

Just before 6.30 pm the *Ville de Paris* struck; no less than 400 men aboard her were killed. Hood in *Barfleur* (90) accepted the surrender.

De Vendreuil took command of the remainder of the French fleet and, establishing some sense of order, led the fleet away. Rodney pursued, but a little half-heartedly, and then gave up the chase, allowing Hood the criticism that many more ships could have been taken if the pursuit had been more vigorous. Indeed, most of Rodney's officers considered that he had "botched his battle".

Captain Cornwallis later wrote: "I could think of nothing for a week . . . but what could be the motive of his forbearance, having such an opportunity thrown in his way, not to take advantage of it."

Nevertheless it was a substantial victory for Rodney. The French losses amounted to five ships and over 2,000 men killed and wounded, and many more taken prisoner. The British lost no ships and their casualties amounted to just over 1,000 men.

Battle Honour:

Agamemnon	Ajax	Alarm	Alcide
Alecto	Alert	Alfred	America
Andromache	Anson	Arrogant	Barfleur
Bedford	Belliqueux	Canada	Centaur

Champion	Conqueror	Duke	Endymion
Eurydice	Fame	Flora	Formidable
Hercules	Magnificent	Marlborough	Monarch
Montagu	Namur	Nonsuch	Prince George
Prince William	Prothée	Repulse	Resolution
Royal Oak	Russell	St Albans	Torbay
Triton	Warrior	Yarmouth	Zebra

THREE DAYS' BATTLE – see PORTLAND 1653

TRAFALGAR 1805
21 October
Napoleonic War 1803–15
The Trafalgar campaign started more than seven months before the famous sea battle which was fought on 21 October off Cape Trafalgar on the south-west coast of Spain. Apart from Admiral Codrington's battle at Navarino Bay in 1827, it was the last major fleet encounter of the days of sail.

The victory of the British Fleet at Trafalgar, and the defeat of the combined French and Spanish fleet, effectively put an end to the hopes of Napoleon's invasion of Britain by his Grand Army. It gave to Britain naval dominance in the Channel, the Atlantic ports and the Mediterranean for the remaining ten years of the Napoleonic War. Thus, Trafalgar had far-reaching consequences both in the short term and the long term.

The actual battle came about as the result of a complex French plan to keep the Channel clear to allow passage of Napoleon's invasion by his Grand Army. To ensure this it was necessary to secure the Straits of Dover and the Western approaches to the Channel by defeating Admiral William Cornwallis's watching fleet.

To accomplish this the Comte de Villeneuve broke Nelson's blockade of Toulon, then intended to release squadrons from blockaded Cadiz and Cartagena, though in the event he only picked up a few Spanish ships in Cadiz. Then he made haste to the West Indies to collect more warships before hastening back to European waters. Off Finisterre he was engaged by Sir Robert Calder (see CALDER'S ACTION p. 247), then made sail for Cadiz, where Collingwood blockaded him.

Nelson had followed Villeneuve to the West Indies and back, and by the end of September 1805 was with his fleet off Spain. He had a battle plan which enthused his captains. He made no secret of the plan, and when Villeneuve eventually left Cadiz to head south Nelson's fleet was ready for the encounter.

Nelson's fleet consisted of twenty-seven of the line. Villeneuve had thirty-three, with his flag in the *Bucentaure* (80). Commanding the Spanish (rear) division was Admiral Gravina, while the French van was commanded by Admiral Dumanoir. As soon as the enemy fleet was sighted Nelson implemented his plan of attacking the Franco-Spanish line in two columns with the intention of breaking the enemy line in two places.

"The whole impression of the British fleet," Nelson had written, "must be to overpower from two or three ships ahead of their C-in-C (supposed to be in the centre) to the rear of the fleet."

The *Victory* (100) and the rest of his division would hold the enemy centre and the flagship in battle while Collingwood would engage the enemy rear, giving Nelson the advantage of powerful strength at the enemy's centre and rear. The enemy van would thus be prevented from aiding the centre. True, the leading ships of the British columns would be subjected to the full force of the enemy broadsides during the hazardous approach and for that reason the toughest ships would lead each column: Nelson in *Victory* with *Temeraire* and *Neptune*, while Collingwood would lead the other column in *Royal Sovereign*. Collingwood had fifteen ships in his rear, or lee, division. Nelson had twelve in his van, or weather, column.

Three minutes before midday Collingwood came under fire and remained so for ten minutes without support. But soon the enemy line was pierced, and once Nelson could bring his broadsides to bear the effect was devastating.

In the next four hours the battle continued furiously: at one time no less than twenty of the enemy ships had struck or been taken in prize. The massive four-decker *Santissima Trinidad* (136) was taken and Gravina mortally wounded aboard the *Asturias*. Villeneuve

SHIPS ENGAGED AND BATTLE HONOURS

BRITISH WEATHER DIVISION

Victory	(100)	Vice-Admiral
		Nelson
Temeraire	(98)	
Neptune	(98)	
Conqueror	(74)	
Leviathan	(74)	
Britannia	(100)	
Agamemnon	(64)	
Ajax	(74)	
Orion	(74)	
Minotaur	(74)	
Spartiate	(74)	
Africa	(64)	

BRITISH LEE DIVISION

Royal		Vice-Admiral
Sovereign	(100)	Collingwood
Belleisle	(74)	
Mars	(74)	
Tonnant	(80)	
Bellerophon	(74)	
Colossus	(74)	
Achilles	(74)	
Polyphemus	(64)	
Revenge	(74)	
Swiftsure	(74)	
Defiance	(74)	
Thunderer	(74)	
Defence	(74)	
Dreadnought	(98)	
Prince	(98)	

Battle Honour also awarded to:

Euryalis
Entreprenant
Naiad
Phoebe
Pickle
Sirius

FRANCO-SPANISH FLEETS

FRANCE

Bucentaure	(80)	Vice-Admiral
Redoutable	(74)	Villeneuve
Indomptable	(80)	
Neptune	(80)	
Fougueux	(74)	
Pluton	(74)	
Intrépide	(74)	
Algéciras	(74)	Rear-Admiral
Berwick	(74)	Magon
Aigle	(74)	
Swiftsure	(74)	
Argonaute	(74)	
Achille	(74)	
Scipion	(74)	
Formidable	(80)	Rear Admiral
		Dumanoir
Mont Blanc	(74)	
Duguay		
Trouin	(74)	
Héros	(74)	

SPAIN

Principe de		Admiral
Asturias	(112)	Gravina
Montanes	(74)	
Argonauta	(80)	
Bahama	(74)	
San Juan		
Nepomuceno	(74)	
San Ildefonso	(74)	
San Justo	(74)	
Santissima		Rear Admiral
Trinidad	(136)	de Cisneros
San Leandro	(64)	
Santa Ana	(112)	Vice Admiral
		de Alavo
Monarco	(74)	
Neptuno	(74)	
San Agustin	(74)	
Rayo	(100)	
San Francisco		
de Asis	(74)	

himself was captured when his flagship *Bucentaure* struck.

But early in the action, at about 1.15 pm, *Redoubtable* grappled with *Victory* and a marksman in her rigging shot Nelson as he was pacing the quarterdeck with his flag captain, Hardy. He was taken below, where he lived for a few hours.

The *Temeraire* (98), commanded by Captain Sir Eliab Harvey, came to *Victory*'s assistance and captured *Redoubtable* (74). *Neptune* (74) and *San Augustino* (74) both struck, and later in the afternoon the burning French *Achille* blew up and sank.

By 4.30 Nelson knew that he had won a great victory and died. The Franco-Spanish fleet lost eighteen ships, seventeen of which were in British hands. Only four finally reached Gibraltar, the remainder being run ashore, sunk or re-captured; they suffered 2,600 dead and wounded and 7,000 prisoners on prizes. No British ships were lost, but half were severely damaged, and 1,700 men were killed or wounded. Five of the damaged ships failed to survive the night storm which deprived Britain of several of its prizes.

The battle's outcome gave Britain undisputed mastery at sea. (See BAY OF BISCAY 1805, p. 46, for a Trafalgar postscript.)

TRINCOMALEE 1782
3 September
American War of Independence 1775–83
This was the fourth action between Vice-Admiral Sir Edward Hughes and Admiral Pierre Suffren in their series of battles in the East Indies. It took place off Ceylon's (Sri Lanka's) eastern anchorage of Trincomalee.

When Hughes arrived off Trincomalee with twelve of the line on 2 September 1782 it was to find that Suffren had already captured the base, one of the world's largest and attractive natural harbours. Suffren, ever ready for action, weighed anchor and set sail with fourteen of the line and battle was joined 25 miles south-east of Trincomalee. In the ensuing three-hour battle, during which Suffren failed to receive the support from some of his captains, his flagship *Héros* (74) lost her mainmast and the *Illustre* (74) and *Ajax* (74) were both severely damaged. Later *L'Orient* (74) grounded on a reef and was totally wrecked.

Despite Hughes's success in the action, it was Suffren who returned to Trincomalee and Hughes who had to retire north to Madras.

Battle Honour:

Burford	Eagle	Exeter	Hero	Isis
Magnanime	Monarch	Monmouth	Sceptre	Sultan
Superb	Worcester			

Frigates:

Active	Combustion	Coventry	Medea
San Carlos	Seahorse		

U

USHANT 1747 (Second Battle of Finisterre)
14 October
War of the Austrian Succession 1739–48
Rear-Admiral Sir Edward Hawke's Western Squadron endured eight weeks of fruitless and exhaustive patrolling between Ushant and Finisterre hoping to intercept a French convoy known to be assembling for the West Indies. Patience was rewarded at 7 am on 14 October when a massive 242-ship convoy came into sight escorted by a squadron of warships which he outnumbered by about two to one.

The French Commodore, the Marquis de l'Étenduère, commanded eight ships of the line and the Indiaman *Content* (64) which he despatched with frigates to shepherd the dispersing convoy. Although fewer in numbers (eight to fourteen) the French ships were more powerfully armed. At 10 am Hawke made the signal for line of battle but an hour later changed it to general chase and at 11.30 the leading British ships were in action.

The French Admiral fought his ships courageously in a nine-hour running battle, enabling the whole of the convoy to escape. But the price he paid for the convoy's safety was high. By nightfall only his flagship, the 80-gun *Tonnant*, and *Intrépide* (74), both badly damaged, escaped the ferocious British attacks, and limped into Brest. The other six were all taken by the British.

Hawke despatched *Weazle* (14) to the West Indies to warn Commodore George Pocock of the convoy's approach. Subsequently thirty-eight of the convoy were captured.

Battle Honour:

Kent	(64)	Captain Thomas Fox
Eagle	(60)	George Rodney
Defiance	(60)	John Benley

Portland	(50)	Charles Steevens
Nottingham	(60)	Philip Saumarez
Edinburgh	(64)	Thomas Cotes
Devonshire	(66)	Adml Edward Hawke
		Capt John Moore
Yarmouth	(64)	Charles Saunders
Windsor	(60)	Thomas Hanway
Gloucester	(50)	Philip Durell
Tilbury	(60)	Robert Harland
Lyon	(60)	Arthur Scott
Monmouth	(64)	Henry Harrison
Princess Louisa	(60)	Charles Weston
Weazle	(14)	No name

Note: Captain Philip Saumarez was killed on the day of the battle. Apart from himself, Hanway and Scott, all the British captains attained flag rank, an indication of the quality of fighting commanding officers available at that time.

USHANT 1781
12 December
American War of Independence 1775–83

This battle took place about 150 miles west of Ushant. Rear-Admiral Kempenfelt, with twelve of the line from the Channel Fleet, intercepted a large and valuable French convoy from Brest to the West Indies, escorted by nineteen of the line commanded by Admiral de Guichen. Undeterred, Kempenfelt ordered his squadron to chase the enemy. He noticed that de Guichen stationed himself far from the convoy. Kempenfelt took advantage of this and skilfully positioned his squadron between de Guichen and the convoy. He cut out no fewer than fifteen of the French merchantmen and got clean away without loss.

Battle Honour:

Agamemnon	Alexander	Arethusa	Britannia	Courageux
Duke	Edgar	Medway	Monsieur	Ocean
Prudente	Queen	Renown	Tartar	Tisiphene
Valiant	Victory			

V

VELEZ MALAGA 1704
13 August
War of the Spanish Succession 1702–13

This was a grand battle fought between an Anglo-Dutch fleet of fifty-three ships of the line and a Franco-Spanish fleet of fifty of the line plus about twenty-four galleys, though little use was made of these.

Admiral Sir George Rooke commanded the Anglo-Dutch fleet, with Admiral Cloudesley Shovel leading the van and the Dutch Admiral Callenburgh the rear squadron.

The Allies had captured Gibraltar only the previous month. The French Admiral Comte de Toulouse sailed from Toulon with the purpose of gaining a naval victory and recapturing Gibraltar.

Battle was joined about 25 miles south-east of Marbella on 13 August and it developed into a long day's artillery duel with no ships being taken, burnt or sunk except a French frigate and two Spanish galleys, but casualties were heavy. The British lost 695 killed and 1663 wounded. The Dutch had 400 casualties. In the Franco-Spanish fleet 1,500 were killed and 3,000 wounded.

The following day Toulouse made no attempt to renew the battle and Rooke was content to return to Gibraltar for extensive repairs.

Despite being a drawn battle, the engagement left Britain and the Netherlands with the ascendancy, for the Allied superiority at sea was not seriously challenged again for the rest of the war, which ran for another nine years. The retention of Gibraltar as a base helped Britain dominate and command the western basin of the Mediterranean.

Battle Honour:

Assurance	*Barfleur*	*Bedford*	*Berwick*
Boyne	*Burford*	*Cambridge*	*Centurion*

Charles Galley	Dorsetshire	Eagle	Essex
Firebrand	Firme	Garland	Grafton
Griffin	Hare	Hunter	Jefferies
Kent	Kingston	Lark	Lenox
Lightning	Monck	Monmouth	Montagu
Namur	Nassau	Newark	Newport
Norfolk	Nottingham	Orford	Panther
Phoenix	Prince George	Princess Anne	Ranelagh
Roebuck	Royal Katherine	Royal Oak	St George
Shrewsbury	Somerset	Suffolk	Swallow
Swiftsure	Tartar	Terror	Tilbury
Torbay	Triton	Vulcan	Vulture
Warspite	William and Mary		Yarmouth

VIETNAM 1964–73

The Vietnam War 1964–73

Dates for the Vietnam War are not easy to assign. For example, in 1964 American aircraft first bombed North Vietnam, and although 1973 is often regarded as the ending of the war it was not until 1975 that the fall of Saigon took place.

On 2 August 1964 a minor naval incident precipitated a bloody and long-drawn-out war, hedged about with political as well as military overtones. The US destroyer *Maddox* was attacked by North Vietnamese MTBs *in error* in what became known as the Gulf of Tonkin Incident. It gave rise to retaliatory attacks by aircraft from the US carrier *Ticonderoga* resulting in a ten-year war of increasing severity and bitterness. It was this war that saw the introduction of surface-to-air missiles and the use for the first time of hovercraft on the extensive Vietnamese inland waterways.

British ships – all four Australian – came under the operational command of the US Seventh Fleet. The fleet gave considerable support with coastal fire, aircraft strikes and naval blockade over the years. The war of attrition ended with the signing of an armistice in 1973.

<u>Campaign Honour:</u>

Brisbane	Hobart	Perth	Vendetta

<u>FAA Squadron:</u> 723

VIGO 1702
12 October
War of the Spanish Succession 1702–13

Admiral Sir George Rooke, returning from an abortive raid on Cadiz, undertook an attack upon a Spanish treasure fleet with its escorting French naval squadron of thirteen ships of the line commanded by Admiral Châteaurenault.

The treasure ships lay protectively behind a harbour boom with fortified batteries guarding the approaches to Vigo in Spain. Vigo Bay is one of the finest naval anchorages of Europe. It has attracted many marauders throughout history – it was twice attacked by Sir Francis Drake – but the most wounding action was in 1702 when the combined Anglo-Dutch fleet which Rooke commanded assaulted the shipping in its bay.

Rooke's force totalled twenty-five Anglo-Dutch ships of the line. Vice-Admiral Hopsonn commanded *Torbay* (80) and it was she who broke through the boom and opened the way for his squadron to enter the harbour. The Dutch Admiral Van der Goes in the 90-gun *Zeven Provincien* landed troops to secure and silence the gun batteries ashore.

In a fierce and furious battle the French squadron was savaged. Châteaurenault ordered his ships to be burnt rather than be seized and taken as prizes, but even so the French losses were enormous: ten of the line were captured or destroyed, and about eleven treasure ships were taken as rich prizes. (It is only fair to report that figures vary in almost every account of the battle.) It is reported that every ship in harbour was sunk, burnt or destroyed. Treasure to the value of £1 million was captured.

The Allied losses in ships were nil and casualties are described as light.

Battle Honour:

Association	Barfleur	Bedford	Berwick	Cambridge
Essex	Grafton	Griffin	Hawk	Hunter
Kent	Lightning	Mary	Monmouth	
Northumberland		Oxford	Pembroke	Phoenix
Ranelagh	Royal Sovereign		Somerset	Swiftsure
Terrible	Torbay	Vulture		

W

WALCHEREN 1944
1 November
World War II 1939–45

Operation Infatuate was launched in an effort to capture Walcheren Island (heavily fortified by the Germans) in order to open up the Scheldt and the port of Antwerp (necessary for logistics), thus giving support to the Allied armies advancing into Flanders.

When the bombers of the strike force became fog-bound and unable to soften up the considerable German defences the naval support vessels sailed close inshore attracting the barrage of German gunfire. Nine vessels were sunk and 372 men killed. The Royal Marine Commandos stormed the shore in the face of strong opposition. Even the Supreme Commander, Eisenhower, observed: "Credit for the success of the amphibious operation is largely due to the support craft of the British Navy."

180 landing craft carried the Marines and troops ashore, supported by the monitors *Erebus* (7,200 tons, 2 × 15") and *Roberts* (7,970 tons, 2 × 15"). *Kingsmill* and the 15" guns of the battleship *Warspite* added to the support.

<u>Battle Honour:</u>

Erebus	*Kingsmill*	*Roberts*	*Warspite*
ML146	*ML902*		

In addition there were about 180 landing craft of various classes.

WARREN'S ACTION – see DONEGAL 1798

Z

ZEEBRUGGE 1918
23 April
World War I 1914–18

Zeebrugge and Ostend were two strategically and logistically important ports in Belgium, vital, too, for the sustenance and movement of German U-boats. Vice-Admiral Roger Keyes (later Admiral of the Fleet Lord Keyes of Zeebrugge and Dover) led an assault on these two harbours.

The two-fold plan was to deny the Germans the use of the advanced base at Bruges and of the harbour refuge at Ostend. This would have the effect of immobilizing forty or fifty U-boats refitting in these waters.

These aims would be achieved by sinking blockships at Bruges, Zeebrugge and Ostend, and by simultaneously assaulting the mole at Zeebrugge.

No fewer than 140 HM ships of all classifications were used in the operation, with another twenty-three ships of Tyrwhitt's destroyer force from Harwich giving distant support.

Central to the plan was placing the old cruiser *Vindictive* (5,750 tons) alongside the mole at Zeebrugge. The cruiser secured alongside and the marines aboard her stormed ashore. Captain A.F.B. Carpenter commanded. Roger Keyes wore his flag in the destroyer *Warwick*.

The mole was a daunting objective. It was a vast construction of concrete blocks paved over with granite; it was nearly 1½ miles long and 80 yards wide, carrying a motley collection of warehouses, a railway station, a lighthouse and gun emplacements for 4" and 5.9" batteries; it carried barbed wire entanglements, a considerable number of machine-gun emplacements and AA guns, and 1,000 troops manned the mole. Alongside the inner mole there were secured some destroyers and smaller craft.

Three British minelayers, filled with concrete, were sunk. *Vindictive* inched alongside under fierce fire and was held in position by the Mersey ferries *Iris II* and *Daffodil*. Both added *Royal* to their names at the command of King George V.

So much gallantry was displayed this day that eight VCs were awarded.

Two British submarines, *C 1* and *C 3*, were sacrificed to prevent German reinforcements reaching the mole.

At Ostend the operation fared less well. The blockships were sunk prematurely.

Vindictive sailed again despite her serious damage, as another blockship for Ostend, where a second attack took place on 10 May 1918. Her bows are still there preserved as a war memorial.

Battle Honour:

Attentive	*Daffodil*	*Erebus*	*Intrepid*	*Iphigenia*
Iris II	*Lingfield*	*Manly*	*Mansfield*	*Melpomeme*
Moorsom	*Morris*	*Myngs*	*North Star*	*Phoebe*
Scott	*Stork*	*Teazer*	*Termagant*	*Terror*
Thetis	*Trident*	*Truculent*	*Ullswater*	*Velox*
Vindictive	*Warwick*	*Whirlwind*		

Submarines: *C 1, C 3.*

CMBs: *5, 7, 15A, 16A, 17A, 21B, 22B, 23B, 24A, 25BD, 26B, 27A, 28A, 29A, 30B, 32A, 34A, 35A.*

MLs: *79, 110, 121, 128, 223, 239, 241, 252, 258, 262, 272, 280, 282, 308, 314, 345, 397, 416, 420, 422, 424, 513, 525, 526, 533, 549, 552, 555, 557, 558, 560, 561, 562.*

OSTEND:

Afridi	*Brilliant*	*Faulknor*	*General Crauford*
Lightfoot	*Lord Clive*	*Marshal Soult*	*Mastiff*
Matchless	*Mentor*	*Prince Eugene*	*Sirius*
Swift	*Tempest*	*Tetrarch*	*Zubian*

Monitors: *M 21, M 24, M 26.*

CMBs: *2, 4, 10, 11, 19A, 20A*

MLs: *11, 16, 17, 22, 23, 30, 60, 105, 512, 532, 551, 556*

SECTION TWO

Battles Not Awarded Honours

A

ABOUKIR, CRESSY and HOGUE SINKINGS 1914
22 September
World War I 1914–18
The German U-boat *U-9* sank three British armoured cruisers off the Maas light vessel in position 52° 18' N, 3° 41' E in the Hoofden Shallows, 30 miles west of Ijmuiden. Weddington, her commander, achieved this incredible success in less than an hour.

All three ships were old armoured cruisers of 12,000 tons, carrying 2 × 9.2" and 12 × 6" guns.

Aboukir was torpedoed and sank almost immediately. Her two sister ships stopped to pick up survivors, presenting good targets for the U-boat which promptly torpedoed and sank both cruisers. Over 1,400 men were drowned and a little over 800 survived.

U-boat warfare was in its infancy. *U-9* was a small coastal boat, one of the few commissioned into the German navy. It is evident that her forward tubes each fired a torpedo and all three of them hit their target. There would not have been time for her to re-load with the spare torpedoes, a lengthy process in such confined surroundings. The episode was an incredibly skilled piece of work.

AIX, ÎLE D' 1758
4 April
Seven Years' War 1756–63
Several naval battles highlighted the Seven Years' War, that war of complex alliances, intrigues and mistrust: Britain and Prussia ranged themselves against the might of Russia, France, Poland, Sweden, Austria and Spain. The war spread to Africa, to India (The

Black Hole of Calcutta and Clive's victory at Plassey), Canada (the capture of Quebec), America (the conquest of Pittsburgh) and the major naval success at Quiberon Bay near Lorient.

The confused action of Île d'Aix took place in 1758. Admiral Sir Edward Hawke prevented a French squadron from quitting Rochefort to escort a valuable convoy to America. Hawke had seven ships of the line and three frigates when he came upon the convoy on 4 April lying off the Île d'Aix. Forty merchantmen were escorted by five 74s and 64s and possibly seven frigates. Battle was joined but the conditions never allowed it to get too damaging. In the confusion many French ships were driven into shoal water and grounded. But most of them lightened ship and got clear. The convoy never re-formed.

B

BANTRY BAY 1689
1 May
War of the English Succession 1689–97
This was an unhappy engagement for the English commander, Admiral Arthur Herbert (later Earl of Torrington), who found his force outnumbered, badly positioned to leeward of the enemy in narrow waters with little searoom.

In 1688 William of Orange was offered the English throne and he was crowned William III in 1689. He soon formed a coalition of European states to counter the power of Louis XIV of France. In the resulting war a French invasion force of 8,000 men with supplies and reinforcements set out to establish a strong beachhead in Bantry Bay as a springboard for invading England in force.

When it was known that this force was at sea Admiral Herbert hurriedly assembled a fleet in Portsmouth. He hoisted his flag in the

70-gun *Elizabeth* and finally commanded a fleet of sixteen more ships of the line (mainly smaller 50s and 60s) and three bomb vessels.

The French force was commanded by the Comte de Châteaurenault. It was a powerful force comprising twenty-four ships of the line and ten fireships.

The two forces met on 1 May 1689. Châteaurenault weighed swiftly and with a favourable wind bore down on Herbert's ships. but despite holding all the trump cards he failed to win a victory. Only one ship was lost to each side. Uncooperative subordinates and the absence of his fireships (which continued to unload stores) led the Frenchman to break off the engagement prematurely. Herbert, hardly believing his good fortune, turned about and got clear away. The attempted invasion had been thwarted, and some years later William III landed near Belfast and all of Ireland fell to the English.

BARHAM, HM BATTLESHIP, 1941
25 November
World War II 1939–45
HM Battleship *Barham* (31,00 tons, 8 × 15") was torpedoed and sunk by the German U-boat *U-331* in the Mediterranean in position 32° 34' N, 26° 24' E, off Sidi Barrani, with enormous loss of life.

BEACHY HEAD 1690
30 June
War of the English Succession 1689–97
This battle won for the French temporary ascendancy in the Channel and disgrace for the English commander, Arthur Herbert, later Earl of Torrington. Herbert's Channel Fleet had been weakened by despatching a squadron to the Mediterranean and other ships to support William III's vainglorious expedition to Ireland. Support came from an unlikely source – the Dutch, for they were allies of the English, and their van squadron under Admiral Cornelis Evertsen [The Youngest] helped build Torrington's combined fleet

BRITISH SHIPS ENGAGED		
BRITISH CENTRE		**BRITISH REAR**
Sovereign (flag)	Grafton	Anne
Plymouth	Windsor Castle	Bonaventure
Deptford	Lenox	Edgar
Elizabeth	Stirling Castle	Exeter
Sandwich	York	Breda
Expedition	Suffolk	St Andrew
Warspite	Hampton Court	Coronation
Woolwich	Duchess	Royal Katherine
Lion	Hope	Cambridge
Rupert	Restoration	Berwick
Albemarle	Constant Warwick	Swallow
Plus 8 fireships		Defiance
		Captain
		Plus 9 fireships

to fifty-six ships. They mounted about 3,850 guns and carried about 23,000 men.

The French commander, Vice-Admiral Comte de Tourville, and his fleet were sighted off the Lizard on 21 June with an awesome fleet of seventy-seven ships bent on blockading the Thames. On 25 June it was off the Isle of Wight. Torrington, exercising his fleet, declined action and retired up Channel, keeping his fleet 'in being'.

Four days later he received direct orders to engage the enemy. On 30 June, with his flag in *Royal Sovereign* (100), he committed his fleet off Beachy Head. The Allied fleet was ill-organized: the Dutch van and English rear made half-hearted attacks independently, and both were mauled. Torrington, at the centre, kept at a long range to windward. In the evening the Allied fleet retired to the eastward, scuttling their own badly damaged ships – a 72, 70, 64, 60 and 50 gun ship. Tourville lost no ships. His gun power was superior, totalling perhaps 4,600 guns and 28,000 men.*

---

* All figures for guns, losses and ships engaged vary in the different accounts of the battle.

246

When the news of the defeat reached London there was panic. However, Tourville abandoned the pursuit, pleaded sickness and lack of supplies: he turned and headed back down the Channel. He burnt Teignmouth as if in a fit of pique.

When Torrington anchored off the Nore he was relieved of his command and, although acquitted at a later court martial, he was never employed again.

The French refer to the battle of Bévésiers, supposedly a corruption of Pevensey.

C

CALDER'S ACTION (CAPE FINISTERRE) 1805
22 July
Napoleonic War 1803–15

Vice-Admiral Calder's lack of resolution lost an opportunity to gain a significant victory – thus found the court martial after his action of 22 July.

The action was the result of elaborate and skilful dispositions by Admiral Lord Barham at the Admiralty, intended to trap Admiral Villeneuve of France and prevent the concentration of Franco-Spanish fleets on Villeneuve's return from the West Indies.

Calder lay off Ferrol with ten ships of the line, soon reinforced by another five. He cruised about 100 miles off Finisterre. Three days after taking up station he made contact with Villeneuve about 150 miles WNW Ferrol leading a fleet of nineteen French and Spanish ships. An indecisive engagement followed in the course of which Calder cut out and took two Spanish ships of the line, *Raphael* (80) and *Firme* (71), and temporarily barred Villeneuve from approaching Ferrol. But he evidently failed to display the offensive spirit the Admiralty deemed necessary. In sending him home for a court martial, Nelson provided, not the usual lowly frigate, but the handsome three-decker *Prince of Wales*, as an unspoken appreciation of Calder's action. Calder was subsequently severely reprimanded at the court martial.

CAPE FINISTERRE – see CALDER'S ACTION 1805

CAPE HENRY, ACTION OFF – see CHESAPEAKE 1781

CAPE TOWN 1810
10 January
Napoleonic War 1803–15
The town capitulated to land forces under the command of Major-General Sir David Baird and seaborne forces commanded by Commodore Sir Home Riggs Popham in *Diadem*. A naval brigade landed. The following ships were engaged:

Belliqueux	*Diadem*	*Diomede*	*Encounter*
Espoir	*Leda*	*Protector*	*Raisonnable*

CARTAGENA (Wager's Action) 1708
28 May
War of the Spanish Succession 1702–13
Commodore Charles Wager, with his flag in the 70-gun *Expedition*, had in company *Kingston* (60), *Portland* (50) and a fireship. This force encountered a Spanish treasure squadron off Cartagena. The enemy force comprised two 64s, two 5th rates and eight smaller vessels.

After sunset on 28 May 1708 Wager brought the enemy flagship to action and after ninety minutes the *San Josef* blew up, taking with her 600 men and a fortune in treasure. Another ship was captured, but she lacked any treasure, while yet another was run aground and lost. The captains of the *Kingston* and *Portland* failed to give Wager the support he expected; they were both court-martialled and dismissed their ships.

CHANNEL DASH 1942
12 February
World War II 1939–45
An audacious and meticulously planned 'escape' of the German battlecruisers *Scharnhorst* and *Gneisenau* (both 31,800 tons, 9 × 11") and the heavy cruiser *Prinz Eugen* (12,750 tons, 8 × 8") occurred in the Channel, as humiliating as Tromp's broom at the masthead.

Vice-Admiral Ciliax commanded the operation, taking the German squadron from the Atlantic port of Brest up-Channel through the narrow waters of the Straits of Dover to Wilhelmshaven and Kiel. The force was escorted by six destroyers, MTBs, minesweepers and aircraft of Luftflotte 3.

British opposition took the form of coastal batteries near Dover, attacks by MTBs, destroyer torpedo attacks from a flotilla of six from Harwich and attacks by Swordfish torpedo-carrying aircraft, in the course of which Lieutenant-Commander Esmonde was awarded a posthumous VC.

All these endeavours failed to stop the warships. *Scharnhorst* was actually struck by three mines and *Gneisenau* by one. The Channel Dash was a masterly German success.

CHINA SEA – 'PRINCE OF WALES' AND 'REPULSE', see FORCE Z

COPENHAGEN 1807
2–4 September
Napoleonic War 1802–15
A powerful British invasion force assaulted Denmark when the latter joined the Continental System. Admiral Lord Gambier

commanded twenty-five ships of the line, forty frigates, 380 transports with 29,000 men and sundry smaller vessels. Cathcart was the military commander.

This enormous invasion fleet entered Copenhagen Sound and demanded a surrender. It was rejected, whereupon the city and the harbour were assaulted and thousands of troops thrown ashore. After two days of intense naval bombardment the Danes capitulated and surrendered their fleet of sixteen ships of the line, ten frigates and forty-three other vessels. The Danes suffered 550 military dead and wounded and 1,600 civilian dead and 1,000 wounded.

CORONEL 1914
1 November
World War I 1914–18
The Battle of Coronel was a decisive defeat for the Royal Navy, redeemed only by the retaliatory victory of the Falklands one month later. (See FALKLANDS 1914, p. 93)

The German Vice-Admiral Graf von Spee wore his flag in the armoured cruiser *Scharnhorst* (11,420 tons, 8 × 8"). He had under his command *Gneisenau*, sister ship of the flagship, and the light cruiser *Nürnberg* (3,350 tons, 10 × 4.1"), the three forming the East Asiatic Squadron. At the outbreak of war von Spee was obliged by British and Japanese naval superiority to operate in South American waters. En route there he was reinforced at the Easter Islands by the light cruisers *Dresden* and *Leipzig* (both 3,544 tons, 12 × 4.1").

Rear-Admiral Sir Christopher Cradock commanded the South American Squadron, comprising the old armoured cruisers *Good Hope* (flagship: 14,100 tons, 2 × 9" and 16 × 6") and *Monmouth* (9,800 tons, 14 × 6"), the light cruiser *Glasgow* (4,800 tons, 2 ×6" and 10 × 4") and the armed merchant cruiser *Otranto* (12,128 tons, 8 × 4.7"). The Admiralty was aware of von Spee's movements and reinforced Cradock with the old and slow pre-dreadnought *Canopus* (12,950 tons, 4 × 12" and 12 × 6").

Cradock sailed without *Canopus* from the Falklands to locate von Spee, and von Spee left Valparaiso and headed south. The opposing squadrons met at nearly 5 pm on 1 November, 50 miles off Coronel, each flagship believing the other to be unaccompanied. Von Spee had every advantage: power, speed, modernity, setting sun silhouetting the British ships.

The accuracy of the German gunnery was awesome, the British futile. By 8 pm *Good Hope* had blown up and an hour later *Monmouth* went down. No one survived. *Glasgow* and *Otranto* managed to escape under cover of darkness.

The German ships suffered neither casualties nor damage to their ships.

CUDDALORE 1783
20 June
American War of Independence 1775–83

It was Vice-Admiral Hughes' misfortune in war to fight no fewer than five naval battles, all of them against the French, but, worst of all, all against that brilliant tactician Admiral Suffren. (See SADRAS, PROVIDIEN, NEGAPATAM and TRINCOMALEE.) Cuddalore was the last of the five.

Sir Edward Hughes wore his flag in *Superb* (74) and had eighteen of the line with him as he sought Pierre André de Suffren with his fifteen of the line outside Cuddalore, which was presently occupied by the French. Nearly three days were spent in manoeuvring for advantage in the unfavourable conditions. Then, on 20 June, battle was joined. It ended three hours later with no losses on either side. Hughes retired north to Madras, having once more failed to gain an advantage over the Frenchman.

Ships engaged were:

Africa	*Bristol*	*Burford*	*Cumberland*
Defence	*Eagle*	*Exeter*	*Gibraltar*
Hero	*Inflexible*	*Isis*	*Magnanime*
Monarch	*Monmouth*	*Sceptre*	*Sultan*
Superb	*Worcester*		

D

DAKAR 1940
23–25 September
World War II 1939–45

An attempt to land troops to take possession of the French African colonies and to take charge of French warships at the fall of France in 1940 led to the action at Dakar.

It was essential for the British to prevent ships of the French Navy falling into German hands. Accordingly the Royal Navy had the distasteful task of immobilizing, capturing or sinking French warships. Vice-Admiral John H.D. Cunningham commanded a force comprising the battleship *Barham* (31,100 tons, 8 × 15"), *Resolution* (29,150 tons, 8 × 15"), the carrier *Ark Royal* (22,000 tons, 36 aircraft), the heavy cruisers *Dorsetshire* (9,850 tons, 8 × 8"), *Cumberland* (9,750 tons, 8 × 8") and *Australia* (9,850 tons, 8 × 8") and six destroyers.

At Dakar the French had an unseaworthy battleship, *Richelieu* (35,000 tons 8 × 15"), the cruisers *Georges Leygues* (7,600 tons, 9 × 6") and *Montcalm* (7,600 tons, 9 × 6"), two destroyers and three submarines.

Over a period of two days the Vichy French submarines *Persée* and *Ajax* and the destroyer *L'Audacieux* (2,569 tons, 5 × 5.5") were sunk and many other ships badly damaged. The destroyer was bombarded into a wreck by the 8" shells of *Australia*.

The *Resolution* received a torpedo hit from the French submarine *Bévéziers*. *Barham* and *Cumberland* were both damaged by gunfire.

Attempts to land troops were repulsed and on the 25th Cunningham abandoned the unhappy operation and the British withdrew.

See also ORAN (MERS EL KEBIR) 1940 – page 277

DARDANELLES 1807
19 February
Napoleonic War 1803–15

Vice-Admiral Sir John Duckworth led a squadron in his flagship *Royal George*, forcing the passage of the Dardanelles and destroying eleven Turkish ships. Two others were taken by the division of ships under Rear-Admiral Sir Sidney Smith in *Pompée*. Duckworth's squadron was roughly handled when it was forced to retreat from Constantinople when the Turks brought up batteries of guns.

DISASTER OF THE SMYRNA CONVOY – see LAGOS 1693

DE RUYTER IN THE THAMES – see MEDWAY 1667

DOMINICA 1780
17 April
American War of Independence 1775–83

The misinterpretation of a crucial signal denied Admiral Rodney a victory over the French Admiral de Guichen in 1780.

Rodney's appointment as C-in-C of the Leeward Islands station coincided with the arrival of strong reinforcements in the West Indies. On 13 April de Guichen left Fort Royal with no fewer than twenty-three ships of the line, five frigates and numerous merchantmen crammed with 3,000 troops to attack Barbados.

Three days later this force was intercepted by Rodney in his flagship *Sandwich* (90), plus twenty of the line. There was plenty of searoom, two great naval tacticians, and the prospect of battle. After much fleet manoeuvring Rodney, whose intention was to attack the enemy's rear and centre, signalled, "Every ship to bear down and steer for her opposite in the enemy's line." It was followed five minutes later with "Engage!" The signals were completely misunderstood. Captain Carkett in *Stirling Castle* leading the van division took it to mean his numerical opposite in the order and maintained full sail to reach that position, followed by the rest of his division.

Rodney intended the signal to mean the opposite in the line at the time of the "Engage!" The result was a scrappy, disjointed attack, lacking concentration.

De Guichen bore up and took advantage by running down wind and making good his escape. No losses were suffered on either side, but Rodney's flagship was severely damaged. Later he bitterly criticized his captains for their actions.

DOMINICA 1782
9 April
American War of Independence 1775–83

All seemed set for a battle royal, yet in the end it fizzled out like a spent flare with the opposing fleets losing no ships at all. The French Admiral de Grasse with thirty-five of the line lay at Fort Royal (now Fort-de-France) in Martinique, preparing to combine with the Spaniards for a joint attack on Jamaica.

Admiral Rodney's lookout frigate kept him informed of the French movements while his thirty-six of the line lay at Castries in St Lucia. As soon as de Grasse weighed anchor Rodney also made his move, and the two fleets were in contact by dusk on 9 April.

The bulk of the French fleet became becalmed in the lee of Dominica, as did Rodney with his centre and rear. Indeed, all twelve of the rear and four of the centre never got into the battle at all. However, both vans, the French under Vendreuil in *Triomphant* and Rear-Admiral Sir Samuel Hood in *Barfleur* (90), engaged in a long-range exchange, with the French failing to employ their advantage in numbers.

De Grasse managed to protect the convoy in his charge, and even to work his ships to windward to attack Hood, but was unable to get to close grips. In the afternoon Rodney contrived to find the wind and came up to support Hood. Both sides were content to break off the action, with neither side having lost a ship.

DOVER SKIRMISH 1917
17–18 March
World War I 1914–18
This engagement results from a German destroyer raid in the Dover Strait. The enemy destroyers were *S 49* and *G 86*. They encountered four Royal Navy destroyers: *Laertes* and *Laforey* (both 1,010 tons, and both 3 x 4"), *Llewellyn* (994 tons, 3 x 4") and *Paragon* (1,000 tons, 3 x 4"). *Paragon* was torpedoed and sank. *Llewellyn* was torpedoed but managed to survive the ordeal.

The following month, April, witnessed a far different result when *Broke* and *Swift* excelled themselves and earned the Battle Honour Dover Strait 1917. (See DOVER STRAIT 1917 p. 84)

DUNGENESS 1652
30 November
First Dutch War 1652–54
The Dutch Admiral de With's failure to defeat the English at the Kentish Knock led to the recall of the enterprising Admiral Marten Tromp as commander of the Dutch fleet. It was a sound decision and led to the defeat of the English at the Battle of Dungeness in 1652.

Tromp's main objective was to safeguard the passage of a large convoy to La Rochelle. He put to sea on 21 November with seventy-eight men-of-war with his flag in *Brederode*. Eight days later Tromp's fleet appeared off the Goodwin Sands.

General-at-sea Robert Blake was in the Downs with a fleet of only forty-two men-of-war. Despite the disparity in the number of ships in the opposing fleets Blake put to sea to engage the enemy. Before the fleets could engage the wind increased to gale force. That night Blake's fleet sought a haven in the Dover Roads and Tromp's lay under the cliffs of the South Foreland.

By the next morning the wind had moderated and both fleets were steering parallel courses along the Kentish coast until, near Dungeness, the coastline forced Blake's fleet to engage Tromp. In the ensuing battle the Dutch soon took an advantage, while many of the English rear failed to engage. Blake's flagship *Triumph* had her fore topmast shot away, and the Dutch took the *Garland* and *Bonaventure*. Three other English ships were sunk.

Patently Tromp had won the day. The Straits were his and he

escorted his outward bound convoy down Channel with ensigns flying. In good time he returned up Channel with a convoy of 150 ships.

English ships engaged were:

Triumph (flag)	Bonaventure	Garland	Happy Entrance
Hercules	Nimble	Sapphire	Ruby
Vanguard	Victory	(List incomplete.)	

Note: In the Netherlands Tromp is always known, and always signed himself, without the "van" or "van der", though his father was van der Tromp. Curiously, too, De Ruyter, known as such to history, always signed and called himself Ruyter, without the "De" *particule*.

E

EAST INDIES STRIKES AND BOMBARDMENTS 1944–45
World War II 1939–45

Over a period of about one year, April 1944 to May 1945, Admiral Sir James Somerville's Eastern Fleet, supplemented by units of the US Navy, Royal Netherland Navy, Free French Navy and the RAN, carried out a series of destructive strikes and bombardments.

(a) Air strike on Sabang, Sumatra (Operation Cockpit) 19 April 1944.

Ships engaged:

Renown	Illustrious	Saratoga (USN)	Ceylon
Gambia	London	Quilliam	Queenborough
Quadrant	Cummings (USN)	Dunlap (USN)	Fanning (USN)
Queen Elizabeth	Valiant	Richelieu (Fr)	Newcastle
Nigeria	Tromp (RNethN)	Tactician	Napier
Nepal	Nizam	Rotherham	Racehorse
Penn	Petard	Van Galen (RNethN)	
Quiberon RAN			

FAA Squadron: *810, 847, 1830, 1833*

(b) Air Strike on Sourabaya, Sumatra, 17 May 1944. An Allied air strike was carried out on the Japanese base at Sourabaya under the codename Operation Transom. Ships engaged were:

Illustrious	*Renown*	*Kenya*	*London*
Suffolk	*Queen Elizabeth*	*Valiant*	*Ceylon*
Gambia	*Saratoga (USN)*	*Richelieu (Fr)*	*Tromp (RNethN)*

Destroyers:

Napier	*Quadrant*	*Quality*	*Quiberon (RAN)*
Cummings (USN)	*Dunlap (USN)*	*Fanning (USN)*	
Van Galen (RNethN)		*Nepal*	*Queenborough*
Quickmatch	*Quilliam*	*Racehorse*	*Rotherham*

FAA Squadron: *832, 851, 1830, 1833*

(c) Air Strike on Sigli, Sumatra (Operation Light) 17 September 1944.

This was a diversionary attack to help reduce the pressure on the US Navy in the Pacific. Ships engaged:

Victorious	*Indomitable*	*Howe*	*Cumberland*
Kenya	*Racehorse*	*Rider*	*Rapid*
Redoubt	*Relentless*	*Rocket*	*Rotherham*

FAA Squadron: *815, 817, 1839, 1844, 822, 1834, 1835*

(d) Air Strike on Nicobar Island, Bay of Bengal, 17–19 October 1944. Japanese installations were struck. Ships engaged:

Renown	*Indomitable*	*Victorious*	*London*
Cumberland	*Phoebe*	*Suffolk*	

Nine destroyers including *Norman* (RAN) and *Van Galen* (RNethN).

FAA Squadron: *815, 817, 1834, 1836, 1839, 1844*

(e) Air Strike at Medan 20 December 1944 (Operation Robson). Medan in Sumatra was the target, with its oil installations and harbour, but the operation was not regarded as a successful strike. Ships engaged were:

Indomitable	*Illustrious*	*Argonaut*	*Black Prince*
Newcastle	*Kempenfelt*	*Wager*	*Wakeful*
Wessex	*Whelp*	*Whirlwind*	*Wrangler*

FAA Squadron: *854, 857, 1830, 1833, 1839, 1844*

(f) Air Strike on Prangkalan Brendan in Sumatra 4 January 1945 (Operation Lentil). Ships engaged were:

Indefatigable   *Indomitable*   *Victorious*   *Argonaut*
Black Prince   *Ceylon*   *Suffolk*
Plus eight destroyers
<u>FAA Squadron:</u>   *849, 857, 1834, 1836, 1770, 888, 1839, 1844, 887, 894*

(g) Strike against oil installations at Palembang: see Honour awarded PALEMBANG 1945.

(h) Strike against Sabang and Oleheh, and against Emmahaven and Padang: Operation Sunfish. Two separate strikes. Ships engaged 11 April 1945:

<u>*Force 63:*</u>   *Queen Elizabeth*   *London*   *Richelieu (Fr)*
<u>26 Destroyer Flotilla:</u>
Venus   *Verulam*   *Vigilant*   *Virago*
Cumberland (cruiser)   *Emperor*   *Khedive*
<u>FAA Squadron:</u>   *808*
Emmahaven and Padang were the targets attacked by the same Force on 16 April 1945.

F

FINISTERRE – see CALDER'S ACTION (Cape Finisterre) 1805

FORCE Z (South China Sea; Gulf of Siam; 'Prince of Wales' and 'Repulse') 1941
10 December
World War II 1939–45
Force Z comprised the battleship *Prince of Wales* (35,000 tons, 10 × 14"), Captain J.C. Leach, the battlecruiser *Repulse* (32,000

tons, 6 × 15"), Captain W. Tennant and four destroyers, *Express* (1,350 tons, 4 × 4.7"), *Vampire* (1,090 tons, 4 × 4"), *Electra* (1,375 tons, 4 × 4.7") and *Tenedos* (905 tons, 1 × 4" and 3").

The C-in-C, Acting Admiral Sir Tom Phillips, wore his flag in the battleship.

In a period of just under two and a half hours, from 11 am till 1.20 pm on 10 December, these two splendid capital ships were sunk in the South China Sea by Japanese bombers and torpedo-bombers of the 22nd Air Flotilla based in Indo-China. In this terrible disaster 327 men were lost in the battleship, in addition to the C-in-C and his flag captain. Another 513 were saved from the *Repulse*'s ship's company. This one strike denied the Navy their operations east of Singapore for three years; naval superiority in the area had been seized by Japanese aircraft. It was a stunning blow.

This loss was the culmination of a series of unfortunate circumstances over the previous months; differences between the Prime Minister, Winston Churchill, and the Admiralty; the grounding in Kingston, Jamaica, of the carrier *Formidable* prevented her presence with Force Z; the under-estimating of Japanese aircraft performance and of the pilots' skills and of air power generally; a false report of Japanese troops landing at Kuantan; Phillips's determination to maintain radio silence; and pure chance, which allowed some Japanese aircraft to make a sighting of the British ships.

But the sinkings had far-reaching repercussions which resulted in the development of new weapons, techniques and tactics, and ultimately in the control of the sea and air by the US Navy in the great battles of the Pacific three years later.

Ships engaged:

Prince of Wales	*Repulse*	*Express*	*Electra*
Vampire	*Tenedos*		

FORT ST DAVID (Negapatam) 1746
25 June
War of 1739–48

Commodore Edward Peyton's feeble efforts off the Coromandel coast of southern India seem hardly worthy of inclusion when compared with many of the everyday battles which occurred almost daily throughout the north Atlantic during the Second World War.

The Frenchman, La Bourdonnais, with his flag in *Achille* (70) and accompanied by seven armed merchantmen, encountered Peyton in his flagship *Medway* (60) with three 50s and two smaller vessels. There was little wind to give either side any advantage, but Peyton failed to use his greater power, and Bourdonnais extricated his force without loss.

The East India Company duly censured Peyton for his conduct and failure to annihilate the French force.

G

GRENADA 1779
6 July
American War of Independence 1775–83
The French Vice-Admiral the Comte D'Estaing in his flagship *Languedoc* was riding high. He had taken the island of St Vincent in the West Indies. Three weeks later, at the beginning of July, he sailed with twenty-five ships of the line and an expeditionary force and took the island of Grenada. The French influence in the Caribbean was about to soar and would remain in the ascendancy for nearly three years.

The recently appointed C-in-C Leeward Islands was Vice Admiral the Hon John Byron. When he learned of the Grenada capture he sailed from St Lucia in his flagship *Princess Royal* with his whole fleet, its main strength being twenty-one ships of the line. He caught the French fleet in some confusion trying desperately to form line of battle in St George's Bay, Grenada, on 6 July.

By 11 am both fleets were in line ahead sailing roughly parallel NNW, though *Lion*, *Fame*, *Grafton* and *Cornwall* were well astern, badly damaged. Both vans became heavily engaged, but later in the afternoon the fire became desultory, the French turned south and broke off the action.

D'Estaing had patently failed to exploit an advantageous situation, for he should have taken the four damaged British ships, yet in spite of this failure the French still enjoyed a naval superiority in the Caribbean.

Ships engaged:

Albion	Boyne	Conqueror	Cornwall	Elizabeth
Fame	Grafton	Lion	Magnificent	Medway
Monmouth	Nonsuch	Prince of Wales		
Princess Royal		Royal Oak	Stirling Castle	Suffolk
Sultan	Trident	Vigilant	Yarmouth	

Frigate: Ariadne

GULF OF GENOA BOMBARDMENT 1941
9 February
World War II 1939–45

Force H, commanded by Vice-Admiral Sir James Somerville, departed Gibraltar to raid the Gulf of Genoa. His force comprised the battleship *Malaya* (31,100 tons, 8 × 15", 12 × 6"); the battlecruiser *Renown* (32,000 tons, 6 × 15", 20 × 4.5"), the aircraft carrier *Ark Royal* (22,000 tons, 72 aircraft), a cruiser and ten fleet destroyers.

The capital ships bombarded Genoa with their 15" guns, and aircraft from *Ark Royal* bombed the installations at Leghorn and dropped mines off the naval base of La Spezia.

The Italian fleet made efforts to intercept Force H with their heavy ships *Vittorio Veneto* (35,000 tons, 9 × 15", 12 × 6"), *Guilio Cesare* (23,622 tons, 10 × 12.6", 12 × 4.7"); *Andrea Doria* (23,622 tons, 10 × 12.6", 12 × 5.3"), but no contact was made.

GULF OF SIAM – see FORCE Z 1941

H

'HAGURO' SINKING 1945
15–16 May
World War II 1939–45

A battle between the 26th Destroyer Flotilla commanded by Captain Manley L. Power and His Imperial Japanese Majesty's heavy cruiser *Haguro* (13,380 tons, 10 × 8") commanded by Captain Kajuh Sugiura during a night action in the Straits of Molucca 55 miles WSW of Penang.

The 26th DF comprised the leader *Saumarez* (1,730 tons, 4 × 4.7"), *Venus*, *Virago*, *Verulam* and *Vigilant* (all 1,710 tons, 4 × 4.7").

The *Haguro* was a fine, powerful, battle-hardened veteran of the Pacific war; she was powerfully armed and well armoured, her 1940 refit leaving her bristling with secondary and tertiary guns. She could not, however, match the high speed (36 knots) of the British destroyers. At the time of the battle she wore the flag of Rear-Admiral Hashimoto.

She had in company the destroyer *Kamikaze* (1,400 tons, 3 × 4.7"), Lieutenant-Commander K. Kasuga in command.

Power's flotilla established contact with *Haguro* by radar after a pursuit of several hours. Battle was joined when Power actioned his plan for a synchronized torpedo attack by the whole flotilla. Within minutes the heavy cruiser had been torpedoed many times. The *Kamikaze* failed to live up to her name and sped off in the confusion of battle and escaped.

Haguro lost way and began to settle. *Venus* administered the coup de grâce. No survivors were picked up, an indication of the fearsome antagonism between Allied and Japanese warships. Later the *Kamikaze* returned to the scene and rescued some 400 survivors.

Saumarez was struck by 8" and 5" shells and suffered severe damage forward, and to a boiler. But the British casualties were minimal. The 26th DF were the victors of the last major torpedo action of the Second World War.

HAVANA 1748
1 October
War of 1739–48

The last battle of this war between Britain and Spain was fought between a squadron of six ships of the line commanded by Rear-Admiral Charles Knowles and a similar squadron (two 74s and four 64s) under Vice-Admiral Reggio about 12 miles north-east of Havana.

Knowles was C-in-C of the Jamaica station. He received intelligence of a Spanish treasure fleet and weighed from Fort Royal in his flagship *Cornwall* (80), leaving part of his squadron to patrol off the Tortuga Banks.

When Knowles sighted Reggio's squadron he had what wind advantage there was. Battle was joined at 2.30 pm, except for *Warwick* and *Canterbury* which were still a couple of hours astern.

After some fierce fighting the Spanish *Conquistador* (64) struck. By 8 pm Reggio was withdrawing towards Havana, but his flagship *Africa* (74) was so badly damaged that she anchored in a cove to make repairs. Two days later she was discovered there by the British ships and her crew burnt her to avoid its capture.

Knowles was subsequently court-martialled and reprimanded for his failure to get his squadron into action earlier and for his poor tactics.

<u>Ships engaged:</u>

Canterbury	*Cornwall*	*Lenox*	*Oxford*
Stratford	*Tilbury*	*Warwick*	

LA HOGUE – see BARFLEUR 1692

HOLMES'S BONFIRE 1666
8–9 August
Second Dutch War 1665–67

Sir Robert Holmes (1622–92) commanded a few 'lesser' frigates, fireships and a considerable number of ketches in a mini-fleet endeavouring to burn a huge fleet of Dutch merchantmen sheltering in the River Vlie. The action took place a fortnight after the victory at the Battle of Orfordness.

A huge assembly of merchant ships, still laden with imports from the east, "that would feed Dutch industry and keep the Dutch export trade going for a year to come, lay at Terschelling."

Holmes attacked them with his mini-fleet of ships and boats manned by carefully picked, skilled commandos, and succeeded in setting ablaze two Dutch warships and no fewer than 165 merchant ships in an unprecedented conflagration. The incident was given the name Holmes's Bonfire.

Troops and marines then went ashore and pillaged and fired the houses, public buildings and richly-stocked warehouses of the town of Terschelling.

HYÈRES (Hotham's Second Action) 1795
13 July
French Revolutionary War 1793–1802

This battle was fought between the British and French Mediterranean fleets. The British fleet was commanded by Vice-Admiral William Hotham with his flag in *Britannia* and the French fleet by Rear-Admiral Pierre Martin. They were old antagonists, having fought the battle in the Gulf of Genoa four months previously.

Hotham had the advantage of twenty-one of the line against Martin's seventeen. The opposing fleets met near Hyères Island off Provence. Hotham again displayed a reluctance to act decisively. Martin, wisely perhaps, attempted to avoid entanglement. Hotham signalled "General Chase", but some of his ships never got to within range of the enemy ships. The British van, including Nelson's *Agamemnon* (60), managed to engage the French ships, and one of them, the *Alcide* (74), struck. She then caught fire and blew up. The wind changed and, fearful of being blown ashore, Hotham ordered his ships to disengage. The British Admiral had lost another opportunity of snatching a victory.

Ships engaged:

Agamemnon	Audacious	Bedford	Blenheim
Bombay Castle	Britannia	Captain	Courageux
Culloden	Cumberland	Defence	Diadem
Egmount	Fortitude	Gibraltar	Princess Royal
St George	Saturn	Terrible	Victory
Windsor Castle			

Frigates:

Ariadne	Comet	Cyclops	Eclair	Fleche
Meleager	Moselle	Mutine	Resolution	

I

INDIAN OCEAN 1942
5–9 April
World War II 1939–45

The marauding Japanese carrier striking force commanded by Vice-Admiral Nagumo carried all before it as it advanced into the Indian Ocean early in April 1942 where Admiral Sir James Somerville was building up the Eastern Fleet, a motley collection of ships, mostly, apart from the carriers, totally ill-equipped to match the Japanese force and engage it in battle.

Somerville's fleet comprised the carriers *Indomitable* and *Formdidable* (both 23,000 tons, 72 aircraft), and elderly *Hermes* (22,000 tons, 72 aircraft), the battleships *Warspite* (30,600 tons, 8 × 15") and the four *Royal Sovereign* class: *Resolution*, *Revenge*, *Ramillies* and *Royal Sovereign* (all 29,150 tons, 8 × 15" and 12 × 6"), seven cruisers and sixteen destroyers. Nagumo's striking force comprised the carriers *Akagi* (26,900 tons, 60 aircraft),

Shokaku and *Zuikaku* (both 25,675 tons, 82 aircraft) and the two smaller ones *Hiryu* and *Soryu* (15,900 tons, 73 aircraft), the battle-cruisers *Kongo, Haruna, Hiei* and *Kirishima* (all 26,330 tons, 8 × 14" and 16 × 6"), four cruisers and eight destroyers.

Somerville withdrew his fleet for much-needed manoeuvres and exercises off the Maldives, south-west of Ceylon, comfortably out of range of Nagumo's carrier aircraft. The Japanese fleet debouched into the Bay of Bengal and the Indian Ocean. Aircraft struck at Colombo and its shipping. The two 8" gun cruisers *Cornwall* and *Dorsetshire* were located and a strike force of about fifty aircraft sank them within minutes.

On 9 April the Japanese carrier aircraft attacked Trincomalee on Ceylon's east coast. The carrier *Hermes* was trying to escape to the south but was spotted and overwhelmed by a huge force of about eighty aircraft. She sank quickly. The small destroyer *Tenedos* was also sunk.

Simultaneous with Nagumo's sortie, Vice-Admiral Ozawa commanded a cruiser force which attacked merchant shipping in the Bay of Bengal. All told, Britain lost one carrier (*Hermes*), two cruisers (*Cornwall* and *Dorsetshire*), a destroyer (*Tenedos*), 150,000 tons of merchant shipping and thirty-three aircraft against seventeen Japanese. It was another demonstration, if further demonstration was needed, of the power of air superiority.

J

JAMAICA, CAPTURE OF, 1655
17 May
Anglo-Spanish War 1654–59
England's prime objective was to break Spanish dominance in the West Indies and her powerful influence on trade in the region.

Admiral William Penn was despatched to take San Domingo, wearing his flag in *Swiftsure* and leading a fleet of thirty-eight ships with an invasion force of troops commanded by General Robert Venables. The two commanders failed to take San Domingo but captured Jamaica instead.

JAVA SEA 1942
27 February
World War II 1939–45

The Battle of the Java Sea was fought between the covering forces for the invasion of the island of Java and an Allied squadron commanded by the Dutch Rear-Admiral Karel Doorman. The Japanese squadron was commanded by Admiral Takagi and the rival forces are shown in the accompanying table.

The Allied force was a makeshift one, without a common signalling plan, and it operated under air dominated by the Japanese.

Doorman led his squadron in the Dutch cruiser *De Ruyter* from Sourabaya to seek out and engage the approaching Takagi force. A long-range gunnery duel developed, with mass torpedo attacks from destroyers. *Exeter* (8,390 tons, 6 × 8") was severely damaged and fell out of line. The RN destroyer *Electra* (1,375 tons, 4 × 4.7") and Dutch *Kortenaer* (1,310 tons, 4 × 4.7") were sunk, obliging Doorman to break off the action and work round the covering force to get at the troop convoy.

The four US destroyers, having expended all their torpedoes, were detached back to Sourabaya. The RN destroyer *Jupiter* (1,690 tons, 6 × 4.7") struck a mine and foundered.

After dark another clash of the cruisers occurred: *De Ruyter* and *Java* both sank with enormous loss of life. The Battle of the Java Sea was at a virtual end.

Captain Waller in HMAS *Perth* (6,830 tons, 8 × 6") took command of the remaining ships and withdrew. The following day *Perth*, *Houston* (USN, 9,050 tons, 9 × 8"), the destroyers *Encounter* (1,375 tons, 4 × 4.7") and *Pope* (1,190 tons, 4 × 4") all tried to escape the Java Sea, but were intercepted. They fought with great gallantry and were sunk with heavy loss of life. (See SUNDA STRAIT 1942 pp. 219–20). The Japanese victory was

JAVA SEA AND SUNDA STRAIT		
ALLIED		**JAPANESE**
Doorman	Commander	Takagi
Houston	Heavy Cruiser	*Nachi*
Exeter		*Haguro*
Perth	Light Cruiser	*Jintsu*
De Ruyter		*Naka*
Java		
3 Royal Navy	Destroyers	
2 Netherland		
4 US Navy		

comprehensive and complete. Java was lost.

The damaged *Exeter*, one of the victorious trio of cruisers at the Battle of the River Plate, was patched and made reasonably seaworthy, and with her accompanying destroyer *Encounter* made an attempt to flee the South Java Sea, but both ships were located and sunk by superior surface forces in position 5° 00' S, 111° 00' E.

K

KOLOMBANGARA 1943
13 July
World War II 1939–45

This was a night action (12–13 July 1943) between a force of US, one RAN and one RNZN cruisers, and destroyers commanded by Rear-Admiral Ainsworth USN, and a similar force of Japanese warships which was giving cover to four destroyer transports, commanded by Rear-Admiral Akiyama. It was almost a repeat performance of the battle of Kula Gulf a week earlier.

The four destroyer transports were en route to Kolombangara in the Solomons. Both sides were aware of each other's presence (by radar and radar/intercept). A torpedo battle ensued. HMNZS *Leander* was torpedoed and retired. The Japanese light cruiser *Jintsu* was overwhelmed by gunfire and was later sunk by torpedoes. *Australia* escaped damage. The Japanese destroyer managed to retire, reload torpedoes and launch a second attack which severely damaged the cruiser *Honolulu* and sank the destroyer *Gwin*, at no loss to themselves.

KÖNIGSBERG SINKING 1940
10 April
World War II 1939–45

The First Battle of Narvik on 10 April 1940 during the German invasion of Norway overshadowed a remarkable achievement by two squadrons of the Fleet Air Arm – the sinking of the first major warship by air attack. The two squadrons, 800 and 803, comprising sixteen Skua aircraft from Hatston air station in the Orkneys were led by Lieutenant W.P. Lucy RN and the Royal Marine pilot Captain R.T. Partridge. The light cruiser *Königsberg* (6,650 tons 9 × 5.9") was part of the invasion force and had been damaged by Norwegian shore batteries. She had been sighted by reconnaissance aircraft of the Royal Air Force lying alongside in Bergen harbour at almost the limit of endurance for a Skua.

The cruiser was struck by three 500 lb bombs in a text-book dive-bombing attack for which the aircraft had been specially designed. The attack was a complete success and the *Königsberg* sank.

Vice-Admiral Sir Hugh Binney (V.A. Orkneys and Shetlands) described the strike as brilliantly executed.

Three years later the cruiser was salved, but she no longer saw service and was finally abandoned in 1944.

L

LAGOS 1693 (Disaster of the Smyrna Convoy)
17–18 June
War of the English Succession 1689–97
This was a battle in defence of an important convoy between an attacking French squadron and a defending Anglo-Dutch squadron.

In June 1693 an attempt was made to pass an extremely large and enormously valuable convoy of 400 merchantmen down Channel to the Mediterranean. The merchant ships were English, German, Dutch, Danish and Swedish.

The escort was provided as far as Ushant by the main Anglo-Dutch fleet which returned to their bases on completion of this phase of the operation.

Vice-Admiral Sir George Rooke and Rear-Admiral van der Goes took over responsibility after Ushant. All went reasonably well until noon on 17 June, when, south of Cape St Vincent, Rooke found himself confronted by a vast fleet of about eighty French warships. Unknown to Rooke, the French were well aware of the passage of the convoy and instructions had been issued to Admiral Tourville in Brest and Admiral D'Estrées at Toulon to rendezvous at Lagos Bay just to the east of Cape St Vincent and there to lie in wait.

Rooke did all in his power to avoid action, and two Dutch ships gallantly sacrificed themselves and were taken, *Zeeland* (64) and *Wapen van Medemblik* (64). In vain; the French ships got in among the convoy and in all sank or captured ninety-two of the vessels. Rooke managed to collect another fifty-four into a small convoy and provided them with an escort. Others scattered to Gibraltar, to Cadiz, Malaga and Madeira.

The total financial loss to the Allies has been variously computed between £1 million and £6 million, a huge sum of money. Whatever the sum, in all senses the battle was a disaster of great proportions.

M

MARTINIQUE 1780
15 May
American War of Independence 1775–83

Admiral Sir George Rodney came close to bringing a French squadron to battle on two occasions in May 1780 but each attempt was thwarted. He commanded a fine squadron of twenty-three ships of the line and wore his flag in *Sandwich*.

The French squadron was commanded by Vice-Admiral Guichen with his flag in *Couronne*. The two squadrons met in a position about twenty miles east of Martinique. Twice Rodney came close to bringing Guichen to action but the Frenchman resolved not to bring his ships to close action despite his having the weather gage, and keeping it, so that only the van of the British squadron came into action with the rear French ships. Each side battered the other for six hours, suffering 500 casualties apiece.

On the 21st Guichen broke off to the northward and Rodney lost sight of the enemy.

Ships engaged:

Ajax	Albion	Boyne	Centurion
Conqueror	Cornwall	Elizabeth	Grafton
Intrepid	Magnificent	Medway	Montagu
Preston	Princess Royal	Sandwich (flag)	Stirling Castle
Suffolk	Terrible	Trident	Triumph
Vengeance	Vigilant	Yarmouth	

Frigates: Andromeda   Deal Castle   Greyhound   Venus

MARTINIQUE 1781
29 April
American War of Independence 1775–83

This naval battle was fought when Rear-Admiral Sir Samuel Hood with eighteen ships of the line, with his flag in *Barfleur*, met a French squadron under the French Admiral the Comte de Grasse leading twenty ships of the line in his flagship *Ville de Paris*, escorting a convoy of 150 sail.

Admiral Sir George Rodney was in command of the naval forces in the Caribbean, with Hood as his second-in-command. Rodney ordered Hood to take his squadron to join Rear-Admiral Drake's squadron at Fort Royal, Martinique, then to cruise to windward of the island in the hopes of intercepting de Grasse.

On 28 April Hood sighted the French fleet and spent that night and the following morning skilfully manoeuvring his ships to gain an advantage. But when battle was joined it was mainly at long range, with the benefit of fire power with the French.

Hood's ships *Russell*, *Centaur* and *Intrepid* (all 3rd rates) suffered severe damage but managed to reach port safely. De Grasse safeguarded his convoy, which reached its destination unscathed, and perhaps for this reason alone he can be regarded as the victor of this battle of Martinique.

Ships engaged:

Ajax	Alcide	Alfred	Barfleur
Belliqueux	Centaur	Gibraltar	Intrepid
Invincible	Monarch	Montagu	Princessa
Prince William	Russell	Shrewsbury	Resolution
Terrible	Torbay		

Frigates:

	Amazon	Lizard	Pacahunta

MEDWAY 1667 (De Ruyter in the Thames)
June
Second Dutch War 1665–67

A Dutch fleet of warships under the command of Admiral De Ruyter audaciously sailed up the Thames and into the Medway, burned or captured many ships, blockaded London and created panic in the streets in the city.

No British forces opposed the marauders, primarily because of a bankrupt Treasury, which had resulted in the ships not being fitted out in the spring of 1667. The ships were left "in ordinary", in other words they were in reserve with all their stores taken ashore. Furthermore, incredible though it may seem, hundreds of English seamen whose pay was months in reserve had deserted to serve in the Dutch navy.

De Ruyter commanded twenty-four ships of the line, twenty smaller vessels and fifteen fireships. A chain boom at Sheerness was broken and Sheerness captured; guardships were battered into submission and shore batteries silenced. Armed parties landed and destroyed more batteries at Upnor.

Nearby, sixteen English of the line were captured or burned. Humiliatingly, the *Royal Charles* (80), Albermarle's flagship in recent battles against the Dutch, was taken and towed back to Holland with the royal standard still flying at the main as a tremendous prize of war. Although the ship was broken up in 1673 the magnificent carving from the stern is still preserved in the Rijksmuseum.

De Ruyter continued to blockade the Thames and London for a month, during which time there were bouts of panic. Samuel Pepys recorded in his Diary that he sent his wife and father out of London with as much gold as they could carry to bury in his father's garden in Huntingdonshire.

MERS EL KEBIR – see ORAN 1940

MINORCA 1758
20 May
Seven Years' War 1757–63
It was this indecisive clash which resulted in the celebrated loss of Minorca and its valuable harbour at Port Mahon, and in the court-martialling and shooting of Vice-Admiral John Byng.

Admiral the Marquis de la Galissonnière captured the island of Minorca in April 1756 with a squadron of twelve of the line and 15,000 French troops. They invested the naval base at Port Mahon, whose garrison held out bravely.

A hard-pressed Admiralty raised a weak and inefficient force of thirteen ships of the line under the command of Vice-Admiral the Hon John Byng to relieve the garrison. The number of ships is often misquoted. Byng set out from Gibraltar with thirteen of the line plus three frigates. The latter were dispatched to contact the garrison ashore. When battle commenced, such was Byng's elementary, childlike knowledge of sea warfare that he had one ship too many in his line to fight ship to ship with the French line; thus he ordered *Deptford* out of the line, so twelve British ships took part in the battle.

On 20 May Byng encountered La Galissonnière's squadron about 30 miles east of Port Mahon and an indecisive action followed, largely due to Byng's tactical error in angle of approach. The French drew off and Byng made no positive effort to engage them again. Neither did he make an effort to relieve the garrison or even to bombard the transports supplying the island.

Byng held a council of war aboard his flagship which resolved to draw back to Gibraltar to await reinforcements from Britain. He therefore retired from Minorca, and as a result the garrison had no option but to surrender, with the loss of Minorca.

The Admiralty did not await Byng's despatch but sent Vice-Admiral Sir Edward Hawke to relieve him and recapture the island. But by now the situation was irretrievable

Byng returned to England to face public outcry and a court martial which found him guilty of neglect of duty and sentenced him to execution. It was a ceremonial occasion with representative officers from every ship in Spithead. A firing squad of six marines executed him on the quarterdeck of the *Monarch*. After the volley "he died with great resolution, not showing the least sign of timidity in the awful moment." The execution provoked great public condemnation. It also gave rise to Voltaire's contemptuous comment that, in this country: "it is good to shoot an admiral from time to time to encourage the others."

MONTECHRISTO 1780
20 March and 20 June
American War of Independence 1775–83
These two actions were fought between Captain William Cornwallis and French commanders in the West Indies off

Montechristo on the northern coast of the island of San Domingo (Dominican Republic).

In the first encounter Cornwallis was cruising with three small ships of the line when he met a French convoy escorted by four of the line and three frigates on its way to nearby Cap François. In the running fight which continued throughout the night the British *Janus* was badly damaged. Reinforcements arrived too late to prevent the French escaping.

The second encounter was similarly lightweight. Cornwallis in *Lion* (64), with four ships of the line in support, fought an inconclusive action with Commodore de Ternay, who had a force of seven of the line escorting a valuable convoy. The Frenchman failed to press home an attack in which he had most advantage and the engagement was noted mainly for the good work Cornwallis put in in rescuing the damaged *Ruby* (64).

N

NASMITH'S PATROL 1915
May–June 1915
World War I 1914–18
Admiral Sir Martin Dunbar Nasmith VC KCB (1883–1965) was less resplendent when he was a young Lieutenant-Commander, nor did he affect a hyphenated surname. There was a dash and élan about him during the patrol by *E 11*, the submarine he commanded in the Sea of Marmara in the Dardenelles campaign, that resulted in the award of the VC, the third submarine commander to earn that award in that theatre.

He entered the Dardenelles on 19 May, submerged to 80 feet off Achi Baba and passed under two minefields, then a third, in order to attack a Turkish battleship, but when he surfaced the target had moved out of range. However, there was no shortage of destroyers, two of which spotted his periscope and attempted to ram. The glassy flat water of the inland sea was a grave hazard for a submarine, so Nasmith captured a dhow and lashed it to the part-submerged conning tower to disguise his progress through the Sea.

The next day he put a boarding party on to a sailing ship, torpedoed a Turkish gunboat and took a bullet right through *E 11*'s periscope.

On the 24th Nasmith intercepted a vessel which he ordered to be abandoned; it was loaded with arms, gun spares and 6" shells. A demolition charge sent it to the bottom: "The vessel exploded with a loud report."

After chasing another loaded vessel into the port of Rodosto Nasmith torpedoed her as she secured alongside. Yet another extraordinary event on this same day was the prize he captured which ran itself ashore; his prize crew was driven off by rifle fire from a cavalry unit ashore!

On the 25th Nasmith was off Constantinople, relishing the prospect of masses of shipping in the Bosporus. One torpedo was fired, but it developed a gyro failure and circled round the harbour, narrowly missing *E 11* herself. Another torpedo exploded against the transport *Stamboul* while she was alongside the harbour wall. Constantinople panicked. Shops shut. Troops aboard transports were disembarked and all sailings were cancelled. The city came to a standstill.

After a day ashore on an island, resting and washing, *E 11* tackled a battleship, but was driven off by a destroyer. She then brushed with a Turkish Q ship, but escaped.

On the 28th a large transport was sunk by demolition charges on the same day that a spent torpedo, complete with live firing pistol, was recovered and safely taken aboard after Nasmith himself had swum to the torpedo to make it safe, taking care not to touch the "whiskers" of the firing pistol.

On his return passage to base Nasmith sank another transport, then passed through some more minefields. A mine's mooring-cable fouled one of the forward hydro-planes but Nasmith managed to get clear. During his twenty-day patrol Nasmith had sunk one gunboat, two transports, two ammunition ships, two supply ships

(a third had been driven ashore), had paralysed lines of communi-
cation and blockaded the Turkish army.

Nasmith won accelerated promotion to commander and an
award of the VC.

NEGAPATAM – see FORT ST DAVID 1746

NEVIS 1667
20 May
Second Dutch War 1665–67
This was an English defeat in the West Indies when a Franco-Dutch
squadron of seventeen ships of the line commanded by Admiral de
la Barre and Admiral Crijnssen encountered Captain Berry's
squadron of twelve ships off Nevis Point in the Leeward Islands.

The Franco-Dutch force was carrying more than 1,000 soldiers
to capture the Island of Nevis itself. In the ensuing battle Captain
Berry in the *Coronation* (56) fought bravely, but lost three of his
ships, while the enemy suffered no loss. Nevertheless the invasion
attempt was thwarted, the enemy force retired to Martinique and
Nevis remained in English hands.

O

ORAN (MERS EL KEBIR) 1940
3 July
World War II 1939–45
A melancholy action between heavy units of the Royal Navy and
the bulk of the French fleet at the naval base of Mers el Kebir near

Oran in Algeria. With the fall of France in 1940 it became imperative that the French Navy should not be surrendered to Germany.

The French Admiral Gensoul commanded the battleships *Dunkerque* (26,500 tons, 8 × 13") and *Strasbourg* (as her sister ship), the old battleships *Bretagne* and *Provence* (22,100 tons, 10 × 13.4"), eleven destroyers and five submarines. Admiral Sir James Somerville commanding Force H offered Gensoul three options on 2 July:

1 Join the British forces.
2 Sail to a British port or the West Indies under escort.
3 Scuttle his ships within six hours.

Otherwise Somerville would be compelled to use force, and he had with him the battlecruiser *Hood* (42,100 tons, 8 × 15"), the battleship *Valiant* (32,700 tons, 8 × 15"), battleship *Resolution* (29,150 tons, 8 × 15") and the carrier *Ark Royal* (22,000 tons, 72 aircraft).

Gensoul rejected the ultimatum and at 6 pm on 3 July Somerville's ships opened fire. A 15" shell from *Hood* struck *Bretagne* and she blew up and sank, killing about 950 men. *Dunkerque* and *Provence* and a 2,884-ton destroyer, *Mogador*, were severely damaged and beached themselves. The *Strasbourg* and four destroyers managed to escape to either Toulon or Algiers.

This tragic rift in Anglo-French naval relationships has left scars that even time finds difficult to heal.

See also DAKAR 1940 – page 252.

P

PONDICHERRY 1759
10 September
Seven Years' War 1756–63
The third and final clash between a squadron of seven of the line
commanded by Vice-Admiral Pocock and a French squadron of
eleven of the line under the Comte D'Aché off the Coromandel coast
in the Indian Ocean. (See CUDDALORE and NEGAPATAM.)

A running battle ensued with both squadrons formed into line
ahead on a parallel course. The accuracy and speed of the British
gunnery outweighed the enemy's superiority in numbers, and the
climax came when D'Aché's flagship *Zodiaque* (74) was severely
damaged and hauled out of line with her captain killed and the
Admiral wounded.

The British ships suffered considerable damage to rigging and
sails. The battle ended with the French managing to get into the
safety of Pondicherry, at a cost of about 1,500 men killed and
wounded.

Soon after this defeat D'Aché's squadron was recalled to France
and he abandoned the Indian Ocean.

PORTO PRAYA 1781
16 April
American War of Independence 1775–83
This action took place in the Porto Praya Roads on the south coast
of St Tiago in the Cape Verde Islands, between a small British
squadron commanded by Commodore Johnstone and an even
smaller squadron under the great French Admiral (then
Commodore) Pierre André de Suffren.

Johnstone's force comprised five of the line, several smaller ships
and some troop transports en route to take the Dutch colony at the
Cape of Good Hope.

Suffren left Brest for India with five of the line. Just two of these ships surprised Johnstone's, and these two, both 74s and one of them Suffren's flagship, the *Héros*, the other the *Annibal*, launched a furious attack, taking Johnstone unawares. After seriously damaging the British ships Suffren wisely broke off the action and retired.

While Johnstone remained to make good the damage, Suffren hurried to the Cape and seized it from the Dutch before Johnstone could interfere.

Ships engaged:

BRITISH		FRENCH	
Hero	(74)	Le Héros (flag)	(74)
Monmouth	(64)	L'Annibal	(74)
Romney (flag)	(50)	Le Vengeur	(64)
Jupiter	(50)	L'Artesien	(64)
Isis	(50)	Le Sphinx	(64)
3 Frigates			
East Indiamen and transports			

'PRINCE OF WALES' AND 'REPULSE'; GULF OF SIAM; SOUTH CHINA SEA – see FORCE Z

R

'RAWALPINDI' v 'SCHARNHORST' 1939
3 November
World War II 1939–45
The Peninsular and Oriental Steam Navigation Company's liner *Rawalpindi* was one of four sister ships requisitioned by the Admiralty for conversion to armed merchant cruisers. She had been

built in 1925, an elegant looking ship. She displaced 16,697 tons when converted and carried 8 × 6" guns. Her maximum speed was 17 knots. She was commanded by Captain E.C. Kennedy and was manned almost exclusively by RNR and RNVR personnel of the Royal Navy.

Rawalpindi was detached for Northern Patrol duties south-east of Iceland, on the lookout for German ships attempting to break out from Germany into the Atlantic and to intercept merchant ships trying to break the British blockade.

On the afternoon of 3 November 1939 the German battlecruisers *Scharnhorst* and *Gneisenau*, both of 26,000 tons and mounting 9 × 11" and 12 × 5.9" guns, were returning to Germany passing south-east of Iceland, having carried out unrestricted warfare in the Atlantic. At 1530 they were sighted by *Rawalpindi*. There was no escape for her. *Scharnhorst* alone had enormous superiority and advantage in every department.

Predictably, in the ensuing battle *Scharnhorst* pounded *Rawalpindi* to destruction, allowed her time to get away some lifeboats, but in the end only thirty-seven seamen survived. Captain Kennedy, thirty-nine officers and 226 ratings lost their lives in a sacrificial engagement which earned Kennedy a posthumous VC. The ship and her crew maintained the highest traditions of the Royal Navy.

S

SANTA CRUZ (Tenerife) 1797
25 July
French Revolutionary War 1793–1802
Horatio Nelson in his 74-gun ship *Theseus* was detached from the Mediterranean to seize a treasure ship believed to be taking refuge

in Santa Cruz. He took with him *Culloden* (74), *Zealous* (74) and *Leander* (50), with the 32-gun frigates *Seahorse*, *Emerald* and *Terpsichore*, and the cutter *Fox*. He had no detachment of troops which he thought necessary. This contributed to the failure of the attack, in the course of which *Fox* was sunk by cannon fire from the mole. All attacks were repulsed with heavy fire. Nelson, himself, lost his right arm and the venture was abandoned. Nelson's force lost 141 officers and men killed or drowned and 105 wounded.

SANTA MARTA (Action off Cartagena) 1702
19–24 August
War of the Spanish Succession 1702–13

This battle displayed the amazing courage of the English Vice-Admiral John Benbow, commanding seven ships of the line, and the cowardice of some of his captains. His adversary was the Frenchman Jean du Casse, commanding four of the line and a frigate.

The two squadrons met on 19 August off Santa Marta, 6 leagues N by W on Colombia's coast, north-east of Cartagena. A running fight ensued which lasted for four days, with Benbow leading his flagship *Breda* (70), supported by the two 48s (barely ships of the line) *Ruby* and *Falmouth*. The rest of his squadron comprised *Defiance*, *Greenwich*, *Pendennis* and *Windsor*.

Their captains ignored Benbow's signals and took no part in the action. Benbow broke off the action after he was severely wounded by a chain shot that smashed his right leg. The squadron returned north to Jamaica, and a few days later Benbow died of his wounds.

The captains of the four ships which took no part in the action were court-martialled. Those of *Defiance* and *Greenwich*, Kirby and Ware, were found guilty and executed by firing squad. The others were cashiered. The Frenchman de Casse wrote to Benbow after the action saying the captains deserved hanging.

SCHOONEVELD 1673
4 June
Third Dutch War 1672–74
Not to be confused with the battle a few days earlier which was awarded a battle honour.

The two opposing fleets at the battle some days earlier had retired to make good what damage they could, the Dutch, of course, having the advantage of home waters.

On 4 June, with an advantageous wind, De Ruyter weighed and suddenly attacked the Anglo-French fleet in almost the same position as the first battle. The Allies scuttled about to weigh and engage but they were driven before the Dutch almost to the English coast. Only Tromp and Spragge entered into some serious fighting, but even their action was not closely joined and after six hours De Ruyter recalled his fleet and gave up the chase.

Both battles has demonstrated De Ruyter's brilliance of handling a fleet at sea and in battle: he had frustrated an invasion attempt of the Netherlands, suffered minimal damage and casualties, and, into the bargain, had opened up Dutch ports to precious overseas convoys.

SIRTE, FIRST BATTLE OF, 1941
17 December
World War II 1939–45
This was a brief engagement in which Rear-Admiral Philip Vian, with a squadron of five cruisers and twenty destroyers, giving cover to a convoy to Malta from Alexandria, skirmished with units of the Italian battle fleet under Admiral Iachino. The action took place in the Gulf of Sirte, 34° 00' N, 18° 30' E.

The Italian force comprised the four battleships *Littorio* (35,000 tons, 9 × 15"), *Caio Duilio* (23,000 tons, 10 × 12"), *Andrea Doria* (23,000 tons, 10 × 12") and *Guilio Cesare* (23,000 tons, 10 × 12"), five cruisers and twenty destroyer escorts covering a convoy to Tripoli.

The Italian force had such enormous superiority in firepower that the British convoy seemed doomed. Despite this inferiority Vian attacked the enemy persistently with destroyer torpedo strikes and cruiser gunfire through smokescreens. This action, in a rising gale, was a fine example of the defence of a convoy in the face of overwhelming superiority.

Iachino preferred not to press home his advantage and was impressed by Vian's aggression. The battle never got to close grips and ended inconclusively.

SMYRNA CONVOY – see LAGOS 1759

SUEZ 1956
6 November
Israeli-Arab Wars: 20th Century
Several days after war broke out between Egypt and Israel Britain and France launched an assault on Egypt in an effort to safeguard the Suez Canal.

On 1 November the *Newfoundland* and *Diana* sank the Egyptian frigate *Domiat* (ex-*Nith*). At the assault on the 6th more than 100 seacraft were involved, including six carriers: *Eagle*, *Albion*, *Bulwark*, *Ocean*, *Theseus* and the French *Lafayette*. *Ocean* and *Theseus* carried Royal Marine Commandos and helicopters. RN aircraft flew about 2,000 sorties, and another 400 by helicopters. No 3 Commando Brigade was landed by LST/LCTs, with 45 Commando by air, all in 91 minutes.

The naval bombardment or "softening up" was restricted to nothing larger than 6" guns in order to minimize damage to civilian properties; wanton damage was carefully avoided.

Suez was the first major helicopter-borne assault from ships. It was politically disastrous and the British and French forces were compelled to withdraw after a short while.

T

TEXEL DESTROYER ACTION 1914
17 October
World War I 1914–18

The light cruiser *Undaunted* (3,500 tons, 2 × 6" and 6 × 4") led her 3rd Destroyer Flotilla in a spirited engagement about 40 miles south-west of the Texel in the Broad Fourteens in which the enemy were overwhelmed by superior power. The flotilla comprised *Lance*, *Lennox*, *Legion* and *Loyal*, all of them 994 tons and mounting 3 × 4" guns. They engaged and destroyed the four small German destroyers of 360 tons, all mounting 3 × 1.9" guns. They were *S 119*, *S 115*, *S 117* and *S 118*.

'TIRPITZ' – THE DESTRUCTION OF A BATTLESHIP 1944
1943–44 and 12 November 1944
World War II 1939–45

Tirpitz was a magnificent ship, virtually unsinkable and almost indestructible. Finally she succumbed to the attentions of the Fleet Air Arm, to the RAF and the earlier attempts of the X Craft – midget submarines – of the Royal Navy. When fully laden *Tirpitz* grossed 52,600 tons, with this impressive set of guns:

8 × 15"   12 × 5.9"   16 × 4.1"   16 × 37 mm   70 × 20 mm

In addition she carried 8 × 21" torpedo tubes and six aircraft. She carried a complement of 2,530 men. Her main waterline armoured belt was 12¾" thick.

Tirpitz remained a threat to the allied North Atlantic convoys as long as she remained afloat. Much of her time was spent at anchor in Kaa Fjord, an inlet of Altenfjord in the north of Norway, and in particular a threat to the North Russian convoys.

On the night of 19–20 September 1943 *Tirpitz* was attacked by midget submarines or X Craft. Four of them were survivors of the six that were towed across the North Sea by fleet submarines. *X 10* aborted her operation and was never heard of again. *X 6* and *X 7* were successful, though the crews were taken prisoner. Their explosions seriously damaged *Tirpitz*, unseating her main engines. She was immobilized for several months.

Another attempt was made to sink her on 3 April 1944. Specially trained FAA pilots and crews from the carriers *Victorious* (23,000 tons, 72 aircraft), *Furious* (22,450 tons, 20 aircraft), and the three 11,420-ton carriers *Pursuer* (18 aircraft), *Searcher* (24 aircraft) and *Emperor* (24 aircraft). They gave co-ordinated and extra cover to a Russian convoy. *Victorious* and *Furious* carried bombers, while the other four carriers provided fighter cover.

The planes attacked in two waves, scoring fifteen hits. But the battleship was saved by the 8" thickness of her armoured main deck. Nevertheless she was extensively damaged. Indeed, she never served as a battleship again. As German dockyard facilities were unable to repair her she was moved to Tromsö where she acted as a floating battery.

Tromsö lay within RAF bomber range, and on 12 November 1944 Lancasters of bomber command loaded with six-ton bombs successfully attacked her. The leviathan capsized. *Tirpitz* was destroyed.

TOULON 1744
11 February
War of the Austrian Succession 1739–48
This battle was fought between the British Mediterranean Fleet of twenty-eight ships of the line commanded by Admiral Thomas Mathews and a combined Franco-Spanish fleet of the same number commanded by the French Admiral La Bruyère de Court, and the Spanish Admiral Don José de Navarro commanding the Spanish contingent.

Mathews, leading the centre division in the *Namur* (90), was supported by Rear-Admiral Sir William Rowley commanding the van, while Vice-Admiral Richard Lestock led the rear division.

After a pursuit of three days battle was finally joined on 11 February, but so poor was Mathews's approach to the enemy line that while the British had wind advantage – it was only a breeze –

and while Mathews' and Rowley's divisions became heavily engaged, Lestock's division was miles astern. His division never in fact took part in the actual battle.

The conflict dragged on throughout the day, and apart from an individual ship action of some consequence the general action ended in some confusion and inconclusively. One such individual success was that of Captain Edward Hawke (of future fame) who set a fine example in his *Berwick* in capturing the Spanish *Poder* (60).

The failure at Toulon stirred the country to deep anger. Mathews resigned and came home, and Lestock returned home under arrest. A parliamentary enquiry led to a flurry of courts martial. Four lieutenants of the *Dorsetshire* were acquitted. Their captain, Burrish, was cashiered. Captain Williams of the *Royal Oak* was found guilty, as was Captain Ambrose of the *Rupert*. Captain Dilk of the *Chichester* was cashiered and Captain Norris of the *Essex* fled to Spain, never to be heard of again. Five other captains received a variety of sentences. Lestock, the real culprit, the reluctant admiral, the man who chose to misread signals and to avoid action if possible, was tried and acquitted. In due time Mathews stood trial and was cashiered, the result of stupidity more than anything else, for he was a brave enough, if dull, man.

What the courts martial did establish, to the detriment of the navy for years to come, was that the *Fighting Instructions* were inviolable, omnipotent. The effect was to stifle all initiative on the part of British admirals and condemned them to fight ineffective and sterile battles for the next fifty years until these formal tactics were flouted by admirals of great character such as Howe, Nelson and Hood.

TOULON 1793
August–December
French Revolutionary War 1793–1802

England declared war on France after the execution of Louis XVI. In August 1793 French royalists surrendered the town of Toulon to the British Mediterranean Fleet under the C-in-C, Sir Samuel Hood. British and Spanish forces occupied the town and harbour to discover an impressive haul of shipping – no less than thirty-one ships of the line and twenty-seven frigates and corvettes.

The French Convention besieged the town and on 17 December the Allies evacuated it. Only three ships were taken, nine others were burnt and the rest eventually went back into service with the French fleet.

TRINIDAD, CAPTURE OF, 1797
18 February
French Revolutionary War 1793–1802
After Spain declared war on Britain plans were made for the British to attack and capture the island of Trinidad, then in the hands of the Spanish.

In February 1797 Rear-Admiral Harvey and General Abercromby, with five ships of the line and troops, seized the island. The Spanish Admiral Ruiz de Apodaca, whose ships were only half-manned, burnt his squadron to prevent it falling into enemy hands. The small garrison put up only a token resistance before surrendering.

TRIPOLI: BOMBARDMENT 1941
21 April
World War II 1939–45
On 18 April 1941 the British Mediterranean Fleet under the command of Admiral Sir Andrew B. Cunningham, its C-in-C, with his flag in *Warspite*, left Alexandria, accompanying the transport *Breconshire* (9,776 tons) to besieged Malta.

On the evening of 20 April the battleships, with the cruiser *Gloucester* which had just joined the fleet, headed for Tripoli, which they bombarded.

In the harbour six freighters and one destroyer were severely damaged by the heavy shelling, and extensive damage was inflicted on the shore installations, many of which were left ablaze. *Valiant* suffered some damage on being mined.

Ships engaged:

Warspite	*30,600 tons*	8 × 15"	12 × 6"
Barham	*31,100*	"	"

288

Valiant	32,700	*8 × 15"*	*12 × 6"*
Gloucester		*9,400 tons*	*12 × 6"*
Hasty, Hereward,			
Havock, Hero, Hotspur		*1,340 tons*	*4 × 4.7"*
Jaguar, Juno, Janus		*1,690 tons*	*6 × 4.7"*
Jervis		*1,695 tons*	*6 × 4.7"*
Truant		*1,090/1,575 tons*	*11 × 21"*
			Torpedo Tubes
Formidable		*23,000 tons*	*72 aircraft*
FAA Squadrons:		826 and 829; 803 and 806	

U

'UPHOLDER'S' PATROL 1941
May
World War II 1939–45

Lieutenant-Commander David Wanklyn VC DSO commanded HM submarine *Upholder* and has been referred to by fellow submarine commander Alastair Mars as "the immortal Wanklyn". He was an outstanding submariner of great skill and daring. By May 1941 he had completed six patrols in the Mediterranean, working out of Gibraltar and Valetta in Malta. In one of these patrols he sank the 5,000-ton *Antonietta Lauro* off Lampedusa, the 2,500-ton German mv *Arta*, which he boarded and set ablaze, and the 8,000-ton *Leverkusen*.

It was his May 1941 patrol which earned him the highest award for gallantry on patrol in the southern approaches to the Straits of Messina. A defect in a torpedo necessitated changing it – a dreadful job in the confines of a cramped submarine's torpedo compartment forward. On 20 May Wanklyn saw a 4,000-ton tanker, two supply ships and an escort. He fired four torpedoes, but the bow cap of the fourth torpedo failed to open. The tanker was hit. In the counter-attacks the Asdic and hydrophones were put out of action by the depth-charging.

Three days later Wanklyn torpedoed the Vichy French tanker *Alberta*.

Only two torpedoes remained: one was the defect and the other was in the tube with the faulty bow cap. But both were prepared for action. At about 8.30 pm on 24 May Wanklyn sighted large vessels while *Upholder* was on the surface charging batteries. There were three ships, all of them liners of about 20,000 tons apiece. They were troopships engaged in a high-speed night-time dash to Libya. They were protected by four or five high-speed escorts.

Wanklyn's attack had to be rapid. The enemy ships altered course, giving a more favourable angle of attack. A moderate sea was running; he had no listening gear and only two torpedoes. He penetrated the escort's screen and got away both torpedoes. Two explosions were heard. The 17,800-ton *Conte Rosso* was torpedoed and sank. When she went down she was so close to *Upholder* that some of her wires probably scraped the submarine's hull.

Upholder endured a heavy and damaging counter-attack by thirty-seven depth charges, but the submarine survived and Wanklyn extricated her and made good the escape to Malta. It was for this exploit that Wanklyn won the VC.

It was almost exactly a year later that *Upholder* herself was sunk with all hands, on 14 April 1942.

Upholder completed twenty-four patrols, sinking two destroyers and two submarines (*Ammiraglio St Bon* and *Tricheo*). Merchant ships totalling about 82,000 tons were also sunk or seriously damaged, and a cruiser was damaged.

On her loss the Admiralty uniquely issued a statement:

"It is seldom proper for Their Lordships to draw distinction between different services rendered in the course of naval duty, but they take the opportunity of singling out those of HMS *Upholder*, under the command of Lieutenant-Commander Wanklyn for special mention. . . . Such was the standard of skill and daring, that the ship and her officers and men became an inspiration, not only to their own flotilla, but the fleet of which it was a part, and Malta, where for so long HMS *Upholder* was based. The ship and her company are gone, but the example and inspiration remain."

USHANT 1778
27 July
American War of Independence 1775–83

This encounter had all the ingredients of a battle royal but in the end it proved inconclusive and left the bitter taste of a prolonged dispute between two British admirals both of whom were court-martialled.

It was the first clash of fleets from Britain and France in this war and it took place about 108 miles NW by N of Ushant.

Admiral the Hon Augustus Keppel in his flagship *Victory* (100) commanded the Channel Fleet comprising twenty-six ships of the line. He had a splendid personal record, having served with distinction at Quiberon Bay (1759) and Havana (1762) and pleaded in vain for Byng's acquittal.

The opposing commander was Admiral the Comte D'Orvilliers who commanded the Brest Squadron of thirty-two ships of the line led by his flagship, the mighty *Bretagne* (110).

Four days of manoeuvring preceded the encounter. On the afternoon of 27 July the two fleets passed each other on opposite tacks, exchanging broadsides and inflicting damage to each other. When Keppel later renewed the action his rear division under the command of Vice-Admiral Hugh Palliser in *Formidable* (90) fell badly astern and seemed to ignore signals to rejoin. By the time Palliser did rejoin D'Orvilliers had retired into the gathering dusk and the battle was at an end. Neither side had lost a ship, but the casualties of killed and wounded were 700 British and 500 French. Damage to the ships was extensive.

Recriminations between Palliser and Keppel followed and would not be dispelled until both were court-martialled. Both were acquitted of the charges brought against them but the recriminations persisted. Palliser is considered to have come off worse than Keppel.

WAGER'S ACTION – see CARTAGENA 170-8

SECTION THREE

Single-Ship and Boat Service Actions

Acasta   SCHARNHORST 1940   8 June

In one disastrous clash of ships during the Norwegian Campaign of 1940 in the Second World War the Royal Navy lost an aircraft carrier and two destroyers with enormous loss of life, while the opposing German battlecruisers *Scharnhorst* and *Gneisenau* escaped virtually unscathed. The Germans, incidentally, always classified these ships as battleships rather than battlecruisers.

The 22,500-ton carrier *Glorious* was being escorted home by *Acasta* (Commander C.E. Glasfurd) and *Ardent* (Lieutenant-Commander J.F. Barker) when they encountered the two battlecruisers. Fire was opened with the German 11" guns at a range of 14 miles. Despite the sensible and courageous use of destroyers' smokescreens the *Glorious*' fate was soon sealed. She was struck many times and sank beneath a pall of smoke, leaving the destroyers at the enemy's mercy. Both launched torpedoes without success. *Ardent* sank first. *Acasta* scored a hit with one of her torpedoes abreast the after turret of *Scharnhorst*, causing some damage. *Acasta* was then overwhelmed and she, too, sank.

The position was logged as 68° 45' N, 4° 30' E.

Only forty-six men survived from about 1,500.

<u>Ships engaged:</u>

BRITISH	GERMAN
Glorious (22,500 tons)	*Scharnhorst* and *Gneisenau*
Acasta (Each of 1,350 tons,	(both 31,800 tons,
Ardent 4 × 4.7" guns,	9 × 11" guns)
8 × 21" TT)	

Achilles   LEOPARD 1917   16 March

Achilles, with a small boarding vessel named *Dundee* in company, was patrolling north of the Shetlands when she intercepted a well-armed German raider, the *Leopard*, disguised as a merchantman. In the ensuing engagement the *Leopard* continued firing until she sank with all hands.

Adventure   TWO LIONS 1681   16 September
During the years of Mediterranean piracy the British ship *Adventure* captured the Algerine ship *Two Lions* off Larache, Morocco.

Adventure   GOLDEN HORSE 1681   29 March
Adventure experienced another encounter with pirates when, in 1681, accompanied by the British ship *Calabash*, she engaged in battle with the Algerine ship *Golden Horse* in a position 25 miles south-west of Cape de Gata on the south coast of Spain. After a brisk battle the *Golden Horse* surrendered to the British ship *Nonsuch*.

Alert   LEXINGTON 1777   19 September
During the War of American Independence Lieutenant John Bazeley of the Royal Navy commanded the 10-gun cutter *Alert*. He encountered the more heavily armed brig the USS *Lexington* (16) off Ushant. After four hours of fighting the brig struck. From a crew of seventy-four she had lost seven killed and eleven wounded. *Alert*'s casualties amounted to two killed and three wounded from her complement of sixty.

Amazon   BELLE POULE 1806   13 March
During the Napoleonic War the British ship *London* captured the French *Marengo* (see MARENGO 1806 p. 305). In the same action the *Amazon* captured the French *Belle Poule* in a position 640 miles W by S of the Canary Islands.

Amethyst   CERBÈRE 1800   29 July
During the French Revolutionary war Jeremiah Goughlan earned immediate promotion to Lieutenant and a Boat Service Award to his ship, *Amethyst* for the capturing of the French *Cerbère*. Three British ships, *Amethyst*, *Viper* and *Impetueux*, carried out a skilled attack on Port Louis, Guadeloupe.

Amethyst   THÉTIS 1808   10 November
Captain Michael Seymour commanded *Amethyst* when she won a
deserved honour for her action in engaging in a two-hour battle
with the French *Thétis*, each of them armed with 36 guns. The
Frenchman was boarded and captured after having suffered 101
men killed and 172 wounded. Seymour's crew had nineteen killed
and fifty-one wounded.

Amethyst   NIEMAN 1809   5 April
Within six months of his success with the *Thétis* capture, Captain
Seymour chased and captured the French frigate *Niéman* (40), an
action which won him a baronetcy. The French ship lost forty-seven
killed and seventy-three wounded. *Amethyst* lost eight killed and
thirty-seven wounded.

Antelope   AQUILON 1757   13 May
In a spirited engagement during the Seven Years' War the British
ship *Antelope* drove ashore the French *Aquilon* where she became
a wreck in Audierne Bay, Brittany.

Ardent   SCHARNHORST 1940   8 June
See entry under *Acasta*.

Artois   RÉVOLUTIONNAIRE 1794   21 October
The French *Révolutionnaire* struck to the British *Artois* during the
French Revolutionary War off Ushant.

Astraea   GLOIRE 1795   10 April
During the French Revolutionary War the French ship *Gloire*
surrendered to the British *Astraea* after an engagement 150 miles
W by S of the Scilly Islands.

Beaulieu   CHEVRETTE 1801   22 July
Boats from the British ship *Beaulieu*, as well as those from *Doris*,
Robust, *Uranie* and *Ville de Paris*, took part in a Boat Service Action
when the French *Chevrette* was cut out in Camaret Bay.

Beaver　　　　ATHALANTE 1804　　　　31 March
See entry under *Scorpion.*

Bellona　　　　COURAGEUX 1761　　　　15 August
During the Seven Years' war the 74-gun *Bellona*, commanded by
Captain R. Faulknor, encountered the French *Courageux* (74) off
Vigo, spain. In 39 minutes the Frenchman was captured, together
with £320,000 worth of cargo, having been overwhelmed by the
British gunnery and marksmanship. 240 dead and 110 wounded
Frenchmen littered her decks. By contrast the British lost six killed
and twenty-eight wounded.

Bengal (Royal　　HOKOKU MARU 1942　　11 November
Indian Navy)
The RIN minesweeper of 650 tons was acting as the sole escort for
the Dutch tanker *Ondina* in the Indian Ocean during the Second
World War when she encountered two Japanese raiders. In the spirited action which followed one of the raiders, the *Hokoku Maru*,
was sunk. The *Aikoku Maru* managed to escape, while the *Bengal*,
although damaged by a torpedo, survived the ordeal and safely
brought her charge to port.

Blanche　　　　PIQUE 1795　　　　5 January
The French vessel *Pique* was taken by the British *Blanche* after a
single ship-to-ship encounter 3 miles to the west of Marie Galante
in the West Indies.

Bonne Citoyenne　　FURIEUSE 1809　　　　6 July
After a brief action during the Napoleonic War the French *Furieuse*
capitulated to the British *Bonne Citoyenne* 700 miles E by S of Cape
Race, Newfoundland.

Calabash　　　　GOLDEN HORSE 1681　　29 March
See entry under *Adventure.*

Carmania   CAP TRAFALGAR 1914   14 September

The 19,524-ton armed merchant cruiser *Carmania* (Captain N. Grant RN) with 8 × 4.7" guns made one of the earliest naval encounters of the First World War when she engaged and sank the German armed liner of the Hambourg-Sud-America company, the *Cap Trafalgar*, off the island of Trinidad. The *Carmania* lost nine killed and twenty-six wounded. Among the German casualties was the commanding officer.

Centaur   CURIEUX 1804   4 February

This Boat Service Action entailed a pull of about 20 miles for the boats' crews of *Centaur* (74). The boarding party, led by Lieutenant R.C. Reynolds, scrambled aboard the French brig/corvette *Curieux* at anchor at Fort Royal, Martinique, and overwhelmed the crew in a well-conducted exercise.

Centaur   SEVOLOD 1808   26 August

See entry under *Implacable*.

Centurion   NUESTRA SENORA DE   20 June
                     COVADONGA 1743

During his formidable circumnavigation of the world in 1740–44, George Anson's squadron of seven ships lost six ships, leaving his own *Centurion* to complete the task. But *Centurion* herself nearly came to an end in June 1743 when she encountered a well-armed Spanish treasure ship off Cape Espiritu Santos, Phillipines. It took Anson just 1½ hours to overcome the opposition and to capture booty of measureless value, which also established his own personal fortune.

Comet   SYLPHE 1808   11 August

Commander C.F. Daly, commanding the 16-gun *Comet*, chased three French vessels in the Bay of Biscay led by the *Sylphe* (16) in a position about 170 miles south of Ushant.

Sylphe was brought to action, and by the time she surrendered she had suffered seven killed and five wounded out of her crew of ninety-eight. *Comet* suffered no casualties.

Comus FREDERIKSCOARN 1807 15 August
This action during the Napoleonic War took just one hour before
the Danish *Frederikscoarn* struck to the Royal Navy *Comus* (22).
The larger Danish ship had a crew of about eighty aboard. She surrendered off Marstrand, north of Gotenberg, Sweden.

Countess of PALLAS 1779 23 September
Scarborough
See entry under *Serapis*.

Crescent RÉUNION 1793 20 October
Captain James Saumarez (later Admiral and 1st Baron) distinguished himself in command of the 36-gun *Crescent* in capturing
the French *Réunion* (36) off Cherbourg during the French
Revolutionary War. After a two-hour fight the Frenchman surrendered having suffered thirty-three killed and eighty-eight wounded.
Crescent suffered no casualties. Saumarez was rewarded with a
knighthood.

Dart DÉSIRÉE 1800 8 July
Commander P. Campbell led a resourceful night raid into Dunkirk's
harbour to attack four French frigates known to be there. His piratical force of brigs and fireships was led by the sloop *Dart*. Her men
boarded the French *Désirée* (40), fought her hand-to-hand to a

standstill and then sailed her out as a prize. The French lost 100
men in killed and wounded. *Dart* suffered just one death and seventeen wounded. Other ships engaged were: *Ann, Biter, Boxer,
Camperdown, Comet, Falcon, Kent, Nile, Rosario, Selby, Stag,
Teaser, Vigilant, Wasp*, and boats of *Andromeda, Babet, Nemesis*
and *Prévoyante*.

Diana ZEFIER 1809 11 September
After a lively engagement near Menado off the Celebes the Dutch
brig *Zefier* of 14 guns surrendered to the 10-gun brig *Diana*.

Dido and *Lowestoft*   MINERVE 1795   24 June
During the French Revolutionary War *Dido* was saved from
destruction at the hands of the French *Minerve* (38) by the timely
arrival of the 5th rate *Lowestoffe*. Captain Towry of the 28-gun
Dido had taken on the heavier *Minerve* off Minorca. The arrival of
Lowestoffe turned the advantage and the Frenchman was taken.
The French *Artemis* was also engaged but managed to escape. The
action took place 150 miles north of Minorca.

Doris   CHEVRETTE 1801   22 July
See entry under *Beaulieu*.

Dorsetshire   RAISONNABLE 1758   29 May
The 3rd rate *Dorsetshire*, only a year old, fought a hard engagement off the French coast against the 64-gun *Raisonnable* before
capturing her.

Dryad   PROSERPINE 1796   13 June
Lord A. Beauclerk, commanding the 36-gun frigate *Dryad* proved
too good a match for the French captain of the 38-gun *Proserpine*
when the two ships fought off Cape Clear. After a short duel
Proserpine surrendered.

Dundee   LEOPARD 1917   16 March
See entry under *Achilles*.

Endymion   (AMERICAN) PRESIDENT 1815   15 July
This action took place 70 miles SE by S of Montauk Point, Long
Island. The *American President* actually surrendered to *Pomone*
and *Tenedos* who came up at the end of the action.

Eurotas   CLORINDE 1814   25 February
Eurotas encountered the French *Clorinde* 180 miles WSW of Ushant
and battered her into submission with accurate gunfire.

Fisgard   IMMORTALITÉ 1798   20 October
This encounter was near the French port of Brest during the French
Revolutionary War. It was fought between two frigates, was bitterly
contested and resulted in many casualties on both sides before the
Frenchman conceded victory. The 38-gun *Fisgard* lost ten killed and
twenty-six wounded. *Immortalité* (40) suffered fifty-four killed and
sixty-one wounded.

Foudroyant   GUILLAUME TELL 1800   30 March
See also *Lion*, *Penelope* and *Vincejo*. *Foudroyant* captured the
French *Guillaume Tell* (80), one of the few ships to escape from
Nelson's victory of the Nile.

Foudroyant   PÉGASE 1782   21 April
Captain Jervis (later Admiral, Earl of St Vincent) distinguished
himself in a relatively rare battle, a ship-to-ship engagement
between large ships. *Foudroyant*, the British ship, carried 80 guns;
she chased and brought to action the 74-gun *Pégase* off Brest. The
French ship was boarded and captured. She had suffered ninety
casualties.

Galatea   LYNX 1807   21 January
During the Napoleonic War Lieutenant W. Coombe RN led boats
from the 32-gun frigate *Galatea* in an 8-hour gruelling pull before
a third attempt to board the French 16-gun *Lynx* succeeded. In this
successful Boat Service Action the *Galatea* lost nine men killed and
another twenty-two wounded. The French lost fourteen killed and
twenty wounded. The action took place 10 miles east of La Guaira,
Venezuela. Coombe was given command of the prize.

Glowworm   ADMIRAL HIPPER 1940   8 April
Lieutenant-Commander Gerald Roope RN conned his 1,345-ton
destroyer *Glowworm* (4 × 4.7") in a suicidal action of ramming the
German 12,600 ton heavy cruiser *Admiral Hipper* (8 × 8"), an
action which won him a posthumous award of the Victoria Cross.

Hebrus   ÉTOILE 1814   27 March

After a spirited ship-to-ship action off the Nez de Cherbourg towards the end of the Napoleonic War the French ship *Étoile* surrendered to the British *Hebrus*.

Hussar   RAISON 1795   16 May

See entry under *Thetis*/PRÉVOYANTE.

Impetueux   CERBÈRE 1800   29 July

See entries under *Viper* and *Amethyst*.

Implacable   SEVOLOD 1808   26 August

Captain Thomas Byam Martin (later Admiral and renowned chronicler) commanded the *Implacable* (74) when he captured the Russian *Sevolod* within sight of the enemy fleet in the Baltic in the Gulf of Finland off Rogervik. *Sevolod* was, in fact, destroyed the following day by fire. The Russian admiral's ship was taken when *Centaur* (74) came to the *Implacable*'s assistance.

Indefatigable   VIRGINIE 1796   21 April

Superior gunnery proved its worth in the encounter and long-running engagement over fifteen hours off the Lizard. The British *Indefatigable* (38) won the day with no casualties, while the French *Virginie* (44) had fifteen killed and twenty-seven wounded.

Indefatigable   DROITS DE L'HOMME 1797   13 January

Captain Sir Edward Pellew (later Viscount and Admiral) commanded *Indefatigable*, and Captain R.C. Reynolds commanded the 36-gun *Amazon*, when they sighted and engaged the 74-gun ship of the line, *Droits de l'Homme*, homeward bound from Bantry Bay. Action began at about 5.30 pm in heavy weather. During the hours of darkness and heavy seas two ships, the Frenchman and *Amazon*, were wrecked on the Penmarch rocks, near Quimper in Audierne Bay, Brittany, with great loss of life. Only *Indefatigable* survived to tell the story.

Jervis Bay   ADMIRAL SCHEER 1940   5 November
In an act of gallant self-sacrifice Captain E.S.F. Fegen gave his life
and those of his crew aboard *Jervis Bay*, an armed merchant cruiser.
She was the sole escort charged with the defence of a convoy of
thirty-seven ships. The German battleship *Admiral Scheer* sank
Jervis Bay and several merchant ships, though most escaped the
scene and reached safety. The crew of *Jervis Bay* suffered heavy loss
of life. Captain Fegen won a posthumous VC.

Kingfisher   SARDINIA 1681   22 May
The sloop *Kingfisher* encountered and brought to battle seven
Algerine piratical men-of-war off Sardinia during the period of
Mediterranean slaving and piracy.

Lion   SANTA DOROTEA 1798   15 July
During the French Revolutionary War the British ship *Lion* (64)
came upon four Spanish frigates which formed line of battle on
identifying the British flag. *Lion* had the weather gage and therefore managed to cut out the rear-most frigate, the *Santa Dorotea*,
and captured her.

Lion   GUILLAUME TELL 1800   30 March
See entry under FOUDROYANT. *Lion* was one of the four British
ships, *Lion*, *Penelope*, *Foudroyant* and *Vincejo*, which intercepted
the French *Guillaume Tell*, escapee from the Nile, as she tried to
escape to Malta.

Lively   MUTINE 1797   29 May
A notable Boat Service Action took place at Santa Cruz, Tenerife,
when boats from the British ships *Lively*, a Fifth Rate, and *Minerve*;
they cut out the French *Mutine* and captured her.

Lively   TOURTERELLE 1795   13 March
The British *Lively* and the French *Tourterelle* encountered each
other about 40 miles north of Ushant. After a brief engagement the
badly damaged French ship struck.

London   MARENGO 1806   13 March
Captain Sir Harry Burrard Neale commanded the 98-gun 1st Rate
London when he encountered the 80-gun Frenchman *Marengo*
homeward bound from the East Indies, about 640 miles W by S of
the Canary Isles. It took four hours of heavy fighting before
Marengo was reduced to surrender after losing her admiral, Rear-
Admiral Linois, and her captain. In addition there were another
fifty-seven killed and fifty-six wounded.

Mars   HERCULE 1798   21 April
During the French Revolutionary War Captain Alexander Hood, of
the famous naval family, commanded the *Mars* which chased and
took the Frenchman *Hercule* (74) near the Brest roads. *Hercule*
suffered 290 killed and wounded. Captain Hood was among the
thirty killed aboard *Mars*.

Mary Rose   THE SEVEN ALGERINES 1669   29 December
During the period of Mediterranean piracy a concentrated attack
by seven Algerine Corsairs which owed allegiance to the Bey of
Algiers was repulsed by the British *Mary Rose*.
 She put up a spirited and successful defence of her convoy and
earned the award of a Single Ship Action honour.

Mersey   KÖNIGSBERG 1915   15 July
The German light cruiser *Königsberg* (3,350 tons, 10 × 4.1")
carried out a series of raids along the River Rufiji in German East
Africa. She was spotted by a reconnaissance aircraft. Two British
naval monitors, *Mersey* and *Severn*, both of 1,260 tons, and each
with 2 × 6" and 2 × 4.7" guns, sought out the cruiser and destroyed
her.
   The monitors were supported by HM ships *Challenger*,
Hyacinth, *Laconia*, *Pioneer*, *Pyramus* and *Weymouth*.

Monmouth   FOUDROYANT 1758   28 February
This was one of the most notable single-ship actions. *Monmouth*
(64) was commanded by Captain Arthur Gardiner. In the ensuing

action, which lasted about four hours, the 80 gun *Foudroyant* lost 100 killed and another ninety of her crew wounded. *Foudroyant* was taken by *Monmouth*.

In a separate action the British *Revenge* and *Berwick* fought and captured the French *Orphée*.

In yet another separate action the British *Monarch* and *Montagu* fought a fierce duel with the French *Oriflame*, driving her ashore.

All of these actions took place about 20 miles south of Cartagena. When Captain Gardiner of *Monmouth* was killed, Lieutenant Carkett assumed command and continued the fight with *Foudroyant*. The latter struck only when *Swiftsure* and *Hampshire* came up. Later she served under the British flag with distinction.

Northumberland   GROIX ISLAND 1812   22 May
The two British ships, *Northumberland* and *Growler*, attacked and destroyed the three French ships *Andromaque*, *Ariane* and *Mameluk* inshore of the Île de Groix.

Nottingham   MAGNANIME 1748   31 January
The award was made to *Nottingham* after the two British ships *Nottingham* and *Portland* captured the French ship *Magnanime* in a position about 250 miles WSW of Ushant.

Nymphe   CLÉOPATRE 1793   19 June
This was the first decisive action in the new war. The French ship *Cléopatre* struck to the British *Nymphe* in a position 20 miles W by S of Start Point.

Nymphe   CONSTANCE 1797   9 March
The British ships *Nymphe* and *St Fiorenzo* engaged the French ships *Constance* and *Resistance* in a position about 10 miles south-west of Brest. *Nymphe* captured the *Constance*.

Onyx   MANLY 1809   1 January
After two and a half hours' battling in heavy weather in the North Sea the small British vessel *Onyx* (Commander C. Gill) mounting

only 8 guns, took the Dutch *Manly* (12). Curiously, casualties were minimal. *Manly* had been taken from the British three years before.

Pearl   SANTA MONICA 1779   14 September
The British *Pearl* overwhelmed the Spanish *Santa Monica* in a sharp encounter. The Spaniard struck about 18 miles S by E of Corvo Island in the Azores.

Pelican   ARGUS 1813   14 August
The brig *Pelican* (16), commanded by Commander J.F. Maples, defeated the American brig-sloop of 18 guns *Argus* in the St George's Channel in a position about 15 miles west of St David's Head.

Penelope   GUILLAUME TELL 1800   30 March
Captain Harry Blackwood (later Vice-Admiral Sir Henry) commanded the frigate *Penelope* and played a notable part in company with *Lion* and *Foudroyant*. The action began with *Penelope* and *Vincejo* just outside Malta's Valetta harbour and ended 20 miles south of Cape Passero, Sicily.

Peterel   LIGURIENNE 1800   21 March
The British *Peterel* came upon the French *Ligurienne* and her convoy, and immediately set about bringing her to action. *Ligurienne* defended as best she could but struck to the *Peterel*. The British ship also captured two ships of the convoy, close off Cape Couronne near Marseilles.

Phaeton   SAN JOSEF 1800   27 October
It is only of recent years the *Phaeton*'s success has merited a Battle Honour award. Her boats cut out and captured the Spanish *San Josef* at Fuengirola near Malaga.

Phoebe   NÉRÉIDE 1797   21 December
Captain Robert Barlow commanded the 36-gun *Phoebe*. He engaged in a long chase and a gallant action 180 miles W of Ushant before taking the *Néréide*. She suffered three killed and ten

wounded. The Frenchman lost twenty killed and fifty-three wounded.

Phoebe   AFRICAINE 1801   19 February
Captain Barlow commanded the 36-gun *Phoebe* in a fierce two-hour ordeal with the French *Africaine* (40) off Ceuta, Spain. *Africaine*, crowded with 400 soldiers, suffered appallingly. She lost 200 men killed and 143 wounded. *Phoebe* lost one killed and twelve wounded. Barlow was rewarded with a knighthood.

Phoebe   ESSEX and ESSEX JUNIOR 1814   28 March
Captain J. Hillyar commanded the *Phoebe* towards the end of the Napoleonic War in an action off Valparaiso, Chile, with the 40-gun American frigate *Essex*. The American and her consort, *Essex Junior*, were taken by *Phoebe* with the help of *Cherub* (16) commanded by Commander Tucker.

Phoenix   DIDON 1805   10 August
Captain Thomas Baker commanded the frigate *Phoenix* (36) when he fought and captured the French *Didon* (44) in the Atlantic. It had been a three-hour struggle. *Didon* suffered twenty-seven killed and forty-four wounded. *Phoenix* lost twelve killed and twenty-eight wounded.

Portland   AUGUSTE 1746   9 February
The British ship *Portland* captured the French *Auguste* in a position 80 miles S by E of the Scilly Isles.

Portland   MAGNANIME 1748   31 January
See entry under *Nottingham*.

Princess   NORTH SEA 1667   20 April
This encounter during the Second Dutch War is sometimes referred to as a Dogger Bank action. The British ship *Princess* fought singly against seventeen men-of-war close by the Dogger Bank.

Revenge   ORPHÉE 1758   28 February
Captain John Storr commanded the *Revenge* when he encountered
the French *Orphée* off Cape Gata. A running battle ensued before
Storr took the Frenchman six miles off Cartagena, but at a cost of
twenty-four British lives and 100 wounded. Storr himself suffered
wounds.

Robust   CHEVRETTE 1801   22 July
See entry under *Beaulieu*.

Romney   SIBYLLE 1794   17 June
The British ship *Romney* captured the French ship *Sibylle* in
Mykoni harbour.

Royalist   WESER 1813   21 October
The small 16-gun *Royalist* fought bravely with Nelsonian valour
against a considerably more powerful enemy ship, the 44-gun
Weser, and would surely have been overwhelmed but for the timely
appearance of the 74-gun *Ripon*. The action took place off
Ushant. *Weser* suffered four killed and fifteen wounded before
being taken.

St Fiorenzo   RESISTANCE 1797   9 March
While the British ship *Nymphe* captured the French *Constance*

(q.v.) the *St Fiorenzo* captured the French *Resistance* 10 miles
south-west of Brest.

St Fiorenzo   PSYCHE 1805   1805
During her commission in the East the *St Fiorenzo* engaged and captured the French *Psyche* 4 miles ESE of Ganjam, Bay of Bengal.

St Fiorenzo   PIEDMONTAISE 1808   8 March
The French *Piedmontaise* struck her colours after enduring the
accurate gunfire of *St Fiorenzo* in an action south of Cape Comorin,
India.

Santa Margarita   TAMISE 1796   8 June
In the action in which the British *Unicorn* captured the French
Tribune, the *Santa Margarita* engaged and captured the French
Tamise to the westward of the Scilly Isles. A third ship, *La Legère*,
managed to escape.

Sappho   ADMIRAL JAWL 1808   2 March
The Danish *Admiral Jawl* surrendered to the British *Sappho* 20
miles north-east of Flamborough Head.

Scorpion   ATHALANTE 1804   31 March
Commander G.N. Hardinge, commander of the 16-gun brig
Scorpion, encountered the Dutch corvette *Athalante*. In a skilled
cutting-out operation boarding parties from *Scorpion* and *Beaver*
captured the *Athalante* in the Vlie Roads in the Netherlands.

Scorpion   ORESTE 1810   21 January
Nearly six years after the *Athalante* honour, *Scorpion* excelled
herself again, under Commander Stanfell, while off Basseterre,
Guadeloupe. She fought the 14-gun French brig *Oreste* for two
hours during which time she was also under the gunfire of shore
batteries. After two hours *Oreste* was taken. Stanfell later won
promotion.

Seahorse   BADERE ZAFFER 1808   6 July
The *Seahorse* engaged and captured the larger Turkish frigate
Badere Zaffer and damaged the corvette *Alis Fezan*.

Seine   VENGEANCE 1800   20 August
The British ship *Seine* captured the French ship *Vengeance* in the
Mona Passage, separating Puerto Rico and the Dominican
Republic.

Serapis   BONHOMME RICHARD 1779   23 September
This was one of the bitterest encounters at sea probably in the whole
of the 18th century. John Paul Jones commanded the *Bonhomme*

Richard, together with the frigate *Alliance* (commanded by a half-mad Frenchman, Pierre Landais), the frigate *Pallas* and two smaller vessels, all flying the American flag. On 23 September 1779 this squadron encountered a British Baltic convoy off Flamborough Head comprising forty-four sail escorted by the frigate *Serapis* (50), commanded by Captain Richard Pearson, and the sloop *Countess of Scarborough*. Pearson gave cover to the convoy which escaped northward. The *Pallas* took the British sloop, but the *Alliance* seems to have taken little or no part in the engagement. The duel between the two major ships was historic. The two ships fought muzzle to muzzle for two hours. The American lost all her guns except two. She was on the brink of defeat when *Serapis* blew up. Pearson struck; he had lost 128 men killed and wounded; the American casualties numbered 150. *Bonhomme Richard* sank two days later. Jones transferred to *Serapis* and put in at the Texel. Pearson was court-martialled, cleared and knighted.

Severn   KÖNIGSBERG 1915   15 July
See entry under *Mersey*.

Shannon   CHESAPEAKE 1813   1 June
A series of inconclusive engagements between British and American frigates during the French Napoleonic War prompted Captain Philip Broke of the *Shannon* (38) to invite Captain Lawrence of the *Chesapeake* (36) to engage in single combat. Lawrence accepted. After only fifteen minutes of battle *Chesapeake* was beaten and captured – all within sight of Boston. Lawrence was mortally wounded. The *Shannon* was eventually brought home to England.

Shannon   LUCKNOW 1858   16 March
During the Indian Mutiny *Shannon*'s naval brigade was placed under the command of General Sir Colin Campbell and contributed, especially with artillery, in the defeat of the mutinous rebels.

Southampton   ÉMERAUDE 1757   12 September
In a curious encounter the British *Southampton* (32) captured the *Émeraude* off Brest with both ships locked foul of each other in a dead calm.

Speedy   GAMO 1801   6 May
This action, resulting in the capture of the Spanish ship *Gamo*, took place 15 miles to the south-west of Barcelona.

Surprise   HERMIONE 1799   25 October
Hermione's story is an astonishing one. Two years before this encounter, in 1797, her mutinous crew handed her over to the Spanish at La Guaira. Now, with a ship's company of 385 men, she lay moored between two batteries at Puerto Cabello. Captain Hamilton in his ship *Surprise* found *Hermione* and pressed home an attack. After some fierce fighting the Spaniards surrendered, but only after having suffered 119 men killed and another ninety-seven wounded. Almost unbelievably *Surprise*'s casualties amounted to only twelve wounded.

Sydney   EMDEN 1914   9 November
The German light cruiser *Emden* (3,544 tons, 10 × 4.1") commanded by Captain von Müller scoured the waters of the Far East sinking and capturing a huge mass of Allied shipping. The British light cruiser HMAS *Sydney* (5,400 tons, 8 × 6"), commanded by Captain Glossop, encountered the *Emden* off the Cocos Islands and with her superior guns could expect to defeat her rapidly. But it took four hours before she sank, taking with her 115 men killed and fifty-six wounded. *Sydney* suffered four killed and twelve wounded.

Sydney   KORMORAN 1941   19 November
In an amazing encounter in Australian waters, the light cruiser *Sydney* (6,830 tons, 8 × 6") engaged the heavily armed German raider *Kormoran* disguised as a merchantman. The raider put up a powerful resistance before being destroyed, but so great was

Sydney's own damage that she, too, sank with all hands.

Sybille   FORTE 1799   1 March
During the French Revolutionary War the French ship *Forte* struck her colours to the British *Sybille* after a fearsome fight in the Balasore Road, Bay of Bengal. Her capture was much facilitated by a detachment of the so-called Brigade which was aboard.

Sylvia   ECHO 1810   26 April
The Dutch *Echo* and two small transports were captured by the British *Sylvia* about ten miles north of Batavia.

Telegraph   HIRONDELLE 1799   18 March
The *Hirondelle* succumbed to *Telegraph*'s superior gunnery and struck her colours about 30 miles north-west of the Île de Bas, Brittany.

Terpsichore   MAHONESA 1796   13 October
The British frigate *Terpsichore* (38) pounded the Spanish frigate *Mahonesa* (34) into submission after a resolute and spirited engagement off Cartagena.

Thetis   BOUFFONNE 1761   17 July
The British *Thetis* captured the French *Bouffonne* west of Cadiz.

Thetis   PRÉVOYANTE 1795   16 May
Two British ships, *Thetis* and *Hussar*, engaged a force of four French ships. *Thetis* captured the *Prévoyante* and *Hussar* took *La Raison*. The other two French ships escaped. The action took place 60 miles E by N of Cape Henry, Virginia.

Thistle   HAVIK 1810   10 February
The British *Thistle* captured the Dutch *Havik* 480 miles SE by S of Bermuda.

Thunderer   ACHILLE 1761   17 July
Captain Charles Proby commanded the new *Thunderer* (74) when she entered into battle with the French *Achille* (64) and took her by boarding 57 miles from Cadiz. During the battle one of *Thunderer*'s forward guns exploded adding considerably to the casualty list. *Thunderer* lost seventeen men killed and 113 wounded.

Unicorn   VESTALE 1761   8 January
Captain J. Hunt commanded the 28-gun, 6th Rate frigate *Unicorn* when she engaged the 30-gun French frigate *Vestale* off Penmarch Point 30 miles south-west of Belle Isle, Brittany. Both captains were killed in the action. Lieutenant Symons replaced Hunt and it was he who captured the *Vestale*.

Unicorn   TRIBUNE 1796   8 June
This Chatham-built 32-gun frigate was a later *Unicorn* than the victor over the *Vestale*. Captain Williams commanded her against the French frigate *Tribune* west of the Scilly Isles. Although it was a one-sided contest, it lasted several hours, and while *Unicorn* suffered no casualties the French frigate lost thirty-seven men killed and another fifteen were wounded. See also entry for *Santa Mararita*.

Uranie   CHEVRETTE 1801   22 July
See entry under *Beaulieu*.

Vestal   BELLONE 1759   21 February
The French *Bellone* was captured by the British *Vestal* after an engagement 600 miles south-west of Lizard Head.

Victorious   RIVOLI 1812   22 February
Victorious was accompanied by *Weazle* in this action. Captain John Talbot commanded the *Victorious* in a contest between two 74-gun ships of the line. The action, fought 14 miles NW by W of Cape Salvore in the Gulf of Trieste, lasted for four hours before the *Rivoli* struck. The French suffered 400 casualties. *Victorious* lost

thirty-two men killed and 109 wounded. She and her consort also destroyed the *Mercure*.

Ville de Paris   CHEVRETTE 1801   22 July
See entry under *Beaulieu*.

Vincejo   GUILLAUME TELL 1800   30 March
See entries under *Foudroyant*, *Penelope* and *Lion*.

Viper   CERBÈRE 1800   29 July
See entries under *Amethyst* and *Impetueux*.

Virginie   GUELDERLAND 1808   19 May
The Dutchman *Guelderland* struck to the British *Virginie* after a spirited action 240 miles north-west of Cape Finisterre.

Weazle   RIVOLI 1812   22 February
See entry under *Victorious*.

Weazle   BOSCALINE BAY 1813   22 April
The *Weazle* destroyed four French gunboats and eight vessels of a convoy in Boscaline (Marina) Bay, near Split, now Croatia.

XE 1 and *XE 3*   TAKAO 1945   31 July
Lieutenant Ian E. Fraser RNR (commanding *XE 1*) and Leading Seaman James J. Magennis (of *XE 3*) were both awarded VCs for their gallantry in a midget submarine attack known as Operation Struggle in attacking and severely damaging the Japanese heavy cruiser *Takao* in the Johore Strait, Singapore.

The midget submarine *XE 4* cut the cable between Saigon and Hong Kong (Operation Sabre) in another gallant exploit.

X 6 and *X 7*   TIRPITZ 1943   22 September
Lieutenant Basil C.G. Place RN (later Rear-Admiral) was awarded a VC for his part in the operation to attack the German battleship *Tirpitz* in her lair in Altenfjord, Norway. German heavy naval units

were a constant threat to the Allied Russian convoys. Place's 35-ton midget submarine was *X 7*. In company were the *X 6* (Lieutenant D. Cameron RNR) who was also awarded the VC; *X 5* was lost; *X 8* had to be scuttled; *X 9* was lost on passage; *X 10* had been sent to attack the *Scharnhorst* in a nearby berth, but the attempt failed and the boat and crew were recovered.

Tirpitz was put out of commission for six months. *Scharnhorst* was sunk some weeks later.

SECTION FOUR

Fleet Air Arm Squadron Honours

Fleet Air Arm Battle Honours which have been promulgated do not cover events prior to the Second World War. This is not to say that naval aviators and their squadrons had not been engaged in battle prior to that period. Indeed, a naval aircraft sank a U-boat as long ago as 1917. It is all to do with nomenclature. The Fleet Air Arm's title was originally the Royal Flying Corps, Naval Wing. It then became the Royal Naval Air Service. In 1918 it lost its identity and became merged into the Royal Air Force. It was not until 1937 that the Fleet Air Arm regained its independence and new title. It is from this date that its battle honours have been awarded.

Until now the accepted source for naval battle honours has been Oliver Warner's *Battle Honours of the Royal Navy**, but his account proved wanting in many respects. Consequently I have resorted to the primary source at the Ministry of Defence Historical Branch Library, and the following compilation can be regarded as the definitive listing. I am also grateful to the staff of the Historical Branch Library for their help and kindness.

* Published by George Philip & Son Ltd, 1956.

700 Squadron
River Plate 1939
Norway 1940
Spartivento 1940
Atlantic 1940–1
Matapan 1941
Mediterranean 1942–3
North Africa 1942–3

701 Squadron
Norway 1940

723 Squadron
Vietnam 1967–71

737 Squadron
Falkland Islands 1982

767 Squadron
Mediterranean 1940

800 Squadron
Norway 1940
Mediterranean 1940–1
Spartivento 1940
Bismarck Action 1941
Malta Convoys 1941–2
Diego Suarez 1942
North Africa 1942
Aegean 1943–4
South France 1944
Burma 1944–5
Korea 1950
Falkland Islands 1982

801 Squadron
Norway 1940–1
Dunkirk 1940

Malta Convoys 1942
Japan 1945
Korea 1952–3
Falkland Islands 1982

802 Squadron
Norway 1940
Atlantic 1941
Arctic 1942
Korea 1952

803 Squadron
North Sea 1939
Norway 1940
Libya 1940–1
Matapan 1941
Mediterranean 1941
Crete 1941

804 Squadron
Norway 1940–4
Atlantic 1941
North Africa 1942
Burma 1945
Korea 1951–2

805 Squadron
Crete 1941
Libya 1941–2
Korea 1951–2

806 Squadron
Norway 1940
Dunkirk 1940
Mediterranean 1940–1
Libya 1940–1
Crete 1941
Matapan 1941

Diego Suarez 1942
Malta Convoys 1942

807 Squadron
Atlantic 1940
Malta Convoys 1941–2
North Africa 1942–3
Sicily 1943
Salerno 1943
South France 1944
Aegean 1944
Burma 1945
Korea 1950–3

808 Squadron
Spartivento 1940
Bismarck Action 1941
Malta Convoys 1941
Atlantic 1943
Salerno 1943
Normandy 1944
Burma 1945
Korea 1951–2

809 Squadron
Arctic 1941
Malta Convoys 1942
North Africa 1942
Salerno 1943
Aegean 1944
South France 1944
Burma 1945
Falkland Islands 1982

810 Squadron
Norway 1940
Mediterranean 1940–1
Spartivento 1940
Bismarck Action 1941

Atlantic 1941
Diego Suarez 1942
Salerno 1943
Korea 1950–3

811 Squadron
English Channel 1942
North Sea 1942
Atlantic 1943–4
Arctic 1944

812 Squadron
North Sea 1940
English Channel 1940–2
Malta Convoys 1941
Mediterranean 1941
Korea 1951–2

813 Squadron
Calabria 1940
Mediterranean 1940–1
Taranto 1940
Libya 1940–1
Malta Convoys 1942
Atlantic 1944
Arctic 1944–5

814 Squadron
Atlantic 1940

815 Squadron
Mediterranean 1940–1
Taranto 1940
Libya 1940–1
Matapan 1941
Burma 1944
Falkland Islands 1982
Kuwait 1991

816 Squadron
Norway 1940
Malta Convoys 1941
Mediterranean 1941
Atlantic 1943
Arctic 1944

817 Squadron
Norway 1941
North Africa 1942
Biscay 1942
Sicily 1943
Korea 1951–2

818 Squadron
Norway 1940
Spartivento 1940
Mediterranean 1940–1
Bismarck Action 1941
Atlantic 1941

819 Squadron
Libya 1940
Taranto 1940
Mediterranean 1940–1
English Channel 1942
Atlantic 1943–4
Arctic 1944

820 Squadron
Norway 1940–4
Spartivento 1940
Mediterranean 1940
Bismarck Action 1941
Atlantic 1941
Malta Convoys 1941
North Africa 1942–3
Salerno 1943
Sicily 1942

Palembang 1945
Okinawa 1945
Japan 1945
Falkland Islands 1982

821 Squadron
Norway 1940
Libya 1942
Mediterranean 1942–3
Korea 1952–3

822 Squadron
North Africa 1942–3
Arctic 1943

823 Squadron
Norway 1940

824 Squadron
Calabria 1940
Mediterranean 1940
Taranto 1940
Libya 1940–1
Malta Convoys 1942
Arctic 1944
Falkland Islands 1982

825 Squadron
Dunkirk 1940
English Channel 1940–2
Norway 1940
Bismarck Action 1941
Malta Convoys 1941
Arctic 1942–5
Atlantic 1944
Korea 1952
Falkland Islands 1982

826 *Squadron*
Dunkirk 1940
North Sea 1940–4
Matapan 1941
Crete 1941
Mediterranean 1941–3
Libya 1941–2
Falkland Islands 1982
Kuwait 1991

827 *Squadron*
Diego Suarez 1942
Malta Convoys 1942
Norway 1944
Korea 1950

828 *Squadron*
Mediterranean 1941–3
Norway 1944
Japan 1945

829 *Squadron*
Matapan 1941
Mediterranean 1941
Crete 1941
Diego Suarez 1942
Norway 1944
Falkland Islands 1982
Kuwait 1991

830 *Squadron*
Mediterranean 1940–2
Norway 1944

831 *Squadron*
Diego Suarez 1942
Malta Convoys 1942
Norway 1944
Sabang 1944

832 *Squadron*
Arctic 1942
Malta Convoys 1942
North Africa 1942

833 *Squadron*
North Africa 1942
Arctic 1944
Atlantic 1944

834 *Squadron*
Atlantic 1942
Salerno 1943

835 *Squadron*
Atlantic 1943–4
Arctic 1944

836 *Squadron*
Atlantic 1943–5

837 *Squadron*
Atlantic 1942–3

838 *Squadron*
Atlantic 1943

840 *Squadron*
Atlantic 1943

841 *Squadron*
English Channel 1943
Norway 1944

842 *Squadron*
Norway 1944
Arctic 1944

845 Squadron
Falkland Islands 1982
Kuwait 1991

846 Squadron
Atlantic 1944
Norway 1944–5
Arctic 1944–5
Falkland Islands 1982
Kuwait 1991

847 Squadron
Falkland Islands 1982

848 Squadron
Okinawa 1945
Japan 1945
Falkland Islands 1981
Kuwait 1991

849 Squadron
Palembang 1945
Okinawa 1945
Japan 1945

851 Squadron
Malaya 1945
Burma 1945

852 Squadron
Norway 1944

853 Squadron
Arctic 1944–5
Norway 1945

854 Squadron
Palembang 1945

Okinawa 1945

856 Squadron
Norway 1944–5
Arctic 1945

857 Squadron
Palembang 1945
Okinawa 1945

860 Squadron
Atlantic 1944–5

878 Squadron
Salerno 1943

879 Squadron
Salerno 1943

880 Squadron
Diego Suarez 1942
North Africa 1942
Sicily 1943
Salerno 1943
Norway 1944
Japan 1945

881 Squadron
Diego Suarez 1942
Norway 1944
Aegean 1944
South France 1944
Atlantic 1944

882 Squadron
Diego Suarez 1942
North Africa 1942
Atlantic 1943–4

South France 1944
Norway 1944–5
Arctic 1945

883 *Squadron*
Arctic 1942
North Africa 1942

884 *Squadron*
Malta Convoys 1942
North Africa 1942

885 *Squadron*
Malta Convoys
North Africa 1942–3
Sicily 1943
Normandy 1944
Okinawa 1945

886 *Squadron*
Salerno 1943
Normandy 1944

887 *Squadron*
Salerno 1943
Norway 1944
Palembang 1945
Okinawa 1945
Japan 1945

888 *Squadron*
North Africa 1942–3
Sicily 1943
Salerno 1943

891 *Squadron*
North Africa 1942

892 *Squadron*
Atlantic 1943

893 *Squadron*
North Africa 1942–3
Sicily 1943
Salerno 1943
Arctic 1943

894 *Squadron*
Salerno 1943
Norway 1944
Palembang 1945
Okinawa 1945

896 *Squadron*
Atlantic 1944
Norway 1944
Burma 1945

897 *Squadron*
Salerno 1943
Normandy 1944

898 *Squadron*
Norway 1944
Atlantic 1944
Korea 1952–3

899 *Squadron*
Sicily 1943
Salerno 1943
South France 1944
Aegean 1944
Falkland Islands 1982

1700 *Squadron*
Burma 1945

1770 Squadron
Norway 1944
Palembang 1945
Okinawa 1945

1771 Squadron
Norway 1944
Japan 1945

1772 Squadron
Japan 1945

1830 Squadron
Sabang 1944
Palembang 1945
Okinawa 1945

1832 Squadron
Atlantic 1944
Norway 1944
Arctic 1944

1833 Squadron
Sabang 1944
Palembang 1945
Okinawa 1945

1834 Squadron
Norway 1944
Sabang 1944
Palembang 1945
Okinawa 1945
Japan 1945

1836 Squadron
Norway 1944

Sabang 1944
Palembang 1945
Okinawa 1945
Japan 1945

1837 Squadron
Sabang 1944

1838 Squadron
Sabang 1944

1839 Squadron
Palembang 1945
Okinawa 1945

1840 Squadron
Norway 1944
Okinawa 1945

1841 Squadron
Norway 1944
Okinawa 1945
Japan 1945

1842 Squadron
Norway 1944
Okinawa 1945
Japan 1945

1844 Squadron
Palembang 1945
Okinawa 1945

1845 Squadron
Okinawa 1945

SECTION FIVE

Royal Marine Awards

GIBRALTAR 1704

The Royal Marines captured the Rock of Gibraltar on 24 July 1704 and held it against repeated attacks before the siege was raised on 9 March 1705. This achievement is symbolized by the Corps' emblazoned colours bearing the globe surrounded by a laurel wreath. The Marines wear 'GIBRALTAR' on their badge – and no other honour.

Instead of Battle Honours as awarded to and displayed by ships of the Royal Navy the Corps and some Units celebrate Memorable Dates. These Memorable Dates were revised in 1987 when citations for the Unit dates were published for the first time.

CORPS MEMORABLE DATES

23 April 1918   The Raid on Zeebrugge
Royal Marines of the 4th Battalian took a leading role in the bold enterprise of blocking the German naval base of Zeebrugge on St George's Day 1918. Ten RM officers and 109 NCOs and men were killed, while another 233 of all ranks were wounded and 13 taken prisoner. Two VCs were awarded to Royal Marines. 50% of the marines were casualties. No other RM Battalion has ever again been numbered the 4th.

28 April 1915   Gallipoli
In a bitterly contested battle for supremacy the Royal Marines suffered serious casualties; during the campaign the RM Brigade's losses amounted to twenty-one officers and 217 men killed.

Another twenty-nine officers and 764 men were wounded and 122 were listed as missing. Lance Corporal R.W. Parker was awarded the VC on 1 May 1915.

6 June 1944   The Landings in Normandy
In the largest amphibious operation in history 16,000 marines served in the initial assault and helped man the landing craft. Detachments manned many guns of the capital ships and five RM Commandos landed during the initial phase. Nine officers and eighty-five men were killed on D-Day itself in making secure beachheads. Awards for gallantry – most of them for gallantry on D-Day – came to: 5 DSO, 3 OBE, 13 DSC, 10 MC, 1 CGM, 26 DSM and 13 MM. See pp. 159–62

7 June 1761   The Battle of Belle Isle
Two battalions of Royal Marines served with heroic distinction at the siege of Belle Isle in Quiberon Bay. The battle was in three phases: seaborne landing, fighting for the island itself, and finally storming the redoubts. See p. 48.

14 June 1982   Recapture of the Falkland Islands
According to the Corps' archives the Corps was involved in virtually every significant aspect of the South Atlantic campaign. A total of 3,520 Royal Marines, approximately 50% of the Corps' strength, took part in the campaign. Two officers and twenty-five men were killed and another sixty-seven wounded.

The battle was unique inasmuch as the fighting for the recapture of the islands was conducted at a range of about 8,000 miles from the Base in the UK. The Argentinians surrendered on 14 June after a campaign of about ten weeks. See pp. 94–5.

17 June 1775   The Battle of Bunker Hill
A rebel American force occupied high ground dominating the British base north of Boston. Two attempts to regain lost ground proved unsuccessful and costly. Only when reinforced by a force of Marines was the attempt to storm the heights successful. Royal Marine Major Pitcairn wrote of his Marines: "The reputation of the

Marines was never more nobly sustained. Their unshaken steadiness was conspicuous." Casualties were twenty-nine killed and eighty-seven wounded.

24 July 1704   The Capture of Gibraltar
Gibraltar surrendered to the British on 24 July 1704. The assault was carried out by a combined force of British and Dutch marines numbering 1,800 men. In the following October the French and Spanish invested Gibraltar. 400 marines reinforced the fortress and held it until March 1705. A contemporary report recorded: "The garrison did more than could be humanly expected, and the English Marines gained an immortal glory." See pp. 103–4

21 October 1805   The Battle of Trafalgar
Ninety-two officers and 3,600 Royal Marines were present at this great sea battle against the combined fleets of France and Spain. Aboard Lord Nelson's *Victory* all four Marine officers and over fifty Marines were killed or wounded. All told the Royal Marine casualties amounted to five officers killed, 121 men killed or died of wounds: another twelve officers and 204 men were wounded. See pp. 227–30.

28 October 1664   The Birth of the Corps
King Charles II sanctioned the formation of the Duke of York and Albany's Maritime Regiment of Foot, a force comprising 12,000 men to be distributed into His Majesty's fleets – "prepared for sea service".

1 November 1944   The Assault of Walcheren
As the advancing Allied armies in Flanders pressed forward it was necessary to assault the heavily defended island of Walcheren to open up a logistics base. The successful seaborne landing was bitterly contested. The Royal Marine contribution to the battle was considerable: the 4th Special Service Brigade comprised Nos 41, 47 and 48 Commandos. The 3 RM Commando attacked Westkapelle supported by RM crews of the Naval Support Craft whose self sacrifice, and two days of heavy fighting ashore, silenced the enemy batteries covering the Scheldt. The capture of Walcheren opened the

river and sustained the Allied armies in their advance into Germany. Winston Churchill later wrote: "The extreme gallantry of the Royal Marines stands forth." See p. 237.

UNIT MEMORABLE DATES

HEADQUARTERS COMMANDO FORCES RM

14 June 1982   The Recapture of the Falklands
On the day of the Argentinian invasion of the Falklands the staff of HQ 3 Commando Brigade were in Denmark, 42 Commando had gone on leave and 45 Commando had half a company in Hong Kong. One of the most remarkable aspects of the campaign was the marshalling of all units of the Commando Brigade. Within 72 hours it had been reinforced by an army battalion, a Rapier battery and two troops of armour, all were embarked and some already sailing south.

Ten weeks or so later came the Argentine surrender. HQ Commando Forces had been involved in the planning and direction of the South Atlantic campaign from the outset and made an invaluable contribution to the victory in the Falklands.

40 COMMANDO RM

3 October 1943   The Landing at Termoli
40 RM Commando with No 3 Commando and elements of the Special Raiding Squadron landed under cover of darkness at Termoli, a seaport on the Adriatic coast north of the River Bifurno and behind the German lines. They gained important tactical objectives, disrupted German supply lines and forced an enemy withdrawal.

6 November 1956   The Assault on Port Said
President Nasser of Egypt nationalized the Suez Canal in the summer of 1956. Great Britain and France determined to re-occupy

the Canal Zone, landed No 3 Commando Brigade as a spearhead, with 40 Commando and 42 Commando on each flank. However, powerful international political pressure compelled total retirement and withdrawal of the British and French forces. This was the first major seaborne assault since the Second World War.

42 COMMANDO RM

31 January 1945   The Battle of Kangaw
This was a hard-fought, hand-to-hand action against the Japanese-held Hill 170 in Burma, described by one historian as "the decisive battle in the whole of the Arakan campaign".

42 COMMANDO RM

11–12 June 1982   The Attack on Mount Harriet
An incident in the Falklands campaign is described in the Marine Museum archives as follows: "Careful planning, resolute leadership and boldness and determination of marines against initially strong resistance and continuous artillery bombardment eventually prevailed." The night action resulted in the capture of Mount Harriet and the surrender of 300 Argentinians.

45 COMMANDO RM

23 January 1945   The Attack on Montiforterbeek
This commemorates a day of hard hand-to-hand fighting against strongly defended German positions behind the Montiforterbeek dyke near Linne in Holland by 45 Commando RM. A Special Order for the day was posted: "Well done Royal Marines! You put up a fine show today." Lance Corporal H.E. Harden RAMC was awarded a posthumous VC.

11–12 June 1982   The Attack on Two Sisters
45 Commando landed at Ajax Bay in the dawn assault on the Falkland Islands and quickly established a beachhead. The Commando's objective – the twin peaks known as the Twin Sisters – was strongly guarded by a well-dug-in enemy. They formed the

centre of the Brigade's three objectives. The Argentinians retreated, lost about fifty men as prisoners and another twenty killed or wounded. The road to Port Stanley lay open.

COMMANDO LOGISTIC REGIMENT RM

22 May 1982   Landing at Ajax Bay
No 3 Commando Brigade's base in Plymouth was about 8,000 miles from the scene of action in the Falklands, stretching the logistic support to its maximum. The enlarged brigade was spread far and wide over more than forty ships. The heavy work load, supporting the landings at San Carlos Water and engaging the enemy, were well executed. Over a period of three weeks a Divisional HQ and two brigades treated 695 casualties, processed 2,000 prisoners of war and handled over 8,000 tons of supplies.

COMACCHIO GROUP RM

2 April 1945   The Battle of Comacchio
43 Commando distinguished itself in this hard won battle in Italy and one of its corporals, Tom Hunter, won a posthumous VC. The Marine archives record that the battle had a considerable strategic effect in the campaign: 43 Commando advanced its front line by 7½ miles and captured 450 prisoners.

3 COMMANDO BRIGADE HEADQUARTERS AND SIGNAL SQUADRON RM

21 May 1982   The Landings at San Carlos Water
Argentinian forces occupied the Falkland Islands in April 1982. No. 3 Commando Brigade RM was the landing element of the amphibious task force with orders to recapture the islands. The landing force comprised 40, 42 and 45 Commandos RM, reinforced by 2nd and 3rd Battalions Parachute Regiment. Landings were effected on 21 May. The British forces were subjected to constant air attack for seven days. The Royal Marines played a major part in the successful recapture of the islands.

COMMANDO BRIGADE AIR SQUADRON RM

14 June 1982 The Recapture of the Falkland Islands
From the first landings on 21 May to the final day of Argentinian surrender on 14 June helicopters of No 3 Commando Brigade Air Squadron supported the land forces, frequently attacked by enemy fighters and ground attack aircraft. The Squadron, of six Scout and nine Gazelle helicopters, was involved in every major ground battle during the campaign, flying a total of 2,110 hours.

OPERATIONAL LANDING CRAFT SQUADRONS

6 June 1944   The Landings in Normandy
The Royal Marines played a prominent part in the successful assault on the Atlantic Wall along the coast of Normandy and the defeat of the German forces in the West. Among their multitude of duties the Royal Marines manned the assault landing craft carrying the first and subsequent waves of the five leading infantry divisions and for weeks thereafter ferried men, stores and vehicles ashore. See pp. 159–62.

21 May 1982 The Landings in San Carlos Water
After the Argentinian occupation of the Falklands a British Task Force was ordered to recapture the islands. On 21 May in San Carlos Water the Marines' landing craft squadrons from *Fearless* and *Intrepid*, with the 1st Raiding Squadron RM, landed No 3 Commando Brigade onto five separate beaches without loss. Thereafter they carried out numberless duties including minesweeping. The Landing Craft Squadron's contribution to the ensuing week's fighting was invaluable to the recovery of the islands.

MEMORABLE DATES OF DISBANDED COMMANDOS		
41 Commando RM	9 September 1943	The Landing at Salerno
43 Commando RM	2 April 1945	The Battle of Comacchio
44 Commando RM	31 January 1945	The Battle of Kangaw
46 Commando RM	11 June 1944	The Attack on Le Hamel and Rots
47 Commando RM	7 June 1944	The Capture of Port-en-Bessin
48 Commando RM	6 June 1944	The Landings in Normandy

Select Bibliography

This is necessarily a selective bibliography. It would be quite impossible because of space limitations to provide a full list of book titles spanning more than four centuries of naval battles. And regrettably there is no recent bibliography of this aspect of naval history to which a reader can be referred. However, the list which follows represents a substantial library of reference works which will serve many purposes. Although it is not comprehensive, it will act as a useful source guide for the general reader, for the student, for the specialist audience and as a general reference list. It serves as a pointer to further reading and includes the books I found most rewarding in compiling this work.

The bibliography is also selective because the number of works about, for example, Trafalgar, Jutland and the Armada are legion. Only a few representative entries of these battles earn an entry here. Other entries listed have stood the test of time and deserve special mention. Sir William Laird Clowes' general work on the history of the Royal Navy and its battles is extensive and most valuable to the researcher. Its seven volumes are currently being reprinted by Chatham Publishing.

Sir Geoffrey A.R. Callendar is more readable but only goes as far as Nelson and Trafalgar. Sir Herbert W. Richmond's "admirable" *Statesman and Sea Power* is almost in a class of its own in providing an "overall consideration of the Royal Navy's place in the life of Great Britain".

A.T. Mahan, that great American, wrote the classic work on the *Influence of Sea Power upon History* and "taught the world the true place of navies in world history." "The Royal Navy," he wrote, was "the prime weapon of Britain's past greatness".

Sir Julian Corbett and Sir Henry Newbolt were historians of high calibre whose five volumes of WW I naval history deserve reading. Nor should Sir Winston Churchill be overlooked for his two world war series of volumes – *World Crisis* covering WW I, and his later History of WW II when he was at the centre of world events.

Admiral of the Fleet Earl Jellicoe's two major works make rewarding reading, as do Captain Stephen Roskill's four-volume history of our naval affairs in WW II. And the serious student should consult Admiral of the Fleet Viscount Cunningham's most readable *Odyssey*.

Special mention is made of the unique contribution to naval history by the library of about 130 volumes by the Navy Record Society, a gradually-growing collection of source books by eminent naval historians.

ALBERT, Marvin H., *Broadsides and Boarders*, Harrap, 1958.

ALLARDICE, Alexander, *Admiral of the Fleet Viscount Keith: Memoir of George Keith Elphinstone*, Blackwood, 1882.

ALLEN, Joseph, *Battles of the British Navy*, 2 vols, Henry G. Bohn, 1852.

ANSON, W.V., *Life of Lord Anson*, John Murray, 1912.

APPS, Michael, *Send Her Victorious*, Kimber, 1971.

ARCHIBALD, Edward H.H., *The Maritime Struggle for India 1871–83*, Ipswich Corporation, n.d.

ASPINALL-OGLANDER, C., *Roger Keyes*, Hogarth, 1951.

BACH, John, *The Australian Station: A History of the Royal Navy in the SW Pacific, 1821–1913*, NSW University Press, 1986.

BACON, Admiral Sir Reginald H., *The Jutland Scandal*, 3rd edition, Hutchinson, 1925.

—— *The Concise Story of the Dover Patrol*, Hutchinson, 1932. Also published later in 2 vols: *Dover Patrol 1915–17* n.d.

—— *The Life of Sir John Rushworth, Earl Jellicoe*, Cassell, 1936.

—— *Lord Fisher*, Cassell, 1945.

BARKER, A.J., *Dunkirk: The Great Escape*, Dent, 1977.

BARNET, Correlli, *Engage the Enemy More Closely: The Royal Navy in the Second World War*, Hodder, 1991.

BARROW, Sir J., *Life of Howe*, John Murray, 1982.

BARTLETT, C.J., *Great Britain and Sea Power, 1815–1853*, The Clarendon Press, 1963.

BASSETT, W.G., *Foundations of the British Navy in the Seventeenth Century*, Harrap, 1939.

Battle of the Atlantic, the official account of the fight Against the U-boats, 1939–45, HMSO, 1946.

BEADON, R., *Robert Blake*, Edward Arnold, 1935.

BEKKER, Cajus, *The Luftwaffe Diaries*, Macdonald, 1964.

—— *Hitler's Naval War*, Macdonald, 1974.

BELL, A.C., *A History of the Blockade of Germany and of the countries associated with her in the Great War, 1914–18*, HMSO, 1961. (Originally published in 1917 for official purposes only).

BENNETT, Captain Geoffrey, *The Battle of Jutland*, David & Charles, 1964.

—— *Naval Battles of the First World War*, Batsford, 1975.

—— *Naval Battles of World War II*, Batsford, 1975.

BERCKMAN, Evelyn, *Creators and Destroyers of the British Navy*, Hamish Hamilton, 1974.

BERESFORD, Rear Admiral Lord Charles, and WILSON, H.W., *Nelson and his Times*, Eyre & Spottiswoode, n.d.

BERTHOLD, Willi, *The Sinking of the Bismarck*, Longmans, 1958. (A thoroughly unreliable propagandist account although it does contain material not published elsewhere.)

BEVAN, Bryan, *The Great Seamen of Elizabeth I*, Robert Hale, 1971.

BLOND, Georges, *Ordeal Below Zero*, Mayflower, 1956.

BLUMENSON, Martin, *Sicily* Macdonald, 1968.

BOLT, Captain, *HMS Theseus in Korean Waters*, RUSI *Journal*, No. 96, 1951.

Brassey's Naval and Shipping Annual.

BRADFORD, Ernle, *The Mighty Hood*, Hodder, 1959.

BRENTON, Captain Edward Pelham, *The Naval History of Great Britain from the year 1783 to 1846*, Henry Colburn, 1847.

BRADLEY, P.B., *Bantry Bay*, Williams & Norgate, 1931.

BRENNECKE, Jochem, *The Hunters and the Hunted*, Burke Publishing, 1958.

BROWN, David, *Carrier Fighters*, Macdonald & Janes, 1977.

BRIDGE, Admiral Sir Cyprian, *Sea Power and Other Studies*, Smith, Elder & Co, 1910.

BRUCE, George, *The Burma Wars 1824–86*, Hart-Davies MacGibbon, 1973.

BUCKLEY, Christopher, *Norway, Commandos, Dieppe*, HMSO, 1977.

BUELL, A.C., *Paul Jones*, 2 vols, Trend, Tubner & Co n.d.

BURROWS, M., *Life of Hawke*, W.H. Allen, 1896.

BUSCH, Harald, *U-boats at War*, Putnam, 1955.

BUSCH, Fritz-Otto, *The Drama of the Scharnhorst*, Robert Hale, 1956.

—— *Prinz Eugen*, Futura, 1960.

CAGLE, Martin and MANSON, Frank, *The Sea War in Korea*, USNI, 1957.

CALLENDAR, Sir Geoffrey, *Nelson's Flagship*, Thomas Nelson, 1919.

—— *Naval Side of British History*, published by Christophers, 1924.

—— *Sea Kings of Britain*, 3 vols, 1939.

Camera at Sea 1939–45, Managing Editor Robert Gardiner, Conway Maritime Press, 1978.

CAMERAN, Ian, *Red Duster, White Ensign*, Frederick Muller, 1959.

CAMPBELL, Vice Admiral Sir Ian, and MACINTYRE, Captain Donald, *The Kola Run*, Frederick Muller, 1958.

Campaigns of World War II (Atlantic, D-Day, Pacific.) Phoebus, 1980.

CAMPERDOWN, Lord, *Admiral Duncan*, Longmans, 1898.

CARPENTER, A.F.B., *The Blocking of Zeebrugge*, Herbert Jenkins, 1921.

CHALMERS, W.S., *Life and Letters of David Beatty*, Hodder, 1951.

—— *Max Horton and the Western Approaches*, Hodder, 1954.

CHATTERTON, E. Keble, *The Auxiliary Patrol*, Sidgwick & Jackson, 1923.

—— *Sailing Ships and Their Story*, Sidgwick & Jackson, 1923.

CHURCHILL, Sir Winston, *World Crisis*, 6 vols, Thornton Butterworth, 1923–1931.

—— *The Second World War*, 6 vols, Cassell 1948–54.

CLOWES, Sir William Laird, *The Royal Navy: A History From Earliest Times to 1900*, 7 vols, published 1897 Sampson Low, Marston Co. Currently being re-printed by Chatham Publications, an imprint of Gerald Duckworth.

—— and BURGOYNE A.H., *Trafalgar Re-Fought*, Thomas Nelson, 1905.

COLLEDGE, J.J. – see LENTON, H.T.

COMPTON-HALL, Richard, *Submarine Warfare*, Michael Joseph, 1986.

CORBETT, Sir Julian, *Drake and the Tudor Navy*, 2 vols, 1898.

—— *England in the Mediterranean*, 1904.

—— *Naval Operations*. 5 vols, first three by Corbett, vols IV and V by Sir Henry Newbolt (q.v.). Longmans, 1920–31.

—— *England in the Seven Years War*, 2 vols, 1907.

—— *The Campaign of Trafalgar*, 1919.

—— *Monk* 1926.

COSTELLO, John and HUGHES, Terry, *Jutland 1916*, Weidenfeld & Nicolson, 1976.

—— *Battle of the Atlantic*, Collins, 1977.

COUTTS, H.B. Money, *Famous Duels of the Fleet*, Blackwood, 1908.

CREMER, Peter, *U-333*, Bodley Head, 1984.

CRESWELL, Captain J., *Sea Warfare 1939–45*, 1950.

CUNNINGHAM, Admiral of the Fleet Viscount Cunningham of Hyndhope, *A Sailor's Odyssey*, Hutchinson, 1951.

CUSTANCE, Admiral Sir Reginald, *The Ship of the Line in Battle*, Blackwood, 1912.

D'ALBAS, Andrieu, *Death of a Navy*, Robert Hale, 1957.

DETTMAR, F.J. and COLLEDGE, J.J., *British Warships 1914–19*, Ian Allan, 1972.

DIVINE, A.D., *Destroyer's War*, John Murray, 1942.

DONALD, Commander, *Stand By For Action*, Kimber, 1956.

DULL, Paul S., *The Imperial Japanese Navy 1941–45*, USNI, 1978.

DUNDONALD, Lord, *The Autobiography of a Seaman*, R. Bentley, 1860.

EDWARDS, Bernard, *Salvo! Classic Naval Gun Actions*, Arms & Armour Press, 1995.

EDWARDS, Kenneth, *Men of Action*, Collins, 1945.

—— *Seven Sailors*, Collins, 1945.

EHRMAN, John, *The Navy in the War of William III*, C.U.P., 1953.

Encyclopedia of Sea Warfare, Spring Books, 1975.

FALK, S., *Liberation of the Philippines*, Macdonald, 1970.

FELL, Captain, *The Sea Our Shield*, Cassell, 1966.

Fighting Ships of World War I and II, Peerage Books, 1976.

FISHER, Lord Fisher of Kilverstone: *Fear God and Dread Nought*: The Correspondence edited by Arthur J. Marder in 3 vols, Jonathan Cape, 1952.

FORBES, Donald, *Two Small Ships: Fortune* and *Pathfinder*, Hutchinson, 1957.

FORD, D., *Admiral Vernon and the Navy*, T. Fisher Unwin, 1907.

FORESTER, C.S., *The Age of Fighting Sail*, Michael Joseph, 1957.

—— *The Naval War of 1812*, Michael Joseph, 1957.

—— *Hunting The Bismarck*, Michael Joseph, 1959.

FOSTER, Thomas, *The Pictorial History of Sea Battles*, Enigma Books, 1977.

FORTESCUE, J., *Dundonald*, Macmillan, 1895.

FRASER, Edward, *The Londons of the British Fleet*, Bodley Head, 1908.

GALLAGHER, Thomas, *Against All Odds*, Cassell, 1971.

GELB, Norman, *Desperate Venture: Operation Torch*, Hodder, 1992.

GIEVE, David W., *Gieves and Hawkes, 1785–1985*.

GILL, G. Hermon, *Royal Australian Navy, 1939–42* vol. I and *1942–43* Vol. II, Australian War Memorial.

GORDON, Captain Oliver, *Fight it Out*, Kimber, 1957.

GRAY, Edwin, *A Damned Un-English Weapon*, Seeley, Service & Co, 1971.

GRENFELL, Captain Russell, *The Bismarck Episode*, Faber & Faber, 1948.

GRETTON, Vice Admiral Sir Peter, *Convoy Escort Commander*, Cassell, 1964.

—— *Former Naval Person*, Cassell, 1968.

—— *Crisis Convoy* (HX 231), Peter Davies, 1974.

GROVE, E., see IRELAND, B.

GROVE, E., Editor in Chief *Great Battles of the Royal Navy*: Britannia Royal Navy College, Dartmouth, Arms & Armour Press, 1994.

HAMPSHIRE, Cecil, *Royal Sailors*, Kimber, 1971.

HANNAY, David, *A Short History of the Royal Navy*: Vol. I 1217–1688; Vol. II 1689–1815, Methuen, 1897 and 1909.

—— *Life of Lord Rodney*, Macmillan, 1903.

HARA, Captain T., PINEAU, Roger, and SAITO, Fred, *Japanese Destroyer Captain*, Ballantine Books, 1961.

HARDY, A.C., *Everyman's History of the War at Sea*, 3 vols, 1948.

HASTINGS, Max and JENKINS, Simon, *The Battle for the Falklands*, Michael Joseph, 1983.

HATTERSLEY, Roy, *Nelson*, Weidenfeld & Nicolson, 1974.

HILL, Captain Roger, *Destroyer Captain*, Grafton, 1979.

HOLMAN, Gordon, *The King's Cruisers*, Hodder, 1947.

HOLT, Edgar, *The Opium Wars in China*, Putnam, 1964.

HOUGH, Richard, *The Hunting of Force Z*, Collins, 1963.

—— *Nelson*, Park Lane Press, 1980.

HOWARTH, David, *Sovereign of the Seas*, Collins, 1974.

HUGHES, Robert, *Through the Waters*, Kimber, 1956. Reprinted as *Flagship to Murmansk*, Kimber, 1975.

HUGHES, Terry see COSTELLO, John.

HUMBLE, Richard, *Japanese High Seas Fleet*, Macdonald, 1973.

—— *Before the Dreadnought*, Macdonald & Janes, 1976.

—— *Fraser of North Cape*, Routledge & Kegan Paul, 1983.

HUMMELCHEN, G. see Rohwer, Jürgen.

IRELAND, Bernard and GROVE, Eric, *Jane's War at Sea 1897–1997*, HarperCollins, 1997

IRVING, David, *Destruction of Convoy PQ 17*, Cassell, 1968.

JACOBSEN, H.A. and ROHWER, J., Editors, *Decisive Battles of World War II: The German View*, Andre Deutsch, 1965.

JAMES, Admiral Sir W., *The British Navy in Adversity*, 1926.

—— *The Naval History of Great Britain 1783–1827, 6 vols*, Macmillan, 1937.

—— *The Durable Monument*, Longmans, 1948.

JONES, Geoffrey, *The Month of the Lost U-boats*, Kimber, 1977.

JONES, Vincent, *Operation Torch*, Macdonald, 1972.

JANES ALL THE WORLD'S FIGHTING SHIPS. The standard annual reference book for ships of the world's navies, a copy of which is probably found on the bridge of every warship of any consequence throughout the world.

JELLICOE, Admiral Viscount, *The Grand Fleet 1914–16*, Cassell, 1920.

—— *The Crisis of the Naval War*, Cassell, 1920.

JERROLD, Douglas, *The Naval Division*, Hutchinson, 1923.

Journal of Strategic Studies, 'Contribution of the Royal Navy to the United Nations Forces during the Korean War' by Stephen Prince, pub. Frank Cass.

KEEGAN, John, *The Price of Admiralty*, Hutchinson, 1988.

KEMP, P.J., Victory at Sea, Frederick Muller, 1947.

—— (Editor) *The Oxford Companion to Ships and the Sea*, Granada Publications, 1976.

KENNEDY, Ludovic, *Nelson's Band of Brothers*, Odhams, 1951.

—— *Pursuit: The Chase and Sinking of the Bismarck*, Collins, 1974.

—— *Menace: The Life and Death of the Tirpitz*, Sidgwick & Jackson, 1979.

KENNEDY, Paul, *Pacific Onslaught*, Macdonald, 1972.

KENT, Graham, *Guadalcanal*, Pan, 1972.

KERR, J. Lennox, and GRANVILLE, Wilfred, *The RNVR*, Harrap, 1957.

LAIRD-CLOWES see CLOWES

LANDSBOROUGH, Gordon, *The Battle of the River Plate*, Panther, 1956.

LANDSDOWN, John, *With the Carriers in Korea 1950–53: The Fleet Air Arm Story*, Square One, 1992.

LANGMAID, Kenneth, *The Blind Eye*, Jarrold, 1972.

LAUGHTON, John Knox, *Studies in Naval History*, Longmans, 1887.

LEASOR, James, *Green Beach* (Dieppe), Heinemann, 1975.

LENTON, H.T. and COLLEDGE, J.J., *Warships of World War II*, Ian Allan, 1973.

LENTON, H.T., *German Warships of the Second World War*, Macdonald and Janes, 1975.

LEWIS, M.A., *The Navy of Britain*, Penguin, 1957.

—— *A Social History of the Navy 1793–1875*, 1960.

LLOYD, Christopher, *The Capture of Quebec 1759*, Batsford, 1959.

—— *Lord Cochrane*, Longmans, 1947.

—— *The Navy of Britain*, 1948.

—— *The Nation and the Navy*, 1954.

—— *St. Vincent and Camperdown*, Batsford, 1963.

MACDONALD, Callum, *Britain and the Korean War,* Blackwell, 1990.

MACINTYRE, Captain Donald, *U-boat Killer,* Weidenfeld & Nicolson, 1956.

—— *Jutland,* Evans Bros, 1957.

—— *The Battle of the Mediterranean,* Batsford, 1964.

—— *Battle of the Atlantic,* Batsford, 1969.

—— *Famous Fighting Ships,* Hamlyn, 1975.

MACKAY, Ruddock, *Admiral Hawke,* 1965.

MACKENZIE, R.H., *The Trafalgar Roll: Men and Ships that took part in the Battle,* George Allen, 1913.

MACKESY, Piers, *The War in the Mediterranean 1803–1810,* Greenwood Press, 1957.

—— *The War For America 1775–83,* Longmans, 1964.

McKIE, Ronald, *Proud Echo,* Robert Hale, 1953.

MAHAN, Alfred Thayer, *Life of Nelson,* Sampson, Low & Marston, 1899.

—— *The Embodiment of the Sea Power of Great Britain,* 2 vols, Little Brown, 1897.

—— *The Influence of Sea Power upon History 1660–1783,* first published 1890: this edition Methuen, 1965.

—— *Sea Power and its Relations to the War of 1812,* 2 vols, Little Brown, 1919.

MANNING, Captain and WALKER, Commander, *British Warship Names,* Putnam, 1959.

MARCUS, Geoffrey, *Quiberon Bay: The Campaign in Home Waters,* Hollis & Carter, 1960.

—— *A Naval History of England,* Allen & Unwin, Vol I, 1961: Longmans, Vol. II, 1941.

MARDER, Arthur, J., *From The Dreadnought to Scapa Flow: The Royal Navy in the Fisher Era,* 5 vols:
Vol. I *The Road to War 1904–14* OUP 1961.
II *The War Years to the eve of Jutland 1914–16,* 1965.
III *Jutland and After: May 1916–Dec 1916,* 1967.
IV *1917: Year of Crisis.* 1969.
V *Victory and Aftermath: Jan 1918–June 1919,* 1970.

—— *Fear God and Dread Nought,* 3 vols. The Correspondence of Admiral of the Fleet Lord Fisher of Kilverstone.

Vol I *The Making of an Admiral* 1952.

II *Years of Power* 1956.

III *Restoration, Abdication and Last Years*, Jonathan Cape, 1959.

MARSHALL, John, *Royal Navy Biography*, Longmans, 1823.

MARS, Alistair, *British Submarines at War 1939–45*, Kimber, 1971.

MARTIENSSEN, Anthony, *Hitler and his Admirals*, Dutton, 1948.

MASTERS, David, *Up Periscope*, Brown Watson, n.d.

MASON, David, *U-boat*, Macdonald, 1968.

—— *Raid on St Nazaire*, Macdonald, 1970.

—— *Salerno: Foothold in Europe*, Macdonald, 1971.

MATHEW, David, *The Naval Heritage*, Collins, 1945.

MATTINGLY, Garrett, *The Defeat of the Spanish Armada*, Jonathan Cape, 1959.

MIDDLEBROOK, Martin, *Convoy*, William Morrow, 1976.

—— *Battleship*, Allen Lane, 1977.

MILLINGTON-DRAKE, Sir Eugen, *The Drama of Graf Spee and the Battle of the River Plate*, Peter Davies, 1964.

MILLOT, Bernard, *The Battle of the Coral Sea*, Ian Allan, 1974.

MORISON, Rear Admiral Samual Eliot, *The History of the United States Naval Operations in World War II*, 15 vols. See in particular Vol I (Atlantic), Vol IX (Salerno and Anzio), Vol XVIII (Java Sea and Sunda Strait), Little Brown, 1947 et seq.

—— *The Two Ocean War*, Little Brown, 1963.

MONSARRAT, Nicholas, *The Cruel Sea*, Cassell, 1951. A fictional work but based on the author's experiences related in three small paperback books published by Cassell: *HM Corvette* (1942), *East Coast Corvette* (1943), and *Corvette Command* (1944).

MULLENHEIM-RECHBERG, Burkard, Baron von, *Battleship Bismarck: A Survivor's Story*.

NAVY RECORDS SOCIETY. Rich source material is found in the publications of this Society. For example, one of the most prominent flag officers of the wars of King William and Queen Anne was Sir John Leake. He played a leading part in the relief of Londonderry in 1688; he fought at Bantry Bay, Beachy Head, La Hogue and Malaga. He relieved Gibraltar twice and captured Cartagena, Alicante, Ibiza, Majorca, Minorca and Sardinia. The publications are listed here in volume numbers:

Defeat of the Spanish Armada, Nos 1 and 2. Reprinted 1981.

Letters of Lord Hood 1781–82. No 3.

Logs of the Great Sea Fights 1794–1805. Nos 16 and 18.

Fighting Instructions 1530–1816. No. 29.

Letters and Papers of Charles Lord Barham. Nos 32, 38, 39.

Views of the Battles of the Third Dutch War. No. 34.

Papers Relating to the loss of Minorca in 1756. No. 42.

The Life of Admiral Sir John Leake. Nos. 52 and 53.

Letters of Lord St. Vincent 1801–04. Nos. 55 and 61.

Letters and Papers of Admiral Viscount Keith. Nos. 62, 90, 96.

Journal of the First Earl of Sandwich. No. 64.

The Private Papers of John Earl of Sandwich, Nos. 69, 71, 75, 78.

The Naval Brigades in the Indian Mutiny. No. 87.

The Private Correspondence of Admiral Lord Collingwood. No. 98.

The Vernon Papers 1739–45. No. 99.

The Jellicoe Papers. Nos. 110 and 111

Siege and Capture of Havana. No. 114.

The Keyes Papers. Nos. 117, 121 and 122.

The Pollen Papers. No. 124.

The Beatty Papers. Nos. 128 and 132.

The Hawke Papers. No. 129.

The Somerville Papers. No. 134.

O'BYRNE, Robert, *James' Naval History*. A narrative of the naval battles, single ship actions, notable sieges and dashing cutting-out expeditions fought in the days of Howe, Hood, Duncan, St. Vincent, Bridport, Nelson, Camperdown, Exmouth . . . and Sir Sydney Smith. W.H. Allen, 1888.

O'BYRNE, William Richard, *A Naval Biographical Dictionary*, John Murray, 1849.

OLLARD, Richard, *Man of War*, Hodder, 1969.

—— *Pepys*, Hodder, 1974.

OMAN, Carola, *Nelson*, Hodder, 1947.

OWEN, J.H., *War at Sea Under Queen Anne*, Cambridge University Press, 1938.

PACK, Captain S.W.C., *Admiral Lord Anson*, Batsford, 1960.

—— *The Battle of Matapan*, Batsford, 1968.

—— *Night Action off Cape Matapan*, Ian Allan, 1972.

—— *Cunningham, The Commander*, Batsford, 1974.

—— *The Battle of Sirte*, Ian Allan, 1975.

—— *Operation Husky: The Allied Invasion of Sicily*, David and Charles, 1977.

PADFIELD, Peter, *Aim Straight*, Hodder, 1966.

—— *The Broke and the Shannon*, Hodder, 1968.

—— *The Battleship Era*, Hart-Davies, 1972.

—— *Doenitz*, Gollancz, 1984.

PARKIN, Ray, *Out of the Smoke*, Hogarth, 1960.

PARKINSON, C., *Lord Exmouth*, Methuen, 1934.

Britannia Rules, Weidenfeld & Nicolson, 1977.

PATERSON, A. Temple, *Tyrwhitt of the Harwich Force*, Macdonald and Janes, 1973.

PEMSEL, Helmut, *An Atlas of Naval Warfare*, Arms and Armour Press, 1977.

PIMLOTT, John and BADSEY, Stephen (Editors), *The Gulf War Assessed*, Arms and Armour Press, 1992.

PHILLIPS, C.E. Lucas, *Victoria Cross Battles of the Second World War*, Heinemann, 1973.

PITT, Barrie, *Zeebrugge*, Cassell, 1958.

—— *Revenge at Sea*, Cassell, 1960.

—— *The Battle of the Atlantic*, Time-Life Books, 1977.

POLLEN, Arthur, *The Navy in Battle*, Chatto and Windus, 1918.

POOLMAN, Kenneth, *Illustrious*, Kimber, 1955.

—— *Ark Royal*, New English Library, 1956.

POPE, Dudley, *Battle of the River Plate*, Kimber, 1956.

—— *73 North* (Battle of the Barants Sea) Weidenfeld and Nicolson, 1958.

PORTEN, Edward P. van der. *The German Navy in World War II*, Arthur Barker, 1970.

POTTER, E.B., and NIMITZ, Chester W., (Editors), *Sea Power: A Naval History*, Prentice Hall, 1960.

POTTER, John Deane, *Fiasco* (The Channel Dash), Heinemann, 1970.

PRESTON, Antony, *History of the Royal Navy*, Bison Books, 1985.

PRIEN, Günther, *I Sank the Royal Oak*, Gray's Inn Press, 1954.

RAEDER, Grand Admiral, Erich *Struggle For the Sea*, Kimber, 1959.

RAWSON, Edward Kirk, *Twenty Famous Naval Battles: Salamis to Santiago*, Crowell, 1899.

REED, Ken, *Hand me Down Ships*: US Cutters with the Royal Navy, Reed, 1993.

RICHMOND, Rear Admiral H.W., *The Navy in the War of 1739–48*, Cambridge University Press, 1920.

—— *Statesmen and Sea Power*, Oxford University Press, 1946.

—— *The Navy in India 1763–83*, Ernest Benn, 1931.

ROBERTSON, Terence, *Walker RN*, Evans Bros, 1956.

ROBINSON, Ernest H., see SHAW, Frank H.

ROHWER, Jürgen, and HUMMELCHEN, G., *The Chronology of the War at Sea*, 2 vols, Ian Allan, Revised edition, 1992.

ROHWER, J., *The Critical Convoy Battles of March 1943*, Ian Allan, 1977.

—— *Axis Submarine Successes of 1939–45*, Patrick Stephens, 1983.

ROSKILL, Captain Stephen W., The Official History of *The War at Sea*, 4 vols, HMSO, 1954–61.

—— *HMS Warspite*, Collins, 1957.

—— *Churchill and the Admirals*, Collins, 1957.

—— *The Strategy of Sea Power*, Collins, 1962.

—— *Earl Beatty*, Collins, 1980.

ROUSE, A.L., *Sir Richard Grenville*, Jonathan Cape, 1937.

RUGE, Vice Admiral Friederich, *Sea Warfare 1939–45: A German Viewpoint*, Cassell, 1957.

SANDERSON, Michael, *Sea Battles*, David & Charles, 1975.

SAINSBURY, A.B. see SHRUBB, R.E.A.

SCHEER, Admiral, *Germany's High Seas Fleet in the World War*, Cassell, 1920.

SCHOFIELD, Vice Admiral B.B., *British Sea Power*, Batsford, 1967.

—— *The Attack on Taranto*, Ian Allan, 1973.

—— *The Arctic Convoys*, Macdonald & Janes, 1977.

SETH, Ronald, *The Fiercest Battle: Convoy ONS 5*, Hutchinson, 1961.

SHANKLAND, Peter and HUNTER, Anthony, *Malta Convoy*, Fontana, 1963.

—— *Dardanelles Patrol*, Collins, 1964.

SHAW, Captain Frank H., and ROBINSON, Ernest H., *The Sea and its Story*, Cassell, 1910.

SHERRARD, O., *Life of Lord St Vincent*, Allen & Unwin, 1933.

SHOWELL, Jak P. Mallmann, *The German Navy in World War II 1939–1945*, Arms and Armour Press, 1977.

SHRUBB, Lieut.-Commander R.E.A., and SAINSBURY, Captain A.B., *The Royal Navy Day by Day*, Centaur Press, 1979.

SMITH, Peter, *Pedestal: The Malta Convoy of August 1942*, Kimber, 1970.

—— *Task Force 57*, Kimber, 1969.

—— *PQ 18: Arctic Convoys*, Kimber, 1975.

—— and WALKER, Edwin, *The Battles of the Malta Striking Forces*, Ian Allan, 1974.

SMITH, Stan, *Battle of Savo*, MacFadden, 1962.

SNYDER, Gerald S., *The Royal Oak Disaster*, Kimber, 1976.

SOUTHEY, Robert, *The Life of Lord Nelson*, Thomas Nelson, n.d. *c*.1914.

SPINNEY, David, *Rodney*, Allen & Unwin.

STEPHEN, Martin, *Sea Battles in Close Up* (Editor E. Grove) Ian Allan, 1988.

SYRETT, David, *The Royal Navy in American Waters 1775–83*, Scolar Press, 1989.

TAFFRAIL (Captain Taprell Dorling) *Endless Story*, Hodder, 1938.

—— *The Navy in Action*, Hodder, 1941.

THOMAS, David A., *Battle of the Java Sea*, Andre Deutsch, 1968.

—— *Crete 1941: The Battle at Sea*, Andre Deutsch, 1972.

—— *Atlantic Star 1939–45*, W.H. Allen, 1990.

—— *The Illustrated Armada Handbook*, Harrap, 1988.

THOMPSON, R.W., *D-Day*, Macdonald, 1968.

THOMPSON, George Malcolm, *Sir Francis Drake*, Secker & Warburg, 1972.

TUCHMAN, Barbara, *The First Salute*, Michael Joseph, 1989.

TUCKER, Gilbert Norman, *The Naval Service of Canada: Its Official History*, 2 Vols. Cloutier, Ottawa, 1952.

TUNSTALL, B., *Admiral Byng*, Philip Unwin, 1928.

TURNER, John Frayn, *Periscope Patrol*, Harrap, 1957.

UHLIG, Frank, Jnr., *Vietnam, The Naval Story*, USNI, Annapolis, 1986.

VAT, Dan van der, *The Atlantic Campaign: The Great Struggle at Sea 1939–45*, Hodder, 1988.
VERE, Francis, *Salt in Their Blood: The Lives of the Famous Dutch Admirals*, Cassell, 1955.
VIAN, *Admiral of the Fleet Sir Philip Vian*, Frederick Muller, 1960.

WARNER, Oliver, *A Portrait of Lord Nelson*, Chatto and Windus, 1958.
—— *Trafalgar*, Batsford, 1959.
—— *The Battle of the Nile*, Batsford, 1960.
—— *The Glorious First of June*, Batsford, 1961.
—— *Great Sea Battles*, Weidenfeld & Nicolson, 1963.
—— *Nelson's Battles*, Batsford, 1965.
—— *Cunningham of Hyndhope*, John Murray, 1967.
—— *Vice Admiral Lord Collingwood*, Oxford University Press, 1968.
—— *Great Battle Fleets*, Hamlyn, 1973.
—— *Fighting Sail*, Cassell, 1979.
WARREN, C.E.T. and BENSON, James, *Above Us The Waves*, Harrap, 1953.
WATTS, Anthony, J., *The U-boat Hunters*, Macdonald & Janes, 1976.
—— *The Loss of the Scharnhorst*, Ian Allen, 1970.
—— and GORDON, Brian G., *The Imperial Japanese Navy*, Macdonald, 1971.
—— *The Royal Navy: An Illustrated History*, Arms and Armour, 1994.
WEIGHTMAN, Alfred E., *Crests and Badges of HM Ships*, Gale and Polden, 1957.
WERNER, Herbert, *Iron Coffins*, Arthur Barker, 1970.
WINN, Godfrey, *PQ 17: A Story of a Ship*, Arrow, 1947.
WINTON, John, *Freedom's Battle: The War at Sea*, Hutchinson, 1967.
—— *The Forgotten Fleet*, Michael Joseph, 1969.
—— *Air Power at Sea 1939–45*, Sidgwick & Jackson, 1977.
—— *Carrier Glorious*, Hutchinson, 1986.
—— *Ultra at Sea*, Leo Cooper, 1988.

WOODHOUSE, C.M., *The Battle of Navarino*, Hodder, 1965.

WOODWARD, Admiral Sir John, *One Hundred Days: The Memoirs of the Falklands Battle Group Commander*, with Patrick Robinson, HarperCollins, 1992.

ZIEGLER, Philip, *Mountbatten, the Official Biography*, Collins, 1985.

Index

355

359